Rehnquist Justice

Rehnquist Justice
Understanding the Court Dynamic

Edited by Earl M. Maltz

 University Press of Kansas

© 2003 by the University Press of Kansas
All rights reserved

Published by the University Press of Kansas (Lawrence, Kansas 66049), which was organized by the Kansas Board of Regents and is operated and funded by Emporia State University, Fort Hays State University, Kansas State University, Pittsburg State University, the
University of Kansas, and Wichita State University

Library of Congress Cataloging-in-Publication Data

Rehnquist justice : understanding the court dynamic / edited by Earl M. Maltz
    p. cm.
Includes index.
    ISBN 0-7006-1243-2 (cloth : alk. paper)—ISBN 0-7006-1244-0 (pbk. : alk. paper)
    1. United States. Supreme Court. 2. Rehnquist, William H., 1924– .
    3. Conservatism—United States. I. Maltz, Earl M., 1950– .
    KF8742 .R475 2003
    347.73'26—dc21
                        2002155411

British Library Cataloguing in Publication Data is available.

Printed in the United States of America

10 9 8 7 6 5 4 3 2 1

The paper used in this publication meets the minimum requirements of the American
National Standard for Permanence of Paper for Printed Library Materials Z39.48-1984.

Contents

Acknowledgments

The secretarial staff of Rutgers Law School provided invaluable assistance in the production of this manuscript. Special thanks are due to Kaeko Jackson and Celia Hazel. In addition, Fred Woodward at the University Press of Kansas provided invaluable advice and showed great patience with a novice and sometimes inept editor.

Part of Chapter 5 is taken from Earl M. Maltz, "Justice Kennedy's Vision of Federalism," *Rutgers Law Journal* 31 (2000):761–770, reprinted with the permission of the *Rutgers Law Journal*.

Introduction

Earl M. Maltz

Chief Justice William Hubbs Rehnquist has presided over the most conservative Court of the late twentieth century. The Rehnquist Court has moved constitutional jurisprudence substantially to the right in cases related to federalism, economic rights, affirmative action, and a number of other important issues. Given the makeup of the Court, this trend is not surprising; even after the appointments of Ruth Bader Ginsburg and Stephen Breyer, seven of the Rehnquist Court justices were selected by Republican presidents, with six chosen during the administrations of Ronald Reagan and George W. Bush, both of whom were committed to reversing what they saw as the liberal excesses of the Warren and Burger Courts. Against this background, it would have been surprising if the political trajectory of constitutional law had not shifted in a conservative direction.

Particularly in the wake of the Court's controversial decision in *Bush v. Gore*,[1] some liberal scholars have described this shift in almost apocalyptic terms, implicitly or explicitly likening it to the jurisprudential revolutions of 1937 and the Warren era. These commentators argue that the evolving approach of the Rehnquist Court has effectively rejected the basic premises on which post-1937 constitutional law has been based.[2] Such characterizations dramatically overstate the magnitude of the changes wrought during the Rehnquist era. To be sure, the revival of conservative activism—even on a relatively modest scale— is a significant jurisprudential event. However, taken as a whole, the constitutional decisions of the Rehnquist Court present a decidedly mixed picture.

The Rehnquist Court's treatment of the religion clauses of the First Amendment is a microcosm of the overall structure of the Court's constitutional jurisprudence. In the years from 1962 through 1986, the Warren and Burger Courts deployed both the Establishment and Free Exercise Clauses to impose a wide variety of restraints on government action. The process began in the early 1960s with the politically explosive decisions that barred schools from sponsoring both

1

prayers and readings from the Bible. Soon thereafter, the Warren Court concluded that states must often grant religious exemptions to the requirements of generally applicable statutes. The Burger Court not only reaffirmed these doctrines but also virtually outlawed government aid to church-related elementary and secondary schools.

The conservative justices of the Rehnquist Court have been successful in modifying some of these doctrines. In *Employment Division, Department of Human Resources v. Smith,*[3] the Court categorically rejected the idea that the government was constitutionally required to provide religious exemptions to generally applicable regulatory statutes. Subsequently, Congress sought to impose such a requirement by statute in the Religious Freedom Restoration Act (RFRA). However, in *City of Boerne v. Flores,*[4] the Court found that Congress had no constitutional authority to pass RFRA.

The decisions in *Smith* and *Boerne* clearly rejected significant elements of an approach that is typically associated with liberal constitutional jurisprudence. Nonetheless, in purely political terms, the divisions on the underlying substantive issue cut across traditional liberal/conservative lines. By contrast, the question of the propriety of government aid to parochial schools was one that generally divided liberals from conservatives. Conservatives were victorious in *Agostini v. Felton*[5] and *Zelman v. Simmons-Harris*[6] as the Court rejected challenges to government programs that provided school vouchers and other forms of aid to parochial schools.

However, conservatives have had little reason to be satisfied with the Rehnquist Court's treatment of the issue of school prayer. The decisions in *Engel v. Vitale*[7] and *Abington School District v. Schempp,*[8] which outlawed state-sponsored prayer and Bible reading, had long been a source of conservative dissatisfaction with the Court's interpretation of the religion clauses. The Rehnquist Court rebuffed efforts to overrule *Engel* and *Schempp;* indeed, in *Lee v. Weisman*[9] and *Santa Fe Independent School District v. Doe,*[10] the Court not only reaffirmed the prohibitions but also marginally expanded the restrictions on state action in this area.

The overall structure of Rehnquist Court jurisprudence replicates the pattern of the religion clause decisions. Viewed in standard political terms, the orientation of the Court's decisions has been somewhat uneven. Without question, in some areas doctrine has moved undeniably rightward. However, in many cases this rightward movement has been somewhat muted, and in some situations doctrine has actually moved in the opposite direction.

To many commentators, the Court's treatment of federalism has come to symbolize the resurgence of conservative jurisprudence in the Rehnquist era. Beginning with the decision in *Seminole Tribe of Florida v. Florida,*[11] the Rehnquist Court has greatly limited the ability of Congress to force state governments to submit to federal regulations. Further, in cases such as *United States v. Printz,*[12] the Court held that Congress could not require state officials to be the agents who enforce federal law. Finally, for the first time in the modern era, in *United States v. Lopez*[13] and *United States v. Morrison,*[14] the Court concluded that Congress had exceeded its enumerated powers in seeking to regulate private activity. Whatever their merits in distinctively legal terms, these decisions clearly advanced the conservative political agenda.

Many of the Court's decisions on race-related issues also reflect the influence of conservative political thought. For example, under Rehnquist's leadership the Court has encouraged lower courts to end judicial supervision of school districts that formerly practiced de jure segregation and for the first time squarely held that race-based affirmative action programs were subject to strict scrutiny. Moreover, the Court has curtailed the states' ability to craft so-called "majority-minority" districts, which are designed to ensure that racial minorities are fairly represented in Congress.[15]

Even in the cases involving federalism and race, however, the Rehnquist Court has not fully vindicated the hopes of many conservatives. For example, none of the federalism cases threatens the authority of the federal government to regulate all private economic activity, even if that activity has no direct connection to interstate commerce. Similarly, in the districting cases, the Court has declined to ban all consideration of race in the districting process. Instead, the justices have held that race may be considered as a factor in drawing congressional districts, so long as it is not the predominant factor in the construction of any district. In addition, the Court has held that race may be used as a proxy for party affiliation in the districting process. Thus, state legislatures exercising a minimum of ingenuity have essentially remained free to craft districts that virtually guarantee the election of members of minority races.[16]

Moreover, in most areas of constitutional jurisprudence, the rightward shift in doctrine has been less pronounced or even nonexistent. The Court's treatment of the abortion issue is typical in this regard. The 1973 decision in *Roe v. Wade*[17] had held that government restrictions on abortions were subject to strict scrutiny and thus were unconstitutional unless necessary to serve a compelling governmental interest. In subsequent cases, this standard proved almost impossible to meet. With the exception of cases involving government funding and parental involvement in the decisions of minors, between 1973 and 1986 the Court struck down almost every government effort to limit or regulate a woman's access to abortions.[18]

Pro-life activists and conservatives generally were outraged by *Roe* and its progeny. They hoped that the justices appointed by Ronald Reagan and George W. Bush would shift the balance of power on the abortion issue and lead to a decision overruling *Roe* outright, leaving the state and federal governments free to outlaw or at least sharply curtail access to abortions. This group was thus sorely disappointed in the 1992 decision in *Planned Parenthood of Southeastern Pennsylvania v. Casey*.[19] Although *Casey* failed to produce an opinion for the Court, a majority of the justices did reject the strict scrutiny test of *Roe;* however, this test was replaced by a requirement that the government not place an "undue burden" on those choosing to seek abortions. In practice, this test gave the government only slightly more leeway to regulate abortions—a point reinforced eight years later when the Court struck down a ban on so-called "partial birth" abortions in *Stenberg v. Carhart*.[20]

Despite the decision in *Carhart,* the Rehnquist Court has clearly moved the jurisprudence of abortion at least marginally to the right. In other contexts, liberals have had even less reason to be dissatisfied with the political direction of the Court's decision-making. The case law dealing with sex discrimination is a prime example. Many liberals were no doubt disappointed with the decision in *Nguyen v. Immigration and Naturalization Service,*[21] where the Court refused to invalidate a gender-based provision governing the right of illegitimate children to claim birthright citizenship; however, this holding appeared to rest in part on the deference historically granted to Congress on decisions related to naturalization. In purely domestic cases—most notably *J. E. B. v. Alabama*[22] and *United States v. Virginia*[23]—the Court has shown little patience for classifications based on sex, denying attorneys the right to exclude jurors on the basis of gender and forcing the state of Virginia to allow women to attend the historically all-male Virginia Military Institute.

The political orientation of the Court's sex discrimination jurisprudence is by no means a unique phenomenon during the Rehnquist era; indeed, on issues related to gay rights and the rights of undocumented aliens, the Court has actually moved the law at least marginally to the left. Given this pattern of decisions, the overall tenor of constitutional jurisprudence during the Rehnquist era is by no means as extreme as some have claimed but rather is perhaps best described as moderately conservative.[24]

The religion clause cases also reflect the basic dynamic that has created the pattern of constitutional law in the late twentieth century. The Rehnquist era has witnessed an ongoing struggle between the partisans of two radically different conceptions of the proper role of the Supreme Court in the American political system. Some of the justices are strongly committed to a refined version of the conservative paradigm of constitutional jurisprudence long associated with the chief justice himself. Others, by contrast, have an equally strong commitment to the liberal approach to constitutional analysis that shaped the Court's doctrines during the Warren and Burger eras. The overall pattern of the Rehnquist Court's decisions has been a by-product of the interaction between these two models.

One of the most striking features of the Rehnquist Court dynamic has been the increasing influence of the conservative paradigm on the evolution of constitutional analysis. During the Burger years, Rehnquist himself was viewed as the personification of right-wing constitutionalism. After he became chief justice, Rehnquist was joined by the even more conservative Antonin Scalia and Clarence Thomas. When Thomas and Scalia joined the Court, conservative jurisprudence took on a sharper edge. Nonetheless, conservative theory remains marked by internal tensions that have never been satisfactorily resolved.[25]

The conservative paradigm evolved in response to the liberal activism of the Warren and early Burger eras. Conservatives framed their objections in jurisprudential as well as political terms. Seeking to justify Warren and Burger Court decisions, liberal justices and theorists had developed a profoundly antiformalist view of constitutional law. They argued that judges were well-positioned to correct legislative "failures" and that the interpretation of the constitutional text should change over time to reflect the evolution of fundamental values in a changing society.[26] Conservatives responded by contending that an activist federal judiciary was usurping the prerogatives of the other branches of government; adopting a formalist approach, they also argued for a jurisprudence based on originalism—the theory that the constitutional text should be seen as having a fixed meaning and that the original understanding of the language should be the touchstone of constitutional interpretation.

Even in theory, originalism is not entirely compatible with a philosophy of judicial restraint. At times the original understanding will mandate a degree of judicial activism that goes well beyond that of the Warren and Burger years. Moreover, in practice the analysis of Rehnquist, Scalia, and Thomas has been further complicated by a preference for conservative political results, even where such results could not plausibly be justified in terms of either originalism or a philosophy of judicial restraint.[27] Indeed, in recent years the conservative justices themselves have implicitly recognized this tension; while formalism remains a significant influence on their approach, deference has become a much less important theme in conservative thought. The conservatives' treatment of *Bush v. Gore* is the most widely discussed example of this phenomenon; *Boerne* illustrates the same point in the context of the religion cases.

In the late Rehnquist era, the conservatives have often been opposed by Justices John Paul Stevens, David H. Souter, Ruth Bader Ginsburg, and Stephen G. Breyer. Each of these justices supports the antiformal approach that marked the jurisprudence of the Warren and Burger era and deploys that approach in support of many of the same causes espoused by liberal politicians in the late twentieth century. Thus, the members of this group have generally opposed both the activist innovations of the conservative justices and the efforts to roll back liberal constitutional doctrine in other areas. In some cases they also have made efforts to move liberal constitutional doctrine beyond the boundaries established by the Warren and Burger Courts.

Most often, the votes of Justices Sandra Day O'Connor and Anthony M. Kennedy have determined the outcome of the ideological struggle between the two opposing factions on the Court. O'Connor and Kennedy are similar in a number of important respects. Both were appointed by President Ronald Reagan, who was committed to reshaping the Court in a conservative image. Moreover, in the case of both justices, the circumstances surrounding their appointments prevented Reagan from selecting the most conservative candidate who was available. O'Connor was chosen to fulfill a campaign pledge to place a woman on the Court, and the Kennedy nomination was made in the wake of the failed effort to place Robert Bork on the Court. Both O'Connor and Kennedy reject the formal, originalist approach that is the jurisprudential benchmark of the conservative paradigm.[28] At the same time, neither is a centrist in the true sense; instead, each is far more likely to align himself or herself with the conservative bloc than with the more liberal members of the Court. Nonetheless, both Kennedy and O'Connor are more likely than the chief justice and Justices Scalia and Thomas to abandon their conservative allies in the cases that divide the Court along ideological lines. When either O'Connor or Kennedy joins the liberals, they are typically victorious.

The pivotal role played by O'Connor and Kennedy is well illustrated by the religion cases. For example, both have supported the constitutionality of a variety of government aid to parochial schools and the students who attended those schools. Thus, such programs have often survived constitutional challenges during the Rehnquist era. At the same time, the opposition of O'Connor and Kennedy has doomed efforts to reverse the ban on prayers in the public schools.

Some of the religion cases also reflect a further complexity in the pattern of Rehnquist Court decision-making. Although the core liberal and conservative coalitions generally hold together in cases raising politically charged issues, the members of those coalitions do not always move in lockstep. Each member of the Court will at times abandon his or her normal coalition partners on specific issues. Given the fact that the Court is often closely divided, even a single defection can be crucial to the outcome of a case.

Smith provides a classic example. In that case, O'Connor rejected the conservative view that simple neutrality was sufficient to insulate a state statute against a Free Exercise Clause attack. If the standard liberal and conservative coalitions had remained intact, O'Connor's vote would have been sufficient to guarantee rejection of the neutrality standard. However, Stevens abandoned his normal allies and joined the conservatives in *Smith,* providing the indispensable fifth vote that established neutrality as the constitutional norm.

The defection of one or more of the liberal justices is by no means a unique event in the Rehnquist era. Indeed, none of the current justices has demonstrated the unswerving devotion to liberal constitutional theory that marked, for example, the jurisprudence of Justices William J. Brennan and Thurgood Marshall during the Warren and Burger eras. Instead, Stevens, Souter, Ginsburg, and Breyer have all demonstrated that on specific issues they are willing to reject the position that is generally advocated by liberal politicians and scholars and join with the conservative members of the Court. Similar fissures also occasionally appear in the conservative bloc. While the chief justice generally takes traditional conservative positions, Justices Scalia and Thomas have a more libertarian perspective. Even Scalia and Thomas themselves—probably the closest ideological allies on the Court—occasionally take different positions on important issues.

Against this background, the overall pattern of Rehnquist era decision-making cannot be seen as the reflection of any single, unified approach to constitutional analysis. Instead, Rehnquist Court jurisprudence can only be understood as the product of the interaction of the views of nine separate individuals, each of whom has an idiosyncratic view of the proper interpretation of the Constitution and appropriate role of the Court in the American political system. The chapters of this book are designed to provide the reader with insight into this interaction by focusing on each of the justices as an individual and analyzing his or her unique approach to constitutional adjudication.

NOTES

1. 531 U.S. 98 (2000).
2. See, for example, Jack M. Balkin and Sanford Levinson, "Understanding the Constitutional Revolution," *Virginia Law Review* 87 (2001): 1034–1110.
3. 494 U.S. 872 (1990).
4. 521 U.S. 507 (1997).
5. 521 U.S. 203 (1997).
6. 122 S.Ct. 2460 (2002).
7. 370 U.S. 421 (1962).
8. 374 U.S. 203 (1963).
9. 505 U.S. 577 (1992).
10. 530 U.S. 290 (2000).
11. 517 U.S. 44 (1996).
12. 521 U.S. 98 (1998).
13. 514 U.S. 99 (1995).
14. 529 U.S. 598 (2000).
15. See, for example, *Missouri v. Jenkins*, 515 U.S. 70 (1995); *City of Richmond v. J. A. Croson Co.*, 488 U.S. 469 (1989); *Shaw v. Reno*, 509 U.S. 630 (1993).
16. *Bush v. Vera*, 517 U.S. 952 (1996); *Hunt v. Cromartie*, 526 U.S. 541 (2001).
17. 410 U.S. 113 (1973).
18. See, for example, *Thornburgh v. American College of Obstetricians and Gynecologists*, 476 U.S. 747 (1986); *Akron v. Akron Center for Reproductive Health, Inc.*, 462 U.S. 416 (1983).
19. 505 U.S. 833 (1992).
20. 530 U.S. 914 (2000).
21. 121 S.Ct. 2053 (2001).
22. 511 U.S. 527 (1994).
23. 518 U.S. 515 (1996).
24. *Romer v. Evans*, 517 U.S. 620 (1996); *Immigration and Naturalization Service v. St. Cyr*, 121 S.Ct. 2271 (2001); *Zadvydas v. Davis*, 121 S.Ct. 2491 (2001).
25. For a concise description of Rehnquist's jurisprudential philosophy in his own words, see William H. Rehnquist, "The Notion of a Living Constitution," *Texas Law Review* 54 (1976): 693–706. Scalia describes and defends his views in Antonin Scalia, *A Matter of Interpretation* (Princeton: Princeton University Press, 1999).
26. This point is made explicitly in *Harper v. Virginia State Bd. of Elections*, 383 U.S. 663 (1966).
27. See, for example, *Lucas v. South Carolina Coastal Council*, 505 U.S. 1003 (1992).
28. *Michael H. v. Gerald D.*, 491 U.S. 110 (1989).

1

William H. Rehnquist: Nixon's Strict Constructionist, Reagan's Chief Justice

Keith E. Whittington

On January 7, 2003, William H. Rehnquist celebrated his thirty-first anniversary of taking the oath to be a justice of the U.S. Supreme Court. This is a long tenure for a Supreme Court justice, but not extraordinarily long. It certainly does not match the nearly thirty-seven years that Justice William O. Douglas served on the Court. But it is well above the average of fifteen years of service, and no current justice has served longer.

During his tenure, Rehnquist has made a substantial contribution to the Court and constitutional law. Unlike great iconoclastic justices such as John Marshall Harlan, Oliver Wendell Holmes, or Antonin Scalia, Rehnquist does not generally write the biting and memorable lines in dissent. Unlike some of his predecessors, he has not been able to speak for a united Court in a historically great case such as *McCulloch v. Maryland* or *Brown v. Board of Education*. Nonetheless, Rehnquist has provided a sustained, intellectually serious, and judicially effective voice for the type of conservative constitutional jurisprudence that for much of the middle of the twentieth century appeared to be decisively defeated. During his time on the bench, he has played a significant role in ushering such a constitutional philosophy back into legitimacy and prominence. Rehnquist's constitutional vision has not quite captured the Supreme Court, but over the course of his time on the bench he has moved from being the symbol of impotent conservative protest against judicial liberalism to being the symbol of the preeminence of a revitalized strand of judicial conservatism.

RICHARD NIXON AND THE CRITIQUE OF THE WARREN COURT

The Warren Court came to a close just as Richard Nixon was being elected to the presidency. Within a week of Robert Kennedy's assassination in the summer of

1968 and the apparent implication that Nixon would soon occupy the White House, Chief Justice Earl Warren decided to retire immediately so that Lyndon Johnson could choose his successor. Nixon and Warren had been old adversaries from their days in California politics, and Nixon's presidential campaign was a running critique of the Warren Court. For his part, Johnson welcomed the opportunity to choose the next chief justice and quickly began marshaling support in the Senate for the elevation of his long-time adviser, Associate Justice Abe Fortas. The confirmation hearings were a disaster for Fortas, as senators assailed the justice's continuing relationship with the administration and the Warren Court itself. After the hearings, Fortas wrote dejectedly to Justice William Douglas, "Every decent constitutional decision in the last three years and for some years prior thereto, has been denounced."[1] His supporters in the Senate could not break a filibuster, and his nomination was withdrawn in October. Seven months later, Fortas resigned from the Court under an ethical cloud. The following month, Nixon's choice of Warren Burger was confirmed as the new chief justice of the United States.

An important aspect of Richard Nixon's 1968 campaign was an attack on the Warren Court. During Warren's tenure, the Court had issued a large number of deeply controversial constitutional decisions. Over the course of the 1960s, the Court waded into or initiated debates over religion, obscenity, and criminal justice, among other things. With its liberalizing tendencies in each of these areas, the Court ran against a public that was increasingly concerned about social issues.[2] Less than half of the public rated the Supreme Court as "excellent" or "good" in 1967. At the time of Warren's retirement in the midst of the 1968 presidential campaign, the Court's support had been pushed down to 36 percent, and it remained at such levels until Nixon left office.[3] Nixon recognized a political opportunity and built on Barry Goldwater's 1964 presidential campaign's southern strategy and appeal for "law and order." Though the strategy had won Goldwater nothing but an embarrassing defeat, the message had broader appeal four years later.

Both Richard Nixon and independent candidate George Wallace featured attacks on the Warren Court as part of their campaigns. Although the federal judiciary came in for criticism on busing, school prayer, and obscenity, the Court's decisions expanding the rights of criminal defendants received the most attention. Wallace was the more strident of the two candidates, often declaring that the criminal "is out of jail before the victim is out of the hospital."[4] Similarly, Nixon repeatedly noted that the "courts have gone too far in weakening the peace forces as against the criminal forces." The Court had "encouraged criminals" and had overlooked the "forgotten civil right" of public safety. It was a winning issue, as the public rated crime as one of the most important problems facing the nation in 1968, and a large majority believed that the courts did not deal with criminals "harshly enough."[5]

In the days before the election, Nixon promised that the appointments to the Court would be different in his administration. Nixon's nominees "would be strict constructionists who saw their duty as interpreting law and not making law. They would see themselves as caretakers of the Constitution and servants of the people, not super-legislators with a free hand to impose their social and political viewpoints on the American people." Although "strict constructionism" was more of a political slogan than a sharply defined analytical concept, both Nixon and his audience understood that it mainly represented an opposition to the innovative judicial decisions of the prior decade, especially those relating to social issues and individual rights. In keeping with this theme, Nixon emphasized that central to the qualifications he would look for in a potential justice would be "experience or great knowledge in the field of criminal justice." He pledged that "any justice I would name would carry to the bench a deep and abiding concern for these forgotten rights" of crime victims.[6] Nixon drew some of his campaign criticisms of the Warren Court's criminal justice rulings from a speech delivered by then judge Warren Burger, who was well known for his support for "the power of law enforcement agencies."[7] Earl Warren himself had guessed that Burger, who had positioned himself as the veritable "anti-Warren," would be his replacement.[8]

Burger may have been a conservative critic of Warren, but like Warren he was not an intellectual leader. In chambers, Burger frequently frustrated his colleagues with his relatively weak understanding of the cases. In public, he was unable to provide deeply reasoned defenses of conservative constitutional understandings.[9] Nixon's next two successful appointments, Harry Blackmun and Lewis Powell, were political compromises, as the president sacrificed ideology for confirmability. After Burger's easy confirmation, Nixon had been determined to find young, conservative, Republican, southern judges to elevate to the Supreme Court and solidify his electoral strategy. Unfortunately, few attractive candidates fit those demanding criteria in the late 1960s, and his selection process was plagued by internal confusion and external embarrassment. Almost by accident, Nixon stumbled on his ideal "strict constructionist" with his final appointment of William H. Rehnquist.

REHNQUIST JOINS THE COURT

Born in 1924, Rehnquist was forty-seven when nominated for the Court. He grew up in a staunchly Republican suburb of Milwaukee. After serving in the Army Air Corps during the Second World War, Rehnquist attended Stanford University on the G.I. Bill. He graduated Phi Beta Kappa in 1948 with a degree in political science, earning an M.A. in the same subject the following year. He received a second master's in government at Harvard University in 1950, before returning to Stanford and graduating first in his class from the law school in December 1951. The following February, he began his sixteen-month service as a clerk for Justice Robert H. Jackson. Afterward, he went back west to practice law in Phoenix, became involved in state and local Republican politics, and aided Barry Goldwater's presidential campaign. With Nixon's victory, Rehnquist returned to Washington to head the prestigious Office of Legal Counsel (OLC) within the Justice Department.

Despite his loyal service at OLC, Rehnquist was not close to the president or an obvious choice for the Supreme Court. Just months before Rehnquist was nominated to the Court, Nixon could not even remember his name. He did not appear on any lists of candidates for vacancies on the Court until the day before his eventual nomination. Nixon had long insisted on judicial experience for his nominees, which Rehnquist lacked, and by the end of his search had been enthralled with the idea of appointing the first woman to the Court. Rehnquist himself had dismissed any chance of being nominated, joking that he had "none at all, because I'm not from the South, I'm not a woman, and I'm not mediocre."[10] But in a prime-time television broadcast on October 21, 1971, the president introduced Rehnquist and Powell to the press as his nominees to the Supreme Court. To this audience, Nixon emphasized two considerations, legal skills and judicial philosophy. He lauded Rehnquist as "having one of the finest legal minds in this whole Nation today," who could be expected to recognize the "duty of a judge to interpret the Constitution . . . not twist or bend the Constitution in order to perpetuate his personal political and social views."[11]

His confirmation as associate justice was contentious. As assistant attorney general, Rehnquist had irritated a number of senators with his aggressive defense of the president's prerogatives and policies. Beginning especially with the failed Fortas nomination in 1968, the Senate had become more aggressive in examining the constitutional views of nominees. Rehnquist had been involved in the White House's unsuccessful efforts to win confirmation for Nixon's earlier nominations of Harrold Carswell and Clement Haynsworth, and he took away from that process a belief that nominees were more likely to make enemies than win friends at the hearings and so kept his answers short at his own.[12] None of the ethical or intellectual questions that damaged earlier Nixon nominees could be credibly raised in Rehnquist's case, but ideological disagreements were sufficient to make the confirmation difficult. A number of organized interests, including most prominently civil rights groups, opposed confirmation and challenged the nominee's commitment to minority rights and individual liberties. The confirmation hearings included charges that Rehnquist had harassed black voters in Phoenix as a Republican poll watcher. The publication of a memorandum upholding segregation that Rehnquist wrote as a clerk for Justice Jackson in preparation for the *Brown* case raised even more controversy before the final Senate vote. On December 10, 1971, the Senate approved his appointment to the Court by a vote of 68 to 26, among the most "no" votes received by a successful nominee to the Supreme Court.

Once on the Court Rehnquist quickly established himself as the premier voice of conservative strict constructionism in the nation. In doing so, he raised methodological concerns with the intent of the constitutional framers that were not a prominent theme in Nixon's rhetoric. During his confirmation hearings, Rehnquist gave more content to the meaning of judicial conservatism as an effort to understand the Constitution "by the use of the language used by the framers, the historical materials available, and the precedents which other Justices of the Supreme Court have decided in cases involving a particular provision."[13] He also noted, however, that precedent carried less weight in constitutional cases than in statutory ones, and recent precedents or those "handed down by a sharply divided court" were less authoritative.[14] Rehnquist tied this commitment to originalism to a concern for judicial constraint and preventing judges from becoming Nixon's "super-legislators."

In a prominent 1976 address, Rehnquist warned against a "notion of a living constitution" by which a judge may substitute "some other set of values for those which may be derived from the language and intent of the framers."[15] A "mere change in public opinion since the adoption of the Constitution" was not sufficient to alter the meaning of the Constitution or be the basis for the exercise of judicial review.[16] Looking back to Oliver Wendell Holmes, Rehnquist argued that the Constitution empowered democratically elected officials to solve new social problems but gave no such power to the courts. In a pluralistic society, people will necessarily differ on judgments of moral values and political principle. Such judgments have a "moral claim . . . upon us as a society" only as they derive from their "having been enacted into positive law." The exercise of judicial review based on value judgments that cannot fairly be derived from the Constitution "is genuinely corrosive of the fundamental values of our democratic society" and "an end run around popular government."[17] Although he admitted that there could be reasonable disagreements about the meaning of some of the Constitution's more general phrasings, Rehnquist argued that judges must resist the temptation "to impose by law their [own] value judgments."[18]

If the Burger Court represented the "triumph of country club Republicanism," then Rehnquist represented the voice of true conservatism.[19] He was as critical of the Burger Court from the right as Warren-era stalwart William Brennan was from the left. Especially during his early years on the Court, Rehnquist earned his nickname as the Lone Ranger. Over the course of the Burger Court, more than 43 percent of his written opinions were dissents and 29 percent of his votes in nonunanimous cases were dissents.[20] He was the least likely justice, by far, to be in a Burger Court majority declaring legislation unconstitutional.[21] During the Burger years, Rehnquist issued solo dissents at a historically torrid pace, accounting for 20 percent of the cases with such dissents. As Alexander Bickel noted, Rehnquist was a "man with first rate independent intellect who would keep the other justices' toes to the fire."[22] He quickly "established himself firmly as a one-man strong right wing . . . seemingly dedicated to cleansing, single-handedly if necessary, the Augean stable that conservative dogma perceives as the Supreme Court of the nineteen-fifties and nineteen-sixties." With the "best mind on the Court," Rehnquist had the capability and the interest in exposing the intellectual weaknesses of the Warren Court's legacy and the Burger Court's drift and keeping the fires burning for a more conservative jurisprudence.[23]

TO LEAD THE REAGAN COURT

As Rehnquist lit the way from above, a conservative legal movement grew from below. Nixon faced limited options in staffing the Court. He was not only constrained by his own elaborate political calculations and a Democratic Senate but also by the relatively small number of qualified conservative candidates during the period. Moreover, the 1960s was a period of great intellectual success for the Warren Court. Although still subject to political criticism in Congress and elsewhere, the Warren Court was no longer troubled by the criticisms from academia and bar associations that had dogged it in the late 1950s. By the late 1960s, it had won over many of the constituencies that would provide or evaluate potential judicial appointments. By contrast, Ronald Reagan had a deeper pool of appealing candidates on which to draw, a Republican Senate, and a more ideologically committed set of criteria for judicial selections. As one judicial scholar observed, "Judgeships, at all levels, have never had greater political symbolism and higher priority for an administration than in the Reagan years," nor was there ever a "more coherent and ambitious agenda for legal reform and judicial selection."[24] The Reagan Justice Department became a magnet for a new generation of legal conservatives, many of whom were at least as critical of the Burger Court as of the Warren Court. After becoming attorney general, Edwin Meese mounted high-profile public campaigns for a "new vision of the Constitution" that emphasized the centrality of the original intent of the constitutional framers and judicial restraint on many of the social issues on which the administration and the Court tended to disagree.[25]

For this younger generation of conservative lawyers, for whom the Burger Court rather than the Warren Court was the primary reference point, Rehnquist was an inspiration and an "intellectual giant."[26] Of the Nixon justices, only Rehnquist "fully lived up to conservative hopes."[27] Within the Reagan Justice Department, Charles Cooper, the head of the Office of Legal Counsel, and William Bradford Reynolds, the head of the civil rights division, led the planning for possible Supreme Court vacancies. For them, Rehnquist was the only logical choice to lead the Court. As Reynolds noted, Rehnquist "was quite clearly the justice who most represented the judicial views of the Reagan administration."[28] Reagan argued on behalf of his nominee that Rehnquist was the "articulate spokesman for straightforward interpretations of the Constitution" and a justice who could be trusted to "interpret the law and not write the law."[29] Elevating the Lone Ranger of the Burger Court to the position of chief justice of the United States would make the strongest possible statement about the Reagan administration's understanding of the Constitution and the Supreme Court.

A Rehnquist appointment was not just symbolic. He was also viewed as the perfect chief justice for a Reagan Court. Through the years, Rehnquist had amply demonstrated his intellectual leadership and his ability to go head-to-head with the ideological leader of the Court's left wing, William Brennan.[30] His high dissent rate called into question his willingness to compromise and forge majorities on the Burger Court, but that ideological purity was readily seen as a virtue rather than a vice by the Reagan administration. By the early 1980s, Rehnquist had already emerged as a leader "on a generally rudderless Court," and given more supportive justices, he could be expected to advance the same ideals with even greater success.[31] Moreover, Rehnquist's legal acumen and clear vision could be a welcome change for his colleagues as well. It was well known that they viewed Chief Justice Burger's motives with mistrust and disdained his skills. By contrast, as the justice who "carries more constitutional law in his head" than any other, Rehnquist guided the Court through its work with remarkable efficiency and could not be accused of manipulating the prerogatives of his position, such as opinion assignments.[32] Administration officials thought Rehnquist had demonstrated the intellectual and social skills to maintain "warm collegial relationships" with and the sincere respect of all of the other justices.[33] His tenure as chief justice has borne out such expectations. Even Thurgood Marshall could praise Rehnquist as "a great chief justice," and Brennan regarded him as "the most all-around successful" chief justice in his experience.[34]

After one of the longest gaps between vacancies in the Court's history, Chief Justice Burger decided to retire from the Court in order to lead preparations for celebrating the bicentennial of the Constitution. Once questions about Rehnquist's health and desire to remain on the Court were resolved, his nomination in June 1986 to be chief justice was assured. His confirmation by the Senate, however, proved no easier the second time around. Two justices had been nominated and confirmed since Rehnquist's first time in the Senate, and they had passed through the process with relative ease. The symbolism of Reagan's elevation of Rehnquist to the center seat on the Court provoked substantial opposition on the left and presaged the ideologically polarizing confirmation fight over Judge Robert Bork in 1987. With a record of more than fourteen years on the Court, there was little doubt about how he would behave as chief justice.

Senator Edward Kennedy led the charge against the 1986 confirmation, as he had in 1971, denouncing Rehnquist as "outside the mainstream" and "too extreme to be Chief Justice."[35] The second confirmation hearings largely replayed the battles of the first, focusing on the justice's conservative judicial philosophy and charges of hostility to minorities and civil rights prior to joining the Court. After a full two weeks of hearings, thirteen members of the Senate Judiciary Committee recommended his confirmation, with five Democratic members dissenting. Another month of rancorous floor debate passed before the full Senate approved his confirmation by a vote of 65 to 33, up to that time the largest number of "no" votes cast against a successful nominee to the Court.

As the Senate Judiciary Committee's report recommending his confirmation as chief justice observed in response to the charges of extremism, "Justice Rehnquist is very much in the mainstream of the current Court." In the context of the "present Court, Justice Rehnquist has proven himself a leader of majorities."[36] Since Justice O'Connor joined the Court, Rehnquist had voted with the majority in over 80 percent of its cases. In the 1990s, he was in the majority in nearly 90 percent of the Court's decisions.[37] Dissents account for a mere 5 percent of his written opinions since becoming chief justice, and he has cast the lone dissenting vote in only a handful of cases during that period. As an associate justice, Rehnquist was often writing dissents laying the intellectual foundations for the future. As chief justice, he writes for the present rather than the future, and if he does not write for the majority, then he rarely writes at all. When Rehnquist first arrived at the Court, he may have thought the "boat was kind of heeling over in one direction" such that his "job was, where those sort of situations arose, to kind of lean the other way."[38] He apparently has not found that necessary as chief justice.

INDIVIDUAL RIGHTS

Rehnquist's approach to individual rights is perhaps best seen as a response to the perceived excesses of the Warren Court and the jurisprudential tendencies it encouraged. In his controversial memorandum to Justice Jackson, a young Rehnquist wrote that "in the long run it is the majority who will determine what the constitutional rights of the minority are. One hundred and fifty years of attempts on the part of this Court to protect minority rights of any kind . . . have been sloughed off, and crept silently to rest." The Court is "well suited to its role as arbiter" between the branches of the national government or the national government and the states, but the justices were likely merely to enact "the sentiments of a transient majority of nine men" when "attempting to interpret these individual rights," as demonstrated by *Dred Scott* and *Lochner.*[39] He echoed and elaborated those thoughts in a 1980 address, explaining that "it is no more accurate to say of our Court that it is the ultimate guardian of individual rights than it is to say that it is the ultimate guardian of national authority or of states' rights." The "people of this country" are the "source of *all governmental authority,*" and they have made their own constitutional balancing between the power of government and the rights of individuals.[40]

"The goal of constitutional adjudication is surely not to remove inexorably 'politically divisive' issues from the ambit of the legislative process, whereby the people through their elected representatives deal with matters of concern to them. The goal of constitutional adjudication is to hold true the balance between that which the Constitution puts beyond the reach of the democratic process and that which it does not."[41] The Court may be too likely to recognize the values on only one side of the scales. As he warned in dissent in a death penalty case, "While overreaching by the Legislative and Executive Branches may result in the sacrifice of individual protections that the Constitution was designed to secure against the State, judicial overreaching may result in sacrifice of the equally important right of the people to govern themselves."[42] As a justice, Rehnquist has generally been skeptical of expanding individual rights, and especially of claims that do not have a fairly firm grounding in the constitutional text or historical practice. Although he has accommodated some of these expansions, he has resisted many others, including some favored by conservative colleagues with more libertarian tendencies.

Most claims of individual constitutional rights arise in cases involving state or local governments. Rehnquist is mistrustful of judges substituting their judgments of contested constitutional rights for the judgments of popularly elected representatives and thus urges a strong presumption of constitutionality for acts of government challenged in such cases.[43] Such a presumption, he argues, must be particularly strong when the individual rights being claimed are not firmly rooted in clear constitutional text and accepted historical understandings, for such judicial constitutional innovations are most likely to be affected by personal preferences. With fewer checks and balances on the Court's use of its own powers, "judicial self-restraint is surely an implied, if not an expressed, condition of the grant of authority of judicial review."[44] This approach to controversial constitutional rights converges with Rehnquist's structural concern for protecting the role of the states in the federal system. In both instances, the tendency is to maximize the latitude of state governments to respond to local majorities.[45]

The Court's incorporation doctrine runs afoul of these considerations. "Incorporation" represents the Court's effort to give definition to the Fourteenth Amendment's due process clause by applying most of the requirements that the Bill of Rights imposes on the national government to the states as well. From one angle, incorporation can appear to be a relatively conservative doctrine, for it ties the meaning of the relatively vague due process clause to the more specific textual rights found in the first eight amendments to the Constitution.[46] At the same time, however, with questionable historical pedigree incorporation doctrine imposes a large number of federally enforced individual rights on the states.[47] Like some New Deal justices such as Felix Frankfurter, Rehnquist prefers a more flexible but limited approach to the due process clause, especially in the context of criminal justice.

Incorporation, he contends, gradually draws "all of the ultimate decision making power over how justice is to be administered" into the Supreme Court, which necessarily "smother[s] the healthy pluralism which would ordinarily exist in a national government embracing fifty states."[48] Except by "the mysterious process of transmogrification" known as incorporation doctrine, reasonable state differences in the administration of justice would not be subject to federal judicial review.[49] Rather than simply preventing "violations of the Constitution's commands," the Court increasingly exercises an illegitimate "general supervisory power" over the "administration of criminal justice in the various States [that] is properly a matter of local concern."[50] The due process clause, in Rehnquist's reading, does not authorize the Court to go beyond "an examination for the constitutional minimum of 'fundamental fairness'" in judicial proceedings in areas that "had been left to the States from time immemorial."[51]

In interpreting the substantive rights of individuals, Rehnquist urges that the Court adhere closely to the historical understanding of the lawmakers. This approach is perhaps most clearly illustrated in an early affirmative action case, though the law in question is a federal statute rather than the Constitution. In a biting dissent, Rehnquist accused the majority of Orwellian manipulations of the clear statutory language. He details how "taken in its normal meaning, and as understood by all Members of Congress who spoke to the issue during the legislative debates" and as unanimously interpreted in prior decisions of the Court, the language of the Civil Rights Act of 1964 "prohibits a covered employer from considering race when making an employment decision, whether the race be black or white."[52] Nonetheless, "by a tour de force reminiscent not of jurists such as Hale, Holmes, and Hughes, but of escape artists such as Houdini, the Court eludes clear statutory language, 'uncontradicted' legislative history, and uniform precedent in concluding that employers are, after all, permitted to consider race in making employment decisions."[53] The judicial task "is to give effect to the intent of Congress," and by skirting that intent the Court is more likely to reveal "the spirit animating the present [judicial] majority" than the spirit of the legislative majority that produced the act.[54]

Rehnquist brings a similar skepticism to his interpretation of substantive constitutional rights. Especially when earlier doctrinal statements have not led to resolution, the Court must constantly return to the constitutional fundamentals of text and intent. Precedent cannot alter the meaning of the Constitution: "Our constitutional watch does not cease just because we have spoken before on an issue; when it becomes clear that prior constitutional interpretation is unsound, we are obliged to reexamine the question."[55] Thus, in his opinion in the 1992 *Casey* abortion rights decision, Rehnquist harked back to his initial dissent from the 1973 *Roe* majority. There he argued that the Fourteenth Amendment's due process clause "embraces more than the rights found in the Bill of Rights," but that such "liberty is not guaranteed absolutely against deprivation" but only against deprivation that has no "rational relation to a valid state objective," the standard set down by the New Deal Court for "social and economic legislation" after abandoning the stricter standards of the *Lochner* era.[56] He could find no indication that a stronger right to abortion had been "fundamental," "universally accepted," or even known to the drafters of the Fourteenth Amendment.[57] Recognizing the existence of a modern "substantive due process jurisprudence," Rehnquist has argued that it has "at least been carefully refined by concrete examples involving fundamental rights found to be deeply rooted in our legal tradition. This approach tends to rein in the subjective elements that are necessarily present in due process judicial review."[58]

Similarly, in the context of the Fourteenth Amendment's equal protection clause, Rehnquist has argued that "we are constantly subjected to the human temptation to hold that any law containing a number of imperfections denies equal protection simply because those who drafted it could have made it a fairer or a better law," and indeed the Court had routinely succumbed to those temptations, nullifying "state laws which were merely felt to be inimical to the Court's notion of the public interest."[59] In order to avoid "an endless tinkering with legislative judgments," the Court must return not only to the intent of the drafters of the Fourteenth Amendment but also to "the original understanding at Philadelphia" that limited the proper scope of judicial review.[60] Moving beyond the equal protection clause's core concern with protecting against racial discrimination, the Court has created "out of thin air" doctrines "so diaphanous and elastic as to invite subjective judicial preferences or prejudices relating to particular types of legislation," such as a heightened standard of review for laws discriminating on the basis of gender.[61] It is ultimately "impossible to build sound constitutional doctrine upon a mistaken understanding of constitutional history." Whether in criminal justice, equal protection, or religious establishment, Rehnquist has argued that "any deviation from [the founders'] intentions frustrates the permanence of that Charter and will only lead to the type of unprincipled decision making that has plagued our" constitutional cases.[62] In the context of religious establishment, Rehnquist has emphasized original intent in his critique of the "wall of separation" that the Court has attempted to build between church and state since World War II. He has been an important advocate for a view of the establishment clause of the Constitution that would allow "nondiscriminatory aid to religion."[63]

Though generally consistent, Rehnquist has accommodated some of the expansion of individual rights that he initially resisted. He was the strongest critic on the Court of the heightened standard of constitutional scrutiny that the Court adopted for gender discrimination cases in the 1970s.[64] In 1996, however, the chief justice concurred with the majority in striking down the Virginia Military Institute's male-only policy as unconstitutional. In doing so, he pointedly adopted the heightened standard of scrutiny introduced "two decades ago" and consistently adhered to by the Court "ever since."[65] The Court's earlier decisions had put VMI "on notice," at least by 1982, that its admissions policy "was open to serious question," given the absence of any comparable state institution available to women.[66] By contrast, Justice Antonin Scalia, in a lone dissent in the case, continued to question the foundations of heightened scrutiny for gender discrimination in the historical meaning of the Constitution.[67]

Similarly, in 2000, Rehnquist wrote a strongly worded majority opinion rejecting congressional efforts to modify *Miranda* and defending it as an entrenched constitutional rule.[68] It was left to Scalia and Thomas in dissent to note his own earlier criticisms and modifications of the *Miranda* rules.[69] Somewhat differently, Rehnquist seems to have laid aside his initial doubts about the constitutional protections the Court afforded to commercial speech in the mid-1970s. He initially argued that commercial speech, such as advertisements for services, possessed only the traditional constitutional protections afforded to all economic activity while criticizing the Court for inventing new rights on the basis of nothing but "desirable public policy" and for reading the Constitution to require "the Virginia Legislature to hew to the teachings of Adam Smith."[70] Subsequently, however, Rehnquist argued from those precedents, although often reading them narrowly and in dissent, while still complaining that the Court was returning "to the bygone era of *Lochner*" and failing to recognize the post–New Deal state's "broad discretion in imposing economic regulation."[71] More recently, the chief justice has joined opinions written by others that give greater play to the constitutional protections of commercial speech and evidence little of his initial discomfort with such restrictions on government power.[72]

SEPARATION OF POWERS

For Rehnquist, the structural features of the Constitution—the separation of powers between the different branches of the national government and the federal relations between the national government and the states—are a more appropriate area for judicial interpretation and intervention than are the individual rights features. Though Rehnquist believes that the Court has an important role to play in securing individuals in their clear and traditionally recognized rights, such cases raise the danger of the Court acting undemocratically to impose its own moral preferences. By contrast, he believes the Court is better able to play the role of a neutral arbiter and legal interpreter in the context of disputes over the structural features of the Constitution. In such disputes, Rehnquist has emphasized both the intrinsic powers of the presidency and the distinctiveness of legislative and executive powers while also demonstrating a firm commitment to the authority of the Court.

In evaluating presidential power, Rehnquist has been centrally concerned with protecting the chief executive's ability to successfully perform his constitutional duties. To that end, he has been relatively deferential to the internal administration of the White House. Rehnquist did not participate in the "Watergate tapes" case, given his then recent work in the Office of Legal Counsel. He did, however, unsuccessfully argue in favor of the former president against statutory control over presidential papers. "Any substantial intrusion upon the effective discharge of the duties of the President is sufficient to violate the principle of the separation of powers," and the "candid and open discourse" between the president and his advisers is an "absolute prerequisite to the effective discharge of the duties of that high office."[73] Recognizing the principle that the papers and records of a former president are subject to congressional control necessarily creates an unacceptable risk that such an open discourse might be chilled. Somewhat similarly,

Rehnquist unsuccessfully urged that high-level federal officials beyond the president be recognized to have an absolute immunity against lawsuits arising from their official conduct. Such immunity is thought necessary so that officials can effectively discharge their duties without second-guessing themselves for fear of lawsuits.[74]

Somewhat surprisingly, the chief justice wrote the majority opinion upholding the independent counsel statute, with only Justice Scalia in dissent. Relative to the separation of powers principles noted above, Rehnquist concluded that the independent counsel did not unduly interfere with the president's ability to discharge his own constitutional duties or reflect an effort by Congress to aggrandize its own powers. Ultimately, the "independent" counsel possessed only limited independence, being initiated, jurisdictionally defined, and potentially discharged by the attorney general.[75] The attorney general did not directly appoint the independent counsel, however, but merely initiated the appointment process. A special panel of federal judges appointed a particular individual to serve in this capacity. This unusual procedure gave some independence to the counsel but created its own constitutional difficulties. Rehnquist argued that the procedure neither violated the appointments clause nor imposed unacceptable executive responsibilities on judges. The Constitution grants congressional discretion in allowing a variety of persons to appoint "inferior officers." Although "inferior officers" is not easily defined, the particularly limited nature of the independent counsel's duties, in combination with being ultimately answerable to the attorney general, suggests that the counsel is an inferior officer. Though interbranch appointments of inferior officers are unusual, the independent counsel's appointment by a panel of judges was particularly appropriate to its functions.[76] By excluding the judicial panel from any supervisory role over the independent counsel, the statute preserves the independence of the judiciary and avoids any encroachment on the executive function.[77]

The majority's analysis is surprising, as Scalia points out, in that it allows a purely executive prosecutorial power to be buffered from the president.[78] But Rehnquist's separation of powers analysis had never been purely formal; rather it had been driven by a relatively strong sense of what was necessary to protect the president's ability to perform his constitutional duties. Given the limited and particular functions of the independent counsel and the fact that his or her partial insulation from the president was not accompanied by the encroachment of any other branch into the executive sphere, Rehnquist was not persuaded that the counsel statute in fact created an unconstitutional impediment to the president.[79] But it also seems apparent that the necessarily convoluted scheme of the independent counsel statute was carefully constructed so as to just pass constitutional muster in the eyes of the chief justice.

While seeking to ensure that the president can perform his constitutional duties, Rehnquist has also insisted that Congress meet its own responsibilities. Notably, he suggested the need for a partial revival of the nondelegation doctrine, which had been effectively abandoned during the New Deal. One of the difficulties that the Court initially had found in the New Deal programs was that Congress had effectively delegated its legislative powers to executive officers by empowering them to make important policy with only minimal statutory guidance. In reviewing some labor regulations, Rehnquist encountered similar difficulties. Noting that the justices themselves were deeply divided as to whether the secretary of labor had met statutory guidelines in developing some workplace safety regulations, Rehnquist suggested that the uncertainty was "eminently justified" because in "one of the most difficult issues that could confront a decisionmaker," Congress, "the governmental body best suited and most obligated to make the choice," had "improperly delegated that choice to the Secretary of Labor and, derivatively, to this Court."[80]

Rehnquist recognized a number of acceptable justifications for broad delegations, ranging from technical necessity of the subject matter to joint constitutional responsibilities of the branches, but ruled out cases in which Congress merely sought to avoid political controversy. "It is the hard choices, and not the filling in of the blanks, which must be made by the elected representatives of the people."[81] The legislative history of the provision suggested to him that there was "a fundamental policy disagreement in Congress" and that Congress did not have the political will to speak with any greater clarity than it did. If Congress could not make the "hard policy choices," then no other branch could do so for it.[82] Similarly, Rehnquist cautioned in the legislative veto case that the Court should not be too quick to assume that parts of a statutory compromise were not essential to the passage of the bill and to the legislative policy choice that was made. It could not be presumed that Congress would have delegated the same authority to the executive absent a legislative veto provision that would allow Congress to control how the executive used that authority.[83]

Rehnquist has also claimed an important, if restrained, role for the Court in the constitutional scheme. As noted previously, he has often argued that respect for the Madisonian system of checks and balances necessitates that the Court show self-restraint when faced with essentially political choices regarding the relative balance of individual liberty and public authority. At the same time, however, Rehnquist has insisted that the constitutionally appropriate political body make those choices and that the Court has a role in ensuring that no institution either shirks its responsibilities or encroaches on the proper sphere of another. On occasion, this mandate requires the recognition by the Court that some other institution has primary responsibility for deciding how best to fulfill its constitutional mandates.[84] On many other occasions, the Court has a responsibility to intercede. Interestingly, Rehnquist began his memorandum to Jackson by glossing *Marbury* to read that the Supreme Court is "the ultimate judge" of the various constitutional limits on the government, foreshadowing language that the Court itself would adopt a decade later in expanding its authority over constitutional disputes.[85] He has reemphasized the point more recently as chief justice:

"No doubt the political branches have a role in interpreting and applying the Constitution, but ever since *Marbury* this Court has remained the ultimate expositor of the constitutional text."[86] When other elements of the Constitution "could be defeated" by the efforts of the political branches to interpret and apply the constitutional provisions that have been entrusted to them, then the Court must exercise its "delicate responsibility."[87]

The judicial self-restraint that Rehnquist urged on the Court when facing controversial social issues and innovative rights claims gave way to the judicial duty to intervene when relatively clear rights violations had occurred or the constitutional scheme had otherwise been compromised. Perhaps unsurprisingly, he has not appealed so strongly to the principle of judicial restraint as the chief justice leading a largely conservative Court as he did when in dissent from the Burger Court and the immediate legacy of the Warren era. In practice, the Rehnquist Court in the 1990s has been much more restrained in striking down state laws than has its predecessors over the prior three decades, even as it has aggressively challenged the constitutionality of federal actions.

The chief justice has been assertive on behalf of the primacy of the judicial responsibility for identifying where the authority of one government institution ends and another's begins. In striking down a congressional statute that sought to replace the *Miranda* standard for determining coerced confessions, the chief justice emphasized that "Congress may not legislatively supersede our decisions interpreting and applying the Constitution," even when those decisions have come under criticism from the Court itself.[88] The 1968 statutory provision at issue in that case may have been particularly vulnerable to such a judicial rebuff. Unlike the Court's own later modifications of the *Miranda* rule, the congressional effort was completely unresponsive to the Court's concerns in *Miranda* and simply reflected a hastily written political protest rather than a measured policy response.[89] Similarly, if somewhat uniquely, Rehnquist thought that the U.S. Supreme Court was obliged to intercede if a state judiciary were to "frustrate" a state legislature's exercise of powers delegated specifically to it by the U.S. Constitution.[90] The role of the U.S. Supreme Court in arbitrating interbranch disputes was, to the chief justice, equally important in the context of state institutions selecting presidential electors, though in the instance of *Bush v. Gore* the Court could obviously not escape the kind of direct political controversy that Rehnquist thought more common in the realm of individual rights.

He has also been active in limiting congressional authority to define the constitutional rights enforceable against the states. Though Rehnquist has argued that the judiciary should show restraint relative to legislative decisions about the relationship between government and its citizens, some congressional decisions about rights have additional federalism implications, and the judiciary may be less deferential when the national legislature also seeks to define the relationship between the state governments and their citizens. The Court need not give a final specification of the rights of individuals, but it does need to fix the boundary of authority between the state and federal governments. Rehnquist has emphasized that section five of the Fourteenth Amendment authorizes Congress only to "enforce" the limitations on the states imposed by the amendment. An "enforcement" authority, he has argued, is not equivalent to either a plenary legislative authority or a judicial authority. Congress may only correct "constitutional violations, as this Court has defined them."[91] Otherwise, Congress would be able to enhance its own authority vis-à-vis the states by "altering" the terms of the Fourteenth Amendment. It would be a "topsy-turvy judicial system" that would allow Congress, in the name of remedying constitutional violations, to restrict the states from taking actions that the courts had "affirmatively proved were permissible under the Constitution."[92]

FEDERALISM

Rehnquist may have been most successful in reinvigorating interest in federalism on the Court. Since the New Deal, the Court has been extremely deferential to Congress on matters relating to federalism and the structural limits on the powers of the central government. To most observers, judicially enforceable constitutional limits on the scope of national power seemed of little more than historical interest, as deeply buried as the *Lochner* Court's right to contract. It was, therefore, quite surprising that Rehnquist not only revived the issue but also won a short-lived majority for it in the 1970s. It is perhaps only slightly less surprising, but more consequential, that federalism has taken root on the Rehnquist Court in the 1990s.

The most dramatic statement of Rehnquist's commitment to federalism came in his 1976 majority opinion in *National League of Cities v. Usery.* In *Usery,* he argued that "we have repeatedly recognized that there are attributes of sovereignty attaching to every state government that may not be impaired by Congress."[93] In doing so, he built on one of his own earlier dissenting opinions. In *Fry,* Rehnquist objected to the application of federal wage controls to state employees. Federal law took precedence over state law when they both regulated private "persons or enterprises," but not when the federal regulation is "of the State itself." Federal authority did not extend over activities that are "sufficiently closely allied with traditional state functions."[94] In addition, the Tenth Amendment's recognition of state sovereignty implied an "inherent affirmative constitutional limitation on congressional power" that could exempt state governments from otherwise valid federal regulations, analogous to the rights of individuals guaranteed by other parts of the Bill of Rights.[95] In *Usery,* a majority of the Court supported this view in striking down an extension of the Fair Labor Standards Act to state employees. Even prior majorities had recognized "that Congress may not exercise power in a fashion that impairs the States' integrity or their ability to function in a federal system." Extending federal regulation "not to private citizens but to the States as

States" necessarily hindered state administration and policymaking, essential functions of the states in the federal system.[96] *Usery* was formally overturned in 1985, though in dissent Rehnquist claimed confidence that its principles would "in time again command the support of a majority of this Court."[97]

Some of those principles have indeed regained majority support on the Rehnquist Court, though not in the same form. Rehnquist prefigured some of those later moves in another early opinion in which he suggested the need to reevaluate the Court's approach to the commerce clause. The Constitution authorizes the federal government to regulate interstate commerce, but the identification of the activities that fall into this category has proven complicated. In accepting the New Deal, the Court adopted a very loose standard that gave Congress wide authority over economic activity. In 1981, Rehnquist complained that the Congress had "stretched its authority to the 'nth degree.'" Unlike state police powers, the commerce clause did not provide plenary authority to Congress. The "connection with interstate commerce is itself a jurisdictional prerequisite for any substantive legislation by Congress under the commerce clause," and the Court had a responsibility to take seriously its doctrine that the regulated activity must have a substantial effect on interstate commerce in order to pass constitutional muster.[98] In the late 1990s, the chief justice had the majority to pursue that suggestion.

After a lengthy review of the judicial history of the commerce clause, Rehnquist summarized the postwar doctrine that "requires an analysis of whether the regulated activity 'substantially affects' interstate commerce."[99] In Rehnquist's application, the standard has bite. In the context of the Gun-Free School Zones Act, the chief justice found that by its terms the criminal statute "had nothing to do with 'commerce' or any sort of economic enterprise, however broadly one might define those terms." Where "no such substantial effect was visible to the naked eye," Congress must provide specific legislative findings demonstrating such an effect. Any posited relationship between the regulated activity and interstate commerce would have to be mindful of the inherent limitations on federal power, and the Court would not be willing "to pile inference upon inference in a manner that would bid fair to convert congressional authority under the Commerce Clause to a general police power of the sort retained by the States."[100] The "Constitution requires a distinction between what is truly national and what is truly local," and the "limitation of congressional authority is not solely a matter of legislative grace."[101]

Rehnquist has also sought to protect the states from federal judicial proceedings. As a response to an early Supreme Court decision, the Eleventh Amendment states that the Constitution "shall not be construed" to allow out-of-state citizens to make use of the diversity jurisdiction provision of Article 3 of the Constitution to bring a state government into federal court. In doing so, it recognizes the basic principle that the states were sovereign governments and as such possessed sovereign immunity against lawsuits by individuals without the state's consent. Rehnquist has argued that only the special circumstances of federal protection of Fourteenth Amendment liberties can create exceptions to this principle, and even then Congress has the burden of demonstrating a pattern of constitutional violations by the states.[102]

Notably, "the background principle of state sovereign immunity" cannot be circumvented "even when the Constitution vests in Congress complete lawmaking authority over a particular area," such as congressional power over interstate commerce.[103] Even when Congress has the authority to waive state immunity, the "broader principles" reflected in the Eleventh Amendment require that the congressional intent must be "unmistakably clear."[104] Individual state officials in violation of federal statute or the Constitution cannot be subject to federal suit unless no other remedy is available in either state or federal law.[105]

Similarly, throughout his tenure Rehnquist has struggled with increasing success to pare back federal habeas corpus that had been greatly expanded during the Warren era. In an area such as the criminal law that is so central to the traditional functions of the states, Rehnquist believes that the federal judiciary should be reticent to intercede, reflecting more of an acceptance of diverse local political systems than any special faith in local judges. The "state trial on the merits [should be] the 'main event,'" with federal review justified only in exceptional cases.[106]

CONCLUSION

It is often artificial to name periods of the history of the Supreme Court after the chief justice. The chief justice has relatively little formal power over the Court's work, and the Court is more defined by the cohesiveness and purpose of its majorities than by whoever occupies the center seat on the bench. Thus, the Court under Hughes (after 1937) and Vinson is appropriately known as the New Deal Court. Even when a particular jurisprudential disposition happens to match up with the tenure of a particular chief justice, he or she still may not be the real leader of the Court. Hence, the Warren Court could credibly be known as the Brennan Court. There may be several claimants to the role of namesake for the Court of the late 1980s and 1990s, among them President Ronald Reagan and the often pivotal Justice Sandra Day O'Connor, but Rehnquist has a quite plausible claim to the title himself. Often in dissent for the first decade of his service on the bench, he mapped out the constitutional agenda that would eventually be followed by the White House and the Supreme Court that he ultimately was able to lead. He has not reversed the Warren Court, but rather has developed a distinctly post-Warren conservative constitutional jurisprudence.

In balancing individual rights and democracy, Rehnquist represents a conservative variation on a prominent theme of twentieth-century constitutional thought. The theme appears early—for example, in his controversial memo to

Justice Jackson. Although by the time of his nomination to the Court the arguments in the memo ran contrary to the mythology of the Warren era, there is reason to believe that Rehnquist was not wrong in his assessment that "in the long run it is the majority who will determine what the constitutional rights of the minority are," though he was in error in believing that the antisegregation sentiments of the Court would prove "transient."[107] More generally, Rehnquist tapped into a paradigmatic pragmatist tradition in citing Holmes in support of the view that "where the legislature was dealing with its own citizens, it was not part of the judicial function to thwart public opinion except in extreme cases" and in pointing to *Dred Scott* and *Lochner* as dangerous and illegitimate examples of the Court attempting to read its own political views into the Constitution.[108] In the context of moral disagreement, judges should be skeptical of their confidence in the rightness of their own moral opinions and hesitant to impose their "personal predilections" on their fellow citizens.[109] A commitment to democratic decision-making, in this view, necessitates that the Court exercise judicial restraint except in those instances in which the Constitution clearly limits the authority of elected representatives. In order to avoid the temptation to abuse their power and in order to respect democratic values, judges must bind themselves as closely as possible to the intentions of the lawmakers.[110] Without question, however, the rights that Rehnquist and his conservative colleagues have found clearly embedded in the Constitution, such as a high barrier against government affirmative action, remain controversial to others.

Rehnquist has worked hard to construct a viable post–New Deal conservative philosophy of constitutional law. In his commitment to democratic power and judicial restraint in defining individual rights, he advances a view that was regnant after the New Deal.[111] Though willing to aggressively defend a few fundamental freedoms and clear constitutional requirements, Rehnquist fears the Court being drawn into essentially political decisions about the "substantive business" of government.[112] The activism of the Warren Court necessitated more of a theory of what the Court should be doing than the New Deal justices had initially provided, and a rehabilitation of the founders' intent as a touchstone of constitutional interpretation offered one response.[113] Although an originalist method of constitutional interpretation has the theoretical potential for destabilizing the commitment to judicial restraint—if, for example, the *Lochner* Court was right in its understanding of the historical meaning of the Fourteenth Amendment—Rehnquist has made clear his primary commitment to the latter in the context of controversial individual rights. For Rehnquist, originalism, like Nixon's strict constructionism, has primarily provided a framework for critiquing the expansionistic understanding of individual rights on the part of the Warren and Burger Courts. Even so, as chief justice, he has also been willing to accept entrenched judicial precedents expanding individual rights, even when they conflict with originalist arguments.

Rehnquist sees firmer legal ground among the structural provisions of the

Constitution. Where the legal guidelines are clearer and the temptations to judicial subjectivity are weaker, judicial restraint is less essential (and originalist themes are less prominent). In the areas of federalism and separation of powers, Rehnquist believes that the Court overreacted to the struggle over the New Deal, but he does not question the basic constitutional accommodation that the Court reached with Franklin Roosevelt. He offers a more conservative accommodation, however, one that is more conscious of the basic structural commitments of the founding. Federalism looms large in this context. Although Rehnquist is careful not to challenge the federal government's authority over the national economy, he is insistent that federal power extend no further than is necessary to address the economic transformations of the early twentieth century. The American system embraces both democracy and a communal pluralism. Public values are to be defined in the political arena or else not at all, but the United States leaves space for local communities to reach a variety of different resolutions to our public concerns.

For Richard Nixon, strict construction was a convenient, if ill-defined, label for everything that the Warren Court was not. Despite placing four justices on the Court, Nixon proved unable to fully stop the momentum of the Warren Court.[114] Associate Justice William Rehnquist represented a beacon of hope for conservatives who were disturbed not only by the actions of the Warren Court in the 1950s and 1960s but also by the continuing actions of the Burger Court of the 1970s. Rehnquist's strong voice of dissent indicated that it still might be possible to turn the Court from the path on which it had embarked. His elevation to chief justice of the United States symbolized that the time had finally arrived to take a new path. Although there are limits as to how successfully and how decisively the Rehnquist Court has turned a corner, it seems clear that the chief justice has directed the Court toward a different destination. The Rehnquist Court has sought to play a much less prominent, if still important, role within the political system. It has sought to limit the government less by carving out particular preferred freedoms than by imposing new obstacles on the exercise of central government authority. Its focus is less on achieving its preferred society than on avoiding the perceived mistakes of its own predecessors.

A close student of American political history, Rehnquist may well be taking a lesson from Roger Taney. Ironically, the Rehnquist Court may have stumbled into its own political thicket of presidential politics, even as the chief justice has assiduously sought to avoid forays into social problem-solving and political value judgments where the Taney Court "went totally awry" with *Dred Scott*. But more positively, Rehnquist has urged that *Dred Scott* not obscure Taney's genuine contributions to American constitutional development. Notably, he has praised the Taney Court "at its best" for qualifying rather than overturning the Marshall Court's principal precedents "when common sense seemed to require such qualification" and finding the "necessary authority for states to solve their own problems." It was this "very constructive work" in facilitating the constitutional transformations proceeding elsewhere that

Rehnquist sees as most defining Taney's time on the Court. Strikingly, he concludes his discussion of Taney by repeating the observation of Charles Evans Hughes: "He was a great Chief Justice."[115]

NOTES

1. Quoted in Laura Kalman, *Abe Fortas* (New Haven: Yale University Press, 1990), 348.

2. For discussion, see Donald Grier Stephenson Jr., *Campaigns and the Court* (New York: Columbia University Press, 1999), 168–178.

3. Thomas R. Marshall, *Public Opinion and the Supreme Court* (Boston: Unwin Hyman, 1989), 139.

4. Quoted in Stephenson, *Campaigns and the Court,* 180.

5. Ibid., 181.

6. Ibid.

7. David A. Yalof, *Pursuit of Justices* (Chicago: University of Chicago Press, 1999), 101 (quotation from letter of Herbert Brownell).

8. Lucas A. Powe Jr., *The Warren Court and American Politics* (Cambridge: Harvard University Press, 2000), 482.

9. In terms of opinion writing, Burger was the least productive member of his Court and generally of "average to below-average abilities by Supreme Court standards" (Charles M. Lamb, "Chief Justice Warren E. Burger: A Conservative Chief for Conservative Times," in *The Burger Court,* ed. Charles M. Lamb and Stephen C. Halpern [Urbana: University of Illinois Press, 1991], 133, 159).

10. Quoted in Henry J. Abraham, *Justices and Presidents* (New York: Oxford University Press, 1992), 320.

11. Richard Nixon, *The Public Papers of the President: Richard Nixon, 1971* (Washington, D.C.: Government Printing Office, 1973), 1054, 1056.

12. See also John Anthony Maltese, *The Selling of Supreme Court Nominees* (Baltimore: Johns Hopkins University Press, 1995), 15–16, 74–75, 132–133; David G. Savage, *Turning Right* (New York: John Wiley and Sons, 1992), 42–43.

13. *Nominations of William H. Rehnquist and Lewis F. Powell Jr.: Hearings before the Senate Committee on the Judiciary,* 92d Cong., 1st sess., 1971, 55.

14. Ibid.

15. William H. Rehnquist, "The Notion of a Living Constitution," *Texas Law Review* 54 (1976): 695.

16. Ibid., 696.

17. Ibid., 704, 706.

18. Ibid., 705.

19. Mark Tushnet, "The Burger Court in Historical Perspective: The Triumph of Country Club Republicanism," in *The Burger Court,* ed. Bernard Schwartz (New York: Oxford University Press, 1998).

20. Only Brennan and Marshall were ahead of Rehnquist in either category. The dissent rate is for nonunanimous cases with full opinions.

21. In cases declaring legislation unconstitutional, Rehnquist was in the majority just 38 percent of the time; O'Connor is closest at 66 percent. That basic pattern held through the early Rehnquist Court. Rehnquist was far more likely to be in a majority striking down a congressional statute than state or local legislation. Lee Epstein et al., *The Supreme Court Compendium* (Washington, D.C.: CQ Press, 1996), 550.

22. Quoted in James F. Simon, *In His Own Image* (New York: David McKay, 1973), 241.

23. Warren Weaver, "Mr. Justice Rehnquist Dissenting," *New York Times Magazine,* 13 October 1974, 36. For a perceptive analysis of Rehnquist's constitutional thought during this period, see Sue Davis, *Justice Rehnquist and the Constitution* (Princeton: Princeton University Press, 1989).

24. David M. O'Brien, "The Reagan Judges: His Most Enduring Legacy?" in *The Reagan Legacy,* ed. Charles O. Jones (Chatham, N.J.: Chatham House, 1988), 60, 62.

25. Philip Shenon, "Meese and His New Vision of the Constitution," *New York Times,* 17 October 1985, B10.

26. White House report quoted in Yalof, *Pursuit of Justices,* 153.

27. Savage, *Turning Right,* 8.

28. Quoted in ibid., 9.

29. Ronald Reagan, *Public Papers of the President: Ronald Reagan, 1986* (Washington, D.C.: Government Printing Office, 1988), 819, 829.

30. For one account of that contest, see Peter Irons, *Brennan vs. Rehnquist* (New York: Knopf, 1994).

31. Justice Department report quoted in Yalof, *Pursuit of Justices,* 150. See also Owen Fiss and Charles Krauthammer, "A Return to the Antebellum Constitution: The Rehnquist Court," *New Republic,* 10 March 1982, 14.

32. Unnamed justice quoted in A. E. Dick Howard, "Justice Rehnquist—A Key Fighter in Major Battles," *American Bar Association Journal* 72 (1986): 47. See, for example, O'Brien, "The Reagan Judges," 88; David W. Rohde and Harold J. Spaeth, "Ideology, Strategy, and Supreme Court Decisions: William Rehnquist as Chief Justice," *Judicature* 72 (1989): 247; and Forrest Maltzman and Paul J. Wahlbeck, "May It Please the Chief? Opinion Assignments in the Rehnquist Court," *American Journal of Political Science* 40 (1996): 421.

33. Justice Department report quoted in Yalof, *Pursuit of Justices,* 150.

34. Quoted in O'Brien, "The Reagan Judges," 88; quoted in Abraham, *Justices and the President,* 351.

35. *Nomination of William H. Rehnquist to Be Chief Justice of the United States: Report from the Senate Committee on the Judiciary,* 99th Cong., 2d sess., 1986, 82.

36. Ibid., 30.

37. During his years as chief justice, Rehnquist has also been much more likely to be in the majority when the Court has struck down legislation as unconstitutional (57 percent). It is notable, however, that most of this increase can be accounted for by the relatively greater number of congressional statutes rejected by the Rehnquist Court compared to earlier Courts and the increased likelihood of Rehnquist being in those majorities.

38. Quoted in John A. Jenkins, "The Partisan: A Talk with Justice Rehnquist," *New York Times Magazine,* 3 March 1985, 33.

39. William Rehnquist, "A Random Thought on the Segregation Cases," reprinted in

Nomination of Justice William Hubbs Rehnquist: Hearings before the Senate Committee on the Judiciary, 99th Cong., 2d sess., 1986, 324–325.

40. William H. Rehnquist, "Government by Cliché," *Missouri Law Review* 45 (1980): 393.

41. *Webster v. Reproductive Health Services,* 492 U.S. 490, 521 (1989).

42. *Furman v. Georgia,* 408 U.S. 238, 470 (1972).

43. See, e.g., Rehnquist, "Government by Cliché," 318.

44. *Furman v. Georgia,* 408 U.S. 238, 470 (1972).

45. Cf. Chapter 5 of this book.

46. See especially *Adamson v. California,* 332 U.S. 46, 68 (1947) (Black, J., dissenting).

47. For a recent examination of the historical roots of incorporation, see Akhil Amar, *The Bill of Rights* (New Haven: Yale University Press, 1998).

48. *Richmond Newspapers v. Virginia,* 448 U.S. 555, 606 (1980).

49. *Carter v. Kentucky,* 450 U.S. 288, 309 (1981).

50. Ibid., quoting *Griffin v. California,* 380 U.S. 609, 623 (1965) (Stewart, J., dissenting).

51. *Santosky v. Kramer,* 455 U.S. 745, 771n2, 770 (1982).

52. *Steelworkers v. Weber,* 443 U.S. 193, 220 (1979).

53. Ibid., at 222.

54. Ibid., at 253, 254. Rehnquist has joined important constitutional decisions curtailing affirmative action by state and national governments. See, e.g., *City of Richmond v. J. A. Croson,* 488 U.S. 469 (1989); *Adarand Constructors, Inc. v. Pena,* 515 U.S. 200 (1995).

55. *Planned Parenthood of Southeastern Pennsylvania v. Casey,* 505 U.S. 833, 955 (1992).

56. *Roe v. Wade,* 410 U.S. 113, 172–173 (1973).

57. Ibid., at 175.

58. *Washington v. Glucksberg,* 521 U.S. 702, 722 (1997).

59. *Trimble v. Gordon,* 430 U.S. 762, 779, 778 (1977).

60. Ibid., at 777, 778.

61. *Craig v. Boren,* 429 U.S. 190, 220, 221 (1976).

62. *Wallace v. Jaffree,* 472 U.S. 38, 92, 113 (1985). Especially in the area of criminal justice, Rehnquist's more conservative commitments have led to some divergence between him and the more libertarian originalist arguments of Scalia and Thomas. See, e.g., *Rogers v. Tennessee,* 532 U.S. 451 (2001); *Kyllo v. United States,* 533 U.S. 27 (2001).

63. *Wallace v. Jaffree,* 472 U.S. 38, 106 (1985). See also *Santa Fe Independent School District v. Doe,* 530 U.S. 290, 318 (2000); *Zobrest v. Catalina Foothills School District,* 509 U.S. 1 (1993).

64. *Craig v. Boren,* 429 U.S. 190, 217 (1976); *Califano v. Goldfarb,* 430 U.S. 199, 224 (1977).

65. *United States v. Virginia,* 518 U.S. 515, 559 (1996).

66. Ibid., at 561.

67. Ibid., at 575.

68. *Dickerson v. United States,* 530 U.S. 428 (2000).

69. Ibid., at 451, 462, citing in particular *Michigan v. Tucker,* 417 U.S. 433 (1974).

70. *Virginia State Board of Pharmacy v. Virginia Citizens Consumer Council,* 425 U.S. 748, 784 (1976).

71. *Central Hudson Gas and Electric Corp. v. Public Service Commission of New York,* 447 U.S. 557, 589 (1980).

72. See, e.g., *Glickman v. Wileman Bros. and Elliott,* 521 U.S. 457, 478 (1997); *United States v. United Foods, Inc.,* 533 U.S. 405 (2001); *Lorillard Tobacco Co. v. Reilly,* 533 U.S. 525 (2001).

73. *Nixon v. Administrator of General Services,* 433 U.S. 425, 547 (1977). The same concern with candid discourse drives Rehnquist's defense of the posthumous survival of attorney-client privilege against the efforts of the independent counsel. *Swidler and Berlin v. United States,* 524 U.S. 399 (1998).

74. *Butz v. Economou,* 438 U.S. 478, 517 (1978).

75. *Morrison v. Olson,* 487 U.S. 654, 693 (1988).

76. Ibid., at 670–677.

77. Ibid., at 680–685.

78. Ibid., at 705–710.

79. Ibid., at 693–696.

80. *Industrial Union Department, AFL-CIO v. American Petroleum Institute,* 448 U.S. 607, 672 (1980).

81. Ibid., at 687.

82. *American Textiles Manufacturers Institute v. Donovan,* 452 U.S. 490, 546, 543 (1981).

83. *INS v. Chadha,* 462 U.S. 919, 1015 (1983).

84. See *Goldwater v. Carter,* 444 U.S. 996, 1002 (1979), treaty abrogation nonjusticiable; *Nixon v. United States,* 506 U.S. 224 (1993), impeachments nonjusticiable; *Raines v. Byrd,* 521 U.S. 811 (1997), no generic legislative standing.

85. Rehnquist, "A Random Thought," 324; *Baker v. Carr,* 369 U.S. 186, 211 (1962), "responsibility of this Court as ultimate interpreter of the Constitution."

86. *U.S. v. Morrison,* 120 S.Ct. 1740, 1753n7 (2000).

87. *Nixon v. United States,* 506 U.S. 224, 237, 238 (1993).

88. *Dickerson v. United States,* 530 U.S. 428, 437 (2000).

89. For a brief description of the passage of the legislation, see Powe, *The Warren Court,* 407–410. See also Neal Devins, "How Not to Challenge the Court," *William and Mary Law Review* 39 (1998): 645, on the Religious Freedom Restoration Act.

90. *Bush v. Gore,* 531 U.S. 98, 113 (2000).

91. *City of Rome v. United States,* 446 U.S. 156, 218 (1980). See also *University of Alabama v. Garrett,* 531 U.S. 356 (2001). In the later case, Rehnquist accepts the subsequent argument that the congressional power to enforce Fourteenth Amendment rights against the states includes a constrained power "both to remedy and to deter violation of rights guaranteed thereunder" (*Garrett,* at 365; quoting *City of Boerne v. Flores,* 521 U.S. 507, 536 (1997).

92. *City of Rome v. United States,* 446 U.S. 156, 214, 215 (1980).

93. *National League of Cities v. Usery,* 426 U.S. 833, 845 (1976).

94. *Fry v. United States,* 421 U.S. 542, 552, 558 (1975).

95. Ibid., at 553.

96. *National League of Cities v. Usery,* 426 U.S. 833, 852, 845 (1976). Rehnquist

has more recently noted that states may be regulated as market participants, as long as it does not affect them "in their sovereign capacity" (*Reno v. Condon*, 528 U.S. 141 [2000]).

97. *Garcia v. San Antonio Metropolitan Transit Authority*, 469 U.S. 528, 580 (1985).

98. *Hodel v. Virginia Surface Mining and Reclamation Association*, 452 U.S. 264, 311 (1981).

99. *United States v. Lopez*, 514 U.S. 549, 559 (1995).

100. Ibid., at 561, 563, 567.

101. *United States v. Morrison*, 529 U.S. 598, 618, 616 (2000).

102. Ibid., at 619–627; *University of Alabama v. Garrett*, 531 U.S. 536 (2001).

103. *Seminole Tribe of Florida v. Florida*, 517 U.S. 44, 72 (1996).

104. Ibid., at 56.

105. Ibid., at 74–75; *Florida Prepaid Postsecondary Education Expense Board v. College Savings Bank*, 527 U.S. 627, 643 (1999); *Parratt v. Taylor*, 451 U.S. 527, 539–541 (1981).

106. *Wainwright v. Sykes*, 433 U.S. 72, 91 (1977).

107. Rehnquist, "A Random Thought," 325. For skepticism of the countermajoritarian capacity of the Court, see Robert A. Dahl, "Decision-Making in a Democracy: The Supreme Court as a National Policy-Maker," *Journal of Public Law* 6 (1957): 284; Gerald Rosenberg, *The Hollow Hope* (Chicago: University of Chicago Press, 1991); Barry Friedman, "Dialogue and Judicial Review," *Michigan Law Review* 57 (1993): 91; Mark A. Graber, "The Passive-Aggressive Virtues: *Cohens v. Virginia* and the Problematic Establishment of Judicial Power," *Constitutional Commentary* 12 (1995): 67; James A. Stimson, Michael B. MacKuen, and Robert S. Erikson, "Dynamic Representation," *American Political Science Review* 89 (1995): 543; Michael Klarman, "Rethinking the Civil Rights and Civil Liberties Revolution," *Virginia Law Review* 82 (1996): 1; and Powe, *The Warren Court*, 484–501.

108. Rehnquist, "A Random Thought," 324–325.

109. Ibid., 324.

110. See also Howard Gillman, "The Collapse of Constitutional Originalism and the Rise of the Notion of the 'Living Constitution' in the Course of American State-Building," *Studies in American Political Development* 11 (1997): 191.

111. Tellingly, Rehnquist frequently references one of the seminal post–New Deal cases on individual rights, *Williamson v. Lee Optical* (348 U.S. 483 [1955]). See, e.g., *Weber v. Aetna Casualty and Surety Co.*, 406 U.S. 164, 178 (1972); *Cleveland Board of Education v. LaFleur*, 414 U.S. 632, 660 (1974); *Craig v. Boren*, 429 U.S. 190, 218 (1976); *Renton v. Playtime Theatres*, 475 U.S. 41, 53 (1986); *Planned Parenthood of Southeastern Pennsylvania v. Casey*, 505 U.S. 833, 966 (1992); *Greater New Orleans Broadcasting Association v. United States*, 527 U.S. 173, 196 (1999).

112. Rehnquist, "A Random Thought," 324.

113. Notably, Rehnquist has rejected the other significant response, the canonization of the Carolene Products Footnote Four in which the Court committed itself to the heightened protection of "discrete and insular minorities." *United States v. Carolene Products Co.*, 304 U.S. 144, 152n4 (1938). See, e.g., *Sugarman v. Dougall*, 413 U.S. 634, 656 (1973).

114. Nonetheless, Nixon's four appointees were relatively cohesive and conserva-

tive. See Stefanie A. Lindquist, David A. Yalof, and John A. Clark, "The Impact of Presidential Appointments to the U.S. Supreme Court: Cohesive and Divisive Voting within Presidential Blocs," *Political Research Quarterly* 53 (2000): 795.

115. William H. Rehnquist, *The Supreme Court* (New York: William Morrow, 1987), 133, 150.

2

Text and Tradition: The Originalist Jurisprudence of Antonin Scalia

Ralph A. Rossum

On June 24, 1986, Antonin Scalia—at the time a judge on the U.S. Court of Appeals for the District of Columbia Circuit—was nominated by President Ronald Reagan to serve as an associate justice of the U.S. Supreme Court. On September 17 (Constitution Day), he was confirmed by the Senate by a vote of 98 to 0 and took his seat on September 26. His majority, concurring, and dissenting opinions—all carefully wrought, powerfully argued, highly principled, and filled with well-turned phrases—provide a rich source of instruction on his approach to constitutional interpretation and on the emerging dimensions of his jurisprudence.

Antonin Scalia was born on March 11, 1936, in Trenton, New Jersey. The only child of an Italian immigrant father who became a professor of Romance languages at Brooklyn College and of an Italian-American mother who taught public school, he was educated at Georgetown University (where he graduated as valedictorian of his class in 1957) and Harvard Law School (where he served as notes editor of the *Harvard Law Review* and from which he received his L.L.B. in 1960). He is married and has nine children.

Upon graduation from law school, Scalia practiced law in Cleveland, Ohio, for Jones, Day, Cockley, and Reavis until 1967, when he became professor of law at the University of Virginia. He joined the law faculty at the University of Chicago in 1977 and served there until his appointment to the D.C. Circuit by President Reagan in 1982. Often on leave from his academic posts, he served as general counsel for the Office of Telecommunications Policy, chairman of the Administrative Conference of the United States, assistant attorney general for the Office of Legal Counsel, chairman of the ABA Section of Administrative Law, and chairman of the ABA Conference of Section Chairmen. With Murray Weidenbaum, he was founding co-editor of *Regulation.* What is particularly noteworthy about Scalia's background is his extensive experience in the practice of law, the teaching of law, "inside the beltway" Washington politics, and ABA politics. Scalia knows how law is practiced, taught, and used for corporate, political, and constitutional objectives.

SCALIA'S TEXTUALIST JURISPRUDENCE

Since his elevation to the high bench, Justice Scalia has assiduously and consistently pursued a textualist jurisprudence. He argues that primacy must be accorded to the text, structure, and history of the document being interpreted and that the job of the judge is to apply the clear textual language of the Constitution or statute[1] or the critical structural principle[2] necessarily implicit in the text.[3] If the text is ambiguous, yielding several conflicting interpretations, he turns to the specific legal tradition[4] flowing from that text—to "what it meant to the society that adopted it."[5] "Text and tradition" is a phrase that fills Justice Scalia's opinions.[6] Judges are to be governed only by the "text and tradition of the Constitution," not by their "intellectual, moral, and personal perceptions." As he remarked in his concurring opinion in *Schad v. Arizona*, "When judges test their individual notions of 'fairness' against an American tradition that is deep and broad and continuing, it is not the tradition that is on trial, but the judges."[7]

For Scalia, reliance on text and tradition is a means of constraining judicial discretion. He believes that "the main danger in judicial interpretation of the Constitution—or, for that matter, in judicial interpretation of any law[8]—is that the judges will mistake their own predilections for the law."[9] Faithful adherence to the text of a constitutional or statutory provision or, if that is ambiguous, to the traditional understanding of those who originally adopted it reduces the danger that judges will substitute their beliefs for society's.[10] As Scalia observed in response to a question by Senator Howard Metzenbaum during his Senate confirmation hearings:

> A constitution has to have ultimately majoritarian underpinnings. To be sure a constitution is a document that protects against future democratic excesses. But when it is adopted, it is adopted by democratic process. That is what legitimates it. . . . [I]f the majority that adopted it did not believe this unspecified right, which is not reflected clearly in the language, if their laws at the time do not reflect that that right existed, nor do the laws at the present date reflect that the society believes that right exists, I worry about my deciding that it exists. I worry that I am not reflecting the most fundamental, deeply felt beliefs of our society, which is what a constitution means, but rather, I am reflecting the most deeply felt beliefs of Scalia, which is not what I want to impose on the society.[11]

For Scalia, the Court's opinions in the companion cases of *Board of County Commissioners, Wabaunsee County v. Umbehr*[12] and *O'Hare Truck Service v. Northlake*[13] fully demonstrate the justices' willingness to substitute their beliefs for the traditional beliefs of society. In his combined dissent in these cases, he ridiculed the "Court's Constitution-making process"[14] that prompted his colleagues to declare that the freedom of speech clause of the First Amendment protects private contractors from government retaliation for their exercise of political speech (in the former case, a trash hauler alleged that he had lost a county contract after he criticized the board in a letter to the editor of a local newspaper; in the latter, a towing firm alleged that it was barred from getting towing referrals after the owner refused to contribute to the mayor's reelection). Scalia noted that "rewarding one's allies" while "refusing to reward one's opponents" is "an American political tradition as old as the Republic." Zeroing in on this old tradition, he asked: "If that long and unbroken tradition of our people does not decide these cases, then what does? The constitutional text is assuredly as susceptible of one meaning as of the other; in that circumstance, what constitutes a 'law abridging the freedom of speech' is either a matter of history or else it is a matter of opinion. Why are not libel laws such an 'abridgment'? The only satisfactory answer is that they never were." Scalia's anger was palpable: "What secret knowledge, one must wonder, is breathed into lawyers when they become Justices of this Court, that enables them to discern that a practice which the text of the Constitution does not clearly proscribe, and which our people have regarded as constitutional for 200 years, is in fact unconstitutional?" [15]

Scalia understands that the Constitution creates two conflicting systems of rights: one is democratic—the right of the majority to rule individuals; the other is antidemocratic—the right of individuals to have certain interests protected from majority rule. He relies on the Constitution's text to define the respective spheres of majority and minority freedom, and when that fails to provide definitive guidance, Scalia turns to tradition. He argues that tradition, and not the personal values of the justices, is to tell the Court when the majoritarian process is to be overruled in favor of individual rights.[16] He believes that by identifying those areas of life traditionally protected from majority rule, the Court can objectively determine which individual freedoms the Constitution protects.[17] As he argued in his dissent in *Umbehr* and *O'Hare Truck Service,* "I would separate the permissible from the impermissible on the basis of our Nation's traditions, which is what I believe sound constitutional adjudication requires."[18]

Scalia therefore would overrule the majority only when it has infringed upon an individual right explicitly protected by the text of the Constitution or by specific legal traditions flowing from that text.[19] In his dissent in *United States v. Virginia,*[20] in which the Court proclaimed that the exclusively male admission policy of the Virginia Military Institute violated the equal protection clause of the Fourteenth Amendment, he declared that the function of the Court is to "preserve our society's values, not to revise them; to prevent backsliding from the degree of restriction the Constitution imposed upon democratic government, not to prescribe, on our own authority, progressively higher degrees." The Court is not to "supersede" but rather is to "reflect" those "constant and unbroken national traditions that embody the people's understanding of ambiguous constitutional texts."[21] As he eloquently argued in his dissent in *Rutan v. Republican Party,* in which the Court held that political patronage violates the free speech rights of public employees:

> The provisions of the Bill of Rights were designed to restrain transient majorities from impairing long-recognized personal liberties. They did not create by implication novel individual rights overturning accepted political norms. Thus, when a practice not expressly prohibited by the text of the Bill of Rights bears the endorsement of a long tradition of open, widespread, and unchallenged use that dates back to the beginning of the Republic, we have no proper basis for striking it down. Such a venerable and accepted tradition is not to be laid on the examining table and scrutinized for its conformity to some abstract principle of First Amendment adjudication devised by this Court. . . . When it appears that the latest "rule," or "three-part test," or "balancing test" devised by the Court has placed us on a collision course with such a landmark practice, it is the former that must be recalculated by us, and not the latter that must be abandoned by our citizens.[22]

In *Harmelin v. Michigan,*[23] Scalia's text-and-tradition approach was on full display. In it, he held that the "cruel and unusual punishments" clause of the Eighth Amendment does not prohibit the imposition of a mandatory term of life in prison without possibility of parole for possessing more than 650 grams of cocaine. Announcing the judgment of the Court, he rejected the plaintiff's contention that his sentence was unconstitutional because it was "significantly disproportionate" to the crime he had committed. Scalia noted that "this claim has no support in the text and history of the Eighth Amendment."[24] Concerning the text, he observed that "to use the phrase 'cruel and unusual punishment' to describe a requirement of proportionality would have been an exceedingly vague and oblique way of saying what Americans were well accustomed to saying more directly."[25] Concerning history, he surveyed English constitutional history since the promulgation of the English Declaration of Rights as well as eighteenth- and nineteenth-century American constitutional and legal history to show that the "cruel and unusual punishments" clause was understood only "to outlaw particular modes of punishment" (e.g., drawing and quartering, breaking on the wheel, flaying alive, and so forth), not to require that "all punishments be proportioned to the offense."[26] He was led, therefore, to argue that *Solem v. Helms,*[27] in which the Court had previously held that the Eighth Amendment does contain a proportionality guarantee, was "wrong" and should be overturned.[28]

Although his textualist approach led Scalia in *Harmelin* to reject a criminal defendant's claim, it does not always. Thus, in *Coy v. Iowa,*[29] it led him to uphold the right of a defendant (in this case, a man convicted of two counts of engaging in lascivious acts with a child) literally to "be confronted with the witnesses against him" and to overturn his conviction because Iowa law allowed the two thirteen-year-old girls he was charged with sexually assaulting to testify behind a large screen that shielded them from the defendant. For Scalia, the text was unequivocal and governing: "Simply as a matter of English, it confers at least 'a right to meet face to face all those who appear and give evidence at trial.' Simply as a matter of Latin as well, since the word 'confront' ultimately derives from the prefix 'con-' (from 'contra' meaning 'against' or 'opposed') and the noun 'frons' (forehead). Shakespeare was thus describing the root meaning of confrontation when he had Richard the Second say: 'Then call them to our presence—face to face, and frowning brow to brow, ourselves will hear the accuser and the accused freely speak.'"[30]

Likewise, in *Rogers v. Tennessee,*[31] Scalia's text and tradition approach led him to conclude in his dissent that the Tennessee Supreme Court's retroactive abolition of the common law "year-and-a-day" rule concerning murder convictions (no defendant could be convicted of murder unless the victim died by the defendant's act within a year and a day of the act) violated the due process clause of the Fourteenth Amendment insofar as that clause contains the principle applied against state legislatures by the ex post facto clause of Article I, section 10: "Such retroactive revision of a concededly valid legal rule . . . was unheard-of at the time the original due process clause was adopted."[32]

Scalia does not restrict his text-and-tradition approach to criminal procedural matters; he applies it across the constitutional board. He applied it, for example, in *Pacific Mutual Life Insurance Co. v. Haslip*[33] when he denied that the due process clause places limits on the size of punitive damage awards. He cited Sir Edward Coke, William Blackstone, James Kent, and Joseph Story, all of whom argued that due process means simply the "law of the land," and concluded that the due process clause is met if the trial is conducted according to the settled course of judicial proceedings.[34] "If the government chooses to follow a historically approved procedure, it necessarily provides due process."[35]

He has also applied his text-and-tradition approach to the establishment clause, where it led him to conclude in his dissent in *Lee v. Weisman*[36] that it "was adopted to prohibit such an establishment of religion at the federal level [as in England was represented by the Church of England] and to protect state establishments of religion from federal interference" and that it did not bar nonsectarian prayers at public school graduation ceremonies.[37] Likewise, it led him to complain in *Board of Education of Kiryas Joel v. Grumet*[38] that

> the Founding Fathers would be astonished to find that the Establishment Clause—which they designed "to ensure that no one powerful sect or combination of sects would use political or governmental power to punish dissenters"—has been employed to prohibit characteristically and admirably American accommodation of the religious practices (or more precisely, cultural peculiarities) of a tiny minority sect. I, however, am not surprised. Once this Court has abandoned text and history as guides, nothing prevents it from calling religious tolerance the establishment of religion.

And, concerning the free exercise clause, it led him to conclude in his controversial majority opinion in *Employment Division, Department of Human Resources of Oregon v. Smith*[39] that, "as a textual matter," there is no need to provide a religious exemption to a generally applicable statute, and that "to make an individual's obligation to obey such a law contingent upon the law's coincidence with his religious beliefs, except where the State's interest is 'compelling'—permitting him, by virtue of his beliefs, 'to become a law unto himself,'—contradicts both constitutional tradition and common sense."[40]

Scalia believes deeply in following his text-and-tradition approach. His duty, as he described it in his dissent in *Planned Parenthood v. Casey,* is to "read the text and discern our society's traditional understanding of that text."[41] Discerning the original meaning is, he told the Senate Judiciary Committee during his confirmation hearings, "the starting point and the beginning of wisdom."[42] Nevertheless, Scalia occasionally drifts from his "text-and-tradition" moorings. *Texas v. Johnson,*[43] the flag-burning case in which he joined in Justice Brennan's majority opinion striking down Texas's ban on burning the American flag, is a glaring case in point. It is true that during his Senate confirmation hearings, Scalia defined speech as "any communicative activity,"[44] and, by that definition, flag burning was communicative activity and thereby speech and therefore protected by the First Amendment. What is problematic, however, is not that Scalia's conclusion does not follow logically from his premise but rather the premise itself. There is absolutely no textual or historical evidence to support the contention that the society that adopted the First Amendment understood it to cover all communicative activity. Another glaring case in point is Scalia's unquestioned acceptance of the incorporation doctrine, which is possibly explained by his reluctance to be perceived as a Don Quixote tilting at windmills. As he observed in *Albright v. Oliver,* "Our decisions have included within the Fourteenth Amendment certain explicit substantive protections of the Bill of Rights—*an extension I accept because it is both long established and narrowly limited.*"[45] A third example (and perhaps the most difficult to explain) is Scalia's consistent embrace of the Court's "state sovereignty immunity" jurisprudence. In seven cases since 1996,[46] he has invariably joined in majority opinions that openly dismiss textualism and that repeat the words of Chief Justice Rehnquist first uttered in *Seminole Tribe of Florida v. Florida,* that "a blind reliance upon the text of the Eleventh Amendment" would be "overly exacting" and that the Eleventh Amendment stands, "not so much for what it says, as for the presupposition . . . which it confirms.[47]

Scalia believes that "the rule of law is the law of rules," which reflects the title of his Oliver Wendell Holmes Jr. Lecture delivered at Harvard Law School in 1989.[48] He argues that where the text embodies a rule, judges are simply to apply that rule as the law.[49] Where text and tradition fail to supply a rule, there is no rule; hence there is no law for judges to apply to contradict the actions of the popular branches and, therefore, no warrant for judicial intervention. This was his argument in *Troxel v. Granville,*[50] in which he dissented from the

Supreme Court's invalidation of a Washington State nonparental visitation statute (providing visitation rights for nonparents of a child if a judge found that it would be in the best interests of the child) on the grounds that it unconstitutionally infringed on the fundamental right of parents to rear their children. Scalia found the law offensive, declaring that "in my view, a right of parents to direct the upbringing of their children is among the 'unalienable Rights' with which the Declaration of Independence proclaims 'all Men . . . are endowed by their Creator.'"[51] But, he continued, offensive laws are not unconstitutional in the absence of clear text making them so:

> Judicial vindication of "parental rights" under a Constitution that does not even mention them requires not only a judicially crafted definition of parents, but also—unless, as no one believes, the parental rights are to be absolute—judicially approved assessments of "harm to the child" and judicially defined gradations of other persons (grandparents, extended family, adoptive family in an adoption later found to be invalid, long-term guardians, etc.) who may have some claim against the wishes of the parents. If we embrace this unenumerated right, I think it obvious . . . that we will be ushering in a new regime of judicially prescribed, and federally prescribed, family law. I have no reason to believe that federal judges will be better at this than state legislatures; and state legislatures have the great advantages of doing harm in a more circumscribed area, of being able to correct their mistakes in a flash, and of being removable by the people.[52]

This was also his argument in *Romer v. Evans*,[53] in which he unleashed a powerful attack on the Court for "tak[ing] sides in the culture war"[54] and invalidating Colorado's "Amendment 2" denying preferential treatment to homosexuals. "Since the Constitution of the United States says nothing about this subject, it is left to be resolved by normal democratic means, including the democratic adoption of provisions in state constitutions. This Court has no business imposing upon all Americans the resolution favored by the elite class from which the Members of this institution are selected, pronouncing that 'animosity' toward homosexuality is evil."[55] And this was his argument in his concurring opinion in *Cruzan v. Director, Missouri Department of Health*,[56] in which the Court rejected the petitioner's contention that she had a "right to die." Scalia wrote:

> While I agree with the Court's analysis today, and therefore join in its opinion, I would have preferred that we announce, clearly and promptly, that the federal courts have no business in this field; that American law has always accorded the State the power to prevent, by force if necessary, suicide—including suicide by refusing to take appropriate measures necessary to preserve one's life; that the point at which life becomes "worthless," and the point at which the means necessary to preserve it become "extraordinary" or "inappropriate," are neither set forth in the Constitution nor known to the

nine Justices of this Court any better than they are known to nine people picked at random from the Kansas City telephone directory; and hence, that even when it is demonstrated by clear and convincing evidence that a patient no longer wishes certain measures to be taken to preserve her life, it is up to the citizens of Missouri to decide, through their elected representatives, whether that wish will be honored. It is quite impossible that those citizens will decide upon a line less lawful than the one we would choose; and it is unlikely (because we know no more about "life-and-death" than they do) that they will decide upon a line less reasonable.[57]

In *A Matter of Interpretation,* Justice Scalia succinctly spelled out both the origins of judicial policymaking and his reasons for rejecting it. Judicial policymaking arose, he noted, in the old common-law system in England where judges, unconstrained by statutes or a written constitution, exercised the "exhilarating" function of making law. From there, it eventually spread to modern American law schools where impressionable "law students, having drunk at this intoxicating well," come away thinking that the highest function of the judge is "devising, out of the brilliance of one's own mind, those laws that ought to govern mankind. How exciting!"[58] He noted a key problem with this approach: It is a "trend in government that has developed in recent centuries, called democracy."[59] As Scalia insisted, "It is simply not compatible with democratic theory that laws mean whatever they ought to be mean, and that unelected judges decide what that is."[60]

Scalia has castigated the Court for its contemptuous disregard for the democratic principle in several powerful dissents. Thus, in his dissent in the companion cases of *Umbehr* and *O'Hare Truck Service,* he accused the Court majority of "living in another world. Day by day, case by case, it is busy designing a Constitution for a country I do not recognize." He warned the public that "while the present Court sits, a major, undemocratic restructuring of our national institutions and mores is constantly in progress."[61] Likewise, in his dissent in *United States v. Virginia,* he acerbically noted that much of the Court's opinion concerning Virginia Military Institute and its all-male student body was "devoted to deprecating the closed-mindedness of our forebears with regard to women's education." He therefore felt obliged to "counterbalance" the Court's criticism of our ancestors and to say a word in their praise: "They left us free to change." The virtue of the democratic system with its First Amendment "that we inherited from our forebears" is that "it readily enables the people, over time, to be persuaded that what they took for granted is not so, and to change their laws accordingly." That system, he continued, "is destroyed if the smug assurances of each age are removed from the democratic process and written into the Constitution." But, Scalia charged, that is exactly what "this most illiberal Court" has been doing: it has "embarked on a course of inscribing one after another of the current preferences of the society (and in some cases only the counter-majoritarian preferences of the society's law-trained elite) into our Basic Law."[62]

SCALIA'S UNDERSTANDING OF THE
"WHOLE THEORY OF DEMOCRACY"

Scalia is criticized for a "vulgar majoritarian" understanding of democracy.[63] This criticism is based in large part on a lecture he gave in May 1996 at the Gregorian University in Rome (where his son was a student). During the question-and-answer period that followed, he declared that "it just seems to me incompatible with democratic theory that it's good and right for the state to do something that the majority of the people do not want done. Once you adopt democratic theory, it seems to me, you accept that proposition. If the people, for example, want abortion the state should permit abortion. If the people do not want it, the state should be able to prohibit it." He went on to declare that "the whole theory of democracy . . . is that the majority rules; that is the whole theory of it. You protect minorities only because the majority determines that there are certain minority positions that deserve protection."[64]

This criticism is also based on statements he made in his reply to Laurence Tribe's commentary on his essay in *A Matter of Interpretation.* In dismissing Tribe's "aspirational" theory of constitutional interpretation, Scalia wrote: "If you want aspirations, you can read the Declaration of Independence, with its pronouncements that 'all men are created equal' with 'unalienable Rights' that include 'Life, Liberty, and the Pursuit of Happiness.' Or you can read the French Declaration of the Rights of Man." But, he continued, "There is no such philosophizing in our Constitution, which, unlike the Declaration of Independence and the Declaration of the Rights of Man, is a practical and pragmatic charter of government."[65]

Scalia's critics point out that his theory of democracy bears no relation to the nation's traditional understanding of the limits of the principle of majority rule, so perfectly captured by Thomas Jefferson in his first Inaugural Address: "All, too, will bear in mind this sacred principle, that though the will of the majority is in all cases to prevail, that will to be rightful must be reasonable; that the minority possess their equal rights, which equal laws must protect, and to violate would be oppression."[66] According to Jefferson and the traditional American understanding, "the minority possess their equal rights" independently of the majority; their equal rights are antecedent to majority rule, and majority rule is circumscribed by them. As Harry V. Jaffa has written, the traditional American understanding was that "the foundation of all our free institutions is the doctrine that, under the laws of nature and nature's God, all human beings are endowed with certain unalienable rights, and that it is for the sake of these rights that governments are instituted. As these rights belong *a priori* to every person, they are of necessity the rights of every minority."[67] Scalia's critics also wonder how someone who argues, as he does, that "in textual interpretation, context is everything,"[68] could fail to consider the Declaration of Independence and its theory of democracy in constitutional context.

Scalia is vulnerable to the first criticism. He simply has not developed a well-thought-out understanding of the principles of democracy and, perhaps as a consequence, appears to assume that democracy everywhere operates as it does in the United States at the beginning of the new millennium, where the Constitution, as amended, protects the rights of minorities, where the Constitution itself and its subsequent amendments were ratified by extraordinary majorities, and where the principal threat to democracy is not majority rule trampling on the rights of minorities but the Court itself threatening the right of the majority to rule itself. However, concerning the second criticism—that he has rejected an aspirational theory of constitutional interpretation—Scalia is on firmer ground. He has defended himself by observing that, at least with respect to the Bill of Rights,

> the context suggests that the abstract and general terms, like the concrete and particular ones, are meant to nail down current rights, rather than aspire after future ones—that they are abstract and general references to *extant* rights and freedoms possessed under the then-current regime. The same conclusion follows from the evident purpose of the provisions. To guarantee that freedom of speech will be no less than it is today is to guarantee something permanent; to guarantee that it will be no less than the aspirations of the future is to guarantee nothing in particular at all.[69]

SCALIA'S REJECTION OF LEGISLATIVE HISTORY

As a textualist, Justice Scalia totally rejects reliance on legislative history or legislative intent. He made it very clear during his Senate confirmation hearings that he was not "enamored" with the use of legislative history and reliance on committee reports. As he told Senator Charles Mathias, "Once it was clear that the courts were going to use them [committee reports] all the time, they certainly became a device not to inform the rest of the body as to what the intent of the bill was, but rather they became avowedly a device to make some legislative history and tell the courts how to hold this way or that. Once that happens, they become less reliable as a real indicator of what the whole body thought it was voting on."[70]

He invariably criticizes his colleagues for turning to committee reports, or even floor debates, to ascertain what a law means. His extensive "inside the beltway" experience has made him savvy about how often congressmen will withdraw actual amendments to bills under consideration in the House because they are told by the floor leaders of the bill that they will take care of the congressmen's concerns through the drafting of the legislative history. In *U.S. v. Taylor*,[71] he perspicaciously drew out the consequences:

> By perpetuating the view that legislative history *can* alter the meaning of even a clear statutory provision, we produce a legal culture in which the following statement could be made—taken from a portion of the floor debate alluded to in the Court's opinion:
> MR. DENNIS: "I have an amendment here in my hand which could be

offered, but if we can make up some legislative history which would do the same thing, I am willing to do it."

We should not make the equivalency between making legislative history and making an amendment so plausible. It should not be possible, or at least should not be easy, to be sure of obtaining a particular result in this Court without making that result apparent on the face of the bill which both Houses consider and vote upon, which the President approves, and which, if it becomes a law, the people must obey. I think we have an obligation to conduct our exegesis in a fashion which fosters that democratic process.[72]

Scalia argues that the Court is to interpret the text alone and nothing else.[73] The law should be understood to mean what it says and say what it means. Otherwise, as Scalia noted in his Court of Appeals dissent in *Illinois Commerce Commission v. Interstate Commerce Commission*,[74] compromise, so essential to the legislative process, "becomes impossible." "When there is no assurance that the statutory words in which [the compromise] is contained will be honored," both sides to a compromise "have every reason to fear that any ambiguity will be interpreted against their interests" in subsequent litigation.[75] Likewise, if the law does not mean what it says and does not say what it means, citizens are left at a loss concerning how they should conduct themselves. As he said in *U.S. v. R.L.C.*,[76] "It may well be true that in most cases the proposition that the words of the United States Code or the Statutes At Large give adequate notice to the citizen is something of a fiction, albeit one required in any system of law; but necessary fiction descends to needless farce when the public is charged even with knowledge of Committee Reports."

Scalia insists that the Court should focus its attention on the text alone. As he argued in *Wisconsin Public Intervenor v. Mortier*,[77] "We should try to give the text its fair meaning, whatever various committees might have had to say — thereby affirming the proposition that we are a Government of laws, not committee reports." He took some satisfaction in the fact that "today's decision reveals that, in their judicial application, committee reports are a forensic rather than an interpretive device, to be invoked when they support the decision and ignored when they do not. To my mind that is infinitely better than honestly giving them dispositive effect. But it would be better still to stop confusing [lower courts] and not to use committee reports at all."[78]

Scalia's attack on the use of legislative history is nowhere more sustained and devastating than in his opinion in *Conroy v. Aniskoff*,[79] in which he concurred in the judgment:

The Court begins its analysis with the observation: "The statutory command . . . is unambiguous, unequivocal, and unlimited." In my view, discussion of that point is where the remainder of the analysis should have ended. Instead, however, the Court [Justice Stevens] feels compelled to demonstrate that its holding is consonant with legislative history, including some dating back to 1917 — *a full quarter century* before the provision at issue was enacted. That is not merely a waste of research time and ink; it is a false and disruptive lesson in the law. It says to the bar that even an "unambiguous (and) unequivocal" statute can never be dispositive; that, presumably under penalty of malpractice liability, the oracles of legislative history, far into the dimmy past, must always be consulted. This undermines the clarity of law, and condemns litigants (who, unlike us, must pay for it out of their own pockets) to subsidizing historical research by lawyers. The greatest defect of legislative history is its illegitimacy. We are governed by laws, not by the intentions of legislators. . . . But not the least of the defects of legislative history is its indeterminacy. If one were to search for an interpretative technique that, *on the whole,* was more likely to confuse than to clarify, one could hardly find a more promising candidate than legislative history.[80]

Scalia's contempt for the use of legislative history leads him to some interesting exchanges with his colleagues. In *Chisom v. Roemer,*[81] he was provoked to declare that there is a mistaken "notion that Congress cannot be credited with having achieved anything of major importance by simply saying it, in ordinary language, in the text of a statute, 'without comment' in the legislative history. As the Court colorfully puts it, if the dog of legislative history has not barked, nothing of great significance can have transpired. . . . We have forcefully and explicitly rejected the Conan Doyle approach[82] to statutory construction in the past. . . . We are here to apply the statute, not legislative history, and certainly not the absence of legislative history. Statutes are the law though sleeping dogs lie."[83] And, in *United States v. Thompson/Center Arms Co.,*[84] he ridiculed Justice David Souter for resorting "to that last hope of lost interpretive causes, that St. Jude of the hagiography of statutory construction, legislative history."[85] Souter defended his antitextualist approach by quoting a passage from Justice Frankfurter, a passage that perfectly encapsulates the view that Scalia rejects: "A statute, like other living organisms, derives significance and sustenance from its environment, from which it cannot be severed without being mutilated. Especially is this true where the statute, like the one before us, is part of a legislative process having a history and a purpose. The meaning of such a statute cannot be gained by confining inquiry within its four corners. Only the historic process of which such legislation is an incomplete fragment — that to which it gave rise as well as that which gave rise to it — can yield its true meaning."[86]

Scalia's textualist critique of legislative history has produced dramatic results. Judge Patricia Wald of the U.S. Court of Appeals for the District of Columbia noted in the *Iowa Law Review* that in its 1981–1982 term, the Supreme Court looked at legislative history in virtually every statutory case, regardless of whether it thought that the statute had a clear meaning on its face.[87] In 1995, Gregory E. Maggs, writing in the *Public Interest Law Review,* observed that by the early 1990s, legislative history was being cited in only about 40 percent of statutory cases. He offered a reason:

> With Justice Scalia breathing down the necks of anyone who peeks into the *Congressional Record* or Senate reports, the other members of the Court may have concluded that the benefit of citing legislative history does not outweigh its costs. It is likely for this reason that the percentage of cases citing it has decreased dramatically. No one likes an unnecessary fight, especially not one with as formidable an opponent as Justice Scalia.[88]

Scalia has influenced members of Congress no less than his colleagues on the high bench. When the House Judiciary Committee was drafting a 1991 anticrime bill, *Congressional Quarterly* reported that "some members suggested resolving a dispute by putting compromise language into a committee report, which accompanies a bill to the floor. But Barney Frank, D-Mass., warned off his colleagues with just two words, 'Justice Scalia.'"[89]

SCALIA'S ORIGINALISM

Justice Scalia emphatically rejects legislative history and intent, yet he is described, and describes himself, as an originalist. On the surface, this contradiction suggests a tension: If it is a mistake for his colleagues to consult extrinsic evidence of Congress's intentions as found in a law's legislative history, why is it appropriate for him to consult extrinsic evidence of the framers' intentions as found, say, in *The Federalist*? The tension is heightened further as a result of Scalia's assertion in *Tome v. United States* that "the views of Alexander Hamilton (a draftsman) bear [no] more authority than the views of Thomas Jefferson (not a draftsman) with regard to the meaning of the Constitution."[90]

The answer to that question is that Scalia is a particular kind of originalist. What he means by originalism is revealed by illustration in his Holmes Lecture: "If a barn was not considered the curtilage of a house in 1791, . . . and the Fourth Amendment did not cover it then, unlawful entry into a barn today may be a trespass, but not an unconstitutional search and seizure."[91] For Scalia, originalism is synonymous with the original meaning doctrine. He seeks the original meaning from the text of the document itself and from what it meant to the society that adopted it;[92] at the same time, he ignores altogether the subjective preferences or intentions of those who wrote it. And, of course, for Scalia, originalism means applying that original meaning to the case at hand. His application of originalism in the context of the Fourth Amendment is clearly evident in his majority opinion for the Court in *Kyllo v. United States.*[93] *Kyllo* involved the warrantless use from a public street of a thermal-imaging device aimed at a private residence occupied by someone suspected of growing marijuana. The device detected relative amounts of heat within the residence and whether high-intensity lights were being used to grow marijuana indoors. Scalia held its warrantless use was unreasonable and therefore constituted an unlawful search within the meaning of the Fourth Amendment:

> In the case of the search of the interior of homes—the prototypical and hence most commonly litigated area of protected privacy—there is a ready criterion, with roots deep in the common law, of the minimal expectation of privacy that *exists,* and that is acknowledged to be *reasonable.* To withdraw protection of this minimum expectation would be to permit police technology to erode the privacy guaranteed by the Fourth Amendment. We think that obtaining by sense-enhancing technology any information regarding the interior of the home that could not otherwise have been obtained without physical "intrusion into a constitutionally protected area" constitutes a search—at least where (as here) the technology in question is not in general public use. This assures preservation of that degree of privacy against government that existed when the Fourth Amendment was adopted. On the basis of this criterion, the information obtained by the thermal imager in this case was the product of a search.[94]

Scalia contrasts his originalism with nonoriginalism, which he defines as a method of interpreting the Constitution "not on the basis of what the Constitution originally meant, but on the basis of what judges currently [think] it desirable for it to mean."[95] According to Scalia, the principal defect of nonoriginalism is "the impossibility of achieving any consensus on what, precisely, is to replace original meaning, once that is abandoned." He notes that nonoriginalists invoke "fundamental values as the touchstone of constitutionality" but observes that "it is very difficult for a person to discern a difference between those political values that he personally thinks important, and those political values that are 'fundamental to our society.' Thus, by the adoption of such a criterion judicial personalization of the law is enormously facilitated."[96] He also observes that those values that are "fundamental to our society" can both expand and contract. Describing nonoriginalism as "a two-way street that handles traffic both to and from individual rights," he contrasts it with his originalism as displayed in *Coy v. Iowa,* in which he secured the confrontation rights of a criminal defendant against legislation passed by a state less concerned with the text and tradition of the Sixth Amendment than with the "emotional frailty of children and the sensitivity of young women regarding sexual abuse."[97]

Scalia acknowledges that originalism "is also not without its warts." "Its greatest defect," he argues, "is the difficulty of applying it correctly." He continues:

> It is often exceedingly difficult to plumb the original understanding of an ancient text. Properly done, the task requires the consideration of an enormous

amount of material—in the case of the Constitution and its Amendments, for example, to mention only one element, the records of the ratifying debates in all the states. Even beyond that, it requires an evaluation of the reliability of that material—many of the reports of the ratifying debates, for example, are thought to be quite unreliable. And further still, it requires immersing oneself in the political and intellectual atmosphere of the time—somehow placing out of mind knowledge that we have which an earlier age did not, and putting on beliefs, attitudes, philosophies, prejudices and loyalties that are not those of our day. It is, in short, a task sometimes better suited to the historian than the lawyer.[98]

That very defect, however, is for Scalia a virtue. Because "historical research is always difficult and sometimes inconclusive," originalism will lead to "a more moderate rather than a more extreme result." Scalia argues that since judges inevitably think that "the law is what they would like it to be," their errors in "judicial historiography" will be "in the direction of projecting" upon the past "current, modern values." Originalism ends up as "something of a compromise, . . . not a bad characteristic for a constitutional theory."[99] A better argument for him to have made—one consistent with his criticisms of the "Court's Constitution-making"—would be that, since historical research is often inconclusive and the original understanding is unclear, there is no warrant for the Court to invalidate an act of the popular branches on the grounds that it is inconsistent with the Constitution's original meaning. After all, as Scalia continues, originalism is far more compatible than nonoriginalism with "the nature and purpose of a Constitution in a democratic system":

> A democratic society does not, by and large, need constitutional guarantees to insure that its laws will reflect "current values." Elections take care of that quite well. The purpose of constitutional guarantees . . . is precisely to prevent the law from reflecting certain changes in original values that the society adopting the Constitution thinks fundamentally undesirable. Or, more precisely, to require the society to devote to the subject the long and hard consideration required for a constitutional amendment before those particular values can be cast aside.[100]

As an originalist, Scalia cites and quotes from *The Federalist* to reveal constitutional history—to show how those who drafted and ratified the Constitution saw its various structural provisions and principles as means for achieving the ends that the Constitution was drafted to secure. He studies the framers, and especially *The Federalist,* not to find out what the framers, either individually or collectively, would have done if faced with a specific contemporary constitutional issue but rather to understand (given the words they used) how they designed the Constitution to work and, on that basis, to ascertain how, institutionally, they intended for that issue to be addressed. What he finds from his study is that seldom, if ever, was the judiciary intended to be the branch that would resolve these issues. Just how limited Scalia regards the judicial role is apparent in his criticism of Justice Holmes's famous reply to Chief Justice Marshall's dictum in *McCulloch v. Maryland*[101] that "the power to tax [is] the power to destroy." Holmes qualified Marshall's statement by asserting: "The power to tax is not the power to destroy while this Court sits."[102] While acknowledging that "the notion that predicted evils cannot occur 'while this Court sits' is comforting," Scalia sees no need for the Court to save anyone. Constitutional structure, not an activist Court, will ensure that the power to tax does not result in the destruction of the federal government. "I would have thought it a better response to Marshall's dictum that the power to tax the activities of the federal government cannot constitute the power to destroy the federal government so long as the tax is generally applicable and nondiscriminatory—because it is implausible that the state would destroy its own citizens as well."[103]

In his dissent in *Hoffmann–La Roche v. Sperling*,[104] Scalia admonished his colleagues not to "abandon" their "'passive' role in determining which claims come before them, . . . which I regard as one of the natural components of a system in which courts are not inquisitors of justice but arbiters of adversarial claims." According to him, the role of the Court is not to articulate a theory of justice and discover new rights based on that theory but to ensure that the majority does not contract the sphere of rights traditionally protected. If new theories of justice are to be articulated and if the sphere of protected rights is to be expanded, such expansion should be done by the will of the majority, not the Court.[105]

SCALIA'S RELIANCE ON CONSTITUTIONAL STRUCTURE

What Scalia also finds from his originalist, text-and-tradition approach is that the framers generally and *The Federalist* in particular placed great emphasis on constitutional structure. During his confirmation hearings, he was asked by Senator Strom Thurmond why he thought the Constitution had endured for so long—why he thought it had come to be "the oldest existing Constitution in the world today." Scalia responded as follows:

> I think most of the questions today will probably be about that portion of the Constitution that is called the Bill of Rights, which is a very important part of it, of course. But if you had to put your finger on what has made our Constitution so enduring, I think it is the original document before the amendments were added. Because the amendments, by themselves, do not do anything. The Russian constitution probably has better, or at least as good guarantees of personal freedom as our document does. What makes it work,

what assures that those words [in the Bill of Rights] are not just hollow promises, is the structure of government that the original Constitution established, the checks and balances among the three branches, in particular, so that no one of them is able to 'run roughshod' over the liberties of the people as those liberties are described in the Bill of Rights.[106]

Scalia's response is most instructive. First, he says that our "liberties" are "described" (but not created or secured) by the Bill of Rights. Second and more important, Scalia identifies "the structure of government that the original Constitution established, the checks and balances among the three branches, in particular," as the reason for the Constitution's protection of liberties and, hence, its longevity. His answer to Senator Thurmond is reminiscent of James Madison's argument to the House of Representatives on June 8, 1789, that the Bill of Rights he was proposing did no more than "expressly declare the great rights of mankind secured under this Constitution."[107] Madison believed that rights are secured not by "parchment barriers" (i.e., by prohibitions written into the Constitution) but rather by governmental structure (i.e., that "double security" that arises when power "is first divided between two distinct governments, and then the portion allotted to each, subdivided among distinct and separate institutions").[108] Scalia clearly agrees—at least with regard to separation of powers.

This need to preserve the structure of the Constitution—and especially separation of powers—was central to Justice Scalia's dissent in *Morrison v. Olson,*[109] the independent counsel case. Scalia's textualist jurisprudence generally demands deference to the popular branches, but not in separation of powers cases. As he pointed out in *Morrison,* in such cases, the "caution that we owe great deference to Congress's view that what it has done is constitutional . . . does not apply." He continued:

Where a private citizen challenges action of the Government on grounds unrelated to separation of powers, harmonious functioning of the system demands that we ordinarily give some deference, or a presumption of validity, to the actions of the political branches in what is agreed, between themselves at least, to be within their respective spheres. But where the issue pertains to separation of powers, and the political branches are (as here) in disagreement, neither can be presumed correct. The reason is stated concisely by Madison: "The several departments being perfectly co-ordinate by the terms of their common commission, neither of them, it is evident, can pretend to an exclusive or superior right to settling the boundaries between their respective powers. . . ." *Federalist* No. 49. The playing field for the present case, in other words, is a level one. As one of the interested and coordinate parties to the underlying constitutional dispute, Congress, no more than the President, is entitled to the benefit of the doubt.[110]

Feeling no obligation to presume the constitutionality of the independent counsel statute, Scalia complained that Congress had "effectively compelled a criminal investigation of a high-level appointee of the President in connection with his actions arising out of a bitter power dispute between the President and the Legislative Branch";[111] he further objected that Congress also removed "the decisions regarding the scope of [any] further investigation, its duration, and finally whether or not prosecution should ensue" from "the control of the President and his subordinates" and placed them instead in the hands of a "mini-Executive that is the independent counsel."[112] Quoting the language of Article II, section 1, clause 1, of the Constitution providing that "the executive Power shall be vested in the President of the United States," he declared: "This does not mean some of the executive power, but all of the executive power."[113] He then proclaimed that the independent counsel statute must be invalidated on "fundamental separation of powers principles if the following two questions are answered affirmatively: (1) Is the conduct of a criminal prosecution (and of an investigation to decide whether to prosecute) the exercise of purely executive power? (2) Does the statute deprive the President of the United States of exclusive control over the exercise of that power?" Scalia declared that even the Court majority "appears to concede an affirmative answer to both questions, but seeks to avoid the inevitable conclusion that since the statute vests some purely executive power in a person who is not the President of the United States, it is void."[114] He also noted that "governmental investigation and prosecution of crimes is a quintessentially executive function" and that "the statute before us deprives the President of exclusive control over that quintessentially executive activity."[115]

The Court majority's response conceded that the statute reduced the president's control but insisted that he preserved "sufficient control" to "perform his constitutionally assigned duties"[116] and that it did not "interfere impermissibly with his constitutional obligation to ensure the faithful execution of the laws."[117] Scalia's rejoinder was direct: "It is not for us to determine, and we have never presumed to determine, how much of the purely executive powers of government must be within the full control of the President. The Constitution prescribes that they all are."[118] He accused the Court majority of replacing "the clear constitutional prescription that the executive power belongs to the President with a 'balancing test'" and of abandoning the "text of the Constitution" as the "governing standard" in favor of "what might be called the unfettered wisdom of a majority of this Court, revealed to an obedient people on a case-by-case basis." Waxing indignant, Scalia proclaimed: "This is not only not the government of laws that the Constitution established, it is not a government of laws at all."[119] He chided the Court for adopting an "*ad hoc* approach to constitutional adjudication" whose "real attraction, even apart from its work-saving potential," is that "it is guaranteed to produce a result, in every case, that will make a majority of the Court happy with the law. The law is, by definition, precisely what the majority thinks, taking all things into account, it ought to be."

For his part, however, Scalia preferred "to rely upon the judgment of the wise men who constructed our system, and of the people who approved it, and of the two centuries of history that have shown it to be sound."[120]

Declaring that "if to describe this case is not to decide it, the concept of a government of separate and coordinate powers no longer has meaning,"[121] Scalia bitterly attacked his colleagues for their failure to abide by what "the text of the Constitution seems to require, . . . the Founders seemed to expect, and . . . our past cases have uniformly assumed."[122] He sought to preserve separation of powers because, as he noted, "without a secure structure of separated powers, our Bill of Rights would be worthless, as are the bills of rights of many nations of the world that have adopted, or even improved upon, the mere words of ours."[123] Scalia's argument in *Morrison* is clear: by refusing in this case to defer to Congress and by steadfastly protecting constitutional structure, he can be restrained and deferential elsewhere—i.e., he is spared the need in other cases to protect constitutional rights that are better secured by structure than by judges.

During a 1988 panel discussion on separation of powers, Justice Scalia assessed his legal career and commented that "if there is anyone who, over the years, [has] had a greater interest in the subject of separation of powers [than I], he does not come readily to mind."[124] His dissent in *Morrison* certainly supports his contention; his dissent in *Mistretta v. United States*[125] and his opinions for the Court in *Lujan v. Defenders of Wildlife*[126] and *Plaut v. Spendthrift Farms*[127] do so as well.

Scalia's text-and-tradition jurisprudence was apparent in his vigorous and solitary dissent in *Mistretta v. United States,* in which an eight-member majority upheld the constitutionality of the Sentencing Guidelines Commission, rejecting the argument that Congress had delegated to the commission excessive legislative power and thereby violated separation of powers. He argued that the act established a "sort of junior-varsity Congress"[128] whose guidelines "have the force and effect of laws, prescribing the sentences criminal defendants are to receive. A judge who disregards them will be reversed." Again refusing to defer to Congress, he declared, "I can find no place within our constitutional system for an agency created by Congress to exercise no governmental power other than the making of laws."[129]

He argued that the commission's "power to make law . . . is quite naked. The situation is no different in principle from what would exist if Congress gave the same power of writing sentencing laws to a congressional agency such as the General Accounting Office, or to members of its staff."[130] He especially took exception to the Court majority's treatment of the Constitution "as though it were no more than a generalized prescription that the functions of the Branches should not be commingled too much," with the determination of "how much is too much" left, case by case, to the Court. "The Constitution is not that. Rather, as its name suggests, it is a prescribed structure, a framework, for the conduct of government. In designing that structure, the framers themselves considered how much commingling was acceptable, and set forth their conclusions in the document."[131] For Scalia, then, judgments concerning the degree of acceptable commingling were made, once and for all, by the framers through the "carefully designed structure they created," not by the Court in contemporary decisions. He feared that Court "improvisation of a constitutional structure on the basis of currently perceived utility will be disastrous."[132]

In *Lujan*, Scalia denied that Congress had power to grant legal standing to environmental groups who had suffered no particularized concrete injury but who sought, nonetheless, to sue the executive branch under the Endangered Species Act (ESA) in order to limit use of federal funds for foreign aid projects that could possibly endanger threatened wildlife habitats or species. He declared that Congress in passing the ESA had no more power to violate the Article III concrete-injury requirement than does the Court itself. Vindicating the public interest in government observance of the Constitution and laws is, Scalia asserted, "the function of the Congress and the Chief Executive."[133] Absent evidence of a particularized injury to a plaintiff caused by the government's failure to observe the Constitution and law, the plaintiff has no standing; there is, therefore, no case or controversy—no function for the courts to perform. Providing a lesson on separation of powers, Scalia continued:

> To permit Congress to convert the undifferentiated public interest in executive officers' compliance with the law into an "individual right" vindicable in the courts is to permit Congress to transfer from the President to the courts the Chief Executive's most important constitutional duty, to "take care that the laws be faithfully executed." It would enable the courts, with the permission of Congress, "to assume a position of authority over the governmental acts of another and co-equal department," and to become "virtually continuing monitors of the wisdom and soundness of Executive action." We have always rejected that vision of our role.[134]

Finally, in *Plaut*, he declared for a seven-member majority that Congress violated separation of powers by "requiring the federal courts to exercise 'the Judicial Power of the United States' in a manner repugnant to the text, structure, and traditions of Article III." It did so when it passed a law requiring federal courts to reopen final judgments in private civil actions under the Securities Exchange Act for those plaintiffs whose suits for fraud and deceit in the sale of stock had been dismissed as time-barred because of an earlier Court decision that had the effect of reducing the length of time in which such suits could be filed. Scalia recognized that Congress was motivated by good intentions—the desire to assist defrauded shareholders hurt by the Court's earlier ruling. But, he insisted, "Not favoritism, not even corruption, but power is the object of the separation-of-powers prohibition. The prohibition is violated when an individual final judgment is legislatively rescinded for even the very best of reasons, such as the legislature's genuine conviction (supported by all the law professors in the land) that the judgment was wrong."[135] The doctrine of separation of powers, he insisted, "is a structural safeguard rather than a remedy to be applied only when specific harm, or the risk of specific harm, can be identified. In its major features, it is a prophylactic device, establishing high walls and clear distinctions because low walls and vague distinctions will not be judicially defensible in the heat of interbranch conflict."[136] He likened what Congress had done in *Plaut* to its widespread use of legislative vetoes declared unconstitutional in *Immigration and Naturalization Service v. Chadha*[137] and asserted that "legislated invalidation of judicial judgments deserves the same categorical treatment accorded by *Chadha* to congressional invalidation of executive action." He concluded, "Separation of powers, a distinctively American political doctrine, profits from the advice authored by a distinctively American poet: Good fences make good neighbors."[138]

Scalia's invocation of Robert Frost prompted Justice Stephen Breyer, who concurred only in the judgment and not in Scalia's opinion, to respond in kind: "As the majority invokes the advice of an American poet, one might consider as well that poet's caution, for he not only notes that 'Something there is that doesn't love a wall,' but also writes, 'Before I built a wall I'd ask to know / What I was walling in or walling out.'"[139] Breyer's selection of these particular passages from Frost highlights the chasm that exists between him and Scalia—and more generally between the Court and Scalia—concerning separation of powers. Unlike Breyer and most of Scalia's colleagues, Scalia loves the wall of separation of powers. He loves it because, as he said in his *Morrison* dissent, "Without a secure structure of separated powers, our Bill of Rights would be worthless." He loves this wall and wants it kept high and strong because, as he noted in *Plaut*, "Low walls . . . will not be judicially defensible in the heat of interbranch conflict." He also loves the wall of separation of powers, because, as he said in *Morrison*, it was built by and reflects the "judgment of the wise men who constructed our system, and of the people who approved it, and of the two centuries that have shown it to be sound." Additionally, unlike Breyer and those others, Scalia would never quote a passage that implies that it is his job to build the wall and, therefore, his task to decide what to wall in or wall out. True to his text-and-tradition jurisprudence, Scalia would argue that the justices are to secure the wall of separation of powers built by the framers, not wonder whether it is worthy of their love and certainly not replace it with one of their own design. The decisions of the framers concerning constitutional structure are for the justices to secure, not to alter or to second-guess.

Interestingly, Scalia's interest in preserving separation of powers has not been matched by his interest in preserving federalism.[140] Although he argued in *James B. Beam Distilling Company* that "the division of federal powers" is central to the Constitution and that "those powers must be preserved" as they were understood "when the Constitution was enacted,"[141] Scalia has, in fact, written no important federalism opinions, preferring instead to join the opinions of especially Chief Justice William Rehnquist[142] and Justices Sandra Day O'Connor,[143] Anthony Kennedy,[144] and Clarence Thomas.[145] He has offered two explanations for his lack of interest in preserving federalism. During his confirmation hearings, he argued that the "primary defender of the constitutional balance" between the federal government and the states "is the Congress. It is a principle of the Constitution that there are certain responsibilities that belong to the State and some that belong to the Federal Government, but it is essentially the function of the Congress—the Congress, which takes the same oath to uphold and defend the Constitution that I do as a judge—to have that constitutional prescription in mind when it enacts the laws."[146] Scalia's other explanation is, to put it bluntly, that federalism, as a constitutional principle that can be enforced by the Court, is dead and that he is not interested in expending his own interpretative resources attempting to resuscitate a corpse. As he wrote in *Regulation* magazine in 1979, "Constitutional provisions subsist only as long as they remain not merely imprinted on paper, but also embedded in the thinking of the people. When our people ceased to believe in a federal government of narrowly limited powers, Congress's constitutional interpretation disregarded such limitations, and the courts soon followed."[147] How little interested Scalia is in personally working to protect federalism is apparent in the two "ostensible" federalism opinions he has written: *Printz v. United States*[148] and *College Savings Bank v. Florida Prepaid Postsecondary Education Expense Board.*[149]

In *Printz,* the Court considered the constitutionality of those provisions of the Brady Handgun Violence Prevention Act that commanded the "chief law enforcement officer" of each local jurisdiction to conduct background checks on prospective handgun purchasers on an interim basis until such time as a national instant background check system would become operational in late 1998. Scalia held for a five-member majority that this congressional command was "fundamentally incompatible with our constitutional system of dual sovereignty" and was, therefore, unconstitutional.[150]

However, a careful reading of his opinion makes clear that Scalia's reference to federalism was merely a part of his coalition-building strategy. Ultimately, Scalia found federal commandeering of state officials to be unconstitutional not so much because it violated the principle of federalism but because it violated separation of powers. He noted that "the Constitution does not leave to speculation who is to administer the laws enacted by Congress; the President, it says, 'shall take Care that the Laws be faithfully executed,' personally and through officers whom he appoints." The Brady Act, however, effectively transferred this responsibility to thousands of state and local law-enforcement officers in the fifty states, who, as Scalia pointed out, "are left to implement the program without meaningful Presidential control (if indeed meaningful Presidential control is possible without the power to appoint and remove). The insistence of the Framers upon unity in the Federal Executive—to insure both vigor and accountability—is well known. That unity," he concluded, "would be shattered, and the power of the President would be subject to reduction, if Congress could act as effectively without the President as with him, by simply requiring state officers to execute its laws."[151] This argument comes, of course, directly from his dissent in *Morrison v. Olson.* In *Morrison,* Scalia wrote for himself alone; in *Printz,* by sugarcoating his separation of powers argument with a defense of federalism, he was able to write for a five-member majority.

In *College Savings Bank* (one of three cases handed down by the Court on the same day striking down federal laws for unconstitutionally violating state sovereign immunity), the Court considered the constitutionality of the Trademark Remedy Clarification Act (TRCA), which subjected states to suits brought under the Trademark Act of 1946 for false and misleading advertising. College Savings Bank, a New Jersey institution that offered an annuity contract for financing future college tuition expenses, sued Florida Prepaid Postsecondary Education Expense Board, a state-created entity that provided a similar tuition prepayment contract available to Florida residents, alleging that Florida Prepaid was guilty of misrepresenting its own program. In his opinion for the Court, Justice Scalia first denied that Congress had power under section 5 of the Fourteenth Amendment to pass the TRCA to remedy and prevent state deprivations of property without due process. There simply is no property right, he insisted, to be free from a "competitor's false advertising about its own product."[152] There was, therefore, no constitutional violation for Congress to remedy and, hence, under *City of Boerne v. Flores,*[153] no power under section 5 for Congress to abrogate state sovereign immunity. There was nothing new in that portion of Scalia's opinion; in journeyman fashion, he was dutifully applying a formula already worked out in much greater detail in *Florida Prepaid Postsecondary Education Expense Board v. College Savings Bank*[154] and *Alden v. Maine.*[155]

Scalia then turned, however, to the question of whether Florida had voluntarily waived its immunity by its activities in interstate commerce. College Savings had relied on the Court's 1964 decision in *Parden v. Terminal Railroad Co.*[156] to argue that Florida Prepaid had "'impliedly' or 'constructively' waived its immunity,"[157] since Congress had provided unambiguously in the TRCA that states would be subject to private suit if they engaged in certain federally regulated conduct and Florida Prepaid had thereafter voluntarily elected to engage in that conduct. In by far the most interesting portion of his opinion, Scalia announced that *Parden* was no longer good law. Declaring it to be "expressly overruled,"[158] he argued that it could not be squared with the Court's "cases requiring that a state's express waiver be unequivocal." As Scalia pointed out, "There is a fundamental difference between a State's expressing unequivocally that it waives its immunity, and Congress's expressing unequivocally its intention that if the State takes certain action it shall be deemed to have waived that immunity."[159] Nor, he continued, could it be squared with the principle that a state's waiver must be voluntary; he insisted that "the voluntariness of waiver" is destroyed "when what is attached to the refusal to waive is the exclusion of the

Table 1. Voting Alignments: Scalia and His Colleagues (1986–2000 Terms of the Court)

Justice	Number of opinions*	Total number of cases**	Percentage agreement***
Thomas	765	872	87.7
Rehnquist	1,258	1,587	79.3
Kennedy	866	1,156	74.8
Powell	108	147	73.5
O'Connor	1,140	1,574	72.4
White	644	913	70.5
Souter	617	1,007	61.3
Ginsburg	374	671	55.7
Breyer	311	581	53.5
Blackmun	495	996	49.7
Stevens	753	1,581	47.6
Brennan	268	565	47.4
Marshall	308	685	45.0

*Total number of opinions in which both Scalia and the justice joined, including majority, concurring, and dissenting opinions.
**Total number of cases in which both Scalia and the justice participated.
***Percentage of all cases in which both Scalia and the justice joined the same majority, concurring, or dissenting opinions.

State from otherwise lawful activity" such as, in the instant case, engaging in interstate marketing.[160] This argument is not so much a defense of federalism as a display of the textualist Scalia demanding that words mean what they say.

SCALIA AND HIS COLLEAGUES

The effect of Scalia's textualism on his colleagues is mixed. As noted above, his textualist critique of legislative history has produced a major change in their decision-making. But, in the constitutional realm, his text-and-tradition jurisprudence has generally failed to win converts, even among his conservative colleagues.

Over the years, Scalia has certainly been a consistent vote in the Court's conservative block. From the time of his elevation to the Supreme Court, he has served with thirteen different colleagues. His voting alignments with these justices are presented in Table 1, which records the number of opinions in which Scalia and the other justices were in agreement, the total number of cases in which they participated, and the percentages of these cases in which they joined in the same opinions. It shows, most dramatically, that during their years together on the Court, he has joined in the same opinions with Justice Clarence Thomas 87.7 percent of the time, but it also shows that, over the years, he has joined in the same opinions with each member of the conservative block no less than 72.4 percent of the time.[161]

Nonetheless, his adherence to textualism makes him the least consistent member of the Court's conservative block and the least likely either to join in the

Table 2. Voting Alignments in Nonunanimous Cases (1996–2000 Terms of the Court)*

Justice	Rehnquist	Stevens	O'Connor	Scalia	Kennedy	Souter	Thomas	Ginsburg	Breyer
Rehnquist		20.1	73.8	64.9	75.8	39.3	69.0	37.3	39.1
Stevens	20.1		27.2	11.9	27.8	61.6	15.5	64.8	60.1
O'Connor	73.8	27.2		55.1	69.5	48.2	59.1	44.5	53.2
Scalia	64.9	11.9	55.1		57.2	29.3	77.3	23.8	24.3
Kennedy	75.8	27.8	69.5	57.2		43.2	60.6	41.9	43.0
Souter	39.3	61.6	48.2	29.3	43.2		30.5	77.7	70.1
Thomas	69.0	15.5	59.1	77.3	60.6	30.5		24.1	25.7
Ginsburg	37.3	64.8	44.5	23.8	41.9	77.7	24.1		69.1
Breyer	39.1	60.1	53.2	24.3	43.0	70.1	25.7	69.1	

*Percentage of all cases in which both justices have joined in the same majority, concurring, or dissenting opinions.

opinion of the court or to agree in the disposition of the case. This is apparent in Tables 2 and 3.

Table 2 shows the voting alignments of the entire Court in nonunanimous cases since the publication of *A Matter of Interpretation,* in which Scalia's mature reflections of textualism were so clearly laid out. It shows that Chief Justice Rehnquist and Justices O'Connor and Kennedy (and even Justice Thomas) consistently join in the same majority, concurring, and dissenting opinions far more frequently than Scalia does.

Table 3 compares how often, in these same nonunanimous cases, Scalia, as opposed to the other members of the conservative block, either joins in the opinion of the court or merely agrees in the disposition of the case. In contrast with Justice O'Connor, who joins the opinion of the Court in 80.7 percent of all nonunanimous cases and who agrees in the disposition of the case in 85.0 percent of them, Scalia joins the opinion of the Court only 58.6 percent of the time and agrees in the disposition of the case only 68.9 percent of the time. Not only are Scalia's overall percentages the lowest among the members of the conservative block, but his percentage difference between those occasions in which he joins in the opinion of the Court as opposed to merely agreeing in the case's disposition is the greatest. He agrees with the disposition of a case 10.3 percent more often than he joins in its majority opinion, as opposed to Justice O'Connor, for example, whose percentage difference is only 4.3 percent.[162] Scalia's percentage difference is the direct result of his textualism. It keeps him from joining opinions that rely on legislative history or that expand the words of the Constitution beyond what they meant to those who drafted and ratified them.

As these tables make clear, Scalia's voting is most closely aligned with that of Justice Thomas—despite the fact that Scalia, operating on logical-positivist assumptions, rejects Thomas's natural-rights premises and his willingness to read the Constitution in the light of the principles of the Declaration of Independence. In 87.7 percent of all the cases they have heard together and in 77.3 percent of all recent nonunanimous cases, Scalia and Thomas have joined in the same opin-

Table 3. Voting Patterns in Nonunanimous Cases (1996–2000 Terms of the Court)

Justice	Join in opinion of the Court	Agree in disposition of case	Percentage difference
O'Connor	80.7	85.0	4.3
Kennedy	80.0	85.1	5.1
Rehnquist	76.2	78.0	1.8
Thomas	62.1	71.4	9.3
Scalia	58.6	68.9	10.3

ions. In only eighteen cases over their time together on the Court has one dissented when the other has voted with the majority,[163] and in only two of these cases did one write the majority opinion while the other wrote the dissent. Not surprisingly, both cases involved statutory construction, and what split them apart was Scalia's insistence on pursuing a textualist approach. In *United States v. McDermott,* Thomas dissented from Scalia's opinion for the Court construing a federal tax lien statute,[164] and in *United States v. Rodriguez-Moreno,* Scalia dissented from Thomas's majority opinion construing a federal statute authorizing prosecution for "using or carrying a gun" during the commission of a crime.[165]

CONCLUSION

In *A Matter of Interpretation,* Justice Scalia acknowledged that his textualist jurisprudence is regarded in "some sophisticated circles" of the legal profession as "simpleminded—'wooden,' 'unimaginative,' 'pedestrian.'" He rejected this characterization and denied that he was "too dull to perceive the broader social purposes that a statute is designed, or could be designed to serve, or too hidebound to realize that new times require new laws"; he merely insisted that judges "have no authority to pursue those broader purposes or to write those new laws."[166] During his distinguished career on the Supreme Court, Scalia has remained faithful to the "text and tradition" of our written Constitution and has rejected the intellectual fads and novel theories of interpretation that have the invariable effect of transferring power from the popular branches to the judges. In so doing, he reminds his colleagues of the most important right of the people in a democracy—the right to govern themselves as they see fit and to be overruled in their governance only when the clear text or traditional understanding of the Constitution they have adopted demands it.

NOTES

1. Scalia searches out the ordinary meaning of the words used when the provision was adopted, frequently consulting dictionaries of the era. In fact, he consults dictionar-

ies more often than any of his colleagues. See Note, "Looking It Up: Dictionaries and Statutory Interpretation," *Harvard Law Review* 107 (1994): 1437, 1439.

2. See Antonin Scalia, "Originalism: The Lesser Evil," *University of Cincinnati Law Review* 57 (1989): 849, 851.

3. For Justice Scalia, separation of powers represents such a critical structural principle. As he stated in "Originalism: The Lesser Evil": "Indeed, with an economy of expression that many would urge as a model for modern judicial opinions, the principle of separation of powers is found only in the structure of the [Constitution,] which successively describes where the legislative, executive, and judicial powers shall reside. One should not think, however, that the principle was less important to the federal framers. Madison said of it, in *Federalist* No. 47, that 'no political truth is certainly of greater intrinsic value, or is stamped with the authority of more enlightened patrons of liberty.' And no less than five of the *Federalist Papers* were devoted to the demonstration that the principle was adequately observed in the proposed Constitution" (p. 851).

4. In *Michael H. v. Gerald D.,* 491 U.S. 110, 127n5 (1989), Justice Scalia refers to this as "the most specific level at which a relevant tradition protecting, or denying protection to, the asserted right can be identified."

5. *Hearings before the Senate Committee on the Judiciary on the Nomination of Judge Antonin Scalia to Be Associate Justice of the Supreme Court of the United States,* 99th Cong., 2d sess., J-99-119 (Washington, D.C.: Government Printing Office, 1987), 108. Justice Scalia uses tradition to interpret only ambiguous constitutional texts; as he said in his dissent in *Rutan v. Republican Party,* 497 U.S. 62, 96n1 (1990), "No tradition can supersede the Constitution."

6. See, for example, *Stenberg v. Carhart,* 530 U.S. 914 (2000); *Department of Commerce v. Clinton,* 525 U.S. 316, 349 (1999); *Minnesota v. Carter,* 525 U.S. 83, 92 (1998); *Lewis v. Casey,* 518 U.S. 343, 368 (1996); *Witte v. United States,* 515 U.S. 389, 407 (1995); *Plaut v. Spendthrift Farms,* 514 US. 211, 217 (1995); *Waters v. Churchill,* 511 US. 661, 684 (1994); *Callins v. Collins,* 510 U.S. 1141 (1994); *Herrera v. Collins,* 506 U.S. 390, 427 (1993); *Richmond v. Lewis,* 506 U.S. 40, 54 (1992); *Planned Parenthood of Southeastern Pennsylvania v. Casey,* 505 U.S. 833, 980, 983, 998, 999, 1000, 1001 (1992); *Morgan v. Illinois,* 504 U.S. 719, 751 (1992); *California v. Acevedo,* 500 U.S. 565, 581 (1991); *Cruzan v. Director, Missouri Department of Health,* 497 U.S. 261, 300 (1990); *Rutan v. Republican Party of Illinois,* 497 U.S. 62, 97 (1990); and *McKoy v. North Carolina,* 494 U.S. 433, 466 (1990).

7. 501 U.S. 624, 650 (1991).

8. See Gregory E. Maggs, "Reconciling Textualism and the *Chevron* Doctrine: In Defense of Justice Scalia," *Connecticut Law Review* 28 (1996): 393, and Bradley C. Karkkainen, "Plain Meaning: Justice Scalia's Jurisprudence of Strict Statutory Construction," *Harvard Journal of Law and Public Policy* 17 (1994): 401.

9. Scalia, "Originalism," 863.

10. Scalia's textualism was on display in his dissent in *Troxel v. Granville,* 530 U.S. 57, 91–92 (2000); in this case, the Court struck down a Washington law—permitting "any person" to petition for visitation rights for a child "at any time" and authorizing state superior courts to grant such rights whenever visitation may serve a child's best interest—on the ground that it unconstitutionally infringed on the fundamental right of parents to rear their children. "In my view," he argued, "a right of parents to direct the upbringing of their

children is among the . . . 'other rights retained by the people' which the Ninth Amendment says the Constitution's enumeration of rights 'shall not be construed to deny or disparage.'" However, he continued, "the Constitution's refusal to 'deny or disparage' other rights is far removed from affirming any one of them, and even farther removed from authorizing judges to identify what they might be, and to enforce the judges' list against laws duly enacted by the people. Consequently, while I would think it entirely compatible with the commitment to representative democracy set forth in the founding documents to argue, in legislative chambers or in electoral campaigns, that the state has no power to interfere with parents' authority over the rearing of their children, I do not believe that the power which the Constitution confers upon me as a judge entitles me to deny legal effect to laws that (in my view) infringe upon what is (in my view) that unenumerated right."

11. *Hearings on the Nomination of Judge Antonin Scalia,* 89.

12. 518 U.S. 668 (1996).

13. 518 U.S. 712 (1996).

14. 518 U.S., at 686.

15. Ibid., at 688.

16. "[U]nder either the procedural component or the so-called 'substantive' component of the Due Process Clause[, i]t is precisely the historical practices that *define* what is 'due'" (*Schad v. Arizona,* 501 U.S. at 650).

17. The meanings of those constitutional provisions that are ambiguous are not fixed in time; tradition can evolve, and, for Scalia, the appropriate way for such evolution to take place is through the people via their elected state legislatures and Congress. As he said in *Burnham v. Superior Court,* 495 U.S. 604, 627 (1990): "The difference between Justice Brennan [and me] has nothing to do with whether 'further progress [is] to be made' in the 'evolution of our legal system.' It has to do with whether changes are to be adopted as progressive by the American people or decreed as progressive by the Justices of this Court."

18. 518 U.S., at 695.

19. Timothy Raschke Shattuck, "Justice Scalia's Due Process Methodology: Examining Specific Traditions," *Southern California Law Review* 65 (1992) 2743, 2776–2778.

20. 518 U.S. 515 (1996).

21. Ibid., at 568.

22. 497 U.S., at 95–96.

23. 501 U.S. 957 (1991).

24. Ibid., at 994.

25. Ibid., at 977.

26. 501 U.S., at 981. See also his dissent in *Atkins v. Virginia,* 536 U.S. 304, 371 (2002): "The Eighth Amendment is addressed to always-and-everywhere 'cruel' punishments, such as the rack and the thumbscrew. But where the punishment is in itself permissible, 'the Eighth Amendment is not a ratchet, whereby a temporary consensus on leniency for a particular crime fixes a permanent constitutional maximum, disabling the States from giving effect to altered beliefs and responding to changed social conditions.'"

27. 463 U.S. 277 (1983).

28. Scalia's textualism also led him to conclude in *Payne v. Tennessee,* 501 U.S. 808, 834 (1991), that there is "absolutely no basis in constitutional text, in historical practice, or in logic" to justify using the cruel and unusual punishment clause to ban victim impact statements in capital punishment cases.

29. 487 U.S. 1012 (1988).

30. 487 U.S. at 1016. See also his dissent in *Craig v. Maryland,* 497 U.S. 836 (1990), in which he argued that the Sixth Amendment's confrontation clause also proscribes the use of closed-circuit televised testimony, even in cases involving sexual molestation of children.

31. 532 U.S. 451 (2001).

32. 532 U.S., at 471.

33. 499 U.S. 1 (1991).

34. See also his rejection of substantive due process in *TXO Production Corp. v. Alliance Resources Corp.,* 509 U.S. 443, 471 (1993), when he declared, "It is particularly difficult to imagine that 'due process' contains the substantive right not to be subjected to excessive punitive damages, since if it contains *that* it would surely also contain the substantive right not to be subjected to excessive fines, which would make the Excessive Fines Clause of the Eighth Amendment superfluous in light of the Due Process Clause of the Fifth Amendment." Emphasis in the original.

35. 499 U.S., at 31. Scalia's discussion of "historically approved procedures" needs one important qualification: Broad contemporary societal consensus can purge a "historically approved practice." As he said in *Haslip,* "State legislatures and courts have the power to restrict or abolish the common-law practice of punitive damages, and in recent years have increasingly done so. . . . It is through those means—State by State, and, at the federal level, by Congress—that the legal procedures affecting our citizens are improved. Perhaps, when the operation of that process has purged a historically approved practice from our national life, the Due Process Clause would permit this Court to announce that it is no longer in accord with the law of the land" (ibid., at 39). For his understanding of what constitutes a "broad society consensus" sufficient to purge a "historically approved practice, see his dissent in *Atkins v. Virginia,* 536 U.S. at 363–74.

36. 505 U.S. 577 (1992).

37. Ibid., at 641.

38. 512 U.S. 687, 732 (1994).

39. 494 U.S. 872 (1990).

40. 494 U.S., at 878, 885.

41. 505 U.S., at 1000.

42. *Hearings on the Nomination of Judge Antonin Scalia,* 108.

43. 491 U.S. 397 (1989).

44. *Hearings on the Nomination of Judge Antonin Scalia,* 51.

45. 510 U.S. 266, 275 (1994). Emphasis added.

46. *Seminole Tribe of Florida v. Florida,* 517 U.S. 44 (1996); *Florida Prepaid Postsecondary Education Expense Bd. v. College Savings Bank,* 527 U.S. 627 (1999); *College Savings Bank v. Florida Prepaid Postsecondary Education Expense Bd.,* 527 U.S. 666 (1999); *Alden v. Maine,* 527 U.S. 706 (1999); *Kimel v. Florida Board of Regents,* 528 U.S. 62 (2000); *Trustees of the University of Alabama v. Garrett,* 531 U.S. 356 (2001); and *Federal Maritime Commission v. South Carolina State Ports Authority,* 535 U.S. 743 (2002).

47. 517 U.S., at 54.

48. Antonin Scalia, "The Rule of Law as the Law of Rules," *University of Chicago Law Review* 56 (1989): 1175.

49. This explains why he joined in Chief Justice Rehnquist's concurring opinion in *Bush v. Gore,* 531 U.S. 98 (2000). The gravamen of Rehnquist's concurrence was that the Florida Supreme Court had established new standards for resolving presidential election contests and had thereby violated Article II, section 1, clause 2, of the United States Constitution, which provides that "each State shall appoint, in such Manner as the Legislature thereof may direct," electors for president and vice president (531 U.S., at 112).

50. 530 U.S. 57 (2000).

51. Ibid., at 91.

52. Ibid., at 92–93.

53. 517 U.S. 620 (1996).

54. Ibid., at 651.

55. Ibid., at 636.

56. 497 U.S. 261 (1990).

57. Ibid., at 293.

58. Antonin Scalia, *A Matter of Interpretation: Federal Courts and the Law,* ed. Amy Gutmann (Princeton: Princeton University Press, 1997), 7.

59. Ibid., at 9.

60. Ibid., at 22.

61. 518 U.S., at 711.

62. 518 U.S., at 567.

63. See Larry P. Arnn and Ken Masugi, "The Smoke of a Burning White Flag: Law without a Regime, Form without Purpose," *Perspectives on Political Science* 28, no. 1 (Winter 1999): 16.

64. Antonin Scalia, "Rome Address," *Origins, CNS Documentary Service* 26, no. 6 (27 June 1996).

65. Scalia, *A Matter of Interpretation,* 134. See also *Troxel v. Granville,* 530 U.S., at 91, where Scalia writes: "In my view, a right of parents to direct the upbringing of their children is among the 'unalienable Rights' with which the Declaration of Independence proclaims 'all Men . . . are endowed by their Creator.' . . . The Declaration of Independence, however, is not a legal prescription conferring powers upon the courts." Scalia has invoked the Declaration of Independence in seven of his opinions, including *Troxel.* In the other six instances, however, he has done so merely to support a point he is making. See, for example, his dissent in *Neder v. United States,* 527 U.S. 1, 30–31 (1999), in which he argued that a criminal defendant has the right to have the jury determine his guilt of the crime charged and that this includes his commission of every element of the crime charged: "One of the indictments of the Declaration of Independence against King George III was that he had 'subjected us to a Jurisdiction foreign to our Constitution, and unacknowledged by our Laws' in approving legislation 'for depriving us, in many Cases, of the Benefits of Trial by Jury.'"

By contrast, Justice Clarence Thomas, with whom Scalia votes over 87 percent of the time (see text, p. 57), does take the Declaration of Independence seriously, believes that its principles infuse the Constitution, and grounds his opinions explicitly in them. See Thomas's concurrence in *Adarand Constructors v. Pena,* 515 U.S. 200, 240 (1994), holding that that the strict scrutiny standard applies to all government classifications based on race: "As far as the Constitution is concerned, it is irrelevant whether a government's racial classifications are drawn by those who wish to oppress a race or by those who have a sincere desire to help those thought to be disadvantaged. There can be no doubt that the paternalism that appears to lie at the heart of this program is at war with the principle of inherent equality that underlies and infuses our Constitution. See Declaration of Independence ('We hold these truths to be self-evident, that all men are created equal, that they are endowed by their Creator with certain unalienable Rights, that among these are Life, Liberty, and the pursuit of Happiness')."

66.   Merrill D. Peterson, ed., *Thomas Jefferson: Writings* (New York: Library of America, 1984), 492–493.

67.   Harry V. Jaffa, *Storm over the Constitution* (Lanham, Md.: Lexington Books, 1999), 117.

68.   Scalia, *A Matter of Interpretation,* 134.

69.   Ibid., at 135.

70.   *Hearings on the Nomination of Judge Antonin Scalia,* 106.

71.   487 U.S. 326 (1988).

72.   Ibid., at 345.

73.   As one critic of Scalia's rejection of legislative history complains, individual members of Congress "can no longer express their intentions effectively in any way other than incorporating them in the legislation itself." Note, "Justice Scalia's Use of Sources in Statutory and Constitutional Interpretation: How Congress Always Loses," *Duke Law Journal* 1990 (1990): 160, 188.

74.   749 F.2d 875 (1984).

75.   Ibid., at 893. This Court of Appeals opinion provides further evidence of Scalia's keen appreciation for the workings of the legislative process.

76.   503 U.S. 291, 309 (1992).

77.   501 U.S. 597 (1991).

78.   Ibid., at 621. In his concurring opinion in *Thunder Basin Coal Co. v. Reich,* 510 U.S. 200, 219 (1994), Scalia declared that he found "unnecessary" the majority's discussion of the legislative history of the statute under consideration. "It serves to maintain the illusion that legislative history is an important factor in this Court's deciding of cases, as opposed to an omnipresent makeweight for decisions arrived at on other grounds."

79.   507 U.S. 511 (1993).

80.   Ibid., at 518–519. Emphasis in the original.

81.   501 U.S. 380 (1991).

82.   In Conan Doyle's *Silver Blaze,* Sherlock Holmes solves the mystery on the basis of the dog that did not bark.

83.   501 U.S. at 406. See Ralph A. Rossum, "Applying the Voting Rights Act to Judicial Elections: The Supreme Court's Misconstruction of Section 2 and Misconception of the Judicial Role," in *Affirmative Action and Representation: Shaw v. Reno and the Future of Voting Rights,* ed. Anthony A. Peacock (Durham, N.C.: Carolina Academic Press, 1997).

84.   504 U.S. 505 (1992).

85.   Ibid., at 521.

86.   Ibid., at 516.

87.   Patricia M. Wald, "Some Observations on the Use of Legislative History in the 1981 Supreme Court Term," *Iowa Law Review* 68 (1983): 195.

88.   Gregory E. Maggs, "The Secret Decline of Legislative History: Has Someone

Heard a Voice Crying in the Wilderness?" in *The Public Interest Law Review 1994*, ed. Roger Clegg and Leonard A. Leo (Washington, D.C.: National Legal Center for the Public Interest, 1994), 72.

89. "Congress Keeps Eye on Justices as Court Watches Hill's Words," *Congressional Quarterly Weekly Report* 49 (1991): 2863.

90. 513 U.S. 150, 167 (1995).

91. Scalia, "The Rule of Law as the Law of Rules," 1184.

92. See *Hearings on the Nomination of Judge Antonin Scalia,* 48, 108.

93. 533 U.S. 27 (2001).

94. 533 U.S., at 34. Emphasis in the original. See also Scalia's concurring opinion in *Minnesota v. Dickerson,* 508 U.S. 366, 379 (1993): "I take it to be a fundamental principle of constitutional adjudication that the terms in the Constitution must be given the meaning ascribed to them at the time of their ratification. Thus, when the Fourth Amendment provides that 'the right of the people to be secure in their persons, houses, papers, and effects, against unreasonable searches and seizures, shall not be violated,' it 'is to be construed in the light of what was deemed an unreasonable search and seizure when it was adopted.' The purpose of the provision, in other words, is to preserve the degree of respect for the privacy of persons and the inviolability of their property that existed when the provision was adopted—even if a later, less virtuous age should become accustomed to considering all sorts of intrusion 'reasonable.'"

95. Scalia, "Originalism," 852.

96. Ibid., at 863.

97. Ibid., at 856.

98. Ibid., at 856–857. Scalia also identifies a second "serious objection to originalism: In its undiluted form, at least, it is medicine that seems too strong to swallow" (ibid., at 861). He confesses that "in a crunch I may prove a faint-hearted originalist. I cannot imagine myself, any more than any other federal judge, upholding a statute that imposes the punishment of flogging. But then I cannot imagine such a case arising either" (ibid., at 864). See also his testimony during his Senate confirmation hearing, *Hearings on the Nomination of Judge Antonin Scalia,* 49. In truth, however, Scalia has proven to be anything but a "faint-hearted originalist," as his opinion in *Harmelin v. Michigan* attests (see page 37).

99. Scalia, "Originalism," 864.

100. Ibid., at 862. See also Antonin Scalia, "Assorted Canards of Contemporary Legal Analysis," *Case Western Reserve Law Review* 40 (1990): 581. "To keep government up-to-date with modern notions of what good government ought to be, we do not need a constitution but only a ballot-box and a legislature" (ibid., at 595). "Changes in the Constitution, when thought necessary, are to be proposed by Congress or conventions and ratified by the States. The Founders gave no such amending power to this Court. Our duty is simply to interpret the Constitution, and in doing so the test of constitutionality is not whether a law is offensive to our conscience or to the 'good old common law,' but whether it is offensive to the Constitution" (ibid., at 596).

101. 17 US. 316, 431 (1819).

102. *Panhandle Oil Co. v. Mississippi ex rel. Knox,* 277 U.S. 218, 223 (1928).

103. Scalia, "Assorted Canards of Contemporary Legal Analysis," 590.

104. 493 U.S. 165, 181 (1989).

105. Shattuck, "Justice Scalia's Due Process Methodology," 2782.

106. *Hearings on the Nomination of Judge Antonin Scalia,* 32.

107. Helen E. Veit et al., *Creating the Bill of Rights: The Documentary Record from the First Congress* (Baltimore: Johns Hopkins University Press, 1991), 78. For a detailed analysis of Madison's argument that the Bill of Rights does not create or secure rights but only declares those rights that are secured by constitutional structure, see Ralph A. Rossum, "*The Federalist*'s Understanding of the Constitution as a Bill of Rights," in *Saving the Revolution: The Federalist Papers and the American Founding,* ed. Charles R. Kesler (New York: Free Press, 1987), 219–233.

108. *Federalist* 51: 351.

109. 487 U.S. 654 (1988).

110. Ibid., at 704–705.

111. 487 U.S., at 703.

112. Ibid., at 732. In 1986, while serving on the Court of Appeals for the District of Columbia Circuit, Scalia sat on a special three-judge district court panel that held that the Gramm-Rudman-Hollings Balanced Budget and Emergency Deficit Control Act, which gave to the comptroller of the General Accounting Office (removable only at the initiative of Congress) the ultimate authority in determining what budget cuts would have to be made, unconstitutionally infringed on executive power; *Synar v. United States,* 676 F. Supp. 1374 (D.D.C) (1986). Scalia was widely rumored to be the author of the per curiam opinion. See James G. Wilson, "Constraints on Power: The Constitutional Opinions of Judges Scalia, Bork, Posner, Easterbrook, and Winter," *University of Miami Law Review* 40 (1986): 1200. The Supreme Court subsequently affirmed in *Bowsher v. Synar,* 478 U.S. 714 (1986). See Christopher E. Smith, *Justice Antonin Scalia and the Supreme Court's Conservative Moment* (Westport, Conn.: Praeger, 1993), 40.

113. 487 U.S., at 705. See Scalia's similar formulation of the judicial power in *Freytag v. Commission of Internal Revenue,* 501 U.S. 868, 908 (1991).

114. 487 U.S., at 705.

115. Ibid., at 706.

116. Ibid., at 709.

117. Ibid., at 692.

118. Ibid., at 709. Scalia wondered how willing the Court would be to have a portion of its judicial power given to another branch: "To bring the point closer to home, consider a statute giving to non–Article III judges just a tiny bit of purely judicial power in a relatively insignificant field, with substantial control, though not total control, in the courts. . . . Is there any doubt that we would not pause to inquire whether the matter was '*so central* to the functioning of the Judicial Branch' as really to require complete control, or whether we retained '*sufficient* control over the matters to be decided that we are able to perform our constitutionally assigned duties'? We would say that our 'constitutionally assigned duties' include *complete* control over all exercises of the judicial power " (ibid., at 709–710).

119. Ibid., at 711–712.

120. Ibid., at 734.

121. Ibid., at 703.

122. Ibid., at 734.

123. Ibid., at 697.

124. Quoted in Smith, *Justice Antonin Scalia and the Supreme Court's Conservative Moment*, 39.

125. 488 U.S. 361 (1989).

126. 504 U.S. 555 (1992).

127. 514 U.S. 211 (1995).

128. 488 U.S., at 427.

129. Ibid., at 413.

130. Ibid., at 421.

131. Ibid., at 426.

132. Ibid., at 427.

133. 504 U.S., at 576.

134. Ibid., at 577. See Gene R. Nichols Jr., "Injury and the Disintegration of Article III," *California Law Review* 74 (1986): 1915, 1942: "A judiciary that reviews every claim of government illegality may truly threaten separation of powers." However, see also Nichols, "Justice Scalia, Standing, and Public Law Litigation," *Duke Law Journal* 42 (1993): 1141.

135. 514 U.S., at 228.

136. Ibid., at 239.

137. 462 U.S. 919 (1983).

138. 514 U.S., at 240.

139. Ibid., at 245.

140. According to M. David Gelfand and Keith Werhan, "Federalism and Separation of Powers on a 'Conservative' Court: Currents and Cross-Currents from Justices O'Connor and Scalia," *Tulane Law Review* 64 (1990): 1443, "Justice Scalia has been especially vocal and aggressive in advocating a formalist approach to separation of powers, while showing much less concern for the protection of federalism values."

141. 501 U.S. 529, 549 (1991).

142. See *United States v. Lopez*, 514 U.S. 549 (1995), *Seminole Tribe of Florida v. Florida*, 517 U.S. 44 (1996), *Florida Prepaid Postsecondary Education Expense Board v. College Savings Bank*, 527 U.S. 627 (1999), *United States v. Morrison*, 529 U.S. 598 (2000), and *Trustees of the University of Alabama v. Garrett*, 531 U.S. 356 (2001).

143. See *New York v. United States*, 505 U.S. 144 (1992), and *Kimel v. Florida Board of Regents*, 528 U.S. 62 (2000).

144. See *City of Boerne v. Flores*, 521 U.S. 507 (1997), and *Alden v. Maine*, 527 U.S. 706 (1999).

145. See *Federal Maritime Commission v. South Carolina State Ports Authority*, 335 U.S. 743 (2002).

146. *Hearings on the Nomination of Judge Antonin Scalia*, p. 81.

147. Antonin Scalia, "The Legislative Veto: A False Remedy for System Overload," *Regulation* (November/December 1979): 20. See also Antonin Scalia, "On the Merits of the Frying Pan," *Regulation* (January/February 1985): "The most important, enduring, and stable portions of the Constitution represent such a deep social consensus that one suspects that if they were entirely eliminated, very little would change. And the converse is also true. A guarantee may appear in the words of the Constitution, but when society ceases to possess an abiding belief in it, it has no living effect. Consider the fate of the principle expressed in the Tenth Amendment that the federal government is a government of limited powers" (p. 13).

148. 521 U.S. 898 (1997).
149. 527 U.S. 666 (1999).
150. 521 U.S. 935.
151. Ibid., at 922–923.
152. 527 U.S., at 672.
153. 521 U.S. 507 (1997).
154. Ibid., at 627.
155. 527 U.S. 706 (1999). See Ralph A. Rossum, *Federalism, the Supreme Court, and the Seventeenth Amendment: The Irony of Constitutional Democracy* (Lanham, Md.: Lexington Books, 2001), 36–44.
156. 377 U.S. 184 (1964).
157. 527 U.S., at 676.
158. Ibid., at 676, 680.
159. Ibid., at 681.
160. Ibid., at 687.
161. During the 1991 term of the Court, Scalia found himself on the opposite side of Justices Kennedy and O'Connor in several key cases. He filed or joined in vigorous dissents in *Hudson v. McMillian,* 503 U.S. 1 (1992), in which the Court held that the use of excessive physical force against an inmate may constitute cruel and unusual punishment, even in the absence of significant injury; *Lee v. Weisman,* 505 U.S. 577 (1992), in which the Court held that prayers at public school graduation ceremonies indirectly coerce religious observance and therefore violate the First Amendment; *Doggett v. United States,* 505 U.S. 647 (1992), in which the Court held that the petitioner, who had not been brought to trial until eight and a half years after his indictment, had been denied his Sixth Amendment right to a speedy trial, despite the facts that the petitioner did not even know he had been indicted and that the government believed he was in prison in Panama; and *Planned Parenthood of Southeastern Pennsylvania v. Casey,* 505 U.S. 833 (1992), in which Justices Sandra Day O'Connor, Anthony Kennedy, and David Souter jointly signed an opinion acknowledging that *Roe v. Wade,* 410 U.S. 113 (1973), had been wrongly decided but refusing to overturn it because to do so would result "in profound and unnecessary damage to the Court's legitimacy, and to the Nation's commitment to the rule of law." During that term, Scalia ended up joining in the same opinions with O'Connor only 68.9 percent of the time and with Kennedy only 72.4 percent. And the sharp dissents he filed that term, especially in *Planned Parenthood,* had lingering effects: During the 1992 term of the Court, Scalia joined in the same opinions with O'Connor only 53.5 percent of the time, and with Kennedy only 62.3 percent—both representing the lowest levels of agreement for any of the terms Scalia has served on the Court with these two justices.
162. Among the members of the conservative block, Rehnquist has the lowest percentage difference at 1.8 percent. The very low number, however, may well be attributed to the role he plays as chief justice.
163. *Rowland v. California Men's Colony,* 506 U.S. 194 (1993), *United States v. McDermott,* 507 U.S. 447 (1993), *Musick, Peeler, and Garrett v. Employers Insurance of Wausau,* 508 U.S. 286 (1993), *John Hancock Mutual Life Insurance v. Harris Trust and Savings Bank,* 510 U.S. 86 (1993), *Northwest Airlines v. County of Kent, Michigan,* 510 U.S. 355 (1994), *Powell v. Nevada,* 511 U.S. 79 (1994), *Security Services v. Kmart,* 511 U.S. 431 (1994), *Thomas Jefferson University v. Shalala,* 512 U.S. 504 (1994), *Mas-*

trobuono v. Shearson Lehman Hutton, Inc., 514 U.S. 52 (1995), *Garlotte v. Fordice,* 515 U.S. 39 (1995), *Thompson v. Keohane,* 516 U.S. 99 (1996), *C.I.R. v. Lundy,* 516 U.S. 235 (1996), *Doctor's Associates v. Casarotto,* 517 U.S. 681 (1996), *U.S. v. Bajakajian,* 524 U.S. 321 (1998), *Lopez v. Monterey County,* 525 U.S. 266 (1999), *Cedar Rapids Community School District v. Garret F.,* 526 U.S. 66 (1999), *United States v. Rodriguez-Moreno,* 526 U.S. 275 (1999), and *Sims v. Apfel,* 530 U.S. 103 (2000).

164. See 507 U.S., at 453.

165. 526 U.S., at 281. Scalia's dissent was a textualist classic: "If to state this case is not to decide it, the law has departed further from the meaning of language than is appropriate for a government that is supposed to rule (and to be restrained) through the written word" (ibid., at 285).

166. Scalia, *A Matter of Interpretation,* 23.

3

Clarence Thomas and the Perils of Amateur History

Mark A. Graber

Justice Clarence Thomas is best known jurisprudentially for his apparently steadfast commitment to an originalist theory of the judicial function. This theory maintains that justices should declare unconstitutional only those state actions that are inconsistent, some would claim clearly inconsistent,[1] with the original understandings of the persons responsible for the constitutional provision in question. Originalism, proponents claim, respects both democracy and the rule of law. Popular majorities are free to govern in any way consistent with founding understandings. Constitutional meanings remain stable over time because how the persons responsible for the Constitution understood a particular provision was fixed at the time that provision was ratified.[2]

Justice Thomas's experiences on the Supreme Court provide fertile soil for examining both the status of originalism on that tribunal and the extent to which originalism in practice exhibits the virtues claimed for originalism in theory. The results may dishearten proponents of that historical approach to constitutional interpretation or the judicial function.[3] Originalism does not animate Rehnquist Court majorities. With rare exception, Justice Thomas writes for judicial majorities only when he abandons originalist logic for more conventional doctrinal rhetoric. His separate concurring and dissenting opinions that frequently make extensive use of originalist logic display no virtues claimed for constitutional originalism. Justice Thomas is not more deferential to elected officials than other justices. He would destabilize many areas of constitutional law. His originalism in major cases generally buttresses conservative policy preferences. When history provides little support for some conservative policies, such as the abandonment of affirmative action, he abandons originalism for some other constitutional logic that yields the more conservative result. His originalism in practice yields the sort of outcomes that one would expect of a justice who shared Justice Thomas's political convictions and Justice William Brennan's approach to constitutional adjudication.

This survey of Justice Clarence Thomas's role on the Rehnquist Court is in four parts. The first very briefly details his background and the fight over his confirmation to the Supreme Court. The second section discusses his majority opinions, highlighting both the infrequency with which Justice Thomas writes majority opinions in major constitutional cases and his even more infrequent invocation of original intentions in majority opinions. The relative absence of such rhetoric suggests that his jurisprudence does not guide Rehnquist Court majorities. The dominant philosophy on that tribunal continues to be something more akin to a conservative democratic relativism[4] with a strong federalist twinge. The third part discusses his concurring and dissenting opinions. Often, but not always, Justice Thomas when concurring or dissenting relies on claims about the original meaning of the constitutional provision under debate. He would overrule a remarkable number of cases, some dating back more than two hundred years, in the name of originalism. The last section evaluates Justice Thomas's use of originalism. In his hands that interpretive approach is not particularly democratic or nonpartisan. No good reason exists why he believes conservative historians when historians clash or why he discards originalism completely when that philosophy is hostile to certain conservative interests. Originalism as practiced by Justice Thomas does not seem all that different from aspirationalism as practiced by the more liberal members of the Warren Court.[5]

BACKGROUND AND CONFIRMATION

Justice Clarence Thomas had a relatively undistinguished career by Supreme Court standards before being appointed to the Court in 1991.[6] The future justice was born in Pin Point, Georgia, in 1948. He was raised in Savannah by his grandfather, whom Thomas frequently praises as embodying the traditional virtues associated with hard work.[7] Justice Thomas attended a series of Catholic schools and began studying for the priesthood but abandoned that effort after experiencing substantial racial prejudice at several seminaries. He then attended Holy Cross University and Yale Law School. During these years, motivated partly by his feeling that persons of color accepted on affirmative action programs were perceived as inferior, Thomas abandoned earlier liberal notions for a more conservative political philosophy, After graduating from Yale, he became a staff attorney for John Danforth, who was then the state attorney general of Missouri. In 1980, Thomas went to Washington to work for now Senator Danforth. Although he intended to stay clear of civil rights issues, the young black conservative soon came to the attention of the newly elected Reagan administration. President Reagan appointed Thomas to be assistant secretary for civil rights in the Education Department and then appointed him to the Equal Employment Opportunity Commission (EEOC). Nine years later, President George Bush nominated him to serve on the U.S.Court of Appeals for the District of Columbia.

Justice Thomas clearly demonstrated the skills necessary to rise above an impoverished background, but his career before being nominated to the Supreme Court did not separate him in any way from numerous other peers who faced and overcame similar obstacles. He served on the court of appeals for less than a year, too short a time to leave any mark. He did gain some attention for suggesting that conservatives might adopt a natural rights philosophy rooted in the Declaration of Independence.[8] Still, few persons not identified with the conservative wing of the Republican Party took seriously President Bush's claim that Thomas was the "best person"[9] to replace Justice Thurgood Marshall, unless by "best person" the president meant a "conservative African-American lawyer."

Bush's claim that Clarence Thomas was particularly well qualified for the Supreme Court structured the bitter confirmation fight that followed.[10] Recognizing that Justice Thomas lacked traditional legal qualifications for the high bench, President Bush and other Republicans emphasized his sterling character and capacity for overcoming disadvantage. Following the advice of administration officials, Thomas during the initial stages of the confirmation proceedings kept the character issue foremost in people's minds by emphasizing how his experiences enabled him to empathize with the less fortunate. Thomas denied that he had any thoughts on such issues as whether the Constitution protected abortion rights, claimed that he had no desire to tinker with most existing court precedents on government powers, and generally treated his past speeches on natural law as pure academic speculation that would have only a limited role, at most, in this judicial thinking. Many observers found such claims implausible, even bordering on perjury,[11] but the lack of a written record hampered Senate liberals who hoped to block confirmation on ideological grounds.

Frustrated with the lack of ideological content, Senate Democrats turned to the character issue. Claims that Thomas had some fondness for obscenity and that he misrepresented his sister's experiences on welfare in order to buttress his career merely preached to the choir. Democratic members had more luck when they discovered a rumor that Justice Thomas made improper advances to Professor Anita Hill when both served together on the EEOC. Hill confirmed those allegations to Democratic staffers but insisted they remain private. Despite assurances to the contrary, a member of Senator Howard Metzenbaum's staff leaked the information to National Public Radio. A confirmation imbroglio resulted.

The Thomas/Hill hearings captured public attention, dominated the news for several weeks, and focused public attention on issues of sexual harassment. Professor Hill asserted that while at the EEOC Justice Thomas repeatedly made lewd suggestions to her. She produced witnesses who testified that Hill informed them of these incidents when the alleged behavior took place. Thomas denounced the proceeding as a "high tech lynching" and he produced several witnesses who testified that Hill was mentally unbalanced. That testimony was forcibly championed by the Republicans on the Senate Judiciary Committee. Orrin Hatch publicly speculated about various mental illnesses that might explain Hill's testimony. Senate Democrats, all male, sought a more bipartisan approach, rarely publicly supporting either side of the debate.

Senator Joseph Biden's decision as chair of the Judiciary Committee to analogize the proceeding as a criminal trial (and not to call other witnesses who made similar complaints about Thomas) proved crucial. This decision to focus on whether Justice Thomas had committed a crime biased the confirmation hearings in his favor. No one proved beyond a reasonable doubt that he had harassed Anita Hill. The testimony was largely "he said, she said," and neither side produced a smoking gun. Reasonable persons dispute whether making lewd remarks to a subordinate is or ought to be a crime. Lost in the debate over criminality was the obvious point that persons of good character do not engage in such extraordinarily offensive behavior, an argument that significantly weakened the case for Clarence Thomas's sterling character. Enough Democrats, however, proved willing to give him the benefit of the doubt on the legal issue to enable his nomination to survive the Judiciary Committee and pass the Senate by a 52 to 48 vote.

The events surrounding the Thomas nomination highlight how "politics by other means"[12] derailed any intelligent debate over the principle and policy commitments he has brought to the Supreme Court. Benjamin Ginsberg and Martin Shefter note that "party decline has fostered a stalemate in the national electoral arena." "Rather than seeking to defeat their opponents chiefly by outmobilizing them in the electoral arena," Ginsberg and Shefter observe, "contending fores are increasingly relying on such institutional weapons of political struggle as legislative investigations, media revelations, and judicial proceedings."[13] The debate over the nomination of Judge Bork to the Supreme Court was nasty. Still, the debate focused public attention on Bork's originalist views and on how he would interpret the Constitution in actual cases. The Thomas nomination evoked no similar jurisprudential debate. The Bush administration avoided discussing constitutional law questions by highlighting Judge Thomas's character. Liberal Democrats, after a few feints on the constitutional question, largely played along, preferring debate over whether Thomas had the character necessary for a Supreme Court justice to debate over substantive constitutional issues. The result was a confirmation process that added Justice Thomas's distinctive voice to the Supreme Court without any serious political discussion as to whether this voice is desirable. For those who think democratic values are served by debate over a justice's principles,[14] the nomination process was an unfortunate affair.

MAJORITY OPINIONS

Originalism as practiced by Justice Thomas is not the dominant philosophy of the Rehnquist Court. Thomas writes an average or very slightly below average number of majority opinions every term, but he writes far more majority opinions in statutory cases and substantially fewer majority opinions in constitutional cases than other conservative justices on that tribunal. When he is assigned a majority opinion in a constitutional case, the matter is usually relatively minor. Justice Thomas rarely uses originalist logic when writing those majority opinions. When he does rely on historical understandings, the results fit no ideological pattern. On the 5 to 4 decisions that presently divide the major wings of the Rehnquist Court, Thomas is either not assigned the majority opinion or his majority opinion does not make any reference to the original intentions of the persons responsible for the constitutional provision being debated.

Statutory Opinions

Justice Thomas writes most of his majority opinions in statutory cases. During his first years on the Court, he wrote majority opinions almost exclusively on statutory concerns. The balance of statutory and constitutional cases in subsequent years remains disproportionately tilted to statutory matters. During the 2000 term, he wrote six majority opinions in statutory cases and only one in a constitutional case. The ratio in 2001 was seven statutory opinions to two constitutional opinions.

The statutory cases assigned to Justice Thomas do not raise highly charged political issues or attract substantial national attention. *United States v. Oakland Cannabis Buyers' Co-op*[15] (federal drug law interpreted as having no medical necessity exception for marijuna) is the only prominent statutory case decided by the Rehnquist Court assigned to him. When writing majority opinions in less prominent statutory cases, Justice Thomas refrains from bold assertions about the practice of statutory interpretation or about particular questions of statutory law. *Oakland Cannabis* aside, only two majority opinions in statutory cases have some political significance or contain language with potential political significance. *Robinson v. Shell Oil Co.*[16] held that Title VII of the Civil Rights Act outlawed discrimination against present and former employees. *Farrar v. Hobby*[17] held that civil rights attorneys should rarely be awarded fees under federal law when they only obtain nominal damages for their clients.

More typical were the six majority opinions in statutory cases that Justice Thomas authored in the 2000 term. They limited lawsuits against nonfiduciary parties in cases arising under a particular subsection of the Employee Retirement Income Security Act,[18] declared that the elements of one federal crime were sufficiently distinct from the elements of another federal crime to justify a trial court's decision not to issue a lesser-included offense instruction,[19] ruled that persons who did not raise claims before the Social Securities Appeals Council could nevertheless raise those claims on a court appeal from an adverse administrative ruling,[20] held that public employers under the Fair Labor Standards Act could compel employees to use compensatory time,[21] decided that persons did not have a private cause of action when injured by an act that, while part of a RICO conspiracy, was racketeering,[22] and determined that remittance of estimated taxes would be deemed paid when income taxes were due.[23]

Justice Thomas's majority opinions in statutory cases have a qualified tendency to reach conservative results. He rejects claims of criminal defendants,[24] favors employers over employees,[25] restricts access to courts,[26] and limits official liability.[27] Labeling many of these opinions as "conservative," however, is misleading. Thomas typically writes for a unanimous court in statutory cases. *Tyler v. Cain* (federal statute–barred constitutional claim in habeas corpus appeal),[28] *Lechmere, Inc. v. NLRB* (rejecting claims of an unfair labor practice),[29] *Conrail v. Gottshall* (limiting tort suits under federal law for emotional distress),[30] and *Farrar v. Hobby* are the only instances when a Thomas majority opinion in a statutory case clearly raises issues that presently divide political liberals from political conservatives. Many majority opinions in statutory cases cannot be placed on any meaningful ideological scale. Is the the doctrine of equivalents that Justice Thomas for a unanimous Court upheld in *Warner-Jenkinson Co. v. Hilton Davis Chemical Company*[31] more liberal or conservative? Political scientists automatically label as "liberal" Thomas's conclusion in *Staples v. United States*[32] that the state must prove beyond a reasonable doubt that a criminal defendant was aware his weapon could fire automatically.[33] The voting alignment in that case pitted more conservative members of the Court (Justices Thomas, Rehnquist, Scalia, Kennedy, and the more liberal Souter) against more liberal members (Ginsburg, Breyer, and Stevens).

Constitutional Cases

Justice Thomas's majority opinions in constitutional cases have little political or jurisprudential impact. One study found that *Kansas v. Hendricks* (sexually violent criminal predators can be civilly committed after their prison sentences have ended)[34] was the only major constitutional case in which Thomas authored the majority opinion during his first six years on the Court.[35] He did not write the majority opening in any case excerpted at length in the leading law school constitutional law casebook[36] and wrote only one majority opinion in a case excerpted at length in the leading political science constitutional law casebook.[37] That case, *Oregon Waste Systems v. Department of Environmental Quality of the State of Oregon*,[38] is rarely excerpted at length in other constitutional law casebooks.

Justice Thomas's majority opinions in constitutional cases are minimalist. Issues are decided on as narrow a basis as possible. He does not make bold declarations about law or about methods for interpreting law when writing majority opinions in constitutional cases. He refrains from making strong statements about political policy or political culture. Readers might conclude that Justice Thomas is captivated by the recent jurisprudential writings of Cass Sunstein.[39]

The majority of these opinions reach conservative conclusions. Many side with the state against criminal defendants, prisoners, or persons involved in quasi-criminal proceedings. Justice Thomas in *United States v. Scheffer*[40] held that the military could ban polygraph evidence in court-martial proceedings. In

Godinez v. Moran,[41] he concluded that the standard for pleading guilty or waiving the right to counsel was the same standard used for competency to stand trial. Justice Thomas writes other majority opinions that reach more conventionally liberal outcomes. His unanimous opinion in *Young v. Harper*[42] held that persons in certain preparole programs had the same constitutional rights as persons in parole programs. In *United States v. Bajakajian,*[43] he ruled that the excessive fines clause of the Eighth Amendment was violated by requiring a person to forfeit $150,000 in cash that he failed to declare when leaving the United States. Many majority opinions cannot easily be classified as having liberal or conservative outcomes. Justice Thomas's conclusion in *United States v. IBM*[44] that the export clause of Article 1, section 5, does not permit the federal government to tax goods in export transit cuts in no distinctive ideological direction.

He rarely relies on originalist rhetoric in majority or plurality opinions when reaching conventionally conservative results. *Smith v. Robbins*[45] declares that a prior decision, *Anders v. California,*[46] did not mandate any specific procedures for determining whether an indigent was making a frivolous appeal. *Hopkins v. Reeves*[47] concludes that *Beck v. Alabama*[48] did not "require state trial courts to instruct juries on offenses that were not lesser included offenses of the charged crime under state law."[49] Thomas's opinion in *Rubin v. Coors Brewing Co.*[50] "appl[ies] *Central Hudson*'s test"[51] when overturning a federal law prohibiting beer labels from displaying alcohol content. Only when writing separately does he suggest that *Central Hudson* be limited or modified.[52]

Justice Thomas in *Good News Club v. Milford Central Schools*[53] was "guided . . . by two . . . prior opinions"[54] when holding that religious clubs could meet in public school buildings. His concurring opinion in one of those "prior opinions," *Rosenberger v. Rector and Visitors of the University of Virginia,*[55] relied on the original intentions of the persons who framed the First Amendment.[56] Not a whiff of historicism can be found in his *Milford* majority opinion. *Florida v. White*[57] is the only majority opinion where Justice Thomas reaches a conservative conclusion partly on original grounds. His ruling that the police were not constitutionally required to obtain a warrant when seizing a publicly parked car "was rooted in federal law enforcement practices at the time of the adoption of the Fourth Amendment."[58] No other sentence in a Thomas majority opinion supports a conservative conclusion on historical grounds.

When Justice Thomas uses originalist rhetoric in a majority opinion, he usually reaches more liberal conclusions. His opinion in *Bajakajian* contains a long discussion concluding that the case involved an "in personam, criminal forfeiture" "historically treated as punitive" and subject to the excessive fines clause of the Fourteenth Amendment.[59] He relied on history in *Feltner v. Columbia Pictures TV* when concluding for a unanimous court that the Seventh Amendment protected the right to a jury trial in a copyright case involving statutory damages.[60] "An examination of the common law of search and seizure leaves no doubt," his unanimous opinion in *Wilson v. Arkansas* declares, "that the reason-

ableness of a search of a dwelling may depend in part on whether law enforcement officers announced their presence and authority prior to entering."[61] *United
States v. IBM,* the other majority opinion where Justice Thomas relies on originalist rhetoric, does not divide liberals and conservatives. Both Justices Breyer
and Souter signed Thomas's majority opinion rejecting federal power to tax
goods in export transit.

CONCURRING AND DISSENTING OPINIONS

Thomas's concurring and dissenting opinions reveal a justice entirely different
from the one who crafts his majority opinions. When writing separately, the
mild-mannered judicial minimalist morphs into a crusader for major jurisprudential reform. Justice Thomas in statutory cases maintains that courts must
ignore legislative history when interpreting statutes. He insists that federal
statutes not be interpreted as trenching on state prerogatives. His separate constitutional opinions call for the abolition of affirmative action, dramatic reductions in protections offered to criminal defendants, and substantial constitutional
limitations on federal power. Justice Thomas would overrule numerous Warren
Court precedents as well as precedents more than two centuries old. Many opinions in constitutional cases make extensive use of originalist sources, others do
little more than make passing reference to the past, and some ignore history completely. What unites Thomas's important concurring and dissenting opinions in
constitutional cases is his commitment to conservative or libertarian results
rather than a commitment to any particular theory of the judicial function.

Statutory Opinions

Justice Thomas's separate statutory opinions usually reach more conservative
conclusions than the majority opinion in the case, but this tendency has important exceptions. He exhibits a distinctive liberal strain when writing on one
aspect of criminal law: Justice Thomas interprets criminal statutes strictly. All
elements of a crime must be clearly stated for a conviction to satisfy statutory
norms.[62] Thomas calls on justices to rely on "the traditional canon that construes
revenue raising laws against their drafter."[63] Many separate opinions are devoted
to technical legal concerns that cannot be classified as conservative or liberal.
His first concurring opinion discussed the reasons why federal courts retain jurisdiction in forfeiture cases after the money at issue was deposited in the Treasury
of the United States.[64] Justice Scalia is most likely to join a Thomas opinion, but
every justice on the Rehnquist Court has joined at least one of his separate opinions in statutory cases.

Federalism is often the central theme when Justice Thomas writes separately
in statutory cases. He insists that federal statutes be construed as not infringing

on state prerogatives whenever such a construction is plausible. His dissent in *Evans v. United States* claims that federal laws should not be interpreted as increasing federal criminal jurisdiction over local officials.[65] Joined by Chief Justice Rehnquist and Justice Breyer, Justice Thomas declared in *AT&T Corp. v. Iowa Utils. Bd.* "that Congress consciously designed a system that respected the States' historical role as the dominant authority with respect to intrastate communications."[66] In another separate opinion he concludes that maintaining the autonomy of state courts requires interpreting federal statutes as permitted those tribunals to determine whether binding arbitration agreements are judicially enforceable.[67]

This presumption that federal laws should not be construed as limiting state power has constitutional foundations. Federal habeas corpus statutes, Justice Thomas asserts, must be interpreted in light of the principle that such "review 'disturbs the State's significant interest in repose for concluding litigation . . . and intrudes on state sovereignty to a degree matched by few exercises of federal judicial authority.'"[68] His opinion in *McFarland v. Scott* declares that federal district courts "should not lightly assume that Congress intended to expand federal habeas corpus power by permitting counsel and granting stays before a federal habeas petition was filed."[69] Justice Thomas in *Humphrey v. Heck* wrote that civil rights remedies under section 1983 required similarly narrow readings in light of federalism concerns.[70]

He dissented from a judicial ruling holding that the American Disabilities Act requires community-based legal treatment for some persons with mental illnesses. That decision did not "respect the States' historical roles as the dominant authority responsible for providing services to individuals with disabilities."[71] Federalism principles, his opinion adds, require that "when Congress places conditions on the receipt of federal funds, . . . it must do so unambiguously." The justices should not have interpreted a statute as requiring a public school district to provide certain services to disabled citizens as a condition for receiving federal funds. That decision "blindside[d] unwary States with fiscal obligations that they could not have anticipated."[72]

Justice Thomas insists that federal efforts to "abrogate" the sovereign immunity of states be "unmistakably clear."[73] He maintains that the preclearment provision of the Voting Rights Act must be interpreted narrowly to maintain the constitutional prerogatives of the states. "Section 5 is a unique requirement that exacts significant federalism costs," he wrote in *Lopez v. Monterey County,* and its "interference with state sovereignty is quite drastic."[74] The Constitution might be violated, he declares, if states not covered by the Voting Rights Act may not without federal preclearance change voting practices in state counties previous guilty of race discrimination in voting.[75]

Justice Thomas opposes broad readings of the Votings Rights Act even when federalism concerns are not explicitly implicated. He insists that "the size of a governing body is not a 'standard, practice, or procedure,' within the terms of the

[Voting Rights] Act."[76] The act, in his view, does not cover a legislative reapportionment plan.[77] Justice Thomas claimed that the Voting Rights Act "reach[es] only state enactments that limit citizens' access to the ballot" when dissenting from the Supreme Court's decision requiring parties in covered states to seek preclearance when charging fees for participation in nominating conventions.[78] His dissent indicated that persons had a constitutional right to form white-only political parties, provided their coalition "did not have the stranglehold on the political process that the Democratic Party had in the 1940s."[79]

Justice Thomas repeatedly attacks the Supreme Court's "vote dilution jurisprudence" as "inconsistent"[80] and "disastrous."[81] That jurisprudence is inconsistent, in his view, because the Court sometimes claims and sometimes rejects allegations that reductions in elected officials of color warrant federal intervention.[82] The jurisprudence is disastrous because of "the destructive effects our expansive reading of the Act has had in involving the Federal Judiciary in the project of dividing the Nation into racially segregated election districts." Federal courts, Thomas charges, are engaged in "an enterprise of segregating the races into political homelands that amounts, in truth, to nothing short of a system of 'political apartheid.'" The justices promote this practice "on the implicit assumption that members of racial and ethnic groups must all think alike on important matters of public policy and must have their own 'minority preferred' representatives holding seats in elected bodies if they are to be considered represented at all."[83] Justice Thomas is not above making similar assumptions. Voting rights litigation was not necessary in one county, he observes, because "three blacks were elected from majority-white districts to serve on the Bossier Parish School Board."[84]

Justice Thomas when writing separately advances a prominent theory of statutory interpretation. He declares that justices must interpret only the words of the statute and may not rely on legislative history. The justices should ignore repeated congressional statements that revisions in the Voting Rights Act were intended to endorse past judicial decisions. "The 'authoritative source' for legislative intent was the text of the statute passed by both Houses of Congress and presented to the President, not a series of partisan statements about purposes and objectives collected by congressional staffers and packaged into a committee report."[85] Justice Thomas depends on this theory of statutory interpretation in less contentious cases and condemns judicial reliance on "committee reports and floor statements, which are not law."[86] His opinion in *Carter v. United States* declares, "Our inquiry focuses on an analysis of the textual product of Congress's efforts, not on speculations as to the internal thought processes of its Members."[87] "Congress enacted the [Bankruptcy] Code," he wrote in another case, "not the legislative history predating it."[88]

When Justice Thomas writes separately in statutory cases, he frequently calls on the Court to overrule past precedents. He would have the Supreme Court overrule numerous past precedents finding vote dilution, most notably *Gingles v.*

Thornburg,[89] as well as past decisions impinging on state rights, most notably *Southland Corp. v. Keating*[90] and *Irving Independent School Dist. v. Tatro.*[91] He also urges the overruling and rethinking of judicial decisions relying on the legislative history and purpose of federal statutes. Justice Thomas calls for the overruling of *Sisson v. Ruby*[92] simply on the ground that it was wrongly decided.[93]

Separate Constitutional Opinions

Justice Thomas is best known for his separate opinions in constitutional cases. The vast majority of these opinions take conservative positions. Many, but not all, rely to some degree on claims about the original understanding of the Constitution. Nearly 40 percent of Justice Thomas's separate opinions in constitutional cases maintain that particular decisions or whole doctrinal areas be overruled or rethought. Justice Scalia, Chief Justice Rehnquist, and, recently, Justice Kennedy regularly join Justice Thomas's separate opinions in constitutional cases.[94] Justices White, Blackmun, Ginsberg, and Stevens have never joined a Justice Thomas dissent or concurrence. Justice Souter joined at most two separate Thomas opinions in constitutional cases.[95] Justice O'Connor joined only the dissent Justice Thomas wrote in *Term Limits.*[96]

Free speech is one doctrinal area where Justice Thomas consistently reaches results conventionally labeled as "liberal," although "libertarian" is the better characterization. He provided a crucial vote in *McIntyre v. Ohio Elections Commission*[97] for the constitutional right to distribute anonymous pamphlets. "The historical evidence," he wrote, "indicates that Founding-era Americans opposed attempts to require that anonymous authors reveal their identities on the ground that forced disclosure violated the 'freedom of the press.'"[98] Justice Thomas insists that state laws requiring that persons going door to door with petitions be registered voters and wear name tags do not satisfy the strict scrutiny standard.[99] He opposes hate speech regulations and calls on the Court to lift an injunction barring certain "words deemed offensive to Latino employees."[100] When state legislation increases penalties for hate crimes, he insists that the existence of that motive be determined by a jury using the reasonable doubt standard.[101] Justice Thomas claims that "our First Amendment distinctions between media [were] dubious from their infancy."[102] When appropriate cases come before the Court, he will probably offer far greater constitutional protection to broadcasters than present law provides.

Campaign finance and commercial speech issues evoke the same libertarian spirit. Justice Thomas repeatedly insists that political contributions and advertising merit the same degree of constitutional protection as any other form of expression. Campaign "contributions and expenditures both involve core First Amendment expression," he wrote when defending the right of political parties to engage in unlimited advocacy spending. Both "further the discussion of public issues and debate on the qualifications of candidates . . . integral to the operation of the system of government by our Constitution."[103] Thomas regards as unconstitutional laws imposing individual contribution limits. "Contribution caps," he declares, "which place a direct and substantial limit on core speech, should be met with the utmost skepticism and should receive the strictest scrutiny."[104] He does not "see a philosophical or historical basis for asserting that 'commercial' speech is of 'lower value' than 'noncommercial' speech."[105] "[M]akers of cigarettes," Justice Thomas maintains, "are no different from . . . advocates of harmful ideas."[106] Elected officials have no power to ban advertising of alcohol, gambling, cigarettes, or any other commercial good as a means "to keep legal users of a product or service ignorant in order to manipulate their choices in the marketplace."[107] Government may not "restrict truthful speech or suppress the ideas it conveys."[108] If commercial advertising is speech, then requiring persons to pay for commercial advertising unconstitutionally compels speech.[109]

Justice Thomas defends the free speech rights of religious speakers. His concurring opinion in *Rosenberger v. Rector and Visitors of the University of Virginia* insists that government cannot discriminate between religious and nonreligious viewpoints.[110] The establishment clause permits and may require states to allow religious organizations to enjoy generally available state benefits. The *Rosenberger* concurrence speaks of "our Nation's long tradition of allowing religious adherents to participate on equal terms in neutral government programs." Justice Thomas's dissent from a denial of certorari in *Columbia Union College v. Clark* calls on the justices "to scrap the 'pervasively sectarian' test and reaffirm that the Constitution requires, at a minimum, neutrality not hostility toward religion." Federal practice that excludes institutions that "integrat[e] their religious and secular functions" from government benefits constitutes "invidious religious discrimination."[111] Thomas has convinced a plurality of justices to scrap the pervasively sectarian test when state laws permit religious institutions to enjoy the benefits of general laws. "The religious nature of a recipient should not matter to the constitutional analysis," he wrote in *Mitchell v. Helms*, "so long as the recipient adequately furthers the government's secular purpose." He observes that "if a program offers permissible aid to the religious (including the pervasively sectarian), the areligious, and the irreligious, it is a mystery which view of religion the government has established, and thus a mystery what the constitutional violation would be."[112] "Hostility to aid to pervasively sectarian schools," he concludes, "has a shameful pedigree that we do not hesitate to disavow: . . . [t]his doctrine, born of bigotry, should be buried now."[113]

Justice Thomas is usually a reliable conservative and antilibertarian voice on criminal law matters that do not have free speech dimensions. Persons accused or convicted of crimes rarely gain his vote. His Eighth Amendment does not apply to penal conditions. "Cruel and unusual punishment," his dissent in *Hudson v. McMillan*[114] asserts, was historically understood as "applying only to torturous punishments meted out by statutes or sentencing judges, and not generally to any hardship that might befall a prisoner during incarceration."[115] Prisoners who are beaten up by guards, who claim that they were not protected from other violent prisoners, or who claim health risks from exposure to secondhand smoke have no Eighth Amendment right to relief.[116] Decisions to the contrary convert the "Cruel and Unusual Punishment Clause" into the "National Code of Prison Regulation"[117] and are "yet another manifestation of the pervasive view that the Federal Constitution must address all ills in society."[118] Prisoners seeking affirmative government assistance garner no more support. "Quite simply," Justice Thomas declares, "there is no basis in constitutional text, . . . precedent, history, or tradition for the conclusion that the constitutional right of access [to courts] imposes affirmative obligations on the States to finance and support prisoner litigation."[119]

Justice Thomas reaches conservative conclusions when he writes separately in death penalty and habeas corpus cases. He condemns the Rehnquist Court's "Byzantine death penalty jurisprudence"[120] and regards "a mandatory death penalty scheme [as] a perfectly reasonable legislative response to the concerns expressed in *Furman* [*v. Georgia*[121]]."[122] Juries considering whether death is an appropriate punishment should know that the defendant belonged to a racist gang when in prison,[123] but need not be aware of various mitigating circumstances.[124] Juries also need not know that a capital defendant will not be eligible for parole if given a life sentence, even when the prosecutor's demand for the death sentence emphasized the future dangerousness of that defendant.[125] Justice Thomas regards the writ of habeas corpus as an "affront to a State."[126] In *Thompson v. Keohane,* he declares independent federal review of whether a habeas petitioner was in custody when a confession was made to be an "insult [to] our colleagues in the States."[127] "It seems particularly disrespectful to resolve doubts against the proprietary of state-court judgments," another dissent insists, when the writ was granted after federal justices could not decide whether a clear constitutional error prejudiced the original criminal trial.[128] Federal oversight promotes "uniformity of outcomes" in cases adjudicating constitutional rights, but federalism is the more privileged constitutional value. Consistency in constitutional rights standards, Thomas concludes, "must give way to concerns of comity and finality."[129]

Most cases raising other rights of persons in the criminal process are judged by similar conservative standards. Justice Thomas insists that lengthy periods between indictment and arrest do not violate the speedy trial provision of the Sixth Amendment. That provision was intended only to prevent "'undue and oppressive incarceration' and the 'anxiety and concern accompanying public accusation,'" not capacity to prepare for trial.[130] The Fifth Amendment does not bar negative inferences from a failure to testify.[131] He sees no constitutional problem with giving defendants antipsychotic drugs to ensure competency to stand trial,[132] even when those drugs affect the defendant's demeanor and capacity to assist defense counsel.[133] States may confine forever persons acquitted by reason of insanity, even when those persons are no longer afflicted by mental illness. Justice Thomas's dissent in *Foucha v. Louisiana* declares, that "removing some insanity acquittees from mental institutions may make eminent sense as a policy matter, but the due process clause does not require the State to conform to the policy preferences of federal judges."[134]

Forfeitures for property used in crime "without proof of the owner's wrong-doing" are constitutional. Automatic forfeiture "precludes evasions by dispensing with the necessity of judicial inquiry as to collusion between the wrongdoer and the alleged innocent owner."[135] Justice Thomas is constitutionally untroubled by vague laws that give discretion to police officers. "Laws prohibiting loitering and vagrancy," he writes, "have been a fixture of Anglo-American law at least since the time of the Norman Conquest."[136] Police officers can be trusted to "make spur-of-the-moment determinations" about whether a group of loiterers contains individuals (in this case members of criminal street gangs) whom the city has determined threaten the peace."[137]

Justice Thomas displays some liberal tendencies in cases involving more affluent criminal defendants. His concurrence in *United States v. Hubbell* claims that "the Fifth Amendment privilege protects against the compelled production not just of incriminating testimony, but of any incriminating evidence."[138] He is rethinking the constitutionality of suspicionless roadblock stops,[139] but has not joined Justice Scalia and questioned the constitutionality of suspicionless searches in general.[140]

Social conservatives are pleased that Justice Thomas disavows any intention to use the Due Process Clauses of the Fifth and Fourteenth Amendments to protect privacy rights. He believes that the Supreme Court's "substantive due process cases were wrongly decided and that the original understanding of the Due Process Clause precludes judicial enforcement of unenumerated rights under that constitutional provision."[141] Until that doctrine is overruled, Thomas would follow precedent and allow parents to determine whether grandparents or others should visit their children.[142] He is militantly opposed to supporting abortion rights under any notion of stare decisis. His dissent in *Stenberg v. Carhart* declares, "Nothing in our Federal Constitution deprives the people of this country of the right to determine whether the consequences of abortion to the fetus and to society outweigh the burden of an unwanted pregnancy on the mother."[143] Justice Thomas rejects gay rights even when such rights enjoy legislative support. States cannot constitutionally treat as fundamental the right not to be discriminated against on the basis of marital status when that right conflicts with the rights of religious persons who do not wish to rent housing to unmarried persons.[144] Welfare rights enjoy no constitutional protection. Thomas declares that states may "'discriminate' against citizens who have been domiciled in the State for less than a year in the distribution of welfare benefits."[145]

Property rights rank higher on Justice Thomas's constitutional hierarchy. Such rights, he claims, "are central to our heritage,"[146] and he worries that the Rehnquist Court "has not always placed sufficient stress upon the protection of individuals' traditional rights in real property."[147] He joins majority opinions reinvigorating the takings clause[148] and insists that courts should make no "distinction between sweeping legislative takings and particularized administrative takings" when determining whether a government regulation is a compensable taking.[149] Justice Thomas would reconsider two hundred years of precedent dating from *Calder v. Bull* (1798)[150] holding that the the ex post facto clause does not apply to retroactive civil litigation.[151] The right to bear arms is another constitutional concern. He hopes that "at some future date, this Court will have the opportunity to determine whether Justice Story was correct when he wrote that the right to bear arms 'has been justly considered, as the palladium of the liberties of a republic.'"[152]

Justice Thomas enthusiastically supports and would extend Rehnquist Court efforts to protect state prerogatives. The core of his constitutional thinking is a compact theory of the Constitution many thought rejected by the Supreme Court in *McCulloch v. Maryland*[153] and by the United States during the Civil War. His opinion in *U.S. Term Limits, Inc. v. Thornton* bluntly declared that the "ultimate source of the Constitution's authority is the consent of the people of each individual State, not the consent of the undifferentiated people of the Nation as a whole."[154] Justice Thomas construes the Constitution strictly in favor of state power. "Where the Constitution is silent about the exercise of a particular power," he writes, "the Federal Government lacks the power and the States enjoy it."[155] This presumption in favor of states explains why he treats constitutional silence on whether states have "the power to prescribe eligibility requirements for the candidates who seek to represent them in Congress" as providing sufficient constitutional support for that state power.[156]

Justice Thomas is attempting to reign in numerous federal powers. His concurring opinion in *United States v. Lopez* calls for the justices to "respect a constitutional line that does not grant Congress power over all that substantially affects interstate commerce."[157] The substantial effects test, he complains, "lack[s] any grounding in the original understanding of the Constitution" and "appears to give Congress a police power over the Nation." Pragmatic concerns do not justify broad interpretation. Justice Thomas insists that "our Commerce Clause's boundaries simply cannot be 'defined' as being 'commensurate with the national needs' or self-consciously intended to let the Federal Government 'defend itself against economic forces that Congress decrees inimical or destructive of the national economy.'"[158] He supports recent cases holding that Congress may limit the sovereign immunity of a state only when acting pursuant to federal power under the post–Civil War Amendments[159] and joins recent opinions construing that power quite narrowly in cases not involving race discrimination.[160] He agreed in *Printz v. United States* that the Commerce Clause did "not extend to the regulation of wholly intrastate, point-of-sale transactions," and that "Congress surely lacks the corollary power to impress state law enforcement officers into administering and enforcing such regulations."[161]

Justice Thomas would have courts abandon striking down state legislation that regulates interstate commerce in the absence of federal legislation. His dissent in *Camps Newfound Owatonna v. Town of Harrison* declares, "The negative Commerce Clause has no basis in the text of the Constitution, makes little sense, and has proven virtually unworkable in practice."[162] Dormant commerce clause doctrine is also "unnecessary." He believes "the Constitution would seem to provide an express check on the States' power to levy certain discriminatory taxes on the commerce of other States . . . in the Article I, §10 Import-Export Clause."[163]

These federalism concerns influence Justice Thomas's opinions in equal protection cases. Federalism, in his view, significantly inhibits federal ability to remedy past discrimination. "Federal courts should pause," he writes, "before using their inherent equitable powers to intrude into the proper sphere of the States," and "education is primarily a concern of local authorities."[164] The Voting Rights Act "exacts significant federalism costs" and cannot be constitutionally applied to a state that did not previously engage in race discrimination, even when subunits of the state earlier violated the voting rights of persons of color.[165]

States are not responsible for litigants who discriminate against persons of color when selecting juries. "A criminal defendant's use of peremptory strikes," Justice Thomas asserts, "cannot violate the Fourteenth Amendment because it does not involve state action."[166] Lawyers may strike all jurors from a panel who are members of a different race on the reasonable assumption that jurors have racial prejudices.[167] Prosecutors are similarly immune from judicial scrutiny. Thomas regards "the entire line of cases following *Batson v. Kentucky*[168] as "a misguided effort to remedy a general societal wrong by using the Constitution to regulate the traditionally discretionary exercise of peremptory challenges."[169] He does not believe an association that regulates high school sports is a state actor. "The organization of interscholastic sports," he writes, "is neither a traditional nor an exclusive public function of the States."[170]

Justice Thomas's separate opinions evince an ambivalent attitude on race. He vigorously insists that "strict scrutiny applies to all government classifications based on race."[171] Affirmative action programs are unconstitutional per se: "It is irrelevant whether a government's racial classifications are driven by those who wish to oppress a race or by those who have a sincere desire to help those thought to be disadvantaged."[172] Citing the Declaration of Independence, he declares that "the paternalism that appears to lie at the heart" of affirmative action programs "is at war with the principle of inherent equality that underlies and infuses our Constitution."[173] Government should structure institutions in ways that take private racial preferences into account. He is concerned that judicial efforts to promote integration harm traditional black institutions. Too often, he claims, court-ordered integration is based on the assumption "that anything that is predominantly black must be inferior."[174] "Black schools," he declares, "can function as the center and symbol of black communities, and provide examples of independent black leadership, success, and achievement."[175]

In *United States v. Fordice,* Thomas emphasizes the particular need to ensure that remedying Jim Crow did not destroy black universities. He concurred in the judicial desegregation order only because "it portends neither the destruction of historically black colleges nor the severing of those institutions from their distinctive histories and traditions."[176] "For many," he declares, "historically black colleges have become 'a symbol of the highest attainments of black college.'" Constitutional lawyers should not worry if those "programs might disproportionately appeal to one race or another."[177] Thomas expresses even stronger racial sentiments when objecting to a white defendant's challenge to the exclusion of persons of color from juries. "Regardless of whether black veniremen wish to serve on a particular jury," he states, "they do not share the white defendant's interest in obtaining a reversal of his conviction."[178]

Justice Thomas shows little respect for precedent when writing separately in constitutional cases. During his first year on the bench, he urged the Court to overrule or at least rethink basic confrontation clause doctrine,[179] a minor area of equal protection law,[180] and a series of cases forbidding litigants to use race when exercising peremptory challenges.[181] Approximately two-thirds of the separate opinions he wrote from 1996 to 2000 in constitutional cases challenged stare decisis. Thomas urged the justices to abandon the pervasive sectarian test,[182] overrule past cases limiting state power to permit religious organizations to enjoy certain public benefits,[183] overrule those parts of *Buckley v. Valeo*[184] that permit some regulation of campaign finance,[185] overrule past decisions applying a balancing test to truthful commercial advertising,[186] overrule decisions limiting punitive damages,[187] and rethink judicial decisions providing less protection to broadcast media.[188]

He would overrule or rethink decisions holding that prison conditions may constitute cruel and unusual punishment,[189] decisions providing prisoners with some access to legal materials,[190] the line of cases beginning with *Griffin v. Illinois*[191] providing some assistance to impoverished persons appealing criminal convictions,[192] virtually all limits the Supreme Court has placed on the capital sentencing process,[193] a decision declaring loitering statutes unconstitutionally vague,[194] decisions providing notice of various remedies for persons whose property has been seized during criminal investigations,[195] decisions forbidding adverse commentary on the exercise of Fifth Amendment rights,[196] decisions claiming that the Fifth Amendment does not protect the production of incriminating evidence,[197] and cases justifying some suspicionless roadblock searches.[198] Justice Thomas would overrule past cases holding that the Constitution requires states to give some assistance to civil litigants.[199] He would overrule every judicial case providing constitutional protection for abortion rights[200] and reconsider each judicial decision using the Due Process Clauses of the Fifth and Fourteenth Amendments to protect substantial freedoms.[201] He insists that the entire Commerce Clause doctrine developed after the New Deal be reconsidered,[202] as well as modern decisions on legislative delegation.[203] Age provides little protection for past precedent. Thomas wants the justices to rethink past understandings of the Privileges and Immunities Clause dating back to the

Slaughter-House Cases,[204] overrule the Chase Court's decision in *Woodruff v. Parham*[205] limiting to foreign trade the constitutional prohibition on state efforts to lay duties on imports or exports,[206] abandon dormant Commerce Clause doctrine first developed by the Marshall and Taney Courts,[207] and rethink the Ellsworth Court's decision in *Calder v. Bull* limiting the ex post facto clause to retroactive criminal legislation.[208]

These separate opinions in constitutional cases reveal an erratic originalist. Justice Thomas often supports his conclusions with detailed historical analyses. His opinions in prisoners' rights cases carefully examine how the persons responsible for the Eighth Amendment understood punishment.[209] One finds serious historical assertions in separate opinions on state power to impose term limits on federal representatives, the elements of criminal offenses, the Privileges and Immunities Clause of the Fourteenth Amendment, the right of religious groups not to enjoy state benefits, the Commerce Clause, whether the Fifth Amendment covers incriminating evidence, loitering, and the equity power of federal courts.[210] The originalism is pro forma at most when Justice Thomas discusses commercial speech and other aspects of constitutional criminal procedure.[211] His opinions on campaign finance reform, affirmitive action, voting rights, peremptory challenges, property rights, and other aspects of the criminal process contain much philosophical speculation, but no reference to the original understanding of the persons responsible for the constitutional provision in question.[212]

Originalism as Practiced

Scholars who advocate historical methods of constitutional interpretation for many years had the advantage of comparing originalism in theory to other theories in practice. A theory that might constrain justices seemed more attractive than theories that were not constraining justices. Ten years' experience with Justice Thomas provides constitutionalists with a more level playing field. Scholars may now consider whether justices who purport to be originalists are more constrained and more likely to exhibit other judicial virtues than justices who purport to make decisions on some other basis. Originalists cannot be encouraged by the results. Originalism as practiced by Justice Thomas displays no virtues claimed for that approach to judicial decision-making. He is not particularly deferential to elected officials, and his legal conclusions do not differ substantially from those that might be reached by a conservative aspirationalist with a libertarian strain.

Justice Thomas does not claim his voting patterns can be explained on democratic grounds. He exhibits no tendency to defer to local or national legislators. Elected officials in his constitutional universe may rarely, if ever, regulate political dissent, campaign finance, or commercial advertising. Elected officials may not use race when drawing election districts or when distributing benefits formerly distributed in racially discriminatory manners. Both federal and state officials must include religious organizations when they provide general funds for speech and probably must include religious organizations when they provide any generally available benefit. Neither state nor federal officials may engage in regulatory takings. Elected federal officials may not interfere with certain core state functions, may not regulate matters that merely have a substantial effect on interstate commerce, and may only exercise power under the Fourteenth Amendment when the federal judiciary identifies a constitutional wrong in need of remedy. Justice Thomas defers to legislatures on such matters as abortion and the death penalty. Still, he makes no claim that justices, when interpreting legislative power, have any obligation to defer to the judgment of elected officials.

Thomas defends originalism as the best means for promoting judicial impartiality and constraining judicial choice. He maintains that "justices must be impartial referees who defend constitutional principles from attempts by particular interests (or even the people as a whole) to overwhelm them."[213] "The key to fostering [judicial] impartiality" is "reduc[ing] judicial discretion."[214] Originalism "reduce[s] . . . judicial discretion and . . . maintain[s] judicial impartiality" by "tethering [judicial analysis] to the understanding of those who ratified the text." Justice Thomas proclaims that "originalism recognizes the basic principle of a *written* Constitution." "We as a nation," he asserts, "adopted a written Constitution precisely because it has a fixed meaning, a meaning that does not change."[215]

Justice Thomas the originalist in theory fails to reduce judicial discretion by refusing to be a consistent originalist in practice. History guides only some of his judicial opinions. He votes to declare affirmative action policies unconstitutional, even though scholars believe that such practices were accepted by the persons responsible for the Fourteenth Amendment.[216] He votes to strike down restrictions on commercial speech even though no scholar claims that the persons responsible for the First Amendment intended to protect advertising.[217] A principled originalist eager to overrule ancient precedents might rethink precedents, dubious on historical grounds, treating corporations as persons under the Fourteenth Amendment.[218] Justice Thomas has not. The originalist foundations of *Bush v. Gore*[219] remain a judicial mystery.[220]

Much originalism is premised on the belief that history is more objective than philosophy. Whatever the theoretical merits, this claim is false in practice. "There is simply too much legitimate disagreement within originalism," Christopher L. Eisgruber correctly notes, "for it to constrain judges effectively."[221] History and prominent historians can be cited as supporting virtually every argument made in front of the Rehnquist Court. Rehnquist Court justices who reach more liberal results do not concede history to Justice Thomas. They challenge his beliefs about the original understanding of constitutional provisions. When Justice Thomas in *Rosenberger* asserts that the framers intended to permit religious organizations to receive public moneys,[222] Justice Souter responds by citing history and historians for the proposition that the framers intended to forbid religious organizations from receiving public moneys.[223] Justice Stevens and Justice Kennedy wrote opinions in *U.S. Term Limits v. Thorton* that are as historically detailed as the dissent Justice Thomas wrote in that case.[224] Justice Blackmun and Judge John Noonan challenge Justice Thomas's claim that the persons responsible for the Eighth Amendment were not interested in the conditions of punishment.[225] Many distinguished historians sign legal briefs claiming that originalist logic provides far more support for abortion rights than Justice Thomas and other opponents of *Roe* acknowledge.[226]

Justice Thomas does not offer nonpartisan criteria for resolving disputes among professional historians about the original meaning of constitutional provisions. His opinions in *Rosenberger* and *Lopez* demonstrate his unwillingness to defer to elected officials when competent historians dispute whether the framers granted the federal government a particular power. Thomas uses his judgment as to whose history is right, and these judgments consistently favor historical accounts that support conservative or libertarian policies.

His defense of *Brown v. Board of Education*[227] highlights how he disregards the balance of professional history when most experts reach politically undesirable conclusions. He cites a recent essay by Professor Michael McConnell[228] as demonstrating that *Brown* had originalist foundations.[229] Prominent scholars disagree. Works written before and after McConnell published his findings conclude that the persons responsible for the Fourteenth Amendment did not specifically intend to ban segregated schools.[230] Some of these works are written by persons with special expertise on the original meaning of equal protection. The NAACP during the 1950s asked leading historians to find evidence that the framers intended to abolish Jim Crow. That effort at most concluded that the persons responsible for the Equal Protection Clause may have empowered future generations to abolish school segregation.[231] Michael J. Klarman, McConnell's leading critic in the contemporary legal academy, has an advanced degree in history and has devoted most of his career to studying the constitutional history of civil rights law.[232] Earl M. Maltz, another leading critic, has devoted his scholarly career to exploring the original understanding of the Fourteenth Amendment.[233] Before writing his essay on *Brown,* McConnell had never published historical research on the post–Civil War Constitution or on civil rights law. He was best known previously for essays on the original understanding of the religion clauses and federal funding for abortion.[234]

That Professor McConnell may be right hardly justifies claims that originalism constrains Justice Thomas. Thomas is an amateur historian, and amateurs should rely heavily on expert advice. They should consider both the number and the relative expertise of persons who reach differing conclusions on what constitutional provisions were originally understood to mean. In the case of *Brown,* expert opinion at present clearly favors the view that the persons responsible for the Constitution did not intend to abolish segregated education. Justice Thomas rejects the weight of historical scholarship on *Brown* in favor of less credentialed research that reaches more politically palatable conclusions. Such an originalism does not constrain justices. Progressives and liberals will have little trouble using originalist rhetoric if the only requirement is that they cite one scholar as distinguished as Professor McConnell for their predetermined conclusions.

JUSTICE THOMAS AND JUSTICE BRENNAN

Justice Thomas's constitutional jurisprudence bears a striking resemblance to the constitutional jurisprudence of Justice William Brennan. Professor Lucas A. Powe Jr. in a brilliant study observes that during the 1960s a division of labor existed among liberals in "all three branches of government" who were "working harmoniously to tackle the nation's problems." "It was simply a matter," he notes, "of determining which institution was best suited to handle a specific problem."[235] A similar division of institutional labor presently exists among conservatives. The Rehnquist Court imposes Tenth Amendment limitations on national power, while Congress devolves federal problems to the states.[236] This division of labor hardly requires judicial activism run rampant. The present Supreme Court is no more responsible for achieving all the goals set out in the Contract with America than the Warren Court was responsible for achieving all the goals set out by the Great Society. Judicial institutions have distinctive jurisprudential "missions" in both liberal and conservative regimes largely structured by the intersection of partisan opportunity and the forms of legal discourse at the time.[237] Justices Brennan and Thomas share a wholehearted commitment to the legal missions detailed by their political allies. Justice Brennan pushed the Supreme Court to become more active in every area of constitutional law that prominent liberal scholars thought warranted more judicial intervention. Justice Thomas is pushing the Supreme Court to become more active in every area of constitutional law that prominent conservative scholars think warrants more judicial intervention. These mission commitments, not any abstract theory of the judicial function, provide the glue that unites Brennan and Thomas.

Given the choice between a perfect historian and a perfect philosopher on the Supreme Court, we might well choose the perfect philosopher. Originalists attempt to avoid this choice by postulating that history is more objective than philosophy. Practice does not support this claim. The possibility of objectivity is controversial in both disciplines.[238] If the judge who always gets history right can be posited, so should the judge who always gets justice right. The latter seems preferable. Why be governed by what the framers thought was the best meaning of free speech when we can be governing by the best meaning of free speech?[239]

Our practical choices when staffing the judiciary are between amateur historians and amateur philosophers. Amateur historians often make mistakes about past understandings of constitutional provisions. Amateur philosophers often make mistakes about the best understandings of constitutional provisions.

Forests have been decimated to provide paper used to prove whether Justice Brennan, the amateur philosopher, had a better conception of the judicial function than Justice Thomas, the amateur historian. Ten years of the Rehnquist Court suggest that in practice little difference exists.

NOTES

1. See Keith E. Whittington, *Constitutional Interpretation: Textual Meaning, Original Intent, and Judicial Review* (Lawrence: University Press of Kansas, 1999); Christopher Wolfe, *The Rise of Modern Judicial Review: From Constitutional Interpretation to Judge-Made Law* (New York: Basic Books, 1986).

2. For leading versions of originalism, see Robert H. Bork, *The Tempting of America: The Political Seduction of the Law* (New York: Simon and Schuster, 1990); Antonin Scalia, *A Matter of Interpretation: Federal Courts and the Law* (Princeton: Princeton University Press, 1997); Whittington, *Constitutional Interpretation;* Wolfe, *The Rise of Modern Judicial Review;* Matthew J. Franck, *Against the Imperial Judiciary: The Supreme Court vs. the Sovereignty of the People* (Lawrence: University Press of Kansas, 1996).

3. Most proponents of originalism conflate constitutional interpretation and a theory of the judicial function. Keith Whittington, *Constitutional Interpretation,* especially pp. 5–14, however, maintains that while justices should interpret the Constitution consistently with the original understanding of that text, other governing officials are free to adopt various methods of constitutional interpretation. See also Keith E. Whittington, *Constitutional Construction: Divided Powers and Constitutional Meaning* (Cambridge: Harvard University Press, 1999).

4. See Rogers M. Smith, *Liberalism and American Constitutional Law* (Cambridge: Harvard University Press, 1990), 114–116.

5. For leading versions as aspirationalism, see Frank I. Michelman, *Brennan and Democracy* (Princeton: Princeton University Press, 1999); Sotirios A. Barber, *The Constitution of Judicial Power* (Baltimore: Johns Hopkins University Press, 1993); H. Jefferson Powell, *The Moral Tradition of American Constitutionalism: A Theological Interpretation* (Durham, N.C.: Duke University Press, 1993); Graham Walker, *Moral Foundations of Constitutional Thought: Current Problems, Augustinian Prospects* (Princeton: Princeton University Press, 1990), 154; Ronald Dworkin, *Taking Rights Seriously* (Cambridge: Harvard University Press, 1978); Gary J. Jacobsohn, *The Supreme Court and the Decline of Constitutional Aspiration* (Totowa, N.J.: Rowman and Littlefield, 1986).

6. The biographical details noted in this and the next paragraph were taken from Clare Cushman, "Clarence Thomas," in *The Supreme Court Justices: Illustrated Biographies, 1789–1993,* ed. Clare Cushman (Washington, D.C.: Congressional Quarterly Press, 1993), 526–530.

7. See Clarence Thomas, "Personal Responsibility," *Regent University Law Review* 12 (1999/2000): 317, 325; Clarence Thomas, "Freedom: A Responsibility, Not a Right," *Ohio Northern University Law Review* 21 (1994): 5, 8–11.

8. See Clarence Thomas, "Toward a 'Plain Reading' of the Constitution—The Declaration of Independence in Constitutional Interpretation," *Howard Law Journal* (1987): 691.

9. Cushman, "Thomas," 529.

10. Several forests have been decimated providing paper for books on the Clarence Thomas nomination to the Supreme Court. The leading studies include Christopher E. Smith and Joyce A. Baugh, *The Real Clarence Thomas: Confirmation Veracity Meets Performance Reality* (New York: P. Lang, 2000); Jane Flax, *The American Dream in Black and White: The Clarence Thomas Hearings* (Ithaca, N.Y.: Cornell University Press, 1998); John C. Danforth, *Resurrection: The Confirmation of Clarence Thomas* (New York: Viking, 1994); Timothy M. Phelps and Helen Winternitz, *Capitol Games: The Inside Story of Clarence Thomas, Anita Hill, and a Supreme Court Nomination* (New York: Harper Perennial, 1993); and Jane Mayer and Jill Abramson, *Strange Justice: The Selling of Clarence Thomas* (Boston: Houghton Mifflin, 1994).

11. See Smith and Baugh, *The Real Clarence Thomas.*

12. Benjamin Ginsberg and Martin Shefter, *Politics by Other Means: The Declining Importance of Elections in America* (New York: Basic Books, 1990).

13. Ginsberg and Shefter, *Politics by Other Means,* x, 11.

14. See Terri Jennings Peretti, *In Defense of a Political Court* (Princeton: Princeton University Press, 1999).

15. 532 U.S. 483 (2001).

16. 519 U.S. 337 (1997).

17. 506 U.S. 103 (1992).

18. *Harris Trust and Savings Bank v. Salomon Smith Barney Inc.,* 530 U.S. 238 (2000).

19. *Carter v. United States,* 530 U.S. 255 (2000).

20. *Sims v. Apfel,* 530 U.S. 103 (2000).

21. *Christensen v. Harris County,* 529 U.S. 576 (2000).

22. *Beck v. Prupis,* 529 U.S. 494 (2000).

23. *Baral v. United States,* 528 U.S. 431 (2000).

24. See *Tyler v. Cain,* 533 U.S. 656 (2001); *Carter v. United States,* 530 U.S. 255 (2000); *Shannon v. United States,* 512 U.S. 573 (1994); *United States v. Mezzanatto,* 513 U.S. 196 (1995); *United States v. Alvarez-Sanchez,* 511 U.S. 350 (1994).

25. *Christensen v. Harris County,* 529 U.S. 576 (2000); *Norfolk and W. Ry. v. Hiles,* 516 U.S. 400 (1996); *Conrail v. Gottshall,* 512 U.S. 532 (1994); *Lechmere, Inc. v. NLRB,* 502 U.S. 527 (1992).

26. *Dooley v. Korean AirLines Co.,* 524 U.S. 116 (1998); *Hughes Aircraft Co. v. United States ex rel. Schumer,* 520 U.S. 939 (1997); *Peacock v. Thomas,* 516 U.S. 349 (1996); *Things Remembered v. Petrarca,* 516 U.S. 124 (1995); *National Private Truck Council v. Oklahoma Tax Comm'n,* 515 U.S. 582 (1995).

27. *Bogan v. Scott-Harris,* 523 U.S. 44 (1998); *Molzof v. United States,* 502 U.S. 301 (1992).

28. 533 U.S. 656 (2001).

29. 502 U.S. 527 (1992).

30. 512 U.S. 532 (1994).

31. 520 U.S. 17 (1997).

32. 511 U.S. 600 (1994).

33. See Jeffrey A. Segal and Harold J. Spaeth, *The Supreme Court and the Attitudinal Model* (New York: Cambridge University Press, 1993), 243.

34. 521 U.S. 346 (1997).

35. Smith and Baugh, *The Real Clarence Thomas,* 192.

36. Kathleen M. Sullivan and Gerald Gunther, *Constitutional Law,* 14th ed. (New York: Foundation Press, 2001).

37. Lee Epstein and Thomas G. Walker, *Constitutional Law for a Changing America: Institutional Powers and Constraints,* 4th ed. (Washington, D.C.: CQ Press, 2001), and *Constitutional Law for a Changing America: Rights, Liberties, and Justice,* 4th ed. (Washington, D.C.: CQ Press, 2001).

38. 511 U.S. 93 (1994).

39. See especially Cass R. Sunstein, *One Case at a Time: Judicial Minimalism on the Supreme Court* (Cambridge: Harvard University Press, 1999).

40. 523 U.S. 303 (1998).

41. 509 U.S. 389 (1993).

42. 520 U.S. 143 (1997).

43. 524 U.S. 321 (1998).

44. 517 U.S. 843 (1996).

45. 528 U.S. 259 (2000).

46. 386 U.S. 738 (1967).

47. 524 U.S. 88 (1998).

48. 447 U.S. 625 (1980).

49. 524 U.S., at 90–91.

50. 514 U.S. 476 (1995).

51. Ibid., at 482. See *Central Hudson Gas and Elec. Corp. v. Public Serv. Comm'n of New York,* 447 U.S. 557 (1980).

52. See *Greater New Orleans Broad. Ass'n v. United States,* 527 U.S. 173, 197 (1999) (Thomas, J., concurring).

53. 533 U.S. 98, 121 S.Ct. 2093 (2001).

54. Ibid., at 2100.

55. 515 U.S. 819 (1995) (Thomas, J., concurring).

56. Ibid., at 524–564.

57. 526 U.S. 559 (1999).

58. Ibid., at 564.

59. 524 U.S., at 331–332.

60. 523 U.S. 340, 348 (1998), quoting *Parsons v. Bedford,* 3 Peters 433, 447 (1830).

61. 514 U.S. 927 (1995).

62. See *Evans v. United States,* 504 U.S. 255, 287–290 (1992) (Thomas, J., dissenting); *Caron v. United States,* 524 U.S. 308, 319–320 (1998) (Thomas, J., dissenting); *Holloway v. United States,* 526 U.S. 1, 26 (1999) (Thomas, J., dissenting); *Fischer v. United States,* 529 U.S. 667, 691 (Thomas, J., dissenting).

63. *United Dominion Industries v. United States,* 532 U.S. 822, 121 S.Ct. 1934, 1944 (2001) (Thomas, J., dissenting).

64. *Republic National Bank v. United States,* 506 U.S. 80 (1992).

65. 504 U.S. 255, 291–294 (1992) (Thomas, J., dissenting).

66. 525 U.S. 366, 411 (1999) (Thomas, J., concurring and dissenting).

67. *Allied-Bruce Terminix Cos. v. Dodson,* 513 U.S. 265, 292–293 (1995) (Thomas, J., dissenting). See *Doctor's Assocs v. Casarotto,* 517 U.S. 681, 689 (1996) (Thomas, J.,

dissenting). Justice Thomas sided with Alaska against the United States in a boundary dispute concerning various waters; see *United States v. Alaska,* 521 U.S. 1, 63–73 (1997) (Thomas, J., concurring and dissenting). For the only case I can locate where he was more inclined than his colleagues to find for federal rather than state power, see *PUD No. 1 v. Washington Department of Ecology,* 511 U.S. 700 (1994) (Thomas, J., dissenting), claiming state environmental law inconsistent with federal law authorizing a hydroelectric project. Thomas is more likely to presume federal prerogatives when states are out of the picture. See *Henderson v. United States,* 517 U.S. 654, 673 (1996) (Thomas, J., dissenting), claiming that Congress should not be presumed to have waived sovereign immunity.

68. *McFarland v. Scott,* 512 U.S. 849, 872 (1994) (Thomas, J., dissenting, quoting *Duckworth v. Eagan,* 492 U.S. 195, 210 [1989] [O'Connor, J., concurring]).

69. 512 U.S., at 873.

70. 512 U.S. 477, 491 (1994) (Thomas, J., concurring).

71. *Olmstead v. L.C.,* 527 U.S. 581, 625 (1999) (Thomas. J., dissenting). See ibid., at 624, "the majority's approach imposes significant federalism costs."

72. *Cedar Rapids Community School District v. Garret F. by Chalotte P.,* 526 U.S. 66, 83, 85 (1999) (Thomas, J., dissenting).

73. *Kimel v. Florida Board of Regents,* 528 U.S. 62, 99 (2000) (Thomas, J., concurring and dissenting).

74. 525 U.S. 266, 293–294 (1999) (Thomas, J., dissenting).

75. Ibid., at 295–296.

76. *Holder v. Hall,* 512 U.S. 874, 892 (1994) (Thomas, J., concurring).

77. *Johnson v. DeGrandy,* 512 U.S. 997, 1031–1032 (1994) (Thomas, J., dissenting).

78. 517 U.S. 186, 283 (1996) (Thomas, J., dissenting).

79. *Morse v. Republican Party,* 517 U.S. 186, at 270 (1996) (Thomas, J., dissenting).

80. *Reno v. Bossier Parrish School Board,* 520 U.S. 471, 492 (1997) (Thomas, J., concurring).

81. 512 U.S., at 944.

82. 520 U.S., at 491–492.

83. 512 U.S., at 944, 905, 903.

84. *Reno v. Bossier Parish School Board,* 528 U.S. 320, 341 (2000) (Thomas, J., concurring).

85. 512 U.S., at 933.

86. *United States v. R.L.C.,* 503 U.S. 291, 312 (1992) (Thomas, J., concurring). See *Johnson v. United States,* 529 U.S. 694, 715 (2000) (Thomas, J., concurring).

87. *United States v. R.L.C.,* 503 U.S. 291, 312 (1992) (Thomas, J., concurring). See *Johnson v. United States,* 529 U.S. 694, 715 (2000) (Thomas, J., concurring); *Fogerty v. Fantasy, Inc.,* 510 U.S. 517, 537–538 (1994) (Thomas, J., concurring), describing as "mistaken" claims that "whether we construe a statute in accordance with its plain meaning depends upon the statute's policy objectives and legislative history."

88. *Bank of America Nat'l Trust and Savings Association v. 203 North LaSalle St. PSHP,* 526 U.S. 434, 462n2 (1999) (Thomas, J., concurring).

89. 478 U.S. 30 (1986). See *Holder v. Hall,* 512 U.S. 874, 936–945 (1994) (Thomas, J., concurring).

90. 465 U.S. 1 (1984). See 513 U.S., at 295–297.

91. 468 U.S. 883 (1984). See 526 U.S., at 79–83.

92. 497 U.S. 358 (1990).

93. *Jerome B. Grubart, Inc. v. Great Lakes Dredge and Dock Co.,* 513 U.S. 527, 554–555 (1995) (Thomas, J., concurring).

94. Justice Kennedy did not join a Justice Thomas dissent or concurrence between 1992 and 1999. Since then he has joined five: *Mitchell v. Helms,* 530 U.S. 793 (2000) (opinion of Thomas, J.); *Kimel v. Florida Board of Regents,* 528 U.S. 62 (2000) (Thomas, J., concurring and dissenting); *FEC v. Colorado Republican Federal Campaign Committee,* 533 U.S. 431 (2001) (Thomas, J., dissenting); *Hunt v. Cromartie,* 532 U.S. 234 (2001) (Thomas, J., dissenting); and *Brentwood Academy v. Tennessee Secondary School Athletic Association,* 531 U.S. 288 (2001) (Thomas, J., dissenting).

95. Justice Souter joined that part of Justice Thomas's plurality opinion in *United States v. Scheffer,* 523 U.S. 303 (1998), claiming that forbidding defendants to introduce polygraph evidence "preserve[d] the jury's core function of making credibility determinations in criminal trials" (at 312–313 [opinion of Thomas, J.]). Justice Souter also joined a Thomas dissent in a case raising issues about whether a federal law preempted a state law, a matter sometimes thought to raise Supremacy Clause issues, though usually regarded as a matter of statutory interpretation: *CSX Transp. V. Easterwood,* 507 U.S. 658 (1993) (Thomas, J., concurring and dissenting) (no mention of constitutional issues).

96. 514 U.S. 779 (1995).

97. 514 U.S. 334 (1995) (Thomas, J., concurring).

98. Ibid., at 361.

99. *Buckley v. American Constitutional Law Found,* 525 U.S. 182, 206 (1999) (Thomas, J., concurring).

100. *Avis Rent-A-Car Sys. v. Aguilar,* 529 U.S. 1138 (2000) (Thomas, J., dissenting from denial of cert.).

101. *Apprendi v. New Jersey,* 530 U.S. 466, 499–523 (2000) (Thomas, J., concurring). Justice Thomas is not as forceful in obscenity cases, but his separate opinions exhibit little desire to challenge largely libertarian doctrines. See *United States v. Playboy Entertainment Group,* 529 U.S. 803, 830–831 (2000) (Thomas, J., concurring), agreeing that indecent speech is protected by the First Amendment.

102. *Denver Area Educational Telcommunications Consortium v. FCC,* 518 U.S. 727, 813 (1996) (Thomas, J., concurring and dissenting).

103. *Colorado Republican Federal Campaign Committee v. FEC,* 518 U.S. 604, 636 (1996) (Thomas, J., concurring).

104. *Nixon v. Shrink Mo. Gov't PAC,* 528 U.S. 377, 412 (2000) (Thomas, J., dissenting).

105. *44 Liquormart v. Rhode Island,* 517 U.S. 484, 522 (1996) (Thomas, J., concurring). See *Lorillard Tobacco Company v. Reilly,* 533 U.S. 525, 121 S.Ct. 2404, 2432 (2001) (Thomas, J., concurring).

106. 533 U.S. 525, 121 S.Ct., at 2440.

107. 517 U.S., at 518; *Greater New Orleans Broad. Ass'n v. United States,* 527 U.S. 173, 197 (1999) (Thomas, J., concurring).

108. 533 U.S. 525, 121 S.Ct., at 2431.

109. *Glickman v. Wileman Bros and Elliott,* 521 U.S. 457 (1997) (Thomas, J., dissenting). See *United States v. United Foods, Inc.,* 533 U.S. 405, 121 S.Ct. 2334, 2342 (2001) (Thomas, J., concurring).

110. 515 U.S. 819, 852 (1995).

111. 527 U.S. 1013, 1014–1015 (1999) (Thomas, J., dissenting from a denial of certiorari).

112. 530 U.S. 793, 827 (2000) (opinion of Thomas, J.).

113. Ibid., at 829. Justice Thomas found no Establishment Clause violation when the Klan was permitted to erect a cross on a statehouse square. He nevertheless felt the need to state that "the erection of such a cross is a political act, not a Christian one," *Capitol Square Review and Advisory Board v. Pinette,* 515 U.S. 753 (1995) (Thomas, J., concurring), apparently feeling the need to define religious doctrine.

114. 503 U.S. 1 (1992) (Thomas, J., dissenting).

115. Ibid., at 18–19. See *Farmer v. Brennan,* 511 U.S. 825, 859 (1994) (Thomas, J., concurring).

116. See 503 U.S., at 17–29; 511 U.S., at 858–862; *Helling v. McKinney,* 509 U.S. 25, 37–42 (1993) (Thomas, J., dissenting). Justice Thomas suggests that persons abused in prison have due process claims; 503 U.S., at 28–29. The contours of this due process right have not been delineated.

117. 511 U.S., at 859.

118. 503 U.S., at 28.

119. *Lewis v. Casey,* 518 U.S. 343, 382 (1996) (Thomas, J., concurring).

120. *Knight v. Florida,* 628 U.S. 990, 991 (1999) (Thomas, J., concurring in denial of certiorari). See *Kelly v. South Carolina,* 534 U.S. 246, 122 S.Ct. 726, 737–738 (2002) (Thomas, J., dissenting).

121. 408 U.S. 238 (1972).

122. *Graham v. Collins,* 506 U.S. 461, 487 (1993) (Thomas, J., concurring).

123. *Dawson v. Delaware,* 503 U.S. 159, 171 (1992) (Thomas J., dissenting).

124. *Penry v. Johnson,* 532 U.S. 782, 121 S.Ct. 1910, 1925–1927 (2001) (Thomas, J., concurring and dissenting).

125. 534 U.S. 246 122 S.Ct., at 736–738; *Shafer v. South Carolina,* 532 U.S. 36, 55–58 (2001) (Thomas, J., dissenting).

126. *O'Neal v. McAninch,* 513 U.S. 432, 447 (1995) (Thomas, J., dissenting).

127. 516 U.S. 99, 120 (1995) (Thomas, J., dissenting).

128. 513 U.S., at 448.

129. 516 U.S., at 120n1. Justice Thomas favors judicial intervention when state supreme courts interpret constitutional rights more broadly than the Supreme Court. See *Rainey v. Chever,* 527 U.S. 1044, 1044–1048 (1999) (Thomas, J., dissenting from denial of certiorari).

130. *Doggett v. United States,* 505 U.S. 647, 659–660 (1992) (Thomas, J., dissenting), quoting *United States v. Marion,* 404 U.S. 307, 320 (1971). For other opinions by Justice Thomas urging narrow understandings of Sixth Amendment rights, see *White v. Illinois,* 502 U.S. 346, 365 (1992) (Thomas, J., concurring), confrontation clause may not ban all hearsay, and *Lilly v. Virginia,* 527 U.S. 116, 143–144 (1999) (Thomas, J., concurring), claiming that the Sixth Amendment "does not impose a blanket ban on the government's use of accomplice statements that incriminate a defendant." See also *Campbell v. Louisiana,* 523 U.S. 392, 407 (1998) (Thomas, J., concurring and dissenting), claiming that conviction at trial establishes that "alleged discrimination in grand jury selection could [not] have caused an indictment to have been improperly rendered."

131. *Mitchell v. United States,* 526 U.S.. 314, 343 (1999) (Thomas, J., dissenting).

132. *Riggins v. Nevada,* 504 U.S. 127, 149–150 (1992) (Thomas. J., dissenting).

133. Ibid., at 142.

134. 505 U.S. 71, 125 (1992) (Thomas, J., dissenting).

135. *Bennis v. Michigan,* 516 U.S. 442, 455 (1996) (Thomas, J., concurring).

136. *City of Chicago v. Morales,* 527 U.S. 41, 103 (1999) (Thomas, J., dissenting).

137. Ibid., at 109–110.

138. 530 U.S. 27, 49 (2000) (Thomas, J., concurring).

139. *City of Indianapolis v. Edmond,* 121 S.Ct. 547, 462 (2000).

140. See *National Treasury Employees Union v. Von Raab,* 489 U.S. 656, 680–687 (1989) (Scalia, J., dissenting).

141. *Troxel v. Granville,* 530 U.S. 57, 80 (2000) (Thomas, J., concurring).

142. Ibid., at 80.

143. 530 U.S. 914, 980 (2000) (Thomas, J., dissenting). Justice Thomas considers *Roe* a valid precedent justifying gender distinctions between mothers and fathers who do not support their children. Dissenting from a denial of certiorari, he declared, "The logic of the abortion cases suggesting that the state may not ignore a mother's unique efforts in carrying a child to term, flatly contradicts the Georgia Supreme Court's reasoning that the State must ignore the efforts when deciding whether she, as opposed to the father, is entitled to inherit from the deceased child's estate" (*Rainey v. Chever,* 527 U.S. 1044, 1048 [1999]).

144. *Swanner v. Anchorage Equal Rights Comm'n,* 513 U.S. 979 (1994) (Thomas, J., dissenting from denial of certiorari). See *Boy Scouts of America v. Dale,* 530 U.S. 640 (2000).

145. *Saenz v. Roe,* 526 U.S. 489, 527 (1999) (Thomas, J., dissenting).

146. *United States v. James Daniel Good Real Property,* 510 U.S. 43, 81 (1993) (Thomas, J., concurring and dissenting).

147. Ibid., at 81, 84.

148. See *Dolan v. City of Tigard,* 512 U.S. 374 (1994); *Lucas v. South Carolina Coastal Council,* 505 U.S. 1003 (1992).

149. *Parking Ass'n v. City of Atlanta,* 515 U.S. 1116, 1116–1118 (1995) (Thomas, J., dissenting from a denial of certiorari).

150. 3 U.S. 386 (1798).

151. *Eastern Enters. v. Apfel,* 524 U.S. 498, 538–539 (1998) (Thomas, J., concurring).

152. *Printz v. United States,* 521 U.S. 898, 938 (1997) (Thomas, J., concurring).

153. 17 U.S. 316 (1819).

154. 514 U.S. 779, 846 (1995) (Thomas, J., dissenting).

155. Ibid., at 848. See *Cook v. Gralike,* 531 U.S. 510, 530 (2001) (Thomas, J., concurring).

156. 514 U.S., at 845.

157. 514 U.S. 549, 592 (1995) (Thomas, J., dissenting).

158. Ibid., at 599–600, 602. See *United States v. Morrison,* 529 U.S. 598, 627 (2000) (Thomas, J., concurring).

159. *Kimel v. Florida Board of Regents,* 528 U.S. 62, 99 (2000) (Thomas, J., concurring and dissenting).

160. See *City of Boerne v. Flores,* 521 U.S. 507 (1997); *Board of Trustees of the University of Alabama v. Garrett,* 531 U.S. 356 (2001).

161. 521 U.S., at 937.

162. 520 U.S. 564, 611 (1997) (Thomas, J., dissenting).

163. Ibid., at 610.

164. *Missouri v. Jenkins,* 515 U.S. 70, 131 (1995) (Thomas, J., concurring).

165. *Lopez v. Monterey County,* 525 U.S. 266, 295–296 (1999) (Thomas, J., concurring).

166. *Georgia v. McCollum,* 505 U.S. 42, 60 (1992) (Thomas, J., concurring).

167. Ibid., at 60–62.

168. 476 U.S. 79 (1986).

169. *Campell v. Louisiana,* 523 U.S. 392, 405n1 (1998) (Thomas, J., concurring and dissenting).

170. *Brentwood Academy v. Tennessee Secondary Sch. Ath. Ass'n,* 531 U.S. 288, 309 (2001) (Thomas, J., dissenting).

171. *Adarand Constructors v. Pena,* 515 U.S. 200, 240 (1995) (Thomas, J., concurring). See *Bush v. Vera,* 517 U.S. 592 (1996): "Strict scrutiny applies to all governmental classifications based on race, and we have expressly held that there is no exception for race-based districting."

172. 515 U.S., at 240.

173. Ibid.

174. 515 U.S., at 114.

175. Ibid., at 121.

176. 505 U.S. 717, 745 (1992) (Thomas, J., concurring).

177. Ibid., at 748–749.

178. 523 U.S., at 407.

179. *White v. Illinois,* 502 U.S. 346, 358–363 (1992) (Thomas, J., concurring).

180. *Nordlinger v. Hahn,* 505 U.S. 1, 27–28 (1992) (Thomas, J., concurring), urging the justices to overrule *Allegheny Pittsburgh Coal Co. v. County Com. of Webster County,* 488 U.S. 336 (1989).

181. *Georgia v. McCollum,* 505 U.S. 42, 60–62 (1992) (Thomas, J., concurring), urging the justices to overrule the line of cases beginning with *Batson v. Kentucky,* 476 U.S. 79 (1986). See 523 U.S., at 404–405.

182. *Columbia Union College v. Clark,* 527 U.S. 1013–1015 (1999) (Thomas, J., dissenting from a denial of certiorari).

183. *Michell v. Helms,* 530 U.S. 793, 835 (2000) (opinion of Thomas, J.), urging abandonment of *Meek v. Pittenger,* 421 U.S. 349 (1975), and *Wolman v. Walter,* 433 U.S. 229 (1977).

184. 424 U.S. 1 (1976).

185. *Nixon v. Shrink Mo. Gov't PAC,* 528 U.S. 377, 412–420 (2000) (Thomas, J., dissenting); *Colorado Republican Federal Campaign Committee v. FEC,* 518 U.S. 604, 631 (1996) (Thomas, J., concurring and dissenting).

186. *Glickman v. Wileman Bros. and Elliott,* 521 U.S. 457, 504 (1997) (Thomas, J., dissenting), all commercial speech; *44 Liquormart v. Rhode Island,* 517 U.S. 484, 518 (1996) (Thomas, J., concurring), truthful commercial speech; *Greater New Orleans Broad. Ass'n v. United States,* 527 U.S. 173, 197 (1999) (Thomas, J., concurring).

187. *Cooper Industries v. Leatherman Tool Group, Inc.*, 532 U.S. 424, 443 (2001) (Thomas, J., concurring), asserting that *BMW of North America, Inc. v. Gore*, 517 U.S. 559 (1996), should be overruled.

188. *Denver Area Educational Telecommunications Consortium v. FCC*, 518 U.S. 727, 813 (1996) (Thomas, J., concurring and dissenting).

189. *Heilling v. McKinney*, 509 U.S. 25, 42 (1993) (Thomas, J., dissenting), urging the justices to overrule *Estelle v. Gamble*, 429 U.S. 97 (1976); *Farmer v. Brennan*, 511 U.S. 825, 861–862 (1994) (Thomas, J., concurring).

190. *Lewis v. Casey*, 518 U.S. 343, 373–374 (1996) (Thomas, J., concurring), claiming that *Bounds v. Smith*, 430 U.S. 817 (1977), should be overruled.

191. 351 U.S. 12 (1956).

192. *M.L.B. v. S.L.J.*, 519 U.S. 102, 139 (1996) (Thomas, J., dissenting): "I would be inclined to overrule *Griffin* and its progeny."

193. *Graham v. Collins*, 506 U.S. 461, 487–492 (1993) (Thomas, J., concurring), suggesting that the court rethink or overrule *Roberts v. Louisiana*, 428 U.S. 325 (1976), *Woodson v. North Carolina*, 428 U.S. 280 (1976), *Penry v. Lynaugh*, 492 U.S. 302 (1989), and possibly *Eddings v. Oklahoma*, 455 U.S. 104 (1982); *Knight v. Florida*, 528 U.S. 990, 991 (1991) (Thomas, J., concurring in the denial of certiorari); *Kelly v. South Carolina*, at 736 (Thomas, J., dissenting), urging the court to overrule *Simmons v. South Carolina*, 512 U.S. 154 (1994).

194. *City of Chicago v. Morales*, 527 U.S. 41, 105–106 (1999) (Thomas, J., dissenting), claiming that *Papachistou v. Jacksonville*, 405 U.S. 156 (1972), was wrongly decided.

195. *City of W. Covina v. Perkins*, 525 U.S. 234, 247–248 (2000) (Thomas, J., concurring).

196. *Mitchell v. United States*, 512 U.S. 314, 343 (1999) (Thomas, J., dissenting), urging the justices to reconsider *Griffin v. California*, 380 U.S. 609 (1965), and *Carter v. Kentucky*, 450 U.S. 288 (1981).

197. *United States v. Hubbell*, 530 U.S. 27, 55–56 (2000) (Thomas, J., concurring).

198. *City of Indianapolis v. Edmonds*, 531 U.S. 32, 56 (2000) (Thomas, J., dissenting), suggesting the Court reconsider *Michigan Dept. of State Police v. Sitz*, 496 U.S. 444 (1990), and *United States v. Martinez-Fuerte*, 428 U.S. 543 (1976).

199. 519 U.S. 102, 141, questioning *Boddie v. Connecticut*, 401 U.S. 371 (1971).

200. *Stenberg v. Carhart*, 530 U.S. 914, 980–982 (1999) (Thomas, J., dissenting).

201. *Troxel v. Granville*, 530 U.S. 57, 80 (2000) (Thomas, J., concurring).

202. *United States v. Lopez*, 514 U.S. 549, 601–602 (1995) (Thomas, J., concurring); *United States v. Morrison*, 529 U.S. 598, 627 (2000) (Thomas, J., concurring).

203. *Whitman v. American Trucking Associations*, 531 U.S. 467, 487 (2001) (Thomas, J., concurring).

204. 83 U.S. 36 (1873). See *Saenz v. Roe*, 526 U.S. 489, 527–528 (1999) (Thomas, J., dissenting).

205. 75 U.S. 123 (1869).

206. *Camps Newfound Owatonna v. Town of Harrison*, 520 U.S. 564, 636 (1997) (Thomas, J., dissenting).

207. Ibid., at 636–637.

208. *Eastern Enters. v. Apfel*, 524 U.S. 498, 538–539 (1998) (Thomas, J., concurring).

209. *Hudson v. McMillan,* 503 U.S. 1, 18–20 (1992) (Thomas, J., dissenting); *Helling v. McKinney,* 509 U.S. 25, 38–40 (1993) (Thomas, J., dissenting); 511 U.S., at 859 (Thomas, J., dissenting).

210. See 514 U.S., at 847–916 (Thomas, J., dissenting); 530 U.S., at 499–518 (Thomas, J., concurring); 515 U.S., at 652–663 (Thomas, J., concurring); 520 U.S., at 610–613, 621–625 (Thomas, J., dissenting); 514 U.S., at 586–599 (Thomas, J., concurring); 530 U.S., at 49–55 (Thomas, J., concurring); 527 U.S., at 103–104 (Thomas, J., dissenting); 515 U.S., at 126–131 (Thomas, J., concurring); *McIntyre v. Ohio Elections Commission,* 514 U.S. 334, 359–367 (1995) (Thomas, J., concurring).

211. 517 U.S., at 522–523 (Thomas, J., concurring); *Foucha v. Louisiana,* 504 U.S. 71, 124–125 (1992) (Thomas, J., dissenting), noting briefly that "many States have long provided for the continued detention of insanity acquittees who remain dangerous." *Lewis v. Casey,* 518 U.S. 343, 373–374, 381–382 (1996) (Thomas, J., concurring); 523 U.S., at 405n1 (Thomas, J., concurring and dissenting); 527 U.S., at 143–144 (Thomas, J., concurring).

212. See *Colorado Republican Federal Campaign Committee v. FEC,* 518 U.S. 604 (1996) (Thomas, J., concurring and dissenting); 528 U.S., at 411, claiming that the persons responsible for the Constitution intended to protect political speech, but making no argument that they regarded campaign contributions as a form of free speech; 518 U.S., at 2371–2372; *Adarand Constructors v. Pena,* 515 U.S. 200 (1995) (Thomas, J., concurring); *Doggett v. United States,* 505 U.S. 647 (1992) (Thomas, J., dissenting), speedy trial guarantee does not protect the ability to defend at trial; *Georgia v. McCollum,* 505 U.S. 42 (1992) (Thomas, J., concurring), peremptory challenges are not state action; *Riggins v. Nevada,* 504 U.S. 127 (1992) (Thomas, J., dissenting), forcing a defendant to take antipsychotic drugs does not violate due process; *United States v. James Daniel Good Real Property,* 510 U.S. 43 (1993) (Thomas, J., concurring and dissenting), property rights; *O'Neal v. McAninch,* 513 U.S. 432 (1995) (Thomas, J., dissenting), harmless error rule.

Justice Thomas also does not discuss in detail the original intentions of the persons responsible for the Constitution when writing on the death penalty and abortion. See *Graham v. Collins,* 506 U.S. 461 (1993) (Thomas, J., concurring); *Stenberg v. Carhart,* 530 U.S. 914 (2000) (Thomas, J., dissenting). In these circumstances, the originalist case had previously been laid out by other justices. No previous judicial opinion accounts for his failure to make historical arguments in the cases cited in the above paragraph.

213. Clarence Thomas, "Francis Boyer Lecture," American Enterprise Institute for Public Policy Research, Washington, D.C., February 13, 2001; *www.aei.org/boyer/thomas.htm.*

214. Clarence Thomas, "Judging," *Kansas Law Review* 45 (1996): 1, 6.

215. Ibid., 7.

216. See Stephen A. Siegel, "The Federal Government's Power to Enact Color-Conscious Laws: An Originalist Inquiry," *Northwestern Law Review* 92 (1998): 477; Eric Schnapper, "Affirmative Action and the Legislative History of the Fourteenth Amendment," *Virginia Law Review* 71 (1985): 753.

217. Two recent studies of early free speech theory highlight how eighteenth-century Americans were concerned with political speech. See Michael Kent Curtis, *Free Speech, "The People's Darling Privilege": Struggles for Freedom of Expression in American History* (Durham, N.C.: Duke University Press, 2000); Robert W. T. Martin, *The Free and Open Press: The Founding of American Democratic Press Liberty, 1640–1800* (New

York: New York University Press, 2001). One prominent study of commercial speech during the late nineteenth and early twentieth centuries concludes that "the status of advertising as speech was murky" in those years. See Alex Kozinski and Stuart Banner, "The Anti-History and Pre-History of Commercial Speech," *Texas Law Review* 71 (1993): 768–769.

218. *Santa Clara County v. Southern Pacific Railroad Company,* 118 U.S. 394 (1886). For some historical problems with the conclusion that the persons responsible for the Constitution intended that corporations be considered persons, see Edward A. Hartnett, "The Akhil Amar Bill of Rights," *Constitutional Commentary* 16 (1999): 373.

219. 531 U.S. 98 (2000).

220. See Michael J. Klarman, "*Bush v. Gore* through the Lens of Constitutional History," *California Law Review* 89 (2001): 1721, 1735.

221. Christopher L. Eisgruber, *Constitutional Self-Government* (Cambridge: Harvard University Press, 2001), 43.

222. 515 U.S., at 852–863 (Thomas, J., concurring).

223. Ibid., at 868–872 (Souter, J., concurring).

224. 514 U.S., at 789–828, 832–834; at 838–846 (Kennedy, J., concurring).

225. *Farmer v. Brennan,* 511 U.S. 825, 855–857 (1994) (Blackmun, J., concurring); *Jordan v. Gardner,* 986 F.2d 1521, 1544 (9th Cir. 1993) (Noonan, J., concurring).

226. See "Brief of 250 American Historians as Amici Curiae in Support of Planned Parenthood of Southeastern Pennsylvania," *Planned Parenthood of Southeastern Pennsylvania et al., Petitioners, v. Robert P. Casey,* nos. 91-744 and 91-902, October term, 1991, March 6, 1992.

227. 347 U.S. 483 (1954).

228. Michael W. McConnell, "Originalism and the Desegregation Decisions," *Virginia Law Review* 81 (1995): 947.

229. 515 U.S., at 120 (Thomas, J., concurring).

230. See Alfred H. Kelly, "Clio and the Court: An Illicit Love Affair," in *1965: The Supreme Court Review,* ed. Philip B. Kurland (Chicago: University of Chicago Press, 1965), 142–145; Earl M. Maltz, "Originalism and the Desegregation Decisions," *Constitutional Commentary* 13 (1996): 223; Alexander M. Bickel, "The Original Understanding and the Segregation Decision," *Harvard Law Review* 69 (1955): 1; Michael J. Klarman, "*Brown*, Originalism, and Constitutional Theory: A Response to Professor McConnell," *Virginia Law Review* 81 (1995): 1881; Rogers M. Smith, "The Inherent Deceptiveness of Constitutional Discourse: A Diagnosis and Prescription," in *Nomos XL: Integrity and Conscience,* ed. Ian Shapiro and Robert Adams (New York: New York University Press, 1998), 242–245.

231. See Richard Kluger, *Simple Justice: The History of Brown v. Board of Education and Black America's Struggle for Equality* (New York: Vintage Books, 1975), 617–656.

232. See Michael J. Klarman, "*Brown*, Racial Change, and the Civil Rights Movement," *Virginia Law Review* 80 (1994): 7; and "An Interpretive History of Modern Equal Protection," *Michigan Law Review* 90 (1991): 213.

233. See Earl M. Maltz, *Civil Rights, the Constitution, and Congress, 1863–1869* (Lawrence: University Press of Kansas, 1990), and "Fourteenth Amendment Concepts in the Antebellum Era," *American Journal of Legal History* 32 (1988): 305.

234. See Michael W. McConnell, "The Origins and Historical Understanding of Free Exercise of Religion," *Harvard Law Review* 193 (1990): 1409, and "The Selective Funding Cases: Abortions and Religious Schools," *Harvard Law Review* 104 (1991): 989.

235. Lucas A. Powe Jr., *The Warren Court and American Politics* (Cambridge: Harvard University Press, 2000), 214.

236. Keith E. Whittington, "Taking What They Give Us: Explaining the Court's Federalism Offensive," *Duke Law Journal* 51 (2001): 477.

237. Howard Gillman, "The Court As an Idea, Not a Building (or a Game): Interpretive Institutionalism and the Analysis of Supreme Court Decision-Making," in *Supreme Court Decision-Making: New Institutionalist Approaches,* ed. Cornell W. Clayton and Howard Gillman (Chicago: University of Chicago Press, 1999), 67.

238. For the debates over objectivity in history, see Peter Novick, *That Noble Dream: The "Objectivity Question" and the American History Profession* (New York: Cambridge University Press, 1988); Joyce Appleby, Lynn Hunt, and Margaret Jacob, *Telling the Truth about History* (New York: W. W. Norton, 1994).

239. The perfect philosopher knows when deference to other governing officials is appropriate.

4

Justice Sandra Day O'Connor: Accommodationism and Conservatism

Nancy Maveety

Until her alliance with the pro-Bush majority in the Supreme Court's much-debated decision in the election case of *Bush v. Gore,*[1] most Court scholars and popular commentators would have probably agreed that Justice O'Connor's record on the high bench was one of steering a sound middle course between doctrinaire conservatism and judicial liberalism. However, in the wake of partisan reaction to the Court's involvement in the 2000 presidential election dispute—and in the wake of revelations regarding O'Connor's own allegedly partisan response to early election returns projecting a Gore victory in Florida—her place on the Court and in its juridical history may be questioned.[2] Yet, in many ways, the role she played in the decision in *Bush v. Gore* is consistent with her performance as strategist on the Rehnquist Court.[3]

If hard cases make bad law—in the words of the timeless aphorism of Justice Oliver Wendell Holmes—then O'Connor's vote to support the per curiam ruling that halted the Florida vote recount in *Bush v. Gore* should not be taken as a simple synopsis of her juridical identity.[4] In spite of this conclusion, her vote to join the majority coalition does reflect certain decisional tendencies she has displayed as an associate justice: her judicial "accommodationism," her propensity for majority-side membership, and her political conservatism. What her vote does not adequately express, however, are the complexities of her behavioral accommodationism and the substance of her jurisprudential accommodationism. Both of these latter tendencies constitute her doctrinal place on the Court and illustrate her importance to the Rehnquist Court's right-center-left dynamic of decision-making.

In keeping with the overarching theme of this volume, this chapter will detail O'Connor's critical role on the Rehnquist Court in moving law and policy in a conservative direction while explaining her significance, as a centrist conservative, in moderating the content of that rightward move. My perspective is that because of O'Connor's behavioral and jurisprudential accommodationism, the Rehnquist Court has not moved law and policy as far to the right as ideological appointment effects might lead us to expect.[5] Her independence as a jurist has preserved both centrist conservative policymaking on this Court as well as her own strategic influence in this Court's collegial decision-making.

In arguing for the unique character of O'Connor's influence on the legal policymaking of the Rehnquist Court, in this chapter I will first detail what is meant by her "judicial accommodationism" and how it relates to her philosophy of centrist conservatism. Then I will document the two facets of her accommodationist approach: a behavioral facet, which entails an analysis of her voting record and particularly her record with respect to majority-side membership and majority-opinion coalition membership; and a jurisprudential facet, which includes discussion of certain of her doctrinal innovations and their influence on subsequent decision-making in particular issue areas. I will further examine the uniting of these accommodationist facets, assessing O'Connor's use of the concurring strategy as a substantive tool of influence on a divided bench. Finally, my conclusion will suggest that O'Connor approximates the judicial role identified by Cass R. Sunstein as "judicial minimalism"[6] and can be praised or castigated as such from a normative perspective. From an empirical perspective, O'Connor—the "famous first" whose jurisprudential contributions were once neglected in favor of evaluative concentration on her performance as the first female justice of the Supreme Court—demonstrates the utility of compromise and "anti-bright line" rule-making in particular coalitional settings on multimember courts.

JUDICIAL ACCOMMODATIONISM: CHARACTERISTICS

"Different voice" analyses predominated in early examinations of O'Connor the jurist; Sherry's work is illustrative. For early commentators such as Sherry and Behuniak-Long, the key to O'Connor's work as a jurist lay in her "feminine" decision-making style, a style that emphasizes compromise, empathy, and an orientation toward community. This approach was located in the different voice in which female judges allegedly speak; it stressed the gender-based analysis of a judge's record and decisional approach, contrasting male and female decision-makers.[7]

As the initial lens through which to examine Justice O'Connor, such difference-feminist jurisprudence was a natural choice, given the unusual celebrity of her appointment as the first woman on the Supreme Court in 1981. Yet, in many ways, the feminine voice heuristic obscured as much as it clarified: it revealed little about the specific doctrinal content of her jurisprudence or her substantive impact as a jurist.[8] It also neglected to emphasize two aspects of O'Connor's background that seem salient in accounting for her decision-making style: her state legislative experience and her longtime and active affiliation with the Republican Party of Arizona. Indeed, it was the latter that brought her to the attention of Senator Barry Goldwater and, ultimately, to President Ronald Reagan as a potential nominee to fill the vacancy of retiring Justice Potter Stewart. Of course, it is also true that O'Connor's gender was the critical factor moving her selection: appointing the first woman justice to the Supreme Court fulfilled several political objectives of the Reagan administration and was the product of a 1980 election campaign promise that would allow President Reagan to recover some desired standing with women's rights groups.

Despite the demographic motivations behind her nomination, these state legislative and partisan background characteristics are salient—as salient as her gender—to O'Connor's character as a policymaker. But like the gender factor, the state legislative experience factor could be connected with a certain tendency to prefer compromise solutions, coalition-building, and majority-side membership, for these are the approaches consistent with success as a legislative leader. Compromise—or accommodation—in other words, is not the exclusive province of women decision-makers. But whatever the essential cause of such an approach to collegial decision-making, O'Connor's efforts to balance opposing views and positions must be weighed against another powerful influence in her political background: her Republican ideology.

Certainly, her vote with the majority in the recent decision of *Bush v. Gore* could be taken as dispositive testimony to her GOP leanings. Yet her conservative ideology, even as a member of the Arizona Senate, always coexisted with certain centrist preferences, both substantive and stylistic. Her legislative record from the early 1970s included support for removal of sex-based classifications from state laws, liberalization of state welfare laws and bilingual education programs, and ratification of the Equal Rights Amendment. As a judicial nominee, her "questionable" record on abortion rights and the uncertainty of her pro-family credentials came under fire (albeit fairly gently) from pro-life conservative senators prodded by the National Right to Life Committee. Although O'Connor was successful during her confirmation hearings in deflecting such concerns, the moderate nature of her conservative attitudes was clear. Her centrism as a conservative also had a behavioral dimension: her preoccupation had been with the politics of legislative coalition-building, not with the championing of purist conservative positions. She expressed, in her confirmation hearings and in subsequent, early off-the-bench writings, that her approach to deciding cases would resemble her approach to legislation: her decisional philosophy was atheoretical and practical, fact-based and contextually situated, and incrementalist in seeking results.[9] Her record as a state appellate judge on the Arizona Court of Appeals did not provide much predictive guidance for the senators examining her, but it did illustrate another experience with compromise-oriented decision-making: her practical attitude toward the evolutionary but incrementalist nature of legal policy was the product of a state judge's experience with accommodating state law to federal expectations.

One commentator on O'Connor's Burger Court record labeled her a "preservative conservative" for whom conservative ideology works within the system of precedents without attacking it.[10] This diagnosis of O'Connor's centrist conservatism remains, I think, largely accurate. But it does not tell us everything about the characteristics of her judicial accommodationism.

Elsewhere I have detailed O'Connor's accommodationist approach to judging according to the following attributes. First, her approach to case facts and fact-based decision-making can be described as contextually conservative: she is comparatively restrained when it comes to revisiting or overturning precedent and is likely to reason by exception when faced with a case not adequately covered by an existing rule. Ideologically, then, her conservative preferences are not categorical and rule-bound but sensitive to the particular elements and history of specific fact situations. Jurisprudentially, this predilection entails the use of balancing approaches to resolve certain constitutional rights questions. As O'Connor herself has said about the use of balancing approaches in adjudicating constitutional liberties, "The impulse may be to draw a *bright-line rule,* but such rules may sacrifice one legitimate claim for entitlement for another in the name of simplicity." Rejecting this simplifying impulse, she proposed balancing tests "as a way of overcoming problems associated with historical, bright-line approaches to resolve constitutional ambiguity."[11] Such an orientation distinguishes her approach from the more scholastic, originalist conservatism practiced by some of her fellow Republican appointees.

Second, as a more behavioral aspect of her accommodationism, her coalitional predilections include the propensity to join what political scientists term minimum-winning coalitions on the Court, or 5 to 4 majorities. She seems to consider the influence potential of being part of, if not necessary to, such coalitions on a collegial decision-making body. The tactical maneuver of going along with the majority—though not unconditionally—offers the advantage of influence through bargaining, particularly by a judge uncommitted to any one bloc or a deeply committed judge who appears or is perceived to be unsure. In some ways, O'Connor has been a quintessential compromiser blessed by circumstance: both on the Burger and Rehnquist Courts, she has been a centrist serving under conditions of shifting coalitional alliances where no one ideological bloc could dominate decisional outcomes. In other words, key centrist justices throughout her term of service have frequently held the balance of power in deciding key issues of legal policy. O'Connor has been determined to be one of them, recognizing that the value of compromise is greatly affected by those who consistently ally with a majority coalition. Such a decisional tendency is consistent with the current model of the strategically interdependent nature of judicial choice.[12]

Finally, and perhaps most controversially, part of O'Connor's pragmatic, centrist conservatism includes the pursuit of the alternative leadership tactic of writing concurring opinions as a method of shaping the development of legal doctrine. Clearly, such a tactic is only available to a member of a majority coalition, though not necessarily the majority-opinion coalition. The success of this tactic depends upon the fluidity of judicial choice and the existence of shifting coalitional alliances; hence, a judge whose arguments can appeal to the greatest number of potential coalition partners can wield significant influence over the content of legal policy. Use of the concurring strategy is a way to extend this appeal without completely sacrificing one's status as a member of the controlling majority. Nevertheless, there are risks extant to such a tactic: judges who refuse to join colleagues' opinion coalitions may find themselves punished by similar lukewarm support for their opinions for the Court in subsequent cases. Moreover, the prevalence of concurring opinion–writing has been criticized (even by certain of O'Connor's judicial colleagues, though before ascending to the high bench) as contributing to incoherence within the law, exhibiting a type of willful judicial egoism, and illustrating the demise of consensual norms on the modern Supreme Court.[13] Whether, on balance, her use of the concurring strategy to shape the law has been substantively successful or personally damaging will await detailed examination of particular issue areas in a subsequent section of this chapter.

The thesis of this chapter, then, is that the accommodationist conservative Justice O'Connor has had a definitive impact on both legal policy and the conventions of collegial decision-making on the contemporary Supreme Court. Evaluating the normative implications of that impact must follow establishing it empirically.

BEHAVIORAL ACCOMMODATIONISM: O'CONNOR'S VOTING RECORD

The fact that the Rehnquist Court justices are a divided group hardly requires documentation. Although the left or left-of-center wing of the Court has arguably been on the defensive since the appointment of Justice Kennedy, the right-conservative bloc has not succeeded in dominating decision-making across all issues of concern to conservative jurists. This situation is partly due to the independent voting behavior of centrist justices, including Justice Kennedy, but also, and more germane to our purposes here, to Justice O'Connor.

Definitions of judicial conservatism and judicial liberalism are at once somewhat elastic and a matter of conventional agreement. Judicial ideology, with respect to votes cast, is usually conceptualized as a matter of preferences for certain parties or policy positions: judicial liberals, then, tend to vote in favor of the individual and individual rights' claims in contests against the government and governmental interests; judicial conservatives tend to vote in favor of the opposite.[14] Judicial centrists are notoriously slippery to define; in terms of ideological scaling of judicial votes, centrists often come off as indecisive or uncommitted decision-makers whose convictions are tepid at best. They are frequently identified by what they are not, which is consistent conservatives or liberals. Although ideological labeling and the subsequent projecting of votes—the core of the attitudinal model of judicial decision-making—are of somewhat limited utility in understanding judicial opinion writing, the examination of the ideological dimension of judicial voting behavior reveals important information about patterns of alliance and coalitional membership. The attitudinal model does not speak about the substantive or jurisprudential aspects of such alliance and coalitional membership—and does not pretend to.[15] Such information must be gleaned from reading the opinions themselves.

Yet in order to assess O'Connor's voting behavior on the Rehnquist Court and, significantly, her behavior with respect to majority-side membership, aggregate figures are instructive. Three types of statistics are most relevant: the frequency with which she votes as part of a minimum-winning majority coalition, the comparative ideological directions of those minimum-winning coalitions, and the frequency with which she "disturbs" the majority-opinion coalition with whom she is voting by issuing or joining a "special" concurrence—a concurring opinion agreeing with the majority result but not with the legal reasoning of its opinion for the Court. (Concurring opinions that simply "augment" the majority opinion are known as "regular" concurrences. Arguably, the latter are less divisive, yet both types of concurrence ensure that the Court speaks in a choral voice.) All three statistics help to inform us as to the nature and degree of O'Connor's behavioral accommodationism and her adoption of this strategy as a way of being influential or critical to the Court's disposition of the cases it hears.

To examine the frequency with which she joins the winning side of minimal majorities rulings on the Rehnquist Court, we must look at the breakdown of her votes in 5 to 4 or 4 to 3 orally argued dockets (those with full opinions issued). Table 4 reports these figures, beginning with the first term of the Rehnquist Court and ending with the last term for which such data are available, 1999.[16] As we see, in 337 possible instances, O'Connor voted with the majority or plurality 168 times, filed a regular concurrence 32 times, and wrote the judgment of the Court 7 times. In only 15 instances did she file a special concurrence, joining the majority voting coalition but not the majority-opinion coalition. Clearly, she is more often on the winning side in such situations; therefore, her vote is critical to the resolution of the issue in question. Moreover, she is not a conditional coalition partner—the author of a special concurrence—with great frequency overall.

In the aggregate and since the appointment of Justice Thomas in 1992 and the potential solidification of a right-of-center conservative bloc on the Rehnquist Court, the number of dockets decided by minimum-winning majorities has declined, as has the number of minimum-winning majorities in which Justice O'Connor might participate. From the terms 1986–1991, there were 188 5 to 4 or 4 to 3 orally argued dockets in which she participated; from the terms 1992–1999, there were 149. O'Connor's rate of dissent—her failure to be part of the minimal majority coalition in some capacity—has remained fairly steady: she was in dissent in 5 to 4 or 4 to 3 orally argued dockets 36 percent of the time from 1986–1991, and in dissent 31 percent of the time (in a slightly smaller subset of such dockets) from 1992–1999. Does this suggest that the Rehnquist-Scalia-Kennedy-Thomas axis, plus O'Connor, was successful in gaining additional coali-

Table 4. O'Connor's Votes in 5 to 4 and 4 to 3 Orally Argued Dockets, Rehnquist Court, 1986–1999

Court term	Majority or plurality vote	Dissent	Regular concurrence	Special concurrence	Judgment of the Court	Total
1986	19	19	2	2	1	43
1987	9	10	4			23
1988	21	10	5	4		40
1989	24	15	1	2	2	44
1990	11	9	2	1		23
1991	5	6	2	2		15
1992	8	11	1			20
1993	5	6	1	1		13
1994	5	6	8			19
1995	8	4	1	1	3	17
1996	13	5	3			21
1997	9	6		1	1	17
1998	12	5				17
1999	19	3	2	1		25
	168	115	32	15	7	337

tion partners, or do these figures reveal that O'Connor (and, at times, Kennedy) defected to a more moderate bloc on the Rehnquist Court?

To assess how O'Connor's behavioral accommodationism—her propensity to join the winning side of minimum-winning majority coalitions—interacts with her conservative ideology, we must examine two phenomena: her voting behavior in 5 to 4 orally argued dockets in which she and Rehnquist, Scalia, Kennedy, and Thomas acted as the majority, and the ideological direction of her voting in minimum-winning majority situations in general. Figures for these phenomena will reveal whether her accommodationism includes a swing voting dimension— a shifting of her coalitional alliances—and a compromised or conditional support dimension—the filing of separate opinions to indicate her distance from or partial disagreement with the legal policy of the majority in question.

Table 5 reports her behavior in those 5 to 4 orally argued dockets in which she joins the aforementioned conservative bloc. Figures begin with the 1992 term and the seating of Justice Thomas, the last "reliable conservative" appointed to the high bench. From the terms 1992–1999, there were 71 instances in which the five-member minimal majority consisted of Rehnquist, O'Connor, Scalia, Kennedy, and Thomas. O'Connor filed concurring opinions in 12 situations, and only 2 of these were special concurrences defecting from the majority coalition's opinion and reasoning. She also joined one special concurrence, authored by Rehnquist. I would interpret these figures in the following way.

From 1992–1999, roughly half of the minimal majorities consisted of the conservative wing of the Court plus O'Connor, and she was a compliant member of these majority coalitions: she did not conditionally join them, by filing special concurrences, but was overwhelmingly part of the opinion coalition as well as

Table 5. O'Connor's Votes in 5 to 4 Orally Argued Dockets, Rehnquist-O'Connor-Scalia-Kennedy-Thomas Majority Coalition

Court term	Joins majority opinion	Writes majority opinion	Joins regular concurrence	Writes regular concurrence	Joins special concurrence	Writes special concurrence	Writes Court's judgment	Total
1992	2	1		1				4
1993	4			1		1		6
1994	1	1	1	5				8
1995	6						3	9
1996	7	2		3				12
1997	3	1			1		1	6
1998	7	1						8
1999	12	5				1		18
	42	11	1	10	1	2	4	71

the five-judge voting bloc. On the other hand, as reference to the overall figures for the terms 1992–1999 displayed in Table 4 suggests, she acted as part of the winning side in roughly the same number of minimum-winning majorities that were made up of other groupings of justices; in these instances she filed, proportionally, a somewhat lower number of regular and special concurrences. O'Connor appears to be part of the conservative bloc, at times and across certain issues that generally unite this group of GOP jurists (such as law and order or states' rights questions), but she remains a justice who acts with fluidity in terms of the minimum-winning majorities she joins.

Perhaps her seeming independence, however, is simply that she seeks or acts as part of mixed coalitions that nevertheless support conservative outcomes. To explore this possibility, we must address the ideological direction of her votes in these minimal majority situations. Table 6 reports the figures for all 5 to 4 or 4 to 3 orally argued dockets, with the type of vote that O'Connor cast identified (authoring the opinion of the Court, filing a concurrence or dissent, silently joining the majority, and so on) and the direction of her vote labeled as conservative or liberal, utilizing the coding conventions for judicial ideology of the Supreme Court Judicial Database.

Because 3 of the dockets in the set concerned an issue to which the conservative-liberal label does not apply, the total instances of 5 to 4 or 4 to 3 orally argued dockets reported is 334. Of these, 216 dockets were decided in a conservative direction; for 36 of these, O'Connor was in dissent and thus *not* part of the winning conservative majority coalition. Likewise, 118 of all relevant 5 to 4 or 4 to 3 orally argued dockets were decided in a liberal direction; for 78 of these, she was in dissent and thus *not* part of the winning liberal majority coalition. In other words, in 220 out of 334 5 to 4 or 4 to 3 orally argued dockets, O'Connor was part of the minimum-winning coalition, and in 180 of these minimum-winning majorities she voted in a conservative direction. Clearly, she is more often with the minimum-winning majority than in dissent, and roughly 80 percent of the time, the minimum-winning majority of which she is a part is voting in a conservative direction. Her dissents, or failure to be a part of the winning side, show

Table 6. O'Connor's Votes in 5 to 4 and 4 to 3 Orally Argued Dockets, Sorted by Ideological Direction of Majority Coalition Vote, Rehnquist Court, 1986–1999

	Silent join	Opinion of Court	Dissent*	Regular concurrence	Special concurrence	Court's judgment	Total
Conservative majority coalition	111	29	36	23	11	6	216
Liberal majority coalition	18	8	78	9	4	1	118
	129	37	114	32	15	7	334

*Dissenting votes by O'Connor are those in which she fails to join the minimum-winning majority coalition: in a dissent from a conservative majority coalition, she is therefore casting a liberal vote; in a dissent from a liberal majority coalition, she is casting a conservative vote.

a similar ideological breakdown: proportionally more of her deviations from the winning side come at the cost of casting a conservative, dissenting vote.

Generally speaking, then, she completes minimum-winning majorities that are conservative but not exclusively. Her behavioral accommodationism thus has a conservative cast, and her strategy of being part of the winning side is most successful when (or because) that side is voting conservatively. Certainly this pattern reflects her ideological closeness to the Rehnquist-Scalia-Kennedy-Thomas bloc as well as the predominance of this bloc in close cases. But O'Connor does not shy from joining liberal coalitions and, on occasion, converting them into minimum-winning majority coalitions. However, two-thirds of these liberal, minimum-winning coalitions did not include her.

A look at her concurring behavior in the context of the ideological direction of the minimum-winning coalitions she joins is also instructive as an indicator of the character of her behavioral accommodationism. Referring still to Table 6, we can see that in conservatively decided 5 to 4 or 4 to 3 orally argued dockets, O'Connor files as many concurrences (34) as dissents (36), while in liberally decided dockets, her dissenting votes (78) are far more numerous than her scattered concurrences (13). These figures must be interpreted with caution, as we cannot equate votes with opinions, but her rates of concurrence suggest that she brandishes this decisional tactic more frequently against her conservative judicial colleagues and their minimal majority coalitions. This tendency signals, I think, something about her conservative ideology and her differences from other conservatives on the Rehnquist Court as to how conservatism ought to be applied juridically. Speculatively, her concurring behavior with respect to conservatively decided minimal majorities allows her to open a space for contextual, fact-based, or balancing-oriented conservative jurisprudence. Half of all her concurrences in this situation are, after all, special concurrences.

Before draping O'Connor with the mantle of concurring conservative sentinel, we should reflect a bit on the frequency generally among the Rehnquist justices in writing concurring opinions. Table 7 assists us in doing so.

Table 7. Opinion-Writing Behavior of Current Rehnquist Court Justices, by Career Participations

Justice	Participations	Court opinions	Dissents	Reguar concurrences	Special concurrences
Rehnquist	3,550	402 (11.3%)	289 (8.1%)	44 (1.2%)	53 (1.8%)
Stevens	2,962	302 (10.2%)	495 (16.7%)	132 (4.5%)	171 (5.8%)
O'Connor	2,210	246 (11.1%)	137 (6.2%)	91 (4.1%)	67 (3.0%)
Scalia	1,472	147 (10.0%)	128 (8.7%)	72 (4.9%)	116 (7.9%)
Kennedy	1,245	129 (10.4%)	54 (4.3%)	51 (4.1%)	36 (2.9%)
Souter	901	88 (9.8%)	57 (6.3%)	29 (3.2%)	23 (2.6%)
Thomas	781	73 (9.3%)	57 (7.3%)	32 (4.1%)	26 (3.3%)
Ginsburg	575	61 (10.6%)	38 (6.6%)	26 (4.5%)	13 (2.3%)
Breyer	485	46 (9.5%)	50 (10.3%)	21 (4.3%)	14 (2.9%)

Lifetime figures—total number of concurring opinions filed across a high court career—are of course misleading, as some justices (Breyer, for instance) have had far fewer opportunities to speak in a concurring voice (though Breyer, at least, seems to be rapidly closing the gap in terms of the proportion of his opinions that are concurrences). Not surprisingly, then, the top concurror is Justice Stevens (a grand total of 303), whose years of service on the Supreme Court are only exceeded by Chief Justice Rehnquist, who was appointed an associate justice in Richard Nixon's first term. Yet even when we examine the proportion of a justice's total opinions, Stevens's figures are impressive: 4.5 percent of all his participations are regular concurring opinions, while 5.8 percent are special concurring opinions. But Stevens is easily eclipsed by relative newcomer Scalia: 4.9 percent of all his participations are regular concurring opinions, and a whopping 7.9 percent are special concurring opinions—those that defect from the majority opinion coalition. (Scalia, a former law professor, is noted for speaking his mind.) Measured against such concurring gladiators, O'Connor is no better than average, even though her total number of concurring opinions is quite high (though still third, after the totals logged by Stevens and Scalia, respectively).

Such overall figures, and the limited information they provide, point to the necessity of examining the content of opinions—particularly, the content of O'Connor's concurring opinions—if we are to paint a complete picture of her judicial accommodationism and, specifically, its jurisprudential dimension. It is at this level of influence that we see her importance in shaping the legal policy of the Rehnquist Court.

JURISPRUDENTIAL ACCOMMODATIONISM: O'CONNOR'S OPINIONS AND CONSERVATIVE LEGAL REASONING

In a critical way, voting behavior and opinion writing are linked in terms of influence over one's judicial colleagues and the collective production of legal doctrine; a justice must be part of a winning coalition for his or her voice to affect the Court's policy statements. Although dissents perform an important function as statements of conscience, appeals to the future, or simply mechanisms for "damage control," they are still dissents and not precedents. One might make the same claim regarding concurring opinions and their marginality to case resolution and policymaking, except that they annotate (or delimit) what is ostensibly a majority's view. Moreover, they signal—to future appellants, lower court judges, and fellow justices—that an alternative doctrinal analysis of the issue in question exists and is persuasive to at least one justice on the Court.

The potential persuasiveness or utility of this jurisprudential alternative becomes significant when the concurring opinion author is writing on a divided bench—where minimally winning majorities are frequent or frequent in high-profile cases raising contentious issues. In addition, a concurrence filed by a justice who ideologically is most distant from a majority or a majority-opinion coalition reveals the exact point of fracture in that decisional coalition. Concurrences, as separate opinions, are often said to display the actual attitude of a justice; they are both ideological messages and ideological signals to judicial behavioralists. But to those Court scholars who stress the "court-like" aspects of judicial decision-making—the necessity of producing a legally reasoned justification for a vote—concurring opinions are clearly efforts to influence that legally reasoned justification or to shape its interpretation.[17]

What concurrences are not are instantaneous tools of influence; they are a concession to a loss (jurisprudential) that hopefully is temporary, so in this way they are like dissenting opinions. But, importantly, they do not record a dispositional loss; rather, their presence suggests that doctrinal fine-tuning is necessary to solidify a judicial policy directive. Particularly in closely decided cases, they are threats to a majority coalition in a way that dissents are not. Special concurrences can be wielded as threats, and very direct ones, for their issuance can convert a majority into a plurality and a precedential ruling into an ambiguous mess. But such threats carry the risk of tit-for-tat reprisal in future rulings, which in the judicial setting is a net loss—for clarity of the law and for institutional legitimacy. Regular concurrence is a more gentle device, but still an insistent one, particularly if its content is repeated in subsequent regular concurrences discussing the same issue area or constitutional provision.

All of this discussion is very general, and very unsubstantiated, at least with respect to O'Connor, her concurring opinion writing, and her jurisprudential accommodationism as an influence over the doctrinal output of the Rehnquist Court. To offer some evidence for these observations about the concurring strategy, and for O'Connor's salience as a judicial policymaker, we must examine selected policy areas in which her voice—her moderate conservative voice—is the voice of doctrinal rule-making on the current Court.

In this section I will accomplish three goals: discuss the nature of O'Connor's jurisprudential accommodationism, illustrate its use in her opinions in three issue areas—reproductive rights,[18] church-state relations, and racial affirmative action[19]—and, ultimately, demonstrate that in these areas her jurisprudential formulations, originally initiated in separate/concurring opinions, have been subsequently adopted by decisional majorities on the Rehnquist Court. Use of O'Connor's approaches to the aforementioned issue areas has produced conservative results, but also results that preserve precedents and their balance between individual rights and states' interests.

Rule-driven conservatives like Justice Scalia are fond of condemning their judicial colleagues for engaging in what they term "judicial legislating." O'Connor has sometimes been the target of such accusations, and her juridical method is quite clearly fact-driven and characterized by a "legislative" balancing of interests and balancing standards. Kathleen Sullivan in the *Harvard Law Review* has drawn a distinction between "justices of rules" and "justices of standards," with the former engaging in a bright-line, deductive approach to resolving cases and the latter applying rule-of-thumb, balancing-of-conflicting-values approaches and a more inductive method to judicial lawmaking.[20] A more clear contrast between these approaches to the judicial jurisprudential role could not be found than in the contrast between Court conservatives Scalia and O'Connor.[21] Though both work with and within the same ideological bloc on the Rehnquist Court, their methods of building coalitions and their record in shaping the legal product of those coalitions could not be more different.

Simply put, O'Connor has not adopted a formulaic or categorical jurisprudential philosophy, which may have reflected an awareness, during the Burger and early Rehnquist Courts, of the futility of ideological posturing on a jurisprudentially splintered bench. She avoided the pitfall of ideological sparring over applicable legal standards, which was pragmatic—even strategic—for during much of her tenure of service no consensus existed as to a preferred interpretive philosophy. Centrists and moderates of various stripes held the balance of power on the Court, and it is still the case that the conservative wing of Rehnquist-Scalia-Kennedy-Thomas needs O'Connor to make a majority coalition. As we saw in the previous section, she frequently votes with their minimum-winning coalition, but she also brackets her support with concurring commentary.

The substance of her separate views suggests why she may have been successful in exerting influence over the generation and adoption of juridical standards for deciding various cases. In avoiding ideological solutions to resolve cases, she follows a case-by-case or incrementalist approach to the formulation of doctrinal principles; her judicial "ideology," then, is one of fact-based reductionism of legal problems or issue questions. She leans toward conservative policy outcomes—this is apparent—*but she does not derive the reasons or justifications for those outcomes from conservative ideological or interpretive principles.* Her agenda is one of accommodating divergent interests. O'Connor's opinions frequently justify exceptions within rules, arrive at limited, context-specific solutions, or articulate balancing tests for specific fact situations. Thus, even the balancing tests or standards she offers are loose, flexible, malleable, which is both their weakness and their strength, as is the case with balancing approaches generally. But because her doctrinal policies are nonformulaic and encourage only modest, incremental change, they have broad appeal to moderate conservatives on the Court and can serve as agents of compromise in contentious legal areas. For O'Connor, I would submit, jurisprudential flexibility is both a philosophy of judging and a strategy for collective bargaining.[22]

These decisional tendencies are clearly demonstrated in O'Connor's opinions across a broad range of highly salient issues. Space permits our detailed exploration of only three, but they are three that continue to be important to the contemporary Court's legacy and O'Connor's role in effecting it: reproductive rights, the "separation" of church and state, and affirmative race-based policies. Following analysis of this case law, I will also say a word about federalism and O'Connor-the-former-state-judge's support for states' rights jurisprudence as well as discuss how that support interacts with her accommodationism and her conservatism.

Although O'Connor cannot take creative credit for the doctrinal formulation that now governs abortion regulation disputes, she must be credited with securing its adoption by the current bench. I refer to the now well-known "undue burdens" approach as a method for balancing reproductive rights of pregnant women seeking abortions against state interests in protecting and preserving maternal health and fetal life.[23] The language of this test was first introduced in an amicus brief filed by the then–solicitor general of the Reagan administration in the 1983 case of *Akron v. Akron Center for Reproductive Health.* Speaking on behalf of the appellant, that brief urged the adoption of an "unduly burdensome" standard for state regulations of abortion: a state would have to identify a valid state objective that was rationally related to the regulation in question.[24] Most significant in the brief was the emphasis that the particular stage of pregnancy involved was irrelevant to the standard of review to be applied to the regulation.

This approach contrasted with the trimester-based methodology adopted by the Burger Court in the 1973 ruling of *Roe v. Wade,* which mandated a broader set of protections for the fundamental privacy right that encompassed a woman's decision to terminate a pregnancy. According to the *Roe* framework, only in the period subsequent to the end of the first trimester of pregnancy did the state's "important and legitimate interests" in protecting maternal health (the medical safety of abortion procedures) and fetal life (the preservation of a viable fetus) permit the qualification of the right of reproductive choice. At the stage subsequent to viability—which, according to then-contemporary medical technology, was approximately coincident with the third trimester—the state's regulative protection of fetal life became compelling and could include proscribing abortion except where necessary to protect the life of the mother.[25] In urging a rational basis for all abortion regulations, the *Akron* brief was dismantling this sliding-scale approach to state interference with reproductive liberty and questioning the constitutional legitimacy of *Roe*'s legislatively intrusive and rights-deferential scheme.

The *Akron* case challenged several state regulations, including informed consent and waiting period restrictions on first and second trimester abortions and a requirement of "humane and sanitary" disposal of fetal remains. Although Brennan's conference notes attest to O'Connor's initial vote with the liberal majority to invalidate both these provisions, she would later circulate a memo to indicate that her views differed somewhat from Powell's draft opinion for the Court and that she would be writing separately. Ultimately, she filed a dissent.[26]

It is important to remember that at the time of *Akron,* and even in the subsequent case of *Thornburgh v. American College of Obstetricians*[27] in 1986 (in which O'Connor was also part of a dissenting coalition), her vote was not critically determinative of abortion questions, for liberals and moderate centrists at the close of the Burger era still controlled the Court's disposition of such issues. But what O'Connor was signaling in her early abortion dissents was her attempt to draw a moderate conservative coalition around a revised understanding of *Roe,* with the existence of its precedent as the consensus point. In this way, her formulation of the unduly burdensome standard parted company with the more acutely legislatively deferential version articulated by the solicitor general's *Akron* brief.

In her 1983 *Akron* dissent, and reiterated and expanded in her 1985 *Thornburgh* dissent, O'Connor presented a position that would come to be her trademark as a jurist, in abortion cases and generally: an aversion to bright-line categories and absolutist, unqualified rights or interests and the preference for contextually specific solutions and flexible, balancing-of-interests methods of scrutinizing allegedly violative state action. Her perspective on the *Roe* precedent was twofold: first, its trimester framework was increasingly unworkable and outmoded, even arbitrary, given the advancing state of medical technology regarding fetal viability; and second, the limited nature of the fundamental right in the abortion context was the true ruling of *Roe,* but subsequent majorities had mistakenly derived from it an absolutist right that had prevented reasonable, threshold inquiries as to the burdensomeness of state regulations of abortion conditions and procedures. Although the record of conference memos in the *Thornburgh* case indicates that O'Connor's judicial colleagues were as yet paying little heed to her new doctrinal formulations, her *Akron* dissent had substantially informed the content of the solicitor general's brief for the state in *Thornburgh*.[28] Her pivotal importance—increasing with the aging of the liberal coalition on the high bench—and the potentially mobilizing quality of her legal arguments were definitely being heeded outside of the Court, largely by conservative interests. In a matter of a few years, however, her influence in the issue area of abortion would be heeded by her fellow justices, when she showed the substantive significance of her tie-breaking vote.

The 1989 case of *Webster v. Reproductive Health Services* was an important turning point in terms of both O'Connor's pivotal coalitional position and her contribution to the doctrinal construction of reproductive rights jurisprudence. The tie-breaking nature of her vote in the case was incontrovertible, and it magnified the significance of the views she expressed in what would be the first of many separate concurrences.[29]

O'Connor's interpretation of the state restrictions in the case—which included a requirement for viability testing where fetal viability was possible in the judgment of the attending physician—reprised her view that if the regulations did not unduly burden the choice to obtain an abortion, they were neither impermissible nor inconsistent with the *Roe* precedent. Thus, while she agreed with the conservative coalition regarding the constitutionality of the state regulations in question, she demurred from supplying the fifth vote to revisit and ultimately overturn *Roe*. The *Webster* case also contained an interesting dramatic element: O'Connor's engaging in strategic voting and circulating of separate opinion drafts during the Court's opinion circulation stage of the decision.

Conference memos reveal that O'Connor threatened a partial defection from the Court's opinion authored by Chief Justice Rehnquist, with respect to one of the statutory provisions; her threat combined with her pivotal coalitional position ultimately resulted in certain concessions in Rehnquist's opinion language. In the end, she filed a partial concurrence/concurrence in the judgment, retaining majority-side membership and influencing the content of the *Webster* plurality opinion. Nevertheless, and perhaps because of O'Connor's efforts, the Court's split in *Webster* was multidimensional (the headnotes in the *U.S. Reports* for the Court's vote comprised a full paragraph of description), and the ruling was at best a decisive victory for the forces of muddled compromise. The future status of the *Roe* precedent remained uncertain, and O'Connor's unduly burdensome formulation appeared to preserve not so much that decision's protection of constitutional rights, but the opportunity for conservative, pro-regulative disposition of abortion questions.[30]

It was in the 1992 case of *Planned Parenthood of Southeastern Pennsylvania v. Casey* that the centrality of O'Connor's accommodationist jurisprudence and her influence from the center would prove decisive, both doctrinally and in terms of the formation of a "preservative conservative" coalition on reproductive rights. The personnel of the high court had changed since *Webster:* O'Connor's judicial colleagues now included Bush appointees Souter and Thomas, replacing staunch *Roe* supporters Brennan and Marshall, respectively. Her position was now even more critical, as was her potential influence over fellow centrist conservatives Souter and, even more important, Kennedy, who had indicated his support for abortion restrictions in the past. The anxiety (or anticipation, depending on one's point of view) was only heightened by the fact that in voting to grant certiorari in the case, the Court was arguably signaling that it had "accepted to reverse"—*Roe,* that is.[31] Was O'Connor's centrist option—whatever its specific substantive content might be and allow—the only possible consensus point for the Rehnquist Court?

Foreshadowed perhaps by the observation by the circuit judge in the ruling below in *Casey* that "O'Connor's undue burden standard is the law of the land," the answer for *Casey* was "yes." The Court adhered to O'Connor's jurispruden- tial standard to uphold all but the spousal notification provisions of the statute in question and firmly reaffirmed *Roe* as a precedent. *Casey* was most noteworthy for a rare occurrence: it occasioned the issuance of an unusual, jointly written opinion—the plurality opinion signed by O'Connor, Kennedy, and Souter. The decision represented a victory for O'Connor the jurisprudential coalition builder, for her unduly burdensome test, combined with an avowed concern for institu- tional integrity and citizens' reliance interest in the principle of stare decisis (a section of the opinion allegedly penned by Souter), commanded the allegiance of the two critical votes of moderate conservatives Kennedy and Souter.[32] Yet the decision's political compromise failed to ameliorate the Court's fragmentation and polarization over the abortion rights issue (or to please abortion activists on either side of the debate), even while the collegial effort represented by the plu- rality opinion cemented a centrist alliance committed to the constitutional princi- ple of precedential force—not to mention a commitment to legal decision-making as a contextually sensitive and incrementalist process of doctrinal creation.

The fact-specific nature of the balancing inquiry into the existence of undue burdens was clear, as was the preservation of *Roe*'s "essential holding" to protect a "dimension of personal liberty." But what was clearly not part of *Roe*'s essen- tial holding—and the element of the *Casey* plurality opinion that made it feasible as a point of compromise—was its unnecessarily rigid trimester framework, which "undervalues the state's interest in potential life, as recognized in *Roe*." By reinterpreting *Roe* (by rereading it, a cynic might say), O'Connor preserved its balance of individual rights and state interests, but conservatized its guiding direc- tion. There would be no bright-line rule regarding reproductive freedom. Instead, the test would be this: an abortion regulation would constitute an undue burden if it "has the purpose or effect of placing *a substantial obstacle* in the path of a woman seeking an abortion of a nonviable fetus." Noteworthy in this formulation of a standard for adjudging reproductive rights violations is the factual qualifica- tion—fetal viability—and the fact-based inquiry mandated—the investigation into "substantial obstacles." Nevertheless, the verbal formula, what is "substan- tial" and what is an "obstacle," is clearly a matter of contextual circumstances.[33]

Although the abortion question has hardly been put to rest, the utility and (to date) determinativeness of O'Connor's jurisprudentially accommodationist for- mulation was demonstrated again in the Court's most recent ruling on reproduc- tive rights: *Stenberg v. Carhart,* or the infamous "partial birth abortion" case. A 5 to 4 ruling composed of eight different opinions (the only justice not to file an opinion was Souter), with the minimum-winning coalition made up of "liberals" Stevens, Ginsburg, Breyer (who authored the opinion for the Court), and "mod- erates" Souter and O'Connor, *Stenberg* employed undue burdens analysis to invalidate a state's ban on certain types of late-term abortion procedures as insufficiently accommodative of maternal health exceptions and therefore reproductive rights. O'Connor herself filed a regular concurrence, stressing that the statute in question was insufficiently narrowly tailored to the state's objectives and suggesting that other possible legislative formulations might survive undue burdens inquiry. Signal in the case was that Kennedy—O'Connor's and Souter's erstwhile partner in *Casey*—joined the conservative, dissenting minority. But once again, O'Connor was a part of the minimally winning majority coalition— an opinion coalition that was her jurisprudential standard bearer.[34]

O'Connor's deeply contextual formulation of the right to terminate a pregnancy renders her, in some sense, the "Chauncey Gardiner" of the Court's abortion rulings. Pro-choice and women's reproductive rights' advocates can see in her "undue burdens" standard a preservation of *Roe*'s essential principle of reproductive freedom as an aspect of the right to privacy. Pro-life conservatives and states' rights champions, on the other hand, can find in her limitation of post-viability abortions a protection of state legislative prerogatives and a constricting of the notion of abortion on demand. Indeed, O'Connor displays both these positions, for it is only her joint opinion in *Casey* that makes a strong connection between reproductive autonomy and women's autonomy; in other words, her jurisprudential approach to abortion rights—which has become the Court's— accommodates both sides of the abortion debate in part by downplaying the women's rights' dimension of reproductive freedom policies.

This leads to a side question, one somewhat off the track of the immediate focus on her concurring opinions and their doctrinal innovations, but one that nevertheless allows us to compare O'Connor with other so-called swing voters or centrist justices on the Rehnquist Court. This side question concerns her jurisprudence with respect to sex discrimination. Is her moderate and fact-sensitive balancing approach to reproductive rights indicative of a lukewarm protection for gender-based equality generally? Or is her doctrinal approach to abortion questions of a piece with her doctrinal approach in related issue areas involving women's rights?

The answer is, I think, the latter, and evidence for this proposition can be found in O'Connor's rulings regarding sexual harassment. Unlike abortion, this is not an issue area in which she has been a leader in the sense of generating doctrinal language that ultimately bands a decisional coalition, nor is it an area in which O'Connor has especially utilized the device of concurrence. She has, however, been pivotal in sexual harassment decisions—and behaviorally accommodationist—by her alignment with the winning coalition in these cases. Her vote has been critical in determining liability questions in both Title VII and Title IX actions, and, as in her abortion opinions, in her sexual harassment rulings she effectively balances fundamental rights issues against the need for reasonable administrative flexibility and local policymaking. Thus, her voting and legal reasoning in both these gender-related rights realms exhibit support for the fundamentals of the essentially gender-related right at issue—whether reproductive choice or protection against sexual discrimination—while moderating the consistency of that support with fact-sensitive, context-specific rules of thumb to guide the resolution of actual controversies over tangible policies and manifest actions.

Illustration of these interrelated claims is found in the line of cases beginning with the 1986 ruling in *Meritor Savings Bank v. Vinson,*[35] in which O'Connor joined Rehnquist's opinion for the court. *Meritor,* which was a unanimous decision though not by a unanimous opinion coalition, offered the broad guidelines of what has become sexual harassment law: harassment is a species of actionable sex discrimination under Title VII of the Civil Rights Act, and harassment consists of either unwelcome sexual advances as quid pro quo conditions of employment or sexual conduct that creates an intimidating, hostile, or offensive working environment. In 1993, O'Connor spoke for another unanimous Court in *Harris v. Forklift Systems,*[36] which definitionally expanded actionable sexual harassment under Title VII.

The doctrinal modifications in *Harris* were the quintessentially anti–bright line formulations with which Justice O'Connor is associated: a work environment must "reasonably be perceived as hostile or abusive," an inquiry that "is not, and by its nature cannot be, a mathematically precise test." "Only by looking at all the circumstances" and "no[t at any] single factor" can discriminatory conduct so pervasive and severe that it created a hostile work environment be determined. Such language, and such an approach, found its way into the Court's next Title VII workplace discrimination ruling, also unanimous: *Oncale v. Sundowner Offshore Services, Inc.,* which upheld a claim of same-sex harassment and featured Court opinion author and "bright-liner" Scalia—of all people—arguing that the impact of workplace behavior "depends on a *constellation of surrounding circumstances,* expectations, and relationships" and on "an appropriate sensitivity to social *context.*"[37]

O'Connor has also spoken for the Court—though, here, for minimum-winning coalitions only—in the expansion of sexual harassment principles to discrimination claims under Title IX. In two cases concerning school district officials' liability for sexual harassment that occurred by district employees or in district schools, the Rehnquist justices divided 5 to 4 in applying a "deliberate indifference" test to determine whether the district was liable for damages in sexual harassment actions. In the 1998 case of *Gebser v. Lago Vista Independent School District,* the five-member majority did not find the school district administrators liable for the teacher-on-student harassment, largely because the sexual conduct in question was not known to them and went unreported;[38] in the 1999 case of *Davis v. Monroe County Board of Education,* the five-member majority held that the county board's "deliberate indifference effectively caused the discrimination" in the situation of student-on-student harassment that persisted over several months in spite of complaints brought to teachers and supervisors.[39] Both majority opinions—one for a conservative and the other for a liberal majority coalition—were authored by O'Connor, who employed *Oncale*'s "constellation of surrounding circumstances" test to determine whether actionable sexual harassment had occurred in the student-on-student complaint.

Her concern, in both cases, was that remedies for sexual harassment that causes interference with access to education and educational opportunities coexist with administrative flexibility and be sensitive to specific educational circumstances and local context. This concession, central to the ruling in *Gebser* and present in dicta in *Davis,* should have prepared Court watchers for O'Connor's vote in the 5 to 4 decision of *U.S. v. Morrison.* She silently joined Rehnquist's majority opinion invalidating a federal civil remedy for gender-motivated violence under the Violence against Women Act as an unauthorized exercise of congressional commerce power; because such violence against women bore no direct connection to economic activity and interstate commerce, state criminal law interests were paramount and Congress had no authority to regulate what was legitimately a state matter.[40] Although some Court commentators see *Morrison* as part of a pattern of self-aggrandizing behavior and rhetoric by the Rehnquist Court,[41] O'Connor's part in it is arguably a feature of her contextual approach to sexual harassment questions. The fact that gender-motivated violence—surely more egregiously "abusive" than most harassment—did not rise to the level of a social ill requiring a federal remedy speaks less to the degree of her commitment to gender equality than it does to her jurisprudential approach to most questions in general. There is no core value or higher principle that trumps all others for O'Connor—neither women's rights nor federalism, for that matter. She certainly pays attention to states' rights and the policy needs of local entities, which is evident in both her sexual harassment and abortion rights opinions. But states' claims seem to fare best when they constitute claims about an administrative context addressing fact-specific circumstances that no general, abstract rule can accommodate.

A brief synopsis of a second issue area, church-state relations, reveals a pattern similar to that found in the abortion cases: concurring pressure by O'Connor and subsequent adoption of her version of a jurisprudentially accommodative doctrinal approach to resolve disputes.[42] Like the reproductive rights issue, establishment of religion questions remain very much alive—including a ruling last term upholding the equal access rights of religious groups to the elementary public school setting for after-school Bible study activities *(Good News Club v. Milford Central School)*[43] and a case on the 2001–2002 docket addressing the use of state school vouchers to attend church-affiliated schools *(Zelman v. Simmons-Harris).*[44] Also like the abortion issue area, the Court's most recent legal policy statement to date comes in a majority opinion echoing an O'Connor doctrinal formulation, crafted through a series of concurring opinions in earlier cases.

Her efforts to shape church-state jurisprudence also date back to her earliest years of service on the Burger Court. At that time, the Court was utilizing a tripartite balancing test as a means of conceptualizing the "separation" of church and state with respect to establishment clause claims under the First Amendment:

the "*Lemon* test," which had its origin in previous precedents and tests developed in a twenty-year series of cases involving aid to parochial schools. Announced in the case of *Lemon v. Kurtzman* in 1971, the test[45] was an effort to bridge the divide between strict "separationists" and more religiously accommodative "nonpreferentialists" on the Court; its balancing approach was intended to offer a more systematic, if painfully complex, method of balancing secular needs and sectarian liberties. But its verbal standards were imprecise, and the *Lemon* test failed to provide clear and unambiguous guidelines for application. Both sides — the "high wallers" and the "low wallers" — would come to criticize it.

O'Connor's particular dissatisfaction with the *Lemon* test was first revealed in her concurrence in the 1984 nativity display case of *Lynch v. Donnelly,* the decision that inaugurated the questionable judicial practice euphemistically termed "reindeer counting."[46] Because one element of the *Lemon* test was the search for a secular purpose to state action challenged under the establishment clause, the five-justice majority in *Lynch* held that despite the religious nature of the Christmas nativity scene at issue, the city displaying it had a permissibly secular purpose because it was part of a seasonal exhibit that included Santa Claus, reindeer, and Christmas trees. For O'Connor, the contrived and overly complicated *Lemon* test offered little more than a justificatory artifice to rationalize the Court's decision; while agreeing with the outcome permitting the display, she articulated in a concurring opinion an alternative method of determining whether governmental use of an object with religious meaning violated the First Amendment: whether the state action conveys a "message of endorsement" of religion.

For O'Connor, the key was equally the context in which the symbol or object appeared. Yet her "endorsement test" would simplify the rigidity and complexity of the *Lemon* approach while being explicitly contextually sensitive in its application. A good illustration of how she sought to convey this compromise position in *Lynch* was the way in which she modified the language in her concurring opinion to bridge a divide between majority-opinion author Chief Justice Burger and dissenting Justice Brennan over what context mattered for First Amendment purposes: Brennan's focus on the physical-spatial setting of the display (and, thus, the reindeer count) or Burger's looser attendance to the cultural-seasonal setting. Signaling that her approach could accommodate both sets of contextual concerns, the final draft of her concurrence inserted the word "physical" in a sentence mentioning the nativity's display "in this particular . . . setting," then proceeded to discuss relevant (and permissible) cultural acknowledgments of religion.[47] Although such waffling may not be the best testimony to the clarity of her new approach, it is revealing as to her interest in furthering doctrinal compromise as a member of a minimum-winning coalition.

Beginning in 1985, a sequence of court majority and plurality opinions explicitly acknowledged and employed the endorsement test of O'Connor's *Lynch* concurrence as a viable analytic formula, though no court has, as yet, officially repudiated *Lemon*. For her part, O'Connor persistently proffered her test in successive concurrences since 1984, providing important elaboration on it in her concurrence in the Alabama moment of silence case of *Wallace v. Jaffree* [48] and spirited defense of its validity from her position at the Court's coalitional vortex in a second nativity display case, *County of Allegheny v. ACLU.* Offering correction from the center to the Blackmun plurality's employment of the endorsement test, she also sparred with the Kennedy dissent over its lament that "it has never been my understanding that a concurring opinion [O'Connor's *Lynch* concurrence] suggesting clarification of our doctrine should take precedence over an opinion joined by the Court." Never, that is, until she began displaying her style of judicial accommodationism and attendant concurring influence on the high bench.[49]

Her judicial allies in converting this concurring formulation into a favored doctrinal approach to church-state controversies would prove to be the Rehnquist Court centrists: Stevens, Souter and Breyer (with voting support from Ginsburg) and, somewhat unevenly but surprisingly given his *County of Allegheny v. ACLU* statements, Kennedy. In the 1992 decision in *Lee v. Weisman,* which invalidated the use of a nonsectarian prayer at public school graduation ceremonies, the Kennedy majority opinion sought no guidance in the *Lemon* test and referred to the case only to firmly reject reconsidering it (which garnered him the scorn of Scalia, who snorted in dissent that "the Court today demonstrates the irrelevance of *Lemon* by essentially ignoring it"). While Kennedy focused on the coercive nature of the religious participation at issue, given students' compulsory and generally desired attendance at the graduation event, the concurring opinions of Blackmun and Souter devoted considerable attention to praising the superior merits of the endorsement approach: both argued that its "message of exclusion" principle provided the needed conceptual framework for the Court's holding. Indeed, Souter went further, claiming that "this principle against favoritism and endorsement has become the foundation of Establishment Clause jurisprudence, ensuring that religious belief is irrelevant to every citizen's standing in the political community."[50]

This cautionary language forbidding the government from making religious adherence relevant to a person's standing in or belonging to the political community came straight from O'Connor's concurrence in the *Jaffree* moment of silence case.[51] The endorsement of religion phrasing appeared again in White's majority opinion for the 1993 decision in *Lamb's Chapel v. Center Moriches Union Free School District,* which, confusingly, resurrected the *Lemon* precedent as well.[52] Yet, in the end, this retrograde aspect of *Lamb's Chapel* was less significant for establishment jurisprudence than the door it opened to the religiously expressive complications of state efforts at secular neutrality toward religion.

The school district involved in *Lamb's Chapel* had opened school facilities for use after hours for a wide variety of social, civic, and recreational purposes, but it had specifically rejected offering those same facilities to groups for religious purposes; in this exclusion, the *Lamb's Chapel* Court found a constitutionally impermissible instance of viewpoint discrimination. As such, the ruling, and the case that soon followed on its heels, *Rosenberger v. University of Virginia,* raised the question of what standards would guide the accommodation of establishment of religion and freedom of speech concerns, particularly when protection of the latter was uncomfortably intertwined with a potential violation of the former. *Lemon,* in such circumstances, provided no guide. The 5 to 4 majority that decided *Rosenberger* could agree on no guide itself, but in agreeing that religiously oriented extracurricular student activities could not be excluded from the university's public funding program for such activities generally, Kennedy's opinion for the Court stressed the principle of viewpoint neutrality while largely avoiding direct mention of the *Lemon* precedent.

O'Connor, who not surprisingly was part of the minimum-winning coalition in *Rosenberger,* used the occasion to file a concurrence to argue for the heuristic utility of the endorsement approach to flesh out the meaning of "neutrality" in this kind of establishment clause context. She cautioned against "reduc[ing] to a single test"—i.e., neutrality—any "bedrock principle" of the Constitution, while in the same breath praising the majority for "do[ing] today only what courts must do in many Establishment Clause cases—focus[ing] on specific features of a particular governmental action to ensure that it does not violate the Constitution." The opinion was vintage O'Connor: accommodationist behaviorally and jurisprudentially and, also, only a concurrence, lacking the full impact of a new precedential standard.[53]

In the words of the editors of a popular and influential constitutional law casebook, "Whether the Court kills off *Lemon* once and for all seems to hinge on the justices' ability to agree over a replacement and on the application of that replacement, which . . . they have been unable to do." The Rehnquist Court arguably moved a step closer to such agreement in the recent ruling of *Santa Fe School District v. Doe,* the high school football game prayer case. In invalidating the student-led prayer to open such public school sporting contests, a six-judge majority—led by endorsement-test doctrinal ally Stevens and incorporating O'Connor and Kennedy—relied heavily on the *Lee* precedent to find a "perceived and actual endorsement of religion" as well as an objectionable element of coercion in the state's furtherance of and the provision of the machinery for the communication of the religious message.[54] Clearly, this latter, express concern for coercive religious compliance was an overt overture to gain Kennedy's vote and, ultimately, a successful overture to the author of the "coercion test." This test was—somewhat ironically for its author, the critic of the concurringly spawned endorsement test—first authored in Kennedy's partial, special concurring opinion in *County of Allegheny v. ACLU.* (For Kennedy, in his concurring contest with O'Connor over whose doctrinal formulation for establishment questions will supplant a *Lemon*-based inquiry, separate opinion citing seems to be a matter of "do as I say, not as I do.")

It would be difficult to pronounce a full O'Connor-esque doctrinal victory at this stage in the evolution of church-state jurisprudence,[55] but its development is proceeding much as the process of O'Connor-esque jurisprudential accommodationism might envision: incrementally, contextually, through the force of compromise, and with the device of the concurring opinion figuring prominently. If *Santa Fe* signals anything, it is that Kennedy has been (temporarily, anyway) pulled into a centrist coalition and away from hard-liner absolutists and religious accommodationists Scalia, Thomas, and Rehnquist. The fact that he has even copied O'Connor's concurring strategy to effect his own doctrinal influence suggests that her judicial accommodationism has had an impact on the decisional conventions of the Court on which she has served.

A third and last issue area that illustrates the impact of both O'Connor's jurisprudential accommodationism and concurring strategy is race-based affirmative action—or, more precisely, the use of race as a factor in allocating employment opportunities, admission to educational programs, and electoral district boundaries to remedy conditions of racial discrimination. Constitutionally, the question raised by affirmative racial classifications is their legitimacy under the Equal Protection Clause: the level of judicial scrutiny with which their use should be examined and the types of state purposes that justify their use. Here, O'Connor's contribution is less of a doctrinal innovation than a doctrinal realization of the "danger that a racial classification is merely . . . a form of racial politics."[56] Her "realization" takes the form of an adoption of a strict scrutiny standard of review for all race-based classifications, including those utilized for "benign" or compensatory state purposes.

The jurisprudential accommodationism of her approach lies in its contextual contingency, which has rendered this approach both a basis for coalitional compromise on the Rehnquist Court and a target for attack as an "I know it when I see it" jurisprudence of equal protection violation.[57] Moreover, and in spite of this, O'Connor's opinions on race-based affirmative action policies generally are those most open to the charge that they do craft a "formulaic" jurisprudence where the reasons for conservative policy outcomes are derived from conservative ideological principles. One colleague on the Rehnquist Court so labels her efforts in this area, claiming that "when a court becomes preoccupied with *abstract standards,* it risks sacrificing common sense at the altar of formal consistency."[58]

Arguably, both the utility and the vulnerability of O'Connor's jurisprudence of racial classifications lie in its incremental, fact-specific development. Whether this development is conjoint with its allegedly categorical derivation from a conservative ideological principle, that of constitutional "color blindness," is a matter to consider after summarizing her opinion record. Two concurring opinions in 1986 illustrate the earliest stage of her articulation of what I have previously termed "the definitional parameters of legitimate racial group-based claims." Because both affirmative action remedies and majority-minority redistricting aim to redress group status–based harms suffered by members of racial groups because they are members of racial groups, both raise the specter of racial "group rights" in constitutional theory.[59] This result occurs because both remedies — affirmative action plans and majority-minority redistricting practices—take race into account in order to rectify what are explicitly racial group–based rights violations: discriminatory unfairness in employment consideration or in education selection processes and vote dilution due to the electoral districting system or practice. An individual suffers the discrimination or the dilution of his/her vote, but that individual so suffers because of his/her racial group identity; attention to this fact is a way to satisfy the individual rights claim. Although O'Connor acknowledges the strong "nexus between individual rights and group interests" in political circumstances concerning racial minority groups,[60] she nevertheless rejects an expansive concept of racial group–level harm and prefers a circumspect use of race-based classifications. Her challenge as a jurist has been to come up with a doctrinal formulation of this position of political accommodation.

O'Connor was the key player in two late Burger Court rulings in 1986: the review of a race-based retention plan aimed at increasing (or at least preserving) minority teacher positions in *Wygant v. Jackson Board of Education*[61] and the creation of an evidentiary test for racial vote dilution claims under section 2 of the Voting Rights Act in *Thornburgh v. Gingles.*[62] She was "key" in the sense of using her pivotal voting position in both cases to strategically shape the Court's formulation of the jurisprudential standard that would govern such questions. Significantly, she utilized the separate opinion device in both the opinion circulation and decision on the merits phases of both cases as a method of exerting substantive influence. While neither ruling was a creative or definitive doctrinal benchmark, both are instructive illustrations of O'Connor's accommodationist behavior and the evolutionary development of her views on the constitutional use of racial classifications to reverse the effects of societal- or structural-level discrimination.

The late Burger Court was as polarized over this issue as the current Rehnquist Court is now. O'Connor's separate concurrence in the 1986 *Wygant* case is interesting because intracourt memos reveal that she changed her vote between conference and opinion assignment, converting what had been the dissenting position into a plurality opinion for the Court. Powell's plurality opinion, which invalidated the affirmative action plan as imperfectly tailored to remedying racial discrimination in the context of teacher employment, gained O'Connor's endorsement; yet the language of her concurring opinion attempted to breach the divide between the plurality and Marshall's dissent: her final draft inserted statements recognizing the entire Court's agreement as to "certain core principles" and asserting that the Court's differences "do not preclude a fair measure of consensus."[63] The fact that O'Connor saw these "core principles" as the move toward narrowly tailoring racial classifications in employment to a legitimate remedial purpose[64] was less salient as a "consensus" than as a prognosis of her importance in crafting a future majority coalition position.

This prognosis became a reality in the early Rehnquist Court decision of *City of Richmond v. J. A. Croson,* in which O'Connor wrote for a six-member majority utilizing a strict scrutiny standard to invalidate the municipality's set-aside program for minority contractors. The "core principles" governing affirmative action disputes, for O'Connor, also became clearer in her *Croson* opinion, which one commentator observed was her first unambiguous statement "that Fourteenth Amendment rights attach to the *individual,* thus making membership in any particular group irrelevant to . . . an individual's right of equal treatment."[65] She reprised the position in dissent in the 1990 case of *Metro Broadcasting, Inc. v. FCC,* which upheld a congressionally authorized FCC policy of giving special consideration to minority license applicants for new broadcast stations. Although *Metro*'s application of intermediate-level equal protection scrutiny to such federal "benign race-conscious measures" would have a short shelf life as a precedent, its contemporary relevance lies less in its doctrinal content than in the way discussion of that content was framed by Brennan's five-member majority opinion and O'Connor's dissenting one.

Both likened the affirmative action policy question at issue to the debate surrounding race-based redistricting practices: for Brennan, the state objective in both was guaranteeing a racial diversity of viewpoints, and the state could deliberately create or preserve broadcast frequencies or electoral districts for minority interests in order to do so; for O'Connor, such "outright racial balancing" in either context, "untethered to narrowly confined remedial notions," was a purely political and not legal judgment. In framing their debate in this way, both opinions are starkly continuous with present debates over affirmative racial classifications on the Court—even though O'Connor's dissenting position favoring strict scrutiny in all circumstances has come to guide the Rehnquist Court's most recent ruling on affirmative action.[66] Her position has gained the support of a majority coalition, but the terms of the debate on the Court have changed or progressed little.

O'Connor's self-assumed role of searching out core principles for coalitional agreement also characterize the Court's racial redistricting rulings; her "core principles" have subsequently shaped the Court's jurisprudence on the use of race as a factor in electoral districting. Her first significant foray into this policy area, the 1986 case of *Thornburgh v. Gingles,* was again an exchange with Brennan. *Gingles* concerned the standards to be used to identify racially dilutionary electoral districting, or the drawing of geographic districts that, in light of racially polarized voting, diminish minority voting strength and ultimately impair minority voter choice. As in *Wygant* in 1986, in this late Burger Court case, O'Connor's participation in the opinion-drafting phase produced concessions in Brennan's opinion for the Court on the definition of impermissible racial vote dilution under the Voting Rights Act, but these concessions cost him some support from the liberal bloc and reduced his opinion to a plurality judgement. O'Connor's concurring opinion itself eventually gained three joiners; central to her position was her disagreement with the plurality's ostensible "creation of a *right* to a form of proportional representation in favor of all geographically and politically cohesive minority *groups.*"[67]

Her concern seemed to be that this "group-rights" claim was being elevated to the same constitutional status as individual rights' claims. And indeed, in order to comply with the *Gingles* directives against racially dilutionary districting plans, states began to create majority-minority, race-based, and remedial districts when faced with suits under the Voting Rights Act. These districts eventually faced equal protection challenges, raising the very "racial PR" complaint that O'Connor had lodged in her *Gingles* concurrence, and providing the opportunity for the Court to consider whether such majority-minority, race-based, and remedial districting should be reviewed with the same degree of strict scrutiny as any racial gerrymander or inherently suspect racial classification. Not too surprisingly, she was the justice writing for the Court in the first and pathbreaking holding that majority-minority districting could be so bizarrely shaped and so akin to a discriminatory gerrymander that it should be strictly scrutinized as an attempt to segregate voters into separate districts on the basis of race.

Nonetheless, O'Connor cautioned in her 1993 opinion in *Shaw v. Reno,* the Court had never held and was not holding that race-conscious state decision-making was impermissible in all circumstances. Her fact-specific limiting condition to the *Shaw* ruling invalidating North Carolina's use of racial considerations in redistricting was the notion that a redistricting could be "*so* extremely irregular on its face that it rationally can be viewed *only* as an effort to segregate the races for purposes of voting."[68] That this fact-"specific" limiting condition was somewhat impressionistic and subjective (*how* "extremely irregular"?) was one matter, a matter that has bedeviled its creator (to say nothing of its implementors). Another matter, equally germane for our purposes, is that O'Connor's *Shaw* opinion was a doctrinal completion of her *Gingles* opinion's antipathy for gross and imprecise racial group–level remedies—and the assumptions behind remedies that automatically assess and categorize individuals according to their race.

Thus, it is O'Connor's originally concurring position—that individuals legally enjoy the right to equal treatment irrespective of their race—that has come to be salient in shaping the *Gingles* directives on remedying racial vote dilution,[69] largely because she continues to hold the balance of power on the Court in deciding such issues. Yet it is important to remember that O'Connor holds this balance of power because of the substance of her views: she is ideologically in alliance with the Rehnquist Court's "color-blind," conservative coalition, but she stresses a context-dependent method of applying strict scrutiny analysis to race-based classifications that seek to ameliorate discriminatory conditions in the workplace or in electoral contests. For O'Connor, racial classifications must be subject to strict scrutiny because "racial classifications of any sort pose the risk of lasting harm to our society"; that harm, as she has detailed, is the right to participate in a color-blind society and color-blind institutions. Nevertheless, her application of strict scrutiny is, from her perspective, neither categorical nor fatal in fact.[70]

O'Connor stresses that "government is not disqualified from acting in response" to "both the practice and the lingering effects of racial discrimination against minority groups." Does she put this theoretical stress, and this jurisprudentially accommodationist approach to affirmative racial classifications, into practice? An emphasis on remedies that are narrowly tailored to promote a compelling governmental interest unites her narrow majority/partial plurality rulings of the mid-1990s on affirmative action and race-based districting. In *Adarand Constructors, Inc. v. Pena* in 1995, O'Connor's majority/partial plurality opinion for a 5 to 4 Court invalidated a federal contracts minority set-aside program using strict scrutiny analysis. This overruling of *Metro*'s more relaxed standard of intermediate scrutiny for federally implemented remedial racial classifications was qualified by her observation that governmental action based on race is "in most circumstances irrelevant and therefore prohibited."[71]

Likewise, but perhaps more pointedly, in the electoral redistricting case of *Bush v. Vera* in 1996, O'Connor's narrow majority/partial plurality opinion was explicitly qualified by *her own* separate concurring opinion. Although her opinion for the Court invalidated the Texas redistricting plan for its unconstitutional use of race as the "predominant" factor governing district design, her concurrence stated her view that a state's desire to comply with the requirements of the Voting Rights Act, pace *Gingles,* would constitute a compelling interest justifying race-conscious districting.[72] Notably, these qualifications, at least at a verbal level, cost her coalitional support from the conservative bloc: both Scalia and Thomas concurred only in the judgment and in part in *Adarand* and in *Bush.* Neither could countenance the notion of a "creditor or debtor race" or any legitimate use of "racial demographics."[73] Moreover, O'Connor's costly, contextually sensitive language of compromise has not gained for her opinions support from members of the liberal bloc who favor a more unconditionally expansive use of race-based affirmative action and redistricting. And to date, despite her identification of hypothetical contexts, she has not found an actual occasion where an affirmative racial classification survived strict scrutiny analysis.

To conclude, with respect to the use of racial classifications in affirmative action programs and electoral redistricting plans, I would reiterate that

[O'Connor's] juridical position is one of interest accommodation, where the interests at stake are both those of her judicial colleagues and those on either side of the debate about remedial race-based classifications. Her attempt to appeal to the various interests on the Court has been well-documented. In addition, she has attempted an accommodation between two distinct philosophies of racial identity and civil rights: colorblind individualism and group-conscious community empowerment. Unfortunately, O'Connor's accommodationist jurisprudence seems an all-too-accurate reflection of the contemporary irreconcilability of these two philosophies of racial equality.[74]

If O'Connor fails to craft more than a minimum-winning consensus for her decisions on affirmative racial classifications, it is not due to her lack of trying to present a jurisprudentially accommodationist position, nor is it due to a staunchly ideological and formulaic method of approaching racial affimative action and majority-minority districting practices. Rather, it is due to her desire to find compromise in a policy area where compromise has thus far been elusive, more elusive even than in the contentious areas of reproductive rights and church-state relations.

FEDERALISM, MINIMALISM, AND THE "DANGERS OF A GRAND UNIFIED THEORY"

As both of the preceding sections have shown, O'Connor's judicial accommodationism has been a centrist tactic, allowing her to shift the balance of power on the Court among its moderate-liberal and moderate-conservative wings. Her doctrinal coalition partners in the issue areas examined in the previous section have often been the Court's left-centrists, yet the bloc she most frequently votes with—particularly in minimum-winning coalitions—is conservative. Moreover, the results that her accommodationist doctrinal standards generally lead are moderately conservative as well: permitting greater state regulation of the conditions and availability of abortions, facilitating a balance between secular interests and sectarian concerns in church-state questions, and subjecting all racial classifications to strict but not fatal judicial scrutiny. With the personnel change that has produced the current natural Court,[75] some commentators see the emergence of two clearly defined blocs: a liberal minority composed of Stevens, Souter, Ginsburg, and Breyer and a conservative majority consisting of Rehnquist, O'Connor, Scalia, Kennedy, and Thomas. This was the lineup of the justices in the politically charged case of *Bush v. Gore;* it is also the configuration of the high bench in its most dramatic instance of active policymaking: states' rights federalism.

I comment on this area because no synopsis of the Rehnquist Court or of one of its jurists would be complete without so doing. Additionally, the "new" federalism decisions represent an area in which O'Connor's alliance with the majority—minimally winning—has been crucial and an area that further illustrates the behaviorally accommodationist dimension of her judicial record. Yet, in this Tenth and Eleventh Amendment decision-making, one senses that her majority-side membership is not a matter of strategizing, but sincere conservative belief. One of the few areas in which O'Connor had established a "paper trail" at the time of her nomination to the Supreme Court was federalism.[76] Moreover, her experience as a state judge and a state legislator has no doubt given her a particularly sympathetic perspective on state autonomy in federal-state power relations, a sympathy she reveals with crystal clarity in her voting record on such cases.

The fact that decisions such as *U.S. v. Lopez,*[77] *Seminole Tribe v. Florida,*[78] *Printz v. U.S.,*[79] *Alden v. Maine,*[80] *Kimel v. Florida Board of Regents,*[81] and *Board of Trustees, University of Alabama v. Garrett*[82] reflect a right-of-center ideological position on federal-state power relations is uncontestable; that such decisions reflect "conservatism" is more debatable. These rulings resurrecting a kind of "dual federalism" relationship—the most recent being *Garrett,* which held that states have Eleventh Amendment immunity from private lawsuits for damages under the Americans with Disabilities Act—are, quite unambiguously, judicially led policy change. They are activist legal policymaking from the high bench, dramatically narrowing the regulatory reach of congressional power—both pursuant to the Commerce Clause and to section 5 of the Fourteenth Amendment—against the states. Some Court watchers find in these decisions an ideology of "judicial triumphalism," where the struggle over the allocation of power is less between the federal government and the states than between Congress and the Supreme Court. Whatever one thinks of the constitutional correctness of the substance of this federalism revolution, its progress has not been in keeping with the canons of judicial restraint, to which conservative justices are wont to pay homage. Dissenting *Garrett* justice Breyer did not miss the opportunity to point this out, arguing that the majority's exacting scrutiny of the wisdom of the congressional legislative judgment was standing the principle of judicial restraint "on its head."[83]

It is interesting—perhaps telling—that O'Connor's role in making this revolution has generally been as a silent coalitional partner: she has contributed little original doctrine[84] and few opinions, either for the majority or in concurrence in major decisions. The exception is her opinion for the Court in the Age Discrimination in Employment Act case of *Kimel v. Florida Board of Regents,* in which she closely followed the Court's reasoning in *Seminole Tribe* that the Eleventh Amendment bars Congress from abrogating state immunity from private damage suits under the ADEA, even when pursuant to Congress's section 5 enforcement power of the Fourteenth Amendment. O'Connor's *Kimel* opinion also applied the *Boerne* Court's "congruence and proportionality" test for the appropriateness of (congressional) legislative remedies and repeated that decision's express view that "the ultimate interpretation and determination of the Fourteenth Amendment's substantive meaning remains the province of the judicial branch."[85] States' rights federalism seems to be an area in which her jurisprudential accommodationism[86] takes a back seat to her Republican ideology.

This feature of her judicial record is especially compelling given that the new federalism decisions have displayed the kind of bright-line, legislatively presumptive rule-making to which O'Connor generally objects. In a different jurisprudential context, she has commented that "when bedrock principles collide, they test the limits of categorical obstinacy and expose the flaws and dangers of a Grand Unified Theory that may turn out to be neither grand nor unified." Continuing in this vein and in the same opinion, O'Connor cautioned that "the need for careful judgment and fine distinctions presents itself even in extreme cases."[87] Her acceptance of such a "Grand Unified Theory" to limit the scope of congressional commerce and Fourteenth Amendment enforcement power, and to elevate state sovereignty concerns, is therefore puzzling, troubling, and somewhat self-contradictory.

Judicial attitudinalists would probably reply that O'Connor *is* a conservative, and that her votes generally yield conservative outcomes, even in the areas where she and the Court agonize over the proper balancing standard that should produce those outcomes. My response to this supposition is to agree, but to nevertheless stress that it matters *how* those conservative outcomes are produced. It matters in terms of the theory of the judicial role, and it matters in terms of the sensitivity of judicially crafted rules to complex circumstances in which rights conflict, or rights and governmental interests conflict, or structural principles conflict. In several areas of civil rights and liberties jurisprudence, O'Connor has signaled through her doctrinal formulations that she is cognizant of these matters, *that* they matter. What her generally silent assent to the federalism revolution signals—enthusiasm, tacit consent, discomfort, or a mixture—only she can say.

Judges are not infallible, and they are not even final—apologies to Justice Jackson,[88] and to the *Boerne* Court notwithstanding. But they are political as well as juridical actors. Recognizing this dual identity, law professor Cass Sunstein has recently written in defense of what he calls "judicial minimalism." This judicial philosophy would embrace one-case-at-a-time incrementalism that preserves a space for democratic deliberation and policymaking by the elected branches by not foreclosing subsequent policy decisions. He praises the "constructive use of [judicial] silence" and explicitly compliments judges such as O'Connor who seek to avoid broad rules and abstract theories, even when their rulings reach incompletely theorized agreements. Indeed, were it not for O'Connor's performance in the aforementioned federalism line of cases, Sunstein might be speaking of her record of judicial accommodationism in lauding "democracy-promoting minimalism . . . [whose decisions] involve narrow judgments that leave the largest questions for another day. They also involve judgments on which diverse people may converge. They are highly particularistic . . . they promote constitutional ideals without risking excessive judicial intervention into political domains." Perhaps such praise for judicial minimalism by O'Connor and by the Rehnquist Court in general is wishful thinking on Sunstein's part as he confronts a conservative jurisprudential revolution—in states' rights and federal power, surely—with which he disagrees. The judicial "humility" he wants to see, and the effort to "*accommodate* reasonable disagreement" he finds on the current bench, is displayed by O'Connor, but imperfectly.[89]

Sunstein's call for judicial minimalism, and O'Connor's partial conformity to this judicial role, has not been celebrated in all quarters.[90] The very space that minimalism or accommodationism leaves for incrementalist resolution of disagreement and for contextually based decision-making is a space it also leaves for legal unclearness, normative ambiguity, and functional deference to majoritarian views. For some, jurists and commentators alike, minimalism or accommodationism is an abdication of the judicial role to protect the rights of minority groups and the expression of their views. Given that, at the moment, the greatest judicial solicitude from the high court seems to be reserved for states and their rights, one might well wonder whether, on balance, minimalism or accommodationism is a safer bet than judicial messianism. In O'Connor, at least, it is clear that the former is her general—though not exclusive—approach to the judicial office; that it has been her general—though not exclusive—approach to decision-making explains much of the conservatism of the Rehnquist Court.

NOTES

1. 531 U.S. 98 (2000).

2. Charles Lane, "Watch Is on for Signs O'Connor Will Retire," *Washington Post,* 5 February 2001. Others might argue that *Bush* is consistent with O'Connor's general position as one of the "hubristic" Rehnquist Court justices. As Jeffrey Rosen, "Pride and Prejudice," *New Republic,* 10 July 2000, 16, 18, commented—well before the Court's involvement in the 2000 presidential election dispute—the current Court combines conservative, precedentially preservative rulings with "haughty declarations of judicial supremacy." He concludes with this observation: "Perhaps the justices are so eager for consensus in controversial cases that they are papering over their differences by adopting simplistic reasons rather than grappling with complexity." Whether this verdict applies to the decision in *Bush v. Gore* or to O'Connor's version of consensus-seeking jurisprudence generally is equally a matter for debate.

3. See Nancy Maveety, *Justice Sandra Day O'Connor: Strategist on the Supreme Court* (Lanham, Md.: Rowman and Littlefield, 1996).

4. A corollary to this aphorism might be that "bad cases" are those that overreach and those that abdicate. The Court's decision in *Bush v. Gore* might be condemned on both these grounds, but as O'Connor herself did not file an individually signed opinion in the case (the per curiam opinion is attributed to her and Justice Kennedy, and its narrowly focused holding would seem to confirm this attribution [see Linda Greenhouse, "Election Case a Test and a Trauma for Justices," *New York Times,* 20 February 2001]), I leave it to other commentators in this book to discuss the substance of that ruling, the concurrence, and the dissents.

5. Except, perhaps, in the area of states' rights–federal power. The Rehnquist Court's lurch rightward in federalism jurisprudence is a well-known, and continuing, aspect of its juridical record. I will briefly address O'Connor's role in the Court's federalism rulings in the closing section of the chapter, but it is worth noting at this point that her role in these decisions has generally been confined to a silent vote supporting Rehnquist-led five-judge majorities—she has contributed little jurisprudentially, but much in terms of completing majority opinion coalitions.

6. Cass R. Sunstein, *One Case at a Time: Judicial Minimalism on the Supreme Court* (Cambridge: Harvard University Press, 1999).

7. Suzanna Sherry, "Civic Virtues and the Feminine Voice in Constitutional Adjudi-

cation," *Virginia Law Review* 72 (1986): 543–616; Susan Behuniak-Long, "Justice Sandra Day O'Connor and the Power of Maternal Thinking, *Review of Politics* (1992): 417–444.

8. Political scientists who examined O'Connor's voting record on women's issues and in legal policymaking generally have not found that she speaks in a voice different from her male colleagues. See Beverly Blair Cook, "Justice Sandra Day O'Connor: Transition to a Republican Agenda," in *The Burger Court: Political and Judicial Profiles,* ed. Charles Lamb and Stephen Halperin (Champagne: University of Illinois Press, 1991), and Sue Davis, "The Voice of Sandra Day O'Connor," *Judicature* 77 (1993): 134–139. Her vote to join the five-member majority in the recent decision of *U.S. v. Morrison,* 529 U.S. 598 (2000), would seem to corroborate this pattern: the Court held that a federal civil remedy for gender-motivated violence under the Violence against Women Act could not be authorized under congressional commerce power; in *Morrison,* it seemed, federalism concerns outweighed gender-equity issues for Justice O'Connor. Indeed, she has reserved her strongest invective in her off-the-bench writings for gender-based models of judging. See Sandra Day O'Connor, "Madison Lecture: Portia's Progress," *New York University Law Review* 66 (1991): 1546–1558.

9. Note, "Failing Honorably: Balancing Tests, Justice O'Connor, and Free Exercise of Religion," *St. Louis University Law Review* 38 (1994): 837–897; Sandra Day O'Connor, "Keynote Address: Conference on Compelling State Interests," *Albany Law Review* 55 (1992): 538–547.

10. Note, "Justices Harlan and Black Revisited: The Emerging Dispute between Justice O'Connor and Justice Scalia over Unenumerated Fundamental Rights," *Fordham Law Review* 61 (1993): 895–933.

11. Maveety, *Justice Sandra Day O'Connor;* O'Connor, "Keynote Address," 542–543 (emphasis added).

12. Walter Murphy, *The Elements of Judicial Strategy* (Chicago: University of Chicago Press, 1964), 58, 78; Lee Epstein and Jack Knight, *The Choices Justices Make* (Washington, D.C.: Congressional Quarterly Press, 1998).

13. J. Woodford Howard, "On the Fluidity of Judicial Choice," *American Political Science Review* 62 (1968): 43–56; Jeffrey A. Segal and Harold Spaeth, *The Supreme Court and the Attitudinal Model* (New York: Cambridge University Press, 1993), 294–295; Steven A. Peterson, "Dissent in American Courts," *Journal of Politics* 43 (1981): 412–434; Ruth Bader Ginsburg, "Remarks on Writing Separately," *Washington Law Review* 65 (1990): 133–150; Thomas G. Walker, Lee Epstein, and William Dixon, "On the Mysterious Demise of Consensual Norms in the U.S. Supreme Court," *Journal of Politics* 50 (1988): 361–389.

14. For purposes of the discussion in this section and for the sake of some consistent reference point, I will utilize the judicial liberalism scale of Harold Segal and Jeffrey A. Spaeth, *Majority Rule or Minority Will?* (New York: Cambridge University Press, 1999), a full description of which can be found at p. 243.

15. But see Jeffrey A. Spaeth and Harold Segal, *The Supreme Court and the Attitudinal Model Revisited* (New York: Cambridge University Press, 2002), and their use of the attitudinal approach to "test" the legal model of judicial decision-making, particularly judges' conformity with a precedential model of decision-making.

16. For such figures and to generate other frequency statistics, we can refer to the

Supreme Court voting data collected in the Supreme Court Judicial Database, the most comprehensive source currently available. It is important to note that the data on judicial voting collected in the database are reported by docket number, not by case, which may register and resolve more than one docket. I would like to express my thanks to Harold Spaeth for his invaluable assistance in assembling the quantitative evidence reported here regarding O'Connor's voting patterns on the Rehnquist Court. Although I do no more than report frequency statistics and simple cross-tabulations, my access to even this very limited aggregate data was the product of Harold's generosity with his time and expertise.

17. William J. Brennan, "In Defense of Dissent," *Hastings Law Journal* 37 (1986): 427–438; Robert G. McCloskey, *The American Supreme Court,* 3d ed. (Chicago: University of Chicago Press, 2000). For those partial to sporting metaphors, McCloskey likened the process of producing a legally reasoned justification for a vote to playing baseball with a pool cue (p. 13).

18. With a sidebar as to how these opinions relate to her rulings in the gender-related area of sex discrimination, particularly sexual harassment under Titles VII and IX of the Civil Rights Act.

19. "Affirmative" action here will include consideration of O'Connor's tremendously salient role in shaping the standards for the usage of "majority-minority" districting. Such districting, like "classic" affirmative action programs in employment or admissions, involves the the use of race as a "primary factor" in allocating an opportunity—which, in the electoral districting context, is the opportunity for political representation.

20. Kathleen Sullivan, "The Justices of Rules and Standards," *Harvard Law Review* 106 (1992): 24–123. See also Sunstein, *One Case at a Time,* 41.

21. For a detailed study of Scalia's jurisprudence, see Richard Brisbin, *Justice Antonin Scalia and the Conservative Revival* (Baltimore: Johns Hopkins University Press, 1998).

22. Maveety, *Justice Sandra Day O'Connor.*

23. For its most recent exposition, see the Court's ruling in *Stenberg v. Carhart* (2000), which invalidated a state ban on partial birth abortion procedures as lacking an exception for the health of the mother and thus constituting an undue burden on women's reproductive freedom. O'Connor joined Breyer's five-member majority but filed a concurring opinion as well. Her conservative colleagues Rehnquist, Scalia, Kennedy, and Thomas were all in dissent.

24. 462 U.S. 416 (1983); Lee Epstein and Joseph Kobylka, *The Supreme Court and Legal Change* (Chapel Hill: University of North Carolina Press, 1992).

25. 410 U.S. 113, 153, 162–164 (1973).

26. Maveety, *Justice Sandra Day O'Connor,* 94–95.

27. 476 U.S. 767 (1986).

28. 462 U.S., at 457–459, 461; 476 U.S., at 828–829; Maveety, *Justice Sandra Day O'Connor,* 97; Epstein and Kobylka, *The Supreme Court and Legal Change,* 257.

29. 492 U.S. 502 (1990). Space does not permit intensive analysis of all of O'Connor's concurrences in abortion cases, but through the early 1990s and leading up to her coauthored plurality opinion in *Planned Parenthood of Pennsylvania v. Casey,* 505 U.S. 833 (1992), she reiterated and refined the contextual parameters of her unduly burdensome approach.

30. 492 U.S., at 529–530; Maveety, *Justice Sandra Day O'Connor,* 98–99.

31. 505 U.S. 833 (1992). O'Connor had hinted as much in her *Webster* concurrence, observing that "when the constitutional invalidity of a State's abortion statute actually turns on the constitutional validity of *Roe v. Wade,* there will be time enough to reexamine *Roe.* And to do so carefully" (492 U.S., at 526).

32. Barbara Hinkson Craig and David M. O'Brien, *Abortion and American Politics* (Chatham, N.J.: Chatham House Publishers, 1993), 330, 339.

33. Maveety, *Justice Sandra Day O'Connor,* 102–103; 505 U.S., at 877 (emphasis added).

34. 530 U.S. 914 (2001).

35. 477 U.S. 86 (1986).

36. 510 U.S. 17 (1993).

37. 523 U.S. 75 (1998) (emphasis added).

38. 524 U.S. 274 (1998).

39. 119 S.Ct. 1661 (1999).

40. 529 U.S. 598 (2000).

41. See Sanford Levinson, Coda to the 3d ed. (Sanford Levinson, ed.), of *The American Supreme Court,* by Robert G. McCloskey (Chicago: University of Chicago Press, 2000), 236–246.

42. Although here, perhaps reflective of the complexity of the religious freedom and state entanglement issues involved, her record of success in influencing the doctrinal output of the Court is somewhat more mixed. With respect to state aid to sectarian schools— and the definition of government "neutrality" toward religion—the Rehnquist Court remains confusingly divided jurisprudentially. The most recent aid to parochial schools decision in *Mitchell v. Helms,* 530 U.S. 793 (2000), reflects this division: the Court was split (4 to 2) to 3 with Justices O'Connor and Breyer occupying the middle, concurring position. Though agreeing with the Thomas plurality that the state's lending of library and computing equipment to parochial schools for secular instruction was not a violation of the Establishment Clause, O'Connor's concurrence took issue with Thomas's "near *absolute* position with respect to neutrality," reminded the court that the message of endorsement of religion is the critical test for such cases, and lectured her colleagues about the need for "the hard task of judges sifting through particular *facts*" in deciding cases. Regarding free exercise of religion questions and attendant problems of state infringement thereon, O'Connor has been a critical voice in the Court's dubious power struggle with Congress over the Religious Freedom Restoration Act (RFRA) and the standard of review to be applied to state regulations burdening religious liberty. Although the Rehnquist Court—and its champions of judicial supremacy—is the victor to date in this struggle, two of O'Connor's concurring statements in the decisional saga are noteworthy for their suggestion that an endorsement-type approach should govern this area as well. In her special concurring opinion in *Employment Division v. Smith,* 494 U.S. 872 (1990)—the ruling that sparked the passage of RFRA—and in her dissenting opinion in *City of Boerne v. Flores,* 521 U.S. 507 (1997)— the case that overturned the congressionally mandated protective standard for religious exercise in RFRA—O'Connor urged that the Court remain focused on whether a state law "make[s] abandonment of one's own religion or conformity to the religious beliefs of others the price of an equal place in the civil community" (494 U.S., at 872). Interestingly, her dispute with her judicial colleagues was over the doctrinal standard to employ in religious exercise claims, not over the Court's ultimate authority to decree the substance of such

restrictions on the states and to Congress. On this issue of the Rehnquist Court's "hubris" with respect to separation of powers relations, see note 2 of this chapter.

43. 533 U.S. 98 (2001). O'Connor joined the six-member majority in *Good News;* Scalia and Breyer appended concurrences (Breyer concurred in part) to the majority opinion. Though the case turned on free speech and public forum issues, the Court did rely on the endorsement test to adjudicate the Establishment Clause question. Indeed, Breyer devoted his entire concurrence to a discussion stipulating that the ruling had not altered the meaning and force of the endorsement of religion approach, particularly in the school context.

44. Case 00-1751 was decided on 27 June 2002. A 5 to 4 Court upheld the voucher program; O'Connor filed an opinion concurring in the judgment.

45. The *Lemon* test directed that in order to pass constitutional muster, governmental regulation in regard to religion must evidence (1) a secular legislative purpose, (2) a primary effect that neither advances nor inhibits religion, and (3) no excessive entanglement of governmental and religious institutions; 403 U.S. 602, 612–613 (1971). The background of the *Lemon* test is described in Leonard Levy, *The Establishment Clause: Religion and the First Amendment* (New York: Macmillan, 1986), and Maveety, *Justice Sandra Day O'Connor,* 76–77.

46. 465 U.S. 668 (1984). Michael McGough, "Menorah Wars," *New Republic,* 5 February 1990, 12–14.

47. 465 U.S., at 667, 668, 687, 692; Maveety, *Justice Sandra Day O'Connor,* 79.

48. Maveety, *Justice Sandra Day O'Connor,* 88 n. 9; 472 U.S. 38 (1985). In her *Jaffree* opinion she explained that her endorsement test supplied needed analytical content to the *Lemon*-based inquiry by "requir[ing] courts to examine whether government's *purpose* is to endorse religion and whether the statute actually *conveys a message* of endorsement" (472 U.S., at 38, 69; emphasis added). This approach was necessary, she stressed, because standard Establishment Clause analysis was un- or ill-equipped to deal with potential free exercise problems at times present in such cases. See also note 12 of this chapter. Her commentary was prescient, given the intertwined establishment-free exercise questions that the Rehnquist Court would face in its recent cases *University of Wisconsin v. Southworth,* 529 U.S. 217 (2000), and *Santa Fe School District v. Doe,* 530 U.S. 290 (2000).

49. *County of Allegheny v. ACLU,* 492 U.S. 573, 641 (1989). And "never," that is, until Kennedy himself—having learned the lesson of the influence of concurrence—proffered his own "coercion test" for the Establishment area, gleaned from his own separate opinion in *Allegheny.*

50. 112 S.Ct. 2649, 2665, 2671–2672, 2676 (1992).

51. 472 U.S., at 70.

52. 508 U.S. 334 (1993).

53. 515 U.S. 819 (1995).

54. Lee Epstein and Thomas G. Walker, eds., *Constitutional Law for a Changing America: Rights, Liberties, and Justice,* 3d ed. (Washington, D.C.: Congressional Quarterly Press, 1998), 223; 530 U.S. 290 (2000). The relevant passages in *Lee* can be found in 505 U.S., at 587, 590.

55. The 2001 decision in *Good News Club v. Milford Central School,* 533 U.S. 98, proved to present an ideal opportunity for O'Connor-esque accommodationism. As a melding of the problems addressed and the somewhat conflicting directions charted in the decisions of *Rosenberger* and *Santa Fe, Good News* became the occasion for a ruling protective

of equal access for the speech of religious groups that utilized O'Connor's endorsement test to do so. The conservative result in the case—one reached by using O'Connor's context-sensitive, doctrinal solution—is reminiscent of the operation of her "undue burdens" balancing test in the abortion realm.

56. *City of Richmond v. J. A. Croson Co.,* 488 U.S. 469, 510 (1989).

57. For a particularly irreverent yet evocative illustration of such an attack, see Bernard Grofman, "Redistricting 2000: What's Old, What's New, What Might Happen," a presentation to the Annual Meeting of the National Conference of State Legislatures, August 13, 2001.

58. *Adarand Constructors, Inc. v. Pena,* 115 S.Ct. 2097, 2122 (1995) (Stevens, J., dissenting) (emphasis added).

59. See Tinsley Yarbrough, *The Rehnquist Court and the Constitution* (New York: Oxford University Press, 2000), 264; Maveety, *Justice Sandra Day O'Connor,* 110; Luis Ricardo Fraga and Jorge Ruiz-de-Velasco, "Civil Rights in a Multi-Cultural Society," in *Legacies of the 1964 Civil Rights Act,* ed. Bernard Grofman (Charlottesville: University Press of Virginia, 2000).

60. *Bandemer v. Davis,* 478 U.S. 190, 151 (1986) (O'Connor, J., concurring).

61. 476 U.S. 267 (1986).

62. 478 U.S. 30 (1986).

63. Maveety, *Justice Sandra Day O'Connor,* 111.

64. A position she reiterated in her dissenting opinion in the plurality ruling of *U.S. v. Paradise,* 480 U.S. 149 (1987). Applying strict scrutiny to the court-imposed minority promotion plan for the Alabama state troopers, O'Connor argued that it was insufficiently narrowly tailored because the mandating court had failed to consider alternative, race-neutral forms of relief for the discriminatory practices at issue. Without exploring the efficacy of such alternatives, she noted that it was impossible to determine whether it was truly necessary to take race into account in fashioning a remedy (ibid., at 199–200). O'Connor was thus conceding that it was hypothetically permissible to use race as a factor—even a primary factor—in shaping a classificatory scheme.

65. 488 U.S. 469 (1989); Thomas R. Haggard, "Mugwump, Mediator, Machiavellian, or Majority? The Role of Justice O'Connor in the Affirmative Action Cases," *Akron Law Review* 24 (1990): 47–87.

66. Maveety, *Justice Sandra Day O'Connor,* 116–117. See the discussion of *Adarand Constructors, Inc. v. Pena* (1995), in which an O'Connor-led majority/partial plurality reversed *Metro*'s adoption of the intermediate level of scrutiny for congressionally mandated affirmative action programs.

67. 478 U.S. 30, 85 (1986); Maveety, *Justice Sandra Day O'Connor,* 112–113.

68. 113 S.Ct. 2816, 2824 (1993) (emphasis added).

69. This is true not only in her precedential, five-member majority opinion in *Shaw v. Reno,* 509 U.S. 630 (1993), but also in the Rehnquist Court's rulings in *Johnson v. DeGrandy,* 512 U.S. 997 (1994), *Miller v. Johnson,* 515 U.S. 900 (1995), and *Shaw v. Hunt,* 517 U.S. 899 (1996), as well as in O'Connor's majority/partial plurality opinion in *Bush v. Vera,* 517 U.S. 952 (1996), discussed later. See Maveety, *Justice Sandra Day O'Connor,* 120–121; Yarbrough, *The Rehnquist Court,* 262–264.

70. 113 S.Ct., at 2824, 2832; Yarbrough, *The Rehnquist Court,* 258, citing *Adarand v. Pena,* 115 S.Ct. 2097, 2117 (1995).

71. 115 S.Ct. at 2117.

72. 517 U.S. 952 (1996); Yarbrough, *The Rehnquist Court*, 262–263.

73. The quoted language comes from Justice Scalia's concurring opinion in *Adarand*.

74. Maveety, *Justice Sandra Day O'Connor*, 121. For a depiction of this irreconcil-ability in the context of O'Connor's jurisprudential accommodationism, see Grofman, "Redistricting 2000."

75. A "natural Court" refers to those justices serving together on the bench until a new appointment alters the Court's composition.

76. Sandra Day O'Connor, "Trends in the Relationship between Federal and State Courts from the Perspective of a State Court Judge," *William and Mary Law Review* 22 (1981): 801–819.

77. 514 U.S. 549 (1995).

78. 517 U.S. 44 (1996).

79. 521 U.S. 98 (1998).

80. 527 U.S. 706 (1999).

81. 528 U.S. 62 (2000).

82. 531 U.S. 356 (2001).

83. Linda Greenhouse, "The High Court's Target: Congress," *New York Times*, 21 February 2001; Lisa A. Kloppenberg, *Playing It Safe: How the Supreme Court Sidesteps Hard Cases and Stunts the Development of Law* (New York: New York University Press, 2001).

84. With the only major exception being her 1992 opinion for the Court in *New York v. U.S.* in which she relied on a fairly rich understanding of the Tenth Amendment to inval-idate certain provisions of a federal radioactive waste disposal law as contravening "resid-uary and inviolable" state sovereignty. Commenting that "some truths are so basic that, like the air around us, they are easily overlooked," O'Connor's majority opinion was less a personal doctrinal innovation than the culmination of the states' rights crusade that Rehnquist had been waging since his service as an associate justice. See *National League of Cities v. Usery*, 426 U.S. 833 (1976), and *Garcia v. San Antonio Metropolitan Transit Authority*, 469 U.S. 528 (1985).

85. *City of Boerne v. Flores*, 521 U.S. 507, 519–520 (1997).

86. Or her concern for gender equity issues. Although in *Davis v. Monroe County Board of Education*, 526 U.S. 629 (1999), O'Connor authored the opinion for the five-judge majority upholding the local school district's liability under Title IX for student-on-student sexual harassment, she joined Rehnquist's five-member majority opinion coalition in *U.S. v. Morrison*, 529 U.S. 266 (2000), which held that the federal civil remedy for gen-der-motivated violence under the Violence against Women Act could not be authorized by congressional commerce power. Rather, state criminal law interests were paramount.

87. Rosenberger, 515 U.S., at 850–851 (O'Connor, J., concurring).

88. In Justice Jackson's concurring opinion in *Brown v. Allen*, 344 U.S. 343 (1953), he observed rather trenchantly that "we are not final because we are infallible, but we are infallible only because we are final."

89. Sunstein, *One Case at a Time*, 4–5, 9, 11, 28, 35, 40–41, 262.

90. See, for example, Kloppenberg, *Playing It Safe*.

5
Anthony Kennedy and the Jurisprudence of Respectable Conservatism

Earl M. Maltz

Justice Anthony M. Kennedy has played a pivotal role in the evolution of Rehnquist Court jurisprudence. Particularly since the resignation of Justice Byron R. White, Kennedy and Justice Sandra Day O'Connor have been the swing votes on the Court, holding the balance of power between the conservative bloc composed of the chief justice and Justices Antonin Scalia and Clarence Thomas on the one hand and the more liberal Justices John Paul Stevens, David H. Souter, Stephen G. Breyer, and Ruth Bader Ginsburg on the other. Indeed, one recent study concluded that Kennedy has had more influence on the Court's jurisprudence than any other justice of the Rehnquist era. His influence on the Court's jurisprudence was particularly apparent in the period beginning with the 1991 term and ending with the 1997 term. During those seven terms, the Court disposed of 677 cases by opinion; Kennedy dissented from the disposition on only 43 occasions. Thus, in this period, his positions essentially defined those of the Court as a whole. Although Kennedy has been slightly more likely to dissent in later terms, he remains a critical swing vote in cases where the Court is closely divided.[1]

Kennedy was born on July 26, 1936, in Sacramento, California. The second son of a Sacramento lawyer and lobbyist, he finished at the top of his high school class and went on to attend Stanford University, from which he graduated Phi Beta Kappa in 1958. Kennedy next attended Harvard Law School, graduating in 1961 with a good but not exceptional academic record. He then joined the San Francisco law firm of Thelen, Martin, Johnson, and Bridges; however, when his father died suddenly in 1963, Kennedy returned to Sacramento and took over his father's practice. He also began to teach constitutional law part-time at McGeorge School of Law in Sacramento.[2]

In 1975, Kennedy became professionally acquainted with Edwin Meese, the top adviser to then-governor Ronald Reagan. Meese was impressed with Kennedy's abilities. Thus, when an opening occurred on the U.S. Court of

Appeals for the Ninth Circuit, President Gerald Ford nominated Kennedy on Reagan's recommendation. Kennedy was confirmed without incident, becoming one of the youngest federal appellate judges in the nation.

Kennedy came to the Supreme Court after the resignation of Justice Lewis F. Powell in 1987. However, he was not the first choice to fill Powell's seat. President Ronald Reagan initially nominated Judge Robert H. Bork to succeed Powell. In terms of objective criteria, Bork was by any standard one of the best-qualified candidates that could be found—a sitting judge on the U.S. Court of Appeals for the District of Columbia Circuit who was a former professor at Yale Law School and Solicitor General of the United States. At the same time, however, he was also well known for his conservative views on constitutional law.

Bork's prominence as a conservative theorist proved his undoing. His opponents were successful in characterizing him as an extremist whose views were outside the mainstream of American political and jurisprudential thought, and his nomination was rejected by the Senate after a bitter partisan struggle. The tone of the opposition to Bork was reflected in the hyperbolic description of his views by one well-known liberal senator:

> Robert Bork's America is a land in which women would be forced into back-alley abortions, blacks would sit at segregated lunch counters, rogue police could break down citizens' doors in midnight raids, schoolchildren could not be taught about abortion, writers and artists would be censored at the whim of government, and the doors of the Federal courts would be shut on the fingers of millions of citizens for whom the judiciary is often the only protector of the individual rights that are at the heart of our democracy.[3]

After the Bork nomination was defeated, Reagan selected Douglas Ginsburgs, also a judge on the District of Columbia Circuit. This nomination was soon withdrawn, however, after the discovery of embarrassing revelations about Ginsburgs's personal life. It was only at this point that Reagan turned to Kennedy.

The Kennedy nomination was well suited to calm the furor that had surrounded the Bork nomination and the Ginsburgs debacle. Unlike Ginsburgs, Kennedy's personal life was beyond reproach. Moreover, although his record as a judge had a distinctively conservative tone, it was almost entirely devoid of the kind of sweeping definitive pronouncements on controversial issues that had haunted Bork. Exhausted by the intense struggle over the previous nominees, many of Bork's opponents reluctantly accepted Kennedy. The views expressed by Lane Kirkland, president of the AFL-CIO, were typical.

Although expressing reservations about Kennedy's record, Kirkland nonetheless supported his confirmation because, in Kirkland's view, "Judge Kennedy—in contrast to Judge Bork—shows no sign of being attracted to eccentric and rigid theories of jurisprudence that would freeze the meaning of the Constitution by referring only to a simplified view of original intent." Instead,

Kirkland expressed confidence that Kennedy would follow the "grand tradition of constitutional interpretation" by looking to "our historical experiences and our broadly held social values" to give "practical meaning and modern application" to "the Constitution's expansive civil rights and civil liberties guarantees."[4]

In short, unlike Bork, who liberal forces viewed as a dangerous ideologue, Kennedy was viewed as a kind of respectable conservative—the best that liberals could expect from the archconservative Reagan. Conversely, most conservatives were also willing to support Kennedy, albeit with much less enthusiasm than they had shown for Bork. Against this background, Kennedy was confirmed unanimously, taking his seat on February 18, 1988.

In general terms, Kennedy's constitutional jurisprudence has vindicated the expectations of those who saw him as a moderate conservative. Despite his well-deserved reputation as a swing vote on the Rehnquist Court, he cannot be accurately characterized as a true centrist. Throughout his tenure on the Court, he has been far more likely to have been aligned with the conservatives than with his more liberal brethren. Indeed, Kennedy's most consistent ally among the other justices is the chief justice, who early in his career was himself considered the epitome of judicial conservatism.[5] The difference is that Justice Kennedy's innate conservatism has a more moderate tone than that of the chief justice, let alone the even more conservative Justices Scalia and Thomas.

Kennedy's role in *Bush v. Gore*[6] typifies his position on the Court. Some reports suggest that, during the deliberations, the more liberal members of the Court hoped that he would join them in rejecting the constitutional challenges to the procedures established by the Florida Supreme Court for recounting the state's ballots in the disputed 2000 presidential election. Instead, Kennedy ultimately provided the critical fifth vote in support of a judgment that stopped the recount and ensured the election of George W. Bush. At the same time, however, unlike the chief justice and Justices Scalia and Thomas, he refused to join in an opinion that concluded that the Florida Supreme Court had usurped the powers granted to the state legislature by Article 2 of the Constitution.

In other situations, by contrast, Kennedy has gone beyond simple disagreements with the reasoning of his more conservative colleagues. While seeking to have the Court chart a more conservative course than that of the Warren and Burger eras, Kennedy has been more willing than the chief justice and Justices Scalia and Thomas to accept and at times even expand the liberal initiatives of the preceding Courts. This pattern is reflected in his approach to issues involving both federalism and individual rights.

KENNEDY AND FEDERALISM[7]

Justice Kennedy has played a central role in the Rehnquist Court's effort to protect the prerogatives of state governments by restraining the power of Congress.

He has been an indispensable member of the majorities that have invalidated a number of federal statutes because the statutes were viewed as inconsistent with the structure of American federalism. Although he has often simply joined silently in majority opinions, in cases such as *Alden v. Maine*[8] and *United States v. Lopez*,[9] Kennedy has authored opinions articulating his rationale for placing limitations on congressional authority.

In *Alden,* Kennedy spoke for a five-member majority that concluded that state governments could not constitutionally be subjected to suit under the federal Fair Labor Standards Act, even if the action was filed in state court. The *Alden* opinion is notable for its forceful endorsement of the idea of state sovereignty. For example, Justice Kennedy declared that "[states] are not relegated to the role of mere provinces or political corporations, but retain the dignity . . . of sovereignty" and that "Congress [must] treat the States in a manner consistent with their status as residuary sovereigns and joint participants in the governance of the Union."[10]

Taken alone, this language could suggest that Kennedy might be one of the strongest supporters of state autonomy on the Rehnquist Court. Such an impression would not be entirely accurate. Kennedy has indeed supported states' rights in a variety of different contexts. At the same time, however, he has also made it clear that his vision of federalism is somewhat different from that of the most conservative members of the Rehnquist Court.

One of the clearest examples of the difference in Kennedy's approach came in *U.S. Term Limits, Inc. v. Thornton.*[11] In *Thornton,* Kennedy abandoned his allies in *Alden* to join a five-justice majority that struck down an Arkansas state constitutional provision that prohibited the name of an otherwise qualified candidate for Congress from appearing on the general election ballot if the candidate had already served three terms in the House of Representatives or two terms in the Senate. Providing the crucial fifth vote to invalidate the Arkansas limitation, Kennedy explicitly rejected the dissenters' contention that the Constitution derived its authority from the states, declaring instead that "the National Government . . . owes its existence to the act of the whole people who created it." Moreover, he asserted that "the National Government is and must be controlled by the people without collateral interference by the States" and that "the States have no power, reserved or otherwise, over the exercise of federal authority within its proper sphere."[12]

Justice Kennedy's opinion in *Thornton* reflects a view of federalism in which states' rights enjoy less robust protections than those envisioned by the chief justice and Justices O'Connor, Scalia, and Thomas. However, despite its nationalistic tone, the *Thornton* concurrence is in many respects entirely consistent with Kennedy's opinion in *Alden.* Both opinions posit a system of dual sovereignty in which the internal operations of both the state and federal governments are immune from direct interference from the other party. Although more nationalistic than the philosophy of his more conservative colleagues, this conceptual framework nonetheless provides substantial protection for the institutions of state governments.

By contrast, Justice Kennedy's approach to government regulation of private economic activity poses a more substantial threat to state autonomy. To be sure, in both *Lopez* and *United States v. Morrison*,[13] Kennedy provided the crucial fifth vote to overturn federal laws that he characterized as encroaching on areas of traditionally local concern. However, his opinion in *Lopez* strongly implies that he would vote to uphold any federal law that could plausibly be viewed as regulating the economy.[14] Conversely, Kennedy has supported the aggressive deployment of the Dormant Commerce Clause against state regulation of economic activity. His approach to such problems is markedly different from that of the chief justice and Justices Thomas and Scalia.

First, unlike Rehnquist, Scalia, and Thomas, Kennedy has explicitly endorsed the view that evenhanded state regulations that burden interstate commerce should be invalidated if the magnitude of the state interest does not justify the burden imposed by the regulation.[15] Second, he has taken an expansive view of the principle that state governments may not discriminate against interstate commerce and has been unwilling to carve out exceptions to the antidiscrimination principle in order to vindicate the concept that states remain quasi-independent communities with separate, distinctive identities. This point is dramatically illustrated by Kennedy's position in *C & A Carbone v. Town of Clarkstown*[16] and *Camps Newfound Owatonna, Inc. v. Town of Harrison.*[17]

In *Carbone,* a town agreed to allow a private contractor to construct within the town limits a solid waste transfer station to separate recyclable from nonrecyclable items. The contractor was to operate the facility for five years, after which time it would be transferred to the town for one dollar. To finance the transfer station's cost, the town guaranteed a minimum waste flow to the station for the five-year period of operation, for which the contractor was allowed to charge a fee in excess of the disposal cost of waste on the open market. In order to meet the guarantee, the town required all nonhazardous solid waste to be deposited at the transfer station before leaving the municipality.

A majority of the Court concluded that the ordinance was unconstitutional. Speaking for the Court, Justice Kennedy characterized the ordinance as one that "hoards solid waste, and the demand to get rid of it, for the benefit of the preferred processing facility."[18] Noting that the *Carbone* ordinance on its face prevented all out-of-state processors from competing on equal terms for access to locally produced solid waste, he contended that the ordinance created the type of discrimination that violated the Dormant Commerce Clause.

Despite Justice Kennedy's protestations to the contrary, *Carbone* was far from an ordinary case of discrimination against interstate commerce. The ordinance was not designed to foster local economic growth by excluding out-of-state competition; indeed, in the best of all possible worlds, the town of Clarkston no doubt would have preferred not to have any need for waste management facilities, let alone have a waste processing facility located within its borders. However, because the town had a problem with waste, it was forced to provide for the construction of such a facility. When coupled with the pricing system, the requirement that all waste be delivered to the local facility was nothing more than a mechanism by which the town provided that those responsible for the local problem—the producers of waste—would also be responsible for financing the solution to the problem—the construction of the waste management facility. In short, the town was simply attempting to provide a local solution for a locally created problem.

In striking down the *Carbone* ordinance, Justice Kennedy also implicitly rejected the vision of local self-reliance that underlay the ordinance. Instead, he embraced a nationalist model under which the town was not only permitted but also *required* to draw on the resources of the nation as a whole in order to deal with a local problem. The adoption of such a model is hardly consistent with a strong commitment to state autonomy.

If anything, the implications of *Owatonna* for the concept of state autonomy are even more apparent. *Owatonna* was a challenge to the structure of exemptions to the generally applicable tax on real property that was imposed by a subdivision of the state of Maine. "Benevolent and charitable institutions" incorporated in the state were generally exempt from these taxes; however, if such institutions were "in fact conducted or operated principally for the benefit of persons who are not residents of Maine," their eligibility for the exemption was in fact severely limited. Justice Kennedy joined a five-justice majority that concluded the state could not constitutionally deny the exemption to a summer camp that drew approximately 95 percent of its campers from outside Maine. Justice Stevens's majority opinion argued that the statute discriminated against interstate commerce because it "encourages affected entities to limit their out-of-state clientele, and penalizes the principally nonresident customers of businesses catering to a primarily interstate market." Thus, Stevens concluded that the *Owatonna* law was subject to the stringent standard of review that Kennedy himself had invoked in *Carbone,* and that the Maine statute violated strictures of the Dormant Commerce Clause.[19]

The *Owatonna* statute did indeed discriminate against those nonprofit organizations whose clients primarily resided outside of Maine. However, it was a type of discrimination that must be tolerated under any strong theory of state autonomy. One of the most basic elements of state autonomy is that each state government has a unique obligation to advance the health and welfare of its own citizenry. The property tax exemption was by its terms nothing more than an expression of this obligation—an incentive for nonprofit organizations to provide services to Maine residents and a reward for those organizations that provided such services.

Admittedly, the state of Maine also owes a more limited obligation to nonresidents. For example, the state cannot constitutionally erect barriers to entry by outsiders or to those who might provide services to them. In *Owatonna,* however, there was no such barrier erected; the camp's only complaint was that the state had refused to provide a special incentive to those organizations that chose to serve nonresidents rather than the citizenry of Maine. In essence, the camp was asserting the right to receive a subsidy simply because the state had provided an analogous subsidy to nonprofit camps that catered to Maine residents. It was this claim that the *Owatonna* Court found to be of constitutional magnitude.

To be sure, the *Owatonna* opinion did leave open at least the possibility that the government of Maine might constitutionally reach the same goal by providing a direct subsidy that was limited to camps that primarily served state residents.[20] Despite this concession, the decision has important implications for the position of the states in the federal system. First, a truly autonomous state would have an ability to choose among means as well as ends. Therefore, the potential availability of a direct subsidy only partially vitiates the impact of the limitation on the use of the tax credit. Even more important, the *Owatonna* opinion denigrates the significance of the special relationship between a state and its own citizens, one of the most important elements in any strong theory of state autonomy. Thus, Kennedy's decision to concur in *Owatonna* clearly reflects the relative weakness of his commitment to a federal system characterized by truly autonomous states.

Notwithstanding his approach to term limits and the Dormant Commerce Clause, Justice Kennedy's overall record on issues of federalism would probably be disturbing to many of those senators who supported his nomination after opposing Robert Bork's. By 1988, most liberal senators were undoubtedly convinced that federal power was constitutionally limited only by the Bill of Rights and related provisions and that judicial efforts to restrict the scope of that power usurped the legislative function. However, federalism was simply not an issue in the confirmation hearings; instead, the Senate focused its attention primarily on questions of basic judicial methodology and issues of individual rights. In this context, the opponents of the Bork nomination who supported Kennedy made a number of implicit but pointed comparisons between the approaches of the two nominees. At times, the anti-Bork senators expressed reservations about Kennedy's record as well. However, they expressed a willingness to acquiesce in Kennedy's ascension because they believed he was more likely to support liberal positions in other contexts. The Senate Judiciary Committee report that expressed these fears and hopes has often proved to be a remarkably accurate predictor of Kennedy's actual performance on the Court.[21]

KENNEDY AND RACE DISCRIMINATION

One of the major concerns expressed in the report was that Kennedy's record on the Court of Appeals reflected "an insensitivity to systemic discrimination and a hesitancy to use the courts as an instrument to correct damaging institutional policies."[22] In coming to this conclusion, the committee majority relied in substantial part on Kennedy's opinion in *Spangler v. Pasadena School Board,* a controversial school desegregation case where he had chastised the trial court for being unduly critical of the decision-making process of a school board that had been subject to a wide-ranging school desegregation order.[23] Since taking his seat on the Supreme Court, Kennedy has continued to champion the cause of local school authorities, consistently supporting opinions that have decried unduly broad remedial decrees and paved the way for the dissolution of desegregation orders.[24]

His attitude is exemplified by his reaction to the remedial decree in the Kansas City school desegregation litigation, which came to the Court a number of times as *Missouri v. Jenkins.* As a part of the decree, the district court had ordered the state and the school district to undertake a massive capital improvement program for the Kansas City high schools, including, for example, the construction of a twenty-five-acre farm with an air-conditioned meeting room, a model United Nations wired for language translations, and movie editing and screening rooms. The district court had reasoned that such facilities might improve racial balance in the Kansas City schools by attracting white students from the suburbs. However, Kennedy saw no cognizable relationship between these improvements and the principles of *Brown v. Board of Education* and its progeny. He contended that "these items are a part of legitimate political debate over educational policy and spending priorities, not the Constitution's command of racial equality." Subsequently, he became a member of the five-justice conservative majority that overturned a decree that would have required the state to fund salary increases for employees of the Kansas City district and remedial programs designed to raise student achievement that was at or below national norms.[25]

Kennedy has also been a reliable member of conservative majorities that have invalidated race-based affirmative action programs, which are often characterized by their proponents as necessary antidotes for the effects of the racist structure of society. The depth of his antipathy toward such programs is reflected in his opinion in *City of Richmond v. J. A. Croson Co.* In *Croson,* Justice O'Connor's majority opinion applied strict scrutiny to strike down a city requirement that government contractors set aside at least 30 percent of subcontracts for minority-owned businesses. Concurring, Kennedy suggested that he would prefer a rule that would automatically invalidate all race-based classifications. He was willing to join O'Connor's opinion only because it was more consistent with existing precedents and that "in application, the strict scrutiny standard [will] operate in a manner generally consistent with the imperative of race neutrality."[26]

To be sure, Kennedy has been willing to countenance some consideration of race in the process of drawing legislative districts. In this context, he has abandoned Justices Scalia and Thomas, who would have barred all uses of race in redistricting in favor of the more moderate approach articulated by Justice O'Connor in *Bush v. Vera.*[27] Nonetheless, those who feared that Kennedy would reject the tenets of liberal jurisprudence in race-related cases can find little comfort in his overall record as a justice of the Supreme Court.

SEX DISCRIMINATION

Kennedy's approach to sex discrimination stands in marked contrast to his views on race. During the confirmation process, his record on this issue as a judge on the Ninth Circuit was clearly worrisome to more liberal members of the Senate Judiciary Committee. In particular, they were troubled by Kennedy's decision in *AFSCME v. State of Washington,* in which he had rejected the argument that the theory of "comparable worth" could support a sex discrimination claim under Title VII of the Civil Rights Act of 1964.[28] Nonetheless, the committee report expressed the view that, unlike Judge Bork, Kennedy had become "increasingly sensitive and open-minded" with regard to sex discrimination issues, and that in the future he would view such discrimination with great suspicion.[29]

The hopes of those who took this view have been largely vindicated by subsequent events. Unlike his more conservative colleagues, Kennedy has consistently taken the position that government-imposed sex discrimination should be subjected to enhanced scrutiny under equal protection analysis. Thus, for example, in *United States v. Virginia,*[30] Kennedy joined a majority of the Court that concluded that the state of Virginia could not constitutionally maintain Virginia Military Academy as a single-sex institution. Similarly, in *J. E. B. v. Alabama ex rel. T. B.,* he concluded that peremptory challenges could not be used to exclude men from a jury in a civil case. In *J. E. B.,* Kennedy relied on a "strong presumption that gender classifications are invalid" and declared that "the injury is to personal dignity and the [excluded] individual's right to participate in the political process."[31]

Despite his positions in *Virginia* and *J. E. B,* Kennedy has not fully embraced the feminist position on sex-based classifications. This point emerged clearly in *Tuan Anh Nguyen v. Immigration and Naturalization Service.*[32] In *Tuan Anh Nguyen,* the Court dealt with the constitutionality of the Immigration and Naturalization Act provision governing the acquisition of citizenship by children born out of wedlock to American citizens. The statute differentiated sharply between children whose fathers were American citizens and children whose mothers held that status. A child can only claim citizenship through his or her father if, prior to the child's eighteenth birthday, he or she was either formally legitimated, acknowledged by the father under oath, or obtained a court order proving the father's paternity. By contrast, an illegitimate child can claim American citizenship through his or her mother without the benefit of such formal evidence of maternity. This differential treatment was challenged by both the American father of a child born out of wedlock in Vietnam to a Vietnamese mother and the child himself. They argued that the statute violated the Fifth Amendment's prohibition on unjustified sex discrimination.

A deeply divided Court had considered and rejected a challenge to the same statute in *Miller v. Albright.* However, the circumstances that underlay the decision in *Miller* left the constitutionality of the statute unclear. Only four justices—Chief Justice Rehnquist and Justices Stevens, Scalia, and Thomas—concluded that the sex discrimination challenge should be rejected on its merits. Conversely, Justices Souter, Ginsburg, and Breyer argued that the statute violated equal protection norms. As has often been the case in the Rehnquist era, the balance of power rested with Kennedy and Justice O'Connor. In an opinion written by O'Connor, they argued that, because the father of the child in *Miller* had been held not to have standing as a party to the lawsuit, the sex discrimination claim was not properly before the Court. At the same time, however, the O'Connor opinion clearly indicated that if they had considered the sex discrimination claim on its merits, she and Kennedy would have concluded that the statute could not survive heightened scrutiny. Thus, while the child's claim was rejected in *Miller,* it seemed unlikely that the statute would survive an attack in which the merits of the sex discrimination claim were considered by all of the justices.[33]

Tuan Anh Nguyen was just such a case. All parties conceded that the father had standing to be a party to the lawsuit; thus, O'Connor and Kennedy could not avoid reaching the merits of the sex discrimination claim. Surprisingly, Kennedy broke with O'Connor and, speaking for himself, the chief justice, and Justices Stevens, Scalia, and Thomas, concluded that the statute passed muster under the substantial relationship test. While noting the governmental interest in ensuring that the child was in fact fathered by an American citizen, Kennedy relied largely on "the critical importance of the Governmental interest in ensuring some opportunity for a tie between the citizen father and foreign born child which is a reasonable substitute for the opportunity manifest between mother and child at the time of birth."[34]

Obviously, for a majority of the Judiciary Committee in 1987, issues related to sex discrimination played a significant role in differentiating Robert Bork from Anthony Kennedy. However, more general questions of judicial philosophy were even more significant. Bork was defeated in large measure because he was the most prominent academic supporter of a strict originalist theory and he rejected the notion that the Court should constitutionalize rights that were not specifically enumerated in the Constitution itself. Bork's opponents argued that this constitutional theory was outside the mainstream, particularly insofar as it denied the existence of a constitutionally protected right to privacy.[35] By contrast, they praised what they saw as Kennedy's embrace of the concept of unenumerated rights generally and the right of privacy in particular.[36]

THE JURISPRUDENCE OF PRIVACY

During his tenure on the Court, Kennedy's jurisprudence has clearly reflected his commitment to the protection of unenumerated rights. The difference between his opinion and that of the most conservative members of the Court emerged clearly in *Michael H. v. Gerald D.*[37] *Michael H.* arose from the complicated domestic situation of Carole D., who married Gerald D. in 1976 and then, beginning in 1978, became involved in extramarital sexual relations with Michael H. Against this background, Victoria was born to Carole in 1981. Gerald was listed on the birth certificate as the father and had continuously held out Victoria to the world as his daughter. However, blood tests taken by Carole and Michael showed a 98.07 percent probability that Michael was Victoria's biological father. Moreover, for two different periods of three months and five months, respectively, after Victoria's birth, Michael, Carole, and Victoria lived together, and during these periods Michael held out Victoria to be *his* daughter. Ultimately, however, Carole chose to reestablish her permanent relationship with Gerald.

After his attempts to visit Victoria had been rebuffed, Michael filed a paternity action in November 1982, seeking to establish himself as Victoria's biological father and to obtain legally enforceable visitation rights. Relying on state law, the California courts refused to even consider his petition. Michael argued that this action was inconsistent with both the substantive and procedural due process components of the Fourteenth Amendment.

Kennedy joined with Justice Antonin Scalia in concluding that Michael had no cognizable Fourteenth Amendment liberty interest that might support his constitutional claim. However, Kennedy rejected Scalia's basic analysis of the scope of unenumerated rights. Scalia argued that the Fourteenth Amendment protects only the *specific* interests that have a strong historical pedigree. Kennedy, by contrast, joined with Justice O'Connor in contending that the Court might in some circumstances appropriately refer to general categories of interests that have historically been protected. By its nature, this methodology leaves open the possibility of constitutionalizing a broader range of unenumerated rights.[38]

Against this background, it should not be surprising that Kennedy has been sympathetic to privacy claims in a variety of different contexts. In some cases, his views have provoked relatively little public controversy. For example, while some might quarrel with the details of the approach that he adopted in *Troxel v. Granville,*[39] few would disagree with his conclusion that the parental rights of a biological mother are entitled to special constitutional solicitude. By contrast, in other situations, Kennedy's treatment of privacy-related issues has brought him to the center of some of the most divisive social and legal controversies of the late twentieth century. In particular, he has played a pivotal role in the development of the Rehnquist Court's approach to abortion and gay rights.

Although not explicitly mentioned in the Senate Judiciary report condemning the Bork nomination, the controversy over the constitutional status of abortion played an important role in the defeat of the nomination. In the wake of the Supreme Court's 1973 decision in *Roe v. Wade,*[40] which left little leeway for government regulation of abortion, abortion became a pivotal issue in national politics. Pro-life activists, whose top priority was to overturn *Roe,* became a powerful force in the conservative wing of the Republican party; indeed they were an indispensable element of the coalition that brought Ronald Reagan to power. By contrast, the national Democratic Party was dominated by adherents to the pro-choice philosophy, who sought not only to defend *Roe* itself but also to further restrict the ability of the state and federal governments to limit access to abortions.

As a corollary to his rejection of the theory of unenumerated rights, Bork viewed the decision in *Roe* as completely unacceptable. Not surprisingly, some of the most virulent attacks on his nomination came from strong supporters of the pro-choice position. Indeed, the references to unenumerated rights and privacy in the Judiciary Committee report are best understood as a thinly veiled reference to Bork's views on the abortion issue. Conversely, Kennedy's nomination was largely uncontroversial in part because his public record did not clearly indicate his views on the abortion controversy.

Initially, however, it seemed that the pro-life forces had gained a strong ally on the Court. In *Webster v. Reproductive Health Services,* Kennedy agreed with Chief Justice Rehnquist and Justices White and Scalia in calling for the abandonment of the framework established in *Roe,* joining an opinion describing that framework as "unsound in principle and unworkable in practice."[41] Subsequently, in voting to uphold a requirement that only one parent generally be notified before a minor obtained an abortion in *Ohio v. Akron Reproductive Health Center,* he wrote for the same group of justices in declaring that "the legislature acted in a rational manner. . . . It is both rational and fair for the State to conclude that, in most instances the family will strive to give a . . . minor advice that is both compassionate and mature. The statute in issue here is a rational way to further those ends."[42] Similarly, in defending a two-parent notification requirement in *Hodgson v. Minnesota,* Kennedy described the statute as prescribing "reasonable measures to recognize and promote the primacy of the family tie."[43] His emphasis on reasonableness, together with his consistent alliance with the most pro-life members of the Court, seemed to suggest that he was willing to completely jettison enhanced scrutiny for abortion rights. Against this background, the position ultimately taken by Kennedy in *Planned Parenthood of Southeastern Pennsylvania v. Casey*[44] was something of a surprise.

In 1992, when *Casey* was decided by the Court, it appeared that the pro-life forces had finally succeeded in assembling the majority that was necessary to remove constitutional protection from abortion rights altogether. To be sure, Harry Blackmun—the author of *Roe v. Wade*—remained on the Court, as did John Paul Stevens, whose voting record was also generally pro-choice. In addition, Sandra Day O'Connor had voted to strike down the parental notice requirement in *Hodgson,* and the views of the newly appointed David Souter were unknown. Nonetheless, the pro-life forces seemed to have gained at least one certain vote with the appointment of Clarence Thomas, who had replaced the strongly pro-life Thurgood Marshall. Thus, if the coalition from *Webster, Akron,* and *Hodgson* remained intact, the Court seemed certain to reject the theory that access to abortion merited special constitutional protection.

Kennedy, however, chose to abandon the coalition. Instead, he joined Justices O'Connor and Souter in a joint opinion that changed the standard of review but continued to substantially limit the degree to which states could regulate abortions. The opinion contended that the issues raised by *Casey* transcended the controversy over the constitutional status of abortion, arguing that a total about-face on the abortion issue would undermine public confidence in the Court by making it appear that constitutional adjudication was based on nothing more than ordinary political considerations.

Kennedy's alliance with O'Connor and Souter on the abortion issue proved short-lived. Subsequently, in *Stenberg v. Carhart*,[45] he joined the more conservative members of the Court in concluding that the government could outlaw so-called "partial birth" abortions, writing an opinion that emphasized the authority of the state to make moral judgments on such questions. However, by the time *Stenberg* was decided, Kennedy's vote was no longer pivotal on abortion-related issues; Justice White had been replaced by the pro-choice Ruth Bader Ginsburg, creating a dynamic that left the balance of power in the hands of Justice O'Connor, who voted with the majority in striking down the state law at issue in *Stenberg*.

Despite his opinion in *Stenberg*, Kennedy's overall record in the abortion cases obviously reflects a less absolute commitment to conservative ideology than that of the chief justice and Justices Scalia and Thomas. However, as reflected in the joint opinion in *Casey*, the abortion controversy was complicated by issues of stare decisis. Thus, Kennedy's approach is perhaps best seen as an effort to accommodate his basic political philosophy with his view of the imperatives created by institutional concerns. By contrast, his approach to the issue of gay rights can only be seen as a reflection of an unwillingness to fully embrace political and moral values that are central to conservative ideology.

Kennedy first confronted the issue of gay rights in *Romer v. Evans*.[46] In *Romer*, the Court struck down a Colorado state constitutional provision that barred the state and all of its subdivisions from adopting any regulation, statute, or ordinance that prohibited discrimination on the basis of sexual orientation. Speaking for the six-justice majority, Kennedy did not purport to rely on a privacy argument in reaching his conclusion. Instead, he contended that the state constitutional provision failed even the rational basis test, the most lenient standard for judicial review under the Equal Protection Clause. However, even a cursory analysis of the reasoning of the *Romer* opinion reveals its close relationship to privacy issues.

Kennedy's analysis rested largely on his view that the Colorado provision was based on "animus"—that is, unacceptable prejudice against gay men and lesbians. This argument implicitly assumes that the state is not allowed to implement measures that are based on official disapproval of same-sex relationships. The most plausible basis for such an assumption is that the right to enter into same-sex relationships is a privacy interest deserving of significant constitutional protection under the Fourteenth Amendment.

This conclusion is fundamentally inconsistent with the 1986 decision in *Bowers v. Hardwick.* In *Bowers*—decided before Kennedy was appointed—the Court held that states could constitutionally prohibit sexual relationships between two people of the same gender. Speaking for the majority, Justice White's reasoning was straightforward. While noting that the Court had recognized some rights as fundamental even when not readily identifiable from the constitutional text, he asserted that all such rights were "deeply rooted in this Nation's history and tradition." After reviewing the long history of prohibitions against consensual sodomy as well as the fact that twenty-five states and the District of Columbia continued to provide penalties for such activity, White concluded that homosexual activity could not plausibly claim that characterization. The majority thus adopted the rational basis test and found that "notions of morality" provided a sufficient basis to find the challenged statute constitutional.[47]

In *Romer,* Justice Kennedy dealt with *Bowers* by simply ignoring it. In theory, of course, he may not have recognized the connection between the two cases; however, this seems highly unlikely, particularly given the emphasis that the *Romer* dissent placed on *Bowers.* A more plausible explanation is that Kennedy simply rejected the basic premise underlying Bowers—that the government may constitutionally base its decisions on a simple judgment that same-sex relationships are inherently immoral, and that gay men and lesbians could be subjected to legal disadvantages on that basis alone.

Kennedy's opinion in *Romer* thus stood at the confluence of two strands of elite public opinion in the early 1990s. The first element dealt with the substantive issue of same-sex relationships, maintaining that such relationships should be fully accepted and given the same legal treatment as heterosexual relationships. While continuing to be resisted by committed conservatives, this view gained increasing currency among educated, affluent Americans in the period between the decisions in *Bowers* and *Romer.*[48] The second element was one of the rocks on which the Bork nomination had foundered—the view that the Constitution should be seen as an evolving document that could be deployed in support of values that were neither specifically enumerated in the document itself nor viewed as fundamental by the framers themselves. The decision in *Romer* embodied a combination of these two theories.

Like his votes in *Casey* and the sex discrimination cases, Kennedy's position in *Romer* no doubt pleased those who had opposed the Bork nomination. By contrast, his more conservative instincts reasserted themselves in *Boy Scouts of America v. Dale.*[49] In *Dale,* an avowed homosexual and gay activist was dismissed from the position of assistant scoutmaster by the Boy Scouts. The Scouts based this decision on their view that his sexual orientation and political activities in support of gay rights were incompatible with the mission of the organization. The New Jersey courts concluded that the dismissal violated the state's public accommodation law, which prohibited discrimination based on sexual orientation. In a decision in which the Supreme Court divided sharply on ideological lines, Kennedy joined four other justices in reversing the New Jersey decision, concluding that the decision of the Boy Scouts was protected by the First Amendment right of association.

The holding in *Dale* was greeted with outrage from liberal political forces.[50] However, despite his position in cases such as *Dale* and *Stenberg,* the overall pattern of Kennedy's decisions during his tenure on the Court has no doubt given considerable satisfaction to those who led the struggle against Robert Bork. Given the political context in which the struggle took place, his opponents could not expect to seat a justice who shared all or even most of their views; the best that they could hope for was a justice who would diverge from conservative ideology on a substantial number of key issues. Kennedy's record on issues such as sex discrimination, abortion rights, the constitutional status of sexual orientation, and a variety of other issues clearly meets this criterion. Thus, by any reasonable standard, his jurisprudence must be viewed as that of a truly "respectable" conservative.

NOTES

1. Paul H. Edelman and Jim Chen, "The Most Dangerous Justice Rides Again: Revisiting the Power Pageant of the Justices," *Minnesota Law Review* 86 (2001): 131–226; "The Supreme Court, 1991 Term," *Harvard Law Review* 106 (1992): 163–381, at 378; "The Supreme Court, 1992 Term," *Harvard Law Review* 107 (1993): 144–379, at 372, 373; "The Supreme Court, 1993 Term," *Harvard Law Review* 108 (1994): 139–379, at 372; "The Supreme Court, 1994 Term," *Harvard Law Review* 109 (1995): 111–359, at 340, 341; "The Supreme Court, 1995 Term," *Harvard Law Review* 110 (1996): 135–376, at 367, 368; "The Supreme Court, 1996 Term," *Harvard Law Review* 111 (1997): 197–439, at 431, 432; "The Supreme Court, 1997 Term," *Harvard Law Review* 112 (1998), 122–378, at 371, 372.

2. The description of Kennedy's life and early career is taken from Theodore Eisenberg, "Anthony M. Kennedy," in *The Justices of the Supreme Court of the United States: Their Lives and Major Opinions,* ed. Leon Friedman and Fred L. Israel (New York: Chelsea House Publishers, 1997), 5: 1731–1757.

3. *Nomination of Robert H. Bork to Be Associate Justice of the Supreme Court of the United States: Hearings before the Senate Committee on the Judiciary,* 100th Cong., 1st sess. (1987), 33.

4. Statement of Lane Kirkland, in *The Supreme Court of the United States: Hearings and Reports on Successful and Unsuccessful Nominations of Supreme Court Justices by the Senate Judiciary Committee, 1916–1987,* ed. Roy M. Mersky and Gary M. Hartman (Buffalo, N.Y.: William S. Hein, 1991), 15A: 1031–1037.

5. See, for example, "The Supreme Court, 1999 Term," *Harvard Law Review* 114 (2000): 179–408, at 391, 392, and "The Supreme Court, 2000 Term," *Harvard Law Review* 115 (2001): 396–550, at 540, 541.

6. 531 U.S. 98 (2000).

7. This section is taken from Earl M. Maltz, "Justice Kennedy's Vision of Federalism," *Rutgers Law Journal* 31 (2000): 761–770.

8. 527 U.S. 706 (1999).

9. 567 U.S. 549 (1995).

10. 527 U.S., at 715, 748 (citation omitted).

11. 514 U.S. 779 (1995).

12. Ibid., at 837, 841.

13. 529 U.S. 598 (2000).

14. 567 U.S., at 580 (Kennedy, J., concurring).

15. *Bendix Autolite Corp. v. Midwesco Enterprises, Inc.,* 468 U.S. 368 (1988).

16. 511 U.S. 383 (1994).

17. 520 U.S. 564 (1997).

18. 511 U.S., at 392.

19. 520 U.S., at 576.

20. Ibid., at 589.

21. *Nomination of Anthony M. Kennedy to Be an Associate Justice of the United States Supreme Court,* 100th Cong., 1st sess., 1988, S. Exec. Rept. 100-13.

22. Ibid., iv.

23. 525 F.2d 1326 (9th Cir. 1977).

24. See, for example, *Missouri v. Jenkins,* 495 U.S. 33 (1990) (Kennedy, J., concurring in part and concurring in the judgment).

25. Ibid., at 58, 70; *Missouri v. Jenkins,* 515 U.S. 70 (1995).

26. See, for example, *City of Richmond v. J. A. Croson Co.,* 488 U.S. 469, 519 (1989) (Kennedy, J., concurring in part and concurring in the judgment in part).

27. 517 U.S. 952 (1996).

28. 770 F.2d 1401 (1985).

29. *Nomination of Anthony M. Kennedy,* 30–32.

30. 518 U.S. 515 (1996).

31. 511 U.S. 127, 152 (citation omitted), 153 (citation omitted) (1994).

32. 121 S.Ct. 2053 (2001).

33. 520 U.S. 420, 445–452 (1998) (O'Connor, J., concurring in the judgment).

34. 121 S.Ct., at 2062.

35. *Nomination of Robert H. Bork to Be an Associate Justice of the United States Supreme Court,* 1987, S. Exec. Rept. 100-7, 7–21.

36. *Nomination of Anthony M. Kennedy,* 16–21.

37. 491 U.S. 110 (1989).

38. Ibid., at 127–128n6 (opinion of Scalia, J.); 132 (citation omitted) (opinion of O'Connor, J.).

39. 530 U.S. 57 (2000).

40. 410 U.S. 113 (1973).

41. 492 U.S. 490, 518 (1989) (opinion of Rehnquist, C.J.), quoting *Garcia v. San Antonio Metropolitan Area Transit Authority,* 469 U.S. 528, 546 (1985).

42. 497 U.S. 502, 520 (1990) (opinion of Kennedy, J.).

43. 497 U.S. 417, 501 (1990) (Kennedy, J., dissenting).

44. 505 U.S. 833 (1992).

45. 530 U.S. 914 (2000).

46. 517 U.S. 620 (1996).

47. 478 U.S. 186, 192, 196 (1986), quoting *Moore v. City of East Cleveland,* 431 U.S. 494, 503 (1977) (opinion of Powell, J.).

48. A 1986 Gallup Poll reported that 42 percent of college-educated respondents supported legalization of sexual intercourse between adults of the same sex; in 1992, a similar poll found that 69 percent were in support. See "Sharp Decline Found in Support for Legalizing Gay Relations," *Gallup Report* 354 (1986): 24–26; Larry Hagick, "Public Opinion Divided on Gay Rights," *Gallup Poll Monthly* 321 (1992): 2–7.

49. 530 U.S. 640 (2000).

50. See, for example, "Nation's Largest Jewish Organization Disappointed by Supreme Court Sanction of Boy Scout's Discrimination," *www.uahc.org/reform/rac/news/062800bs.html,* 28 June 2000.

6
Realism, Pragmatism, and John Paul Stevens

Ward Farnsworth

When William Rehnquist became chief justice in 1986, John Paul Stevens seemed an unlikely candidate for status as his Court's leading dissenter; by reputation he was a centrist and too idiosyncratic to be labeled a reliable friend or foe of anyone. In the end, however, Stevens turned out be an ideal foil for the Rehnquist Court's conservative majorities, being nearly their opposite in both substance and method. When the Court went right, Stevens did not follow; when the Court made rules, he wanted standards; when the Court made large pronouncements of law, he tried to confine his decisions to cases. Much can be learned about the Rehnquist Court by considering what it was not, and what it most was not was Stevens.

BACKGROUND AND OVERVIEW

John Stevens finished first in his law school class at Northwestern, clerked for Justice Wiley Rutledge, and then spent twenty years working as a lawyer in Chicago, specializing in antitrust cases. He was appointed to the Seventh Circuit by Richard Nixon in 1970 and was regarded as a moderately conservative judge at the time of his nomination to the Supreme Court by Gerald Ford in 1975. The Senate was then under Democratic control, and as an unelected president Ford was in no position to push through a controversial nominee; he picked Stevens over other candidates for William O. Douglas's slot, such as Robert Bork, partly to ensure a painless confirmation, and that is what he got. The confirmation hearings presented Stevens as intelligent, modest, and not particularly political; his views on various subjects were probed only mildly. The hearings took just two days and ended with a unanimous vote to confirm.

Stevens joined the Court in the middle of its 1975 term, and immediately gained a reputation for unpredictability. Right away he became a frequent issuer of separate opinions, apparently setting a record during his first term for lone dissents by a new justice. He often relied on reasoning that seemed idiosyncratic and that sometimes allowed him to straddle divisions that more usually were sources of consistent opposition; in his first term he voted with Chief Justice Burger to uphold capital sentencing schemes in Georgia and Florida, but with Brennan and Marshall to strike them down in Texas, Louisiana, and North Carolina. By the close of the 1980s, he had come to be viewed as moderately liberal but still essentially a centrist. His continued unpredictability caused commentators to regard him as guided by his own somewhat quirky take on each case and as nearly lacking in politics. The standard account of Stevens, perhaps, is that he was a centrist when appointed to the Court but became a "liberal" by comparison as the rest of the Court moved to the right through a series of replacements, until at last he stood as the Court's left-most member in 1994. This account contains some truth; the Court did move to the right around Stevens, and his role did change in the 1990s when, with the retirement of Justice Blackmun, he became the Court's ranking liberal in both politics and seniority. He will be remembered as a centrist figure on the Burger Court, but as the leader in dissent during the heyday of the Rehnquist Court.

All along, however, Stevens has been liberal in several recognizable senses, even if he did "grow"—i.e., move to the left—a little bit over the years. The meaning of liberalism in this context bears some explanation, for the words "liberal" and "conservative" have nonstandard meanings when applied to Supreme Court justices and may simply be misnomers. Clarence Thomas, who often is said to be conservative, is perhaps the Court's least conservative member on a traditional interpretation of the word; he is a right-winger, but he is readier than any of his colleagues to reconsider settled precedent.[1] "Liberalism" likewise is a placeholder term for a set of preferences that have no rigorous relationship to the word itself. And yet, as we shall see, in many areas there are persistent, predictable differences in the votes the justices cast, and the differences generally can be mapped without much difficulty onto the political preferences conventionally associated with the Republican and Democratic parties. It is useful to have a vocabulary to describe this phenomenon, so for now I will use the "conservative" and "liberal" labels despite their shortcomings.

In the time and place where Stevens has been judging, "liberalism" generally has been associated with broad views of federal congressional power, with a willingness to recognize unenumerated constitutional rights through the doctrine of substantive due process, with support for affirmative action but otherwise with expansive readings of what the "equal protection of the laws" forbids, with robust interpretations of the Establishment Clause, and with solicitude for the rights of criminal defendants. Within these positions there of course is much room for differences of style and degree, and Stevens's own variety of liberalism has had two aspects. The first has consisted of a fairly straightforward set of beliefs about the Constitution's meaning that has put him at odds with the conservative majorities of his time on several of the issues just described. The second and more interesting aspect has been a distinctive judicial method that was itself conservative but that usually generated results that seemed liberal. Most of this inquiry will focus on this second sense of Stevens's liberalism, but first let us briefly review the broad outlines of his positions in a few critical areas.

First, Stevens has fervently resisted the Rehnquist Court's federalism decisions. He has dissented from all of its cases limiting the federal government's ability to legislate using the commerce power,[2] and he has dissented from all of its cases holding that the Eleventh Amendment forbids Congress to use its powers under Article 1 to pass laws subjecting the states to lawsuits for damages. Stevens has protested the latter doctrine with special vigor, finding it "so profoundly mistaken and so fundamentally inconsistent with the Framers' conception of the constitutional order that it has forsaken any claim to the usual deference or respect owed to decisions of this Court."[3]

Second, Stevens has been the bête noire of religious conservatives. He has provided regular support for a constitutional "right to die" and for abortion rights and made the startling claim in *Webster v. Reproductive Health Services* that a statutory preamble stating that human life begins at conception violated the Establishment Clause because it served "no identifiable secular purpose."[4] He has been a rare adherent to views of both the Establishment Clause and the Free Exercise Clause that are unhelpful to religious groups;[5] indeed, Stevens has been the only justice to consistently vote both to single out religious organizations for exclusion from generally available benefits[6] and not to single them out for protection from the burdens of generally applicable laws.[7] And he alone has argued that accommodations of religion are, by their nature, violations of the Establishment Clause.[8] Stevens also has been the author of the rhetoric most mistrustful of religion during his time on the Court.[9]

Third, on race and other questions of equal protection Stevens has had a mixed record. During the first half of his career he regularly voted to invalidate racial preferences in various forms;[10] as time passed he began voting the other way.[11] The shift was accompanied by a change in rhetoric. In *Fullilove v. Klutznick,* the Court held that the use of a minority set-aside program for federal government contractors was a valid means to accomplish legitimate objectives. Stevens dissented, providing a stern lecture on the dangers of racial classifications; in a remarkable footnote, he claimed that the "the very attempt to define with precision a beneficiary's qualifying racial characteristics is repugnant to our constitutional ideals" and advised that the government "study precedents such as the First Regulation to the Reichs Citizenship Law of November 14, 1935"—and then quoted from Nazi Germany's rules defining who was Jewish.[12] But Stevens soon returned to more characteristic form, evaluating affirmative action programs and similar laws based on details of their rationale and effects. Thus in *Wygant v. Jackson Board of Education,*[13] the Court held that a school district could not give preferential treatment to minority teachers in deciding who would be laid off; Stevens dissented, saying that "a school board may reasonably conclude that an integrated faculty will be able to provide benefits to the student body that could not be provided by an all-white, or nearly all-white, faculty." Yet then in *City of Richmond v. J. A. Croson Co.,*[14] he voted to invalidate a city's program that required construction contractors to subcontract 30 percent of their work to minority-owned businesses. He thought that in construction, unlike in education, there was no reason to think there were benefits to racial diversity.

A few years later, in *Adarand Constructors, Inc. v. Pena,* Stevens dissented from a decision striking down preferences that were similar in many ways to those at issue in *Fullilove* fifteen years earlier. He criticized the majority for delivering a "disconcerting lecture about the evils of government racial classifications"[15] and said that its analysis "ignores a difference, fundamental to the idea of equal protection, between oppression and assistance." This made for a striking contrast with the lecture on the dangers of racial classifications that Stevens himself had provided in *Fullilove.* At the same time, he became a perennial dissenter to the Rehnquist Court's decisions of the 1990s limiting the use of race-conscious legislative redistricting under the Voting Rights Act.[16] These votes, along with his opinion in *Adarand* and his votes in a few other cases, have caused him to be considered a fairly reliable liberal on matters of race during the Rehnquist years.

Meanwhile Stevens also has used characteristically fine methods, and reached results typically but not reliably liberal, in evaluating sex discrimination under the Constitution. In *Craig v. Boren,*[17] a majority of the Court struck down an Oklahoma law forbidding the sale of 3.2 percent beer to males under the age of twenty-one and to females under eighteen. The Court adopted that variety of review now commonly known as "intermediate scrutiny": "Classifications by gender must serve important governmental objectives and must be substantially related to achievement of those objectives."[18] This caused Stevens to warn in a concurring opinion that "there is only one Equal Protection Clause";[19] he said that the clause simply "requires every State to govern impartially," and that he opposed the creation of distinct "tiers" of equal protection analysis.[20] But this was not because he wanted a method of reviewing legal classifications in which one size fits all. On the contrary: "Instead of applying a 'mid-level' form of scrutiny in all sex discrimination cases, perhaps the burden is heavier in some than in others."[21] There is "one Equal Protection Clause" for Stevens in the sense that every case about it asks whether the harm done by a classification is out of proportion to its public benefits;[22] as an analytical matter this entailed a sliding scale of review with various analytical distinctions along the way. He suggested that laws connected to physical differences between the sexes might be considered presumptively valid, and those not so connected might be presumptively invalid.[23] The presumptions could then be rebutted with evidence bearing one way or the other on the link between the laws involved and the justifications for them, which in turn would require detailed inquiries into the reasons the laws were passed. In *Califano v. Goldfarb*[24] and *Michael M. v. Superior Court,*[25] Stevens found no permissible justifications for the law involved, and this was a common conclusion for him to reach in sex discrimination cases in subsequent years, but then in *Miller v. Albright*,[26] he voted to uphold a statute providing automatic citizenship to children born out of wedlock to American mothers and foreign fathers, but imposing greater burdens on children born out of wedlock to American fathers and foreign mothers. In this last case he thought the classification reasonable because "the blood relationship to the birth mother is immediately obvious and is typically established by hospital records and birth certificates; the relationship to the unmarried father may often be undisclosed and unrecorded in any contemporary public record." Here as elsewhere, Stevens's preference for evaluating the details of a case rather than deciding it by reference to generalities sometimes has made his votes difficult to predict.

The same penchant for particularity has dominated Stevens's decisions in cases involving the freedom of speech. Broad rules would not do; everything depended on the value and context of the speech involved. Thus Stevens argued in *Young v. American Mini Theatres*[27] and *FCC v. Pacifica Foundation*[28] that indecent speech was of "slight social value" and that "any benefit that may be derived from [it] is clearly outweighed by the social interest in order and morality." The time and place and means of communication all were relevant, too; when the FCC decided that a radio station violated federal law by broadcasting George Carlin reciting his "seven dirty words" monologue, wrote Stevens,

> the Commission's decision rested entirely on a nuisance rationale under which context is all-important. The concept requires consideration of a host of variables. The time of day was emphasized by the Commission. The content of the program in which the language is used will also affect the composition of the audience, and differences between radio, television, and perhaps closed-circuit transmissions, may also be relevant. As Mr. Justice Sutherland wrote, a "nuisance may be merely a right thing in the wrong place,—like a pig in the parlor instead of the barnyard." We simply hold that when the Commission finds that a pig has entered the parlor, the exercise of its regulatory power does not depend on proof that the pig is obscene.[29]

Stevens's jurisprudence of speech is in significant part a matter of distinguishing between parlors and barnyards. His idea that some speech is worth less than other types, and thus easier to regulate, never commanded majority support on the Court, and he did not press the point twenty years later when he wrote a majority opinion in *Reno v. ACLU*[30] striking down restrictions on "indecent transmissions" over the Internet. Here the context was different; Stevens thought the features of the broadcasting spectrum that permitted extensive regulation in that setting did not apply "online." It is less any particular result than this style of decision—microanalysis of the kind of speech at issue and the nature of the restriction on it—that is the constant in Stevens's speech jurisprudence; and again it sometimes has made his decisions hard to predict, though it seems clear that it has left him less inclined to uphold First Amendment claims than some of his colleagues who adhered to more categorical approaches. He prominently staked out positions against protecting hate speech[31] and the burning of American flags[32] and was a consistent vote to uphold restrictive campaign finance laws.[33] When he wrote in these cases, the sound of his thought process tended to be similar, and if it had to be summarized in a few words they would be "it all depends." The extent of the protection depends on the value of the speech, the time and place it is being communicated, and from whom to whom, and then also the value of the other interests involved.[34]

Finally, no inquiry into the Rehnquist Court should fail to take notice of the remarkable divisions it produced in criminal cases. Most such cases may seem minor when considered individually and attract little public attention; taken together, however, they constitute a large and consequential share of the Court's work product. From October Term (OT) 1994 to OT 1999, almost a third of the Court's docket consisted of criminal matters (broadly defined to include review on habeas corpus and other complaints by prisoners),[35] and Stevens's role in them was distinctive. Of the 160 criminal matters the Court decided during that period, about a third resulted in unanimous judgments. In the remaining cases, Stevens voted for the defendant approximately 85 percent of the time; his votes were the mirror image of those cast by Rehnquist, who voted for the government approximately as often. The rate and direction of a justice's dissents likewise are interesting measures of where he stands relative to his colleagues and relative to the Court's center of gravity. In criminal matters decided during the 1994–1999 terms, Stevens wrote or joined dissents in favor of defendants or convicts sixty-four times, including eighteen times by himself. Rehnquist dissented in favor of defendants five times and never by himself. Rehnquist dissented in favor of the government twenty-one times; Stevens dissented in favor of the government in a criminal case just once during this period. (Trivia question: what was the one case?)[36]

For a long time—continuing through the early 1990s[37] and perhaps among some constituencies even now—Stevens nevertheless enjoyed a generally moderate reputation that arose from several sources. The first is that for many years he was sitting next to William Brennan and Thurgood Marshall, whose votes were to the left of Stevens's in some high-profile instances, most notably capital punishment and some cases under the Equal Protection Clause.[38] The second reason is that while Stevens's votes have tended toward the left, his judicial style has tended to be conservative. He generally has favored narrow reasoning and modest holdings. Not always, of course; his dissents to the Court's federalism cases were categorical; likewise his views on religion; and he suggested a broad exemption of campaign finance laws from First Amendment scrutiny on the ground that "money is property; it is not speech."[39] But in many other areas, and when he has been at his most distinctive, Stevens has acted in the model of a common law judge, and this muffled the sound of his liberalism—though in fact his method and politics often have been of a piece, expressing the same values and following from the same vision of the judicial role. The paradox created by Stevens's liberal politics and his conservative methods, in other words, is apparent rather than real. The relationship between them is the most interesting feature of his work and the one that sheds the most light on the majorities he opposed, for it was just this pairing of conservative method and liberal outcomes that has made Stevens the opposite of justices like Antonin Scalia, the most prominent advocate of the expansive method and conservative politics for which the Rehnquist Court is likely to be remembered.

CHARACTERISTIC BEHAVIOR

To consider Stevens's judicial style and its relationship to the substance of his decisions, we need to begin by having a closer look at both. I will illustrate them with some examples from his work in two areas: substantive due process and criminal law.

Substantive Due Process

In *BMW of North America v. Gore,*[40] BMW retouched the paint on the plaintiff's car before selling it to him but did not disclose this. An Alabama jury found BMW liable for fraud and awarded the plaintiff $4,000 in compensatory damages and $4 million in punitive damages. The state's supreme court trimmed the award of punitive damages to $2 million. The Supreme Court reversed, finding the reduced award still excessive; a majority held for the first time that an excessively high award of damages in a civil suit violated the Due Process Clause. Justice Stevens's opinion[41] identified three "guideposts" indicating that BMW did not receive adequate notice of its exposure to such a large award of damages and that the award therefore was grossly excessive. The first guidepost was the reprehensibility of the defendant's conduct; BMW had not shown indifference to public safety, deliberately concealed evidence, or violated any criminal laws. The second guidepost was the ratio between the compensatory damages and punitive damages awarded in the case—500 to 1. Stevens said that "we have consistently rejected the notion that the constitutional line is marked by a simple mathematical formula"; "when the ratio is a breathtaking 500 to 1, however, the award must surely raise a suspicious judicial eyebrow."[42] The third guidepost was the relationship between the size of the punitive damages award and the size of criminal penalties available for comparable misconduct. The maximum criminal penalty for BMW's acts imposed by any state was $5,000–$10,000. Stevens concluded that while "we are not prepared to draw a bright line marking the limits of a constitutionally acceptable punitive damages award," the Court nevertheless was "fully convinced that the grossly excessive award imposed in this case transcends the constitutional limit."[43] The *BMW* analysis is characteristic Stevens: factors are considered that produce a judgment on the facts, rather than a rule; the balancing will have to be repeated by other judges in other cases.

Perhaps more suggestive as an illustration of the intersection between Stevens's method and politics are his opinions in the Court's two leading cases on the existence of a constitutional "right to die." In the *Cruzan* case,[44] he dissented from the Court's decision that the state could forbid the parents of a woman in a vegetative state to withdraw medical support from her. He said that "in answering the important question presented by this tragic case, it is wise not to attempt, by any general statement, to cover every possible phase of the subject,"[45] and that "Nancy Cruzan's liberty to be free from medical treatment must be understood in light of the facts and circumstances particular to her."[46] But his bottom line was broader:

> There is no reasonable ground for believing that Nancy Beth Cruzan has any personal interest in the perpetuation of what the State has decided is her life. As I have already suggested, it would be possible to hypothesize such an interest on the basis of theological or philosophical conjecture. But even to posit such a basis for the State's action is to condemn it. It is not within the province of secular government to circumscribe the liberties of the people by regulations designed wholly for the purpose of establishing a sectarian definition of life.[47]

The sequel to *Cruzan* was *Washington v. Glucksburg,*[48] where the Court held that there is no right to assisted suicide protected by the Constitution. There were eight votes in support of that proposition to a greater or lesser degree. In a solo concurring opinion, however—in many ways a dissent in all but name—Justice Stevens again combined a preference for balancing and case-by-case analysis with indications that he considered physician-assisted suicide a plausible candidate for constitutional protection:

> Although, as the Court concludes today, [the] potential harms [cited by the State] are sufficient to support the State's general public policy against assisted suicide, they will not always outweigh the individual liberty interest of a particular patient. Unlike the Court of Appeals, I would not say as a categorical matter that these state interests are invalid as to the entire class of terminally ill, mentally competent patients. I do not, however, foreclose the possibility that an individual plaintiff seeking to hasten her death, or a doctor whose assistance was sought, could prevail in a more particularized challenge. . . . How such cases may be decided will depend on their specific facts. In my judgment, however, it is clear that the so-called "unqualified interest in the preservation of human life" is not itself sufficient to outweigh the interest in liberty that may justify the only possible means of preserving a dying patient's dignity and alleviating her intolerable suffering.[49]

Stevens also has been a consistent supporter of the notion that the Constitution protects abortion rights.[50] Here his most characteristic work has come in assessing laws that require parental notification or consent when a minor seeks an abortion. When the Court first confronted the issue in *Planned Parenthood of Central Missouri v. Danforth,*[51] Stevens argued in dissent that a state constitutionally could require that a doctor obtain the consent of one of a minor's parents before performing an abortion for her; the state's interest in the welfare of its minors justified such protective measures, he argued, even if that meant parents sometimes would not let the abortion go forward. And a few years later Stevens joined a majority in upholding a state law requiring a physician to notify a minor's parents before performing an abortion.

Ten years after that, however, came *Hodgson v. Minnesota.* In this case the state required that before performing an abortion for a minor, the physician must notify both parents if possible. Stevens, writing for a majority, found the notification requirement unconstitutional. He said that while past cases had approved statutes requiring that a minor's parents be notified, they had not focused specifically on requirements that notification go to *both* parents. Here the district court had taken evidence and found that the two-parent notification requirement could be harmful to a minor when her parents were divorced or separated, or when domestic violence was a problem in the household. Stevens found this compelling.[52] He said that "three separate but related interests—the interest in the welfare of the pregnant minor, the interest of the parents, and the interest of the family unit—are relevant to our consideration of the constitutionality of the 48-hour waiting period and the two-parent notification requirement"; he considered those interests and concluded that "the requirement that both parents be notified, whether or not both wish to be notified or have assumed responsibility for the upbringing of the child, does not reasonably further any legitimate state interest." Either parent presumably would act in the child's best interests and assure that the child's decision would be intelligent; and a two-parent notification requirement "disserves the state interest in protecting and assisting the minor with respect to dysfunctional families."

Thus at various points in his career Stevens has taken the position that it is constitutional to require that a minor obtain *consent* from *one* of her parents before having an abortion (though only if there is a judicial bypass option), but he also took the position that the Constitution forbids a state to require *notification* of *both* parents before a minor has an abortion, regardless of whether there is a judicial bypass option.[53] I will consider later the trends that emerge from Stevens's decisions, but note here his penchant for fine distinctions based on perceived factual consequences and the role of interest balancing as a recurring motif in his work.

Crime: The Rights of Defendants

Capital punishment. Stevens made important contributions to the Court's criminal jurisprudence immediately upon his arrival in 1975. A few years earlier, in *Furman v. Georgia,*[54] the Court had struck down Georgia's death penalty law and generally cast the constitutionality of capital punishment into doubt. Three months after Stevens arrived, the Court heard oral arguments in *Gregg v. Georgia* and companion cases that tested the legality of death penalty statutes passed in response to *Furman.* Stevens delivered joint opinions in the cases with Potter Stewart and Lewis Powell.[55] Taken together, the opinions established several principles: that the decision to impose a death sentence has to be guided by criteria that make its application predictable and reviewable, but that the sentencing court's discretion *not* to impose the death penalty cannot likewise be limited (for example, by mandatory death sentences for certain crimes). Viewed more broadly, the cases introduced a judicial regulatory regime for capital punishment. Certain types of "aggravators" offended the Constitution because they did not sufficiently narrow the class of murderers eligible for execution, but the particulars would need to be considered case by case. Future cases thus established that an instruction that a jury could impose a death sentence if the defendant's crime was "outrageously or wantonly vile, horrible or inhuman" was unconstitutional because it was not narrow enough;[56] likewise the criteria that the crime be "unusually heinous, atrocious, and cruel."[57] But it was all right to impose death sentences for crimes "especially heinous, cruel, or depraved" if those words were construed by the state courts to only cover "depraved" crimes where the perpetrator "relishes the murder, evidencing debasement or perversion," or "shows an indifference to the suffering of the victim and evidences a sense of pleasure in the killing."[58] Also acceptable was another state's limitation of death sentences to defendants who exhibited "utter disregard for human life"—so long as that generality had been narrowed by the state court to refer to a defendant who was a "cold-blooded, pitiless slayer."[59] Stevens did not join all of these opinions; in the last one mentioned, for example, he joined a dissent taking issue with the majority's interpretation of the words "cold-blooded." The point of the examples is to demonstrate the character of the jurisprudence to which Stevens's original position on capital punishment has led. He favored detailed judicial supervision and regulation rather than either abolition or deference, and details are what the Court has argued about ever since.

Habeas corpus. Stevens's tenure on the Court has coincided with a line of decisions constricting the availability of writs of habeas corpus,[60] and he generally has resisted the trend. The question in *Rose v. Lundy,*[61] for example, was what federal judges should do with habeas corpus petitions that contained some claims that had been exhausted in the state courts and some that had not. The Court said such petitions should be dismissed. Stevens alone dissented, arguing that "in considering whether the error in these two exhausted claims was sufficient to justify a grant of habeas corpus relief, the federal court—like the state court—had a duty to look at the context in which the error occurred to determine whether it was either aggravated or mitigated by other aspects of the proceeding," such as the seriousness of the error or the prisoner's failure to exhaust other claims. Said Stevens, "The inflexible, mechanical rule the Court adopts today arbitrarily denies district judges the kind of authority they need to administer their calendars effectively."[62]

Similarly, in *Murray v. Carrier*[63] the question was whether a prisoner should be allowed to bring a claim in a habeas corpus proceeding when his lawyer inadvertently had failed to raise the issue on appeal in the state courts. The Court held that such claims are defaulted; a prisoner must therefore show that the "constitutional violation has probably resulted in the conviction of one who is actually innocent" in order to obtain relief. Stevens dissented from the holding, writing that the inquiry into "cause and prejudice" must be considered "within an overall inquiry into justice,"[64] which in turn "requires a consideration, not only of the nature and strength of the constitutional claim, but also of the nature and strength of the state procedural rule that has not been observed." When a lawyer defaults a claim on appeal, "the state interest in procedural rigor is weaker than at trial, and the transcendence of the Great Writ is correspondingly clearer." In this case—where the petitioner, convicted of rape, claimed that he had been wrongly deprived of a chance to see the victim's statement to the police—Stevens said that the trial judge should hold a hearing to determine whether justice demanded that the petition be considered despite the default.[65]

ASSESSMENT

Stevens and the Common Law

Set to one side the merits of Stevens's decisions examined above and consider more generally the judicial style they represent. Stevens's favored approach at its most characteristic involves identifying the interests bearing on a decision and making an all-things-considered judgment about the balance between them. The judgment may be made by balancing but then take the form of a rule (as in *Hodgson*, the abortion case), or it may involve a kind of balancing that will need to be repeated whenever similar facts arise (as in the *BMW* case). Either way, the resulting judgment—even if it takes the form of a rule—tends to be relatively narrow and fact-specific. Stevens also has a taste for fine constitutional distinctions. The law of abortion rights and the law of capital sentencing are full of niceties supported and often written by him: requiring notification of one of a minor's parents before performing an abortion is constitutional, but requiring notification of both parents is unconstitutional. A judge should be allowed to impose a capital sentence when a jury has declined to do so, but only if he has found by clear and convincing evidence that virtually no reasonable person would have decided otherwise.

Distinctions like these often seem unfathomable as interpretations of constitutional or statutory text; they become comprehensible only by reference to a different model—that of the common law judge. All of the justices must partly

regard themselves in that way at times. The clauses of the Constitution are interpreted by cases; the cases themselves are "constitutional law," and they rather
than the constitutional text routinely become the focus of analysis in later
cases.[66] But not all case-based jurisprudence is quite common law jurisprudence;
even in a system of case law, new questions can be answered generally or specifically. Justice Scalia has praised the generality provided by decisions in the form
of rules and interpretive methods that lend themselves to rule-like holdings.[67]
Stevens, however, favors a common law approach in the strong sense of making
narrow, fact-bound decisions and also in the strong sense of preferring to reason
about reasonableness without being overmuch distracted by the project of interpreting whatever texts are on point. (Against this appraisal it is natural to point
to his opinion in the *Chevron* case, which gave rise to an important rule and has
become one of his most oft-cited decisions; but as later became clear, Stevens did
not intend for that opinion to have quite the meaning that it came to acquire.)[68]

Another aspect of the distinction between case law and common law
involves the extent to which a justice focuses on answering questions or on
deciding *cases,* and—relatedly—the extent to which he gives the facts of a case
in which a question arises a leading role or pushes them into the background. For
most of the Court most of the time, cases are regarded as more or less suitable
"vehicles" for deciding questions that need to be answered for the sake of uniformity or for other reasons. Stevens has seemed less likely than his colleagues
to treat cases as vehicles, however, and more likely just to treat them as cases in
the same way a court of appeals judge would. The most important thing is to get
each case decided right on all its facts; Stevens fit Holmes's description of the
common law judge as one who "decides the case first and determines the principle afterwards."[69]

The common law preferences associated with Stevens are in some respects
an awkward fit on the Supreme Court. In most areas the Court takes too few
cases to close in on the law itself one case at a time; its decisions about any given
subject will not be numerous enough to constitute the sort of edifice or "grown
order" often thought to be a payoff of the common law.[70] Narrow decisions therefore leave the task of working out implications case by case to judges in lower
courts. Especially if those courts are applying standards with discretionary content (think of the *BMW* test or of Stevens's argument in *Murray v. Carrier* that
cases like the petitioner's all necessitate an inquiry into what justice requires),
the resulting decisions are likely to lack uniformity. The disuniformities may be
especially persistent when the Court declines to range into an area—for example,
punitive damages—for many years at a time.[71]

Although the Court's use of a common law approach may not have all the
systemic benefits associated with traditional common law, it may have some
other advantages. One has to do with humility. It may be that judges are better at
deciding how cases should come out than they are at answering general questions
of law and so should prefer the former to the latter whenever there is a choice. A

decision about a *case* can be grounded in factual details that give it a firmer basis than an abstract statement of law is likely to have; true, that leaves more work to be done by other judges in subsequent cases—but then they, too, should be deciding just their cases rather than answering questions. Stevens once put it this way: "When we follow our traditional practice of adjudicating difficult and novel constitutional questions only in concrete factual situations, the adjudications tend to be crafted with greater wisdom. Hypothetical rulings are inherently treacherous and prone to lead us into unforeseen errors; they are qualitatively less reliable than the products of case-by-case adjudication."[72]

The approach that Stevens favors maximizes, however, the importance of the judge; he and his powers of judgment are likely to be necessary in every case, and the quality of the result in a case will depend on his skill at balancing the relevant factors. Stevens's method thus implies both a conservative and an expansive judicial role. He decides little in the case at hand, stating the result on the facts but not saying too much about how the law would apply in other circumstances. In this sense Stevens is a minimalist. There is a different sense of minimalism, of course, that involves limiting the role of the courts and judges in giving restrictive or detailed instructions to other branches of government; minimalism in this sense often can be achieved through rules. But Stevens's approach ensures a large role for other judges in adjudicating similar controversies that arise in the future. He assigns a narrow, case-bound role to himself and to any given judge, but a correspondingly large role to judges generally, who are left with a broad mandate of supervision (for example, of punitive damages, of habeas corpus petitions, and of abortion regulations) and also with substantial discretion in conducting that supervision case by case. Not surprisingly, in many areas of law Stevens then favors deference to judges when they make those calls.[73]

Stevens's favored approach to lawmaking has the benefit of ensuring that no legal decision gets made without at least one judge satisfying himself that it actually makes sense—that the purpose and logic of the doctrine involved are expressed in the outcome of the case. It also means that when a factual variant arises, the judge deciding what to do with it will have a free hand to decide it "right" in view of the interests behind the doctrine; he will not be constrained to mechanically apply a rule that may be a bad fit to unexpected circumstances. But of course there are costs of all this. Maximizing the role of the judge makes it harder for parties to know what the law is, whether they are trying to settle a lawsuit or plan their affairs in advance of litigation; the consequences of their decisions will depend on how the judge they draw balances the interests involved. Second and relatedly, requiring fresh acts of judgment in every case makes it more likely that similar cases will be decided differently just because they are brought before different judges. Like cases may yield different results.[74] Last, although deciding cases narrowly lets future judges adapt the law to new circumstances, it also creates opportunities for inconsistency; the next judge—or indeed the same judge—may be able to wriggle out of the prior holding without much trouble, making it a less valuable precedent. Stevens' own jurisprudence is an example. He was unusually prone to voting differently in cases that appeared similar to the naked eye because he would find the first case a little different from the second; uncharitable observers sometimes felt that his jurisprudence started from scratch each term.

In short, Stevens weights the importance of enabling courts to do precise, individualized justice more heavily than the importance of avoiding the costs and abuses that rules prevent. The large judicial role that he favors implies an idealistic view of the capacities of humans in robes. Thus in his dissent to *Bush v. Gore*,[75] Stevens said he regarded the majority's lack of respect for the impartiality of judges as the most bothersome feature of its decision:

> What must underlie petitioners' entire federal assault on the Florida election procedures is an unstated lack of confidence in the impartiality and capacity of the state judges who would make the critical decisions if the vote count were to proceed. . . . The endorsement of that position by the majority of this Court can only lend credence to the most cynical appraisal of the work of judges throughout the land. It is confidence in the men and women who administer the judicial system that is the true backbone of the rule of law.[76]

Nobody would deny the importance of public confidence in judges, but it is particularly characteristic of Stevens to *identify* the rule of law with a sense of confidence in the frontline people who apply law to fact. A lover of rules like Justice Scalia would identify the rule of law precisely with distrust of any given individuals and with attempts to create rules that constrain their discretion whenever feasible;[77] Stevens likely would consider that emphasis unrealistic. In a speech delivered shortly after his arrival at the Court, Stevens said that his former teacher, Leon Green, had a "special influence on my understanding of the law"; he then described Green's view that "any workable system of law depends as heavily on the quality of the persons who administer it as on the form that particular rules take."[78]

Stevens and Pragmatism: The Value of Facts, Details, and Distinctions

Stevens's judicial style reflects a preference for complexity, subtlety, and accuracy in individual cases over predictability, clarity, finality, and cheapness. He generally is prepared to make an inquiry as complicated as need be to capture the considerations he thinks relevant, even if this approach makes the operation of the resulting test hard to predict; again the *BMW* case is an example. Stevens's preference for accuracy over finality also is visible in his habeas corpus opinions; there and elsewhere he tends to weight accuracy heavily vis-à-vis administrative costs.[79] He revels in doctrinal subtleties and chastises his colleagues when they trade them away for clarity, as *RAV v. City of St. Paul*[80] illustrates. In that case the majority struck down a law punishing "hate speech" because it prohibited "otherwise permitted speech solely on the basis of the subjects the speech addresses."[81] Stevens objected that the majority's approach had "simplistic appeal," but did not do justice to the case law. He also rejected Justice White's argument that "fighting words" are an entirely unprotected category of speech, concluding that this approach "sacrifices subtlety for clarity and is, I am convinced, ultimately unsound," that "the concept of 'categories' fits poorly with the complex reality of expression," and that "the categorical approach does not take seriously the importance of *context.*"[82]

These preferences all bear on the claim often made that Stevens is a "pragmatist"[83]—indeed, that he is the "heir to Holmes"[84] on the contemporary Court. The "pragmatist" label often is used in unhappily vague ways, but it generally is associated with a taste for facts and consequences and distaste for abstractions and theories. Stevens is indeed more likely than his colleagues to pore over the facts in the record of a case and tie his proposed resolution to them snugly. He worries about how legal rules actually will play out, which is why he was ready to say that the Constitution allows a state to require that one parent be notified before a minor gets an abortion but forbids a requirement that both parents be notified: he thought that the practical benefits of notifying one parent rather than two were likely to be small, and that the harm to the child in certain types of families might be great if both parents had to be notified. This is a good example of pragmatism if "pragmatic" is defined in negative form—a disinclination to make decisions by pushing legal concepts around. But in that sense all of the justices probably are pragmatists. Even one who dismisses abortion rights because they are not mentioned in the Constitution can be understood as a pragmatist if the choice of that interpretive strategy can be traced to a concern about consequences, as it can be, at least partially, in Justice Scalia's case.[85]

Pragmatism might be given more specific affirmative content if defined as a close interest in the practical consequences of a decision and the facts bearing on it, and a comparative lack of interest in abstractions like legitimacy or fidelity (except insofar as indifference to those concepts has identifiable concrete consequences of its own). But the facts then of interest to a pragmatist cannot be just the facts of the case; they must also be facts about various ways of making decisions and their consequences. As Judge Posner puts it, "The relevant consequences to the pragmatist are long run as well as short run, systemic as well as individual, the importance of stability and predictability as well as of justice to the individual parties."[86] A constitutional jurisprudence that draws a lot of fine distinctions in the name of practicality creates practical problems of its own. It requires a level of detailed knowledge about the world that is likely to be hard for appellate judges to come by. A member of the Supreme Court is in an especially awkward position to "do" pragmatism, in the sense of crafting minute doctrinal distinctions tailored to the facts of the world being regulated, because he rarely will have the knowledge required to make precise and accurate judgments of that sort. One of the counsels of pragmatism is that judges should make their judgments at a level of abstraction commensurate with their institutional competence. The parental notification cases are an example; if the issue must be constitutionalized, the costs and benefits of notifying one parent or two might seem better estimated by legislatures or by trial judges case by case than by Supreme Court justices speculating in the large. This was a situation where Stevens's preference for distinctions got the better of his preference for leaving judgments in the hands of frontline judges.

It would not be fair to complain that Stevens *isn't* pragmatic. A fair complaint would have to be stated as a criticism of the trade-offs his particular brand of pragmatism entails. Pragmatism, like economics, requires notions about what to value that must be imported from outside itself; otherwise it is just an unhelpful injunction to do what works without criteria for deciding what "works" means when it is controversial.[87] Sometimes a consensus about consequences may be so robust that the pragmatist label has meaning on its own, in the same way that economic analysis of a problem means something clear when, but only when, there is a background consensus about what ends to pursue. But in an environment like the Supreme Court where values and ends are contested as a matter of course, labeling someone a pragmatist is uninformative without more. The more that is needed is a maximand—that is, a specification of the consequences the judge regards as important. Stevens is an example. He is a pragmatist, but of a sort that greatly values accuracy in individual cases and exactitude in doctrine: microperfectionism.

Consider what the following Stevensisms have in common: (1) his decision that punitive damage awards should be reviewed by judges to see if they are unreasonable in view of three factors laid out in his opinion; (2) his opinions arguing that instead of rules denying review in various types of habeas corpus cases, the Court should give trial judges discretion to balance the interests in each case; (3) his frequent preference for deciding cases on their facts rather than answering questions in the large;[88] and (4) his habit of writing separate concurring or dissenting opinions more often than any of his colleagues. What these behaviors evidence is the tremendous significance of correctness in individual cases, and particularly individual *judgments,* in Stevens's vision of law—individual judgment as a duty, a necessity, and an object of faith. He estimates the number of mistakes caused by rules highly or weights them heavily or both; he reckons the "error costs" associated with individual judgments as relatively small or weights them lightly or both. So far as he is concerned, a decision that sacrifices individualized accuracy for clarity and predictability does not work well. Yet of course there are those who think Stevens's opinions are the ones that do not work precisely because they create too much unpredictability. His opinions reduce error costs of one type and increase those of another. When you have decided which types of errors trouble you more—because of their likely size or felt importance—you will know whether to conclude that Stevens was a *good* pragmatist.

Stevens's favored brand of pragmatism fits him into a larger line of twentieth-century debates about how best to do law. It is the difference between those who prefer choice of law rules like *lex loci delicti* and those who prefer the "most significant contacts" test of the Second Restatement, the interest balancing of which resembles many of Justice Stevens's constitutional opinions. The general repudiation of mechanical rules in favor of functional analysis generally is associated with the rise of legal realism[89] and, occasionally, pragmatism.[90] Again, the association with pragmatism makes sense if interest balancing is viewed as a repudiation of formalism—for example, of the understanding that the law of the place of the wrong always governs a tort case for reasons related to natural law. But whether interest balancing is *good* pragmatism depends on how its consequences compare to the consequences of alternatives, including the consequences of the formalistic approach, and a comparison of the consequences requires opinions about which sorts of problems one prefers to have: the crudity of the rule or the indeterminacy of the standard. Stevens often argued for the constitutional equivalent of interest balancing approaches to conflicts of laws; criticisms of his jurisprudence sound very much like the criticisms of the Second Restatement. He seemed to think like a pragmatist of the mid-twentieth-century school, meaning that the values he used to assess consequences were individualized accuracy and fairness, a relatively low degree of concern about administrative cost and predictability, and a high degree of trust in frontline judges to apply standards correctly. His approach to judging did not really catch on for the same reason that the net benefits of the conflict of laws revolution remained controversial by the end of the century[91]—not because either of the approaches reflected a want of pragmatism, but because in their pragmatism they struck a balance between priorities that was in questionable keeping with the mainstream values of the times, which weighted clarity, finality, predictability, and generality as more important virtues than those approaches did.

By the same token, the comparisons of Stevens to Holmes and *his* pragmatism seem inapt. Holmes did often speak of the law as involving matters of degree rather than absolutes; he was a skeptic about grand theories, and Stevens generally did not have much use for those either. But the pragmatism of Holmes was a tougher and more brutal variety than anything in Stevens's work. Holmes had a greater appreciation of the value of predictability: "Precisely my skepticism, my doubt as to the absolute worth of a large part of the system we administer, or of any other system, makes me very unwilling to increase the doubt as to what the court will do." The only legal value that could be "assumed as certainly to be wished," he once said, was "that men should know the rules by which the game will be played."[92]

Holmes also had a large appreciation of the practical value of rules. A good example is the *Goodman* case,[93] where he held that it was contributory negligence as a matter of law for a driver to fail to "stop, look, and listen" before entering onto the railroad tracks where he was hit by the defendant's train; likewise the general discussion that foreshadowed that opinion in *The Common Law.*[94] Holmes worried about judges who excessively left questions of reasonableness to juries, for then they "simply confess their inability to state a very large part of the law which they required the defendant to know, and would assert, by implication, that nothing could be learned by experience."[95] Of course Holmes was speaking of the role of juries in the common law, whereas Stevens fought his battles in the arena of federal statutory and constitutional law; but as we have seen, Stevens has brought a common law approach to his work, and the point of Holmes's argument just quoted is similar to Scalia's criticism of federal judges who, by use of standards rather than rules, leave too many questions to be decided by later judges: "At the point where an appellate judge says that the remaining issue must be decided on the basis of the totality of the circumstances, or by a balancing of all the factors involved, he begins to resemble a finder of fact more than a determiner of law. To reach such a stage is, in a way, a regrettable concession of defeat—an acknowledgment that we have passed the point where 'law,' properly speaking, has any further application."[96]

Meanwhile Stevens has been an antipragmatist in a separate sense: he has shown little interest in sacrificing a full airing of his views of a case to secure a majority. "His concern with procedural safeguards was frequently expressed in separate opinions. The number of such opinions in part reflects his deep interest in issues which were to him fundamental, but it also reflects a quality of integrity that is difficult to describe. . . . His conscience literally *forced* him to add the statement of the real basis for his vote."[97] That description was not written about Stevens; it is a description written *by* Stevens about his old boss, Justice Rutledge, when Stevens was a young lawyer in Chicago. Apparently Stevens admired Rutledge's practice well enough not only to emulate it but to surpass it.[98] This seems to reflect a want of pragmatism more in the colloquial sense of "realpolitik" than in the jurisprudential sense. Stevens's penchant for idiosyncratic grounds of decision may tend to minimize his legacy in the long run; while Holmes was the Great Dissenter, Stevens was the Great Concurrer-in-Part, taking "yes, but" positions that may inspire some others to a similar sort of rigor but do not lend themselves to the creation of schools of thought. Indeed, this approach is consistent with a jurisprudential rather than colloquial pragmatism, so long as it is a pragmatism that values the quest for accurate individual judgments in each case above almost all else.

METHOD AND POLITICS

The remaining issue I want to consider is the relationship between Stevens's methods and his politics. We have seen that his liberalism frequently is expressed through interest balancing, which gives it the look of moderation in any given case and can blunt its consequences. A reading of any one of Stevens's opinions likely would not suggest what his judicial politics are; they emerge from the pattern of results taken together. The natural question is whether his politics are a product of his method (or vice versa) or whether they are independent variables. I do not think they are entirely independent, especially in the criminal cases where Stevens most obviously staked out territory to the left of his colleagues during the 1990s. It is true that rules and standards, and general and specific answers to questions, often can be put in the service of either liberalism or conservatism. The Warren Court often spoke generally and through rules rather than balancing tests, just as the Rehnquist Court did; Justice Brennan often preferred rules to standards.[99] "No capital punishment" is as clear—clearer, actually—as a rule treating capital punishment as no different from imprisonment from the standpoint of the Eighth Amendment. So no particular political pattern necessarily follows from a preference for rules. At a sufficiently general level the same point can be made about standards; as Professor Sullivan has shown, standards have at times been the preferred tools of conservatives.[100] But it would be too strong to infer from this a random relationship between politics and method. Some substantive values are peculiarly suited to expression through certain methods and not through others.

In Stevens's case, we have seen that his preference for standards over rules seems an outgrowth of a larger set of values: a heavy valuation of accuracy in individual cases; a sense that faith in the judgment of judges is justified, necessary, and to be counted upon rather than the occasions for it minimized; and a comparatively low valuation of the clarity, finality, and low administrative costs that rules and generalizations provide. Those values do not always translate into clear substantive preferences, but sometimes they will, especially in the criminal matters where Stevens was the later Rehnquist Court's most liberal member. A judge whose answer always is "sometimes" will consistently tug away from a majority trying hard to give a firm "no"; in any area where new claims are asserted—substantive due process cases are a natural example—Stevens's approach makes it more likely that they will survive and thus seems to pull to the left, because he is unlikely ever to shut the door all the way or say "never." Likewise, a justice who favors a large role for judges in balancing interests will regularly be at odds with a Court trying to reduce the role and significance of federal judges in reviewing state criminal convictions. A court can make rules that erode finality and compel the courts to be more generous to defendants, as well as rules that create finality and limit defendants' right to appeal. But it is difficult to advance the cause of finality and cost savings *without* rules, and those were things the Rehnquist Court cared very much about.

We saw earlier that in criminal cases on which the later Rehnquist Court was not unanimous, Stevens voted for the defendant about 85 percent of the time. Most of the votes he cast for the government in these cases concerned the definition of some element of a crime—for example, whether a defendant "carries a firearm" in violation of 42 U.S.C. 924(c) when he keeps it in the glove compartment of his car.[101] In cases like these,[102] Stevens was not particularly likely to be helpful to defendants, yet Scalia was:[103] he dissented in almost all of those cases where Stevens voted in a majority that favored the government's position. This pattern can be explained largely by reference to the values discussed above that drive the justices' decisions. A decision about whether to define an element of a crime more or less helpfully to a defendant does not bear on the trade-off that causes Stevens and the conservatives to disagree so often; it is not obvious which decision about the gun in the glove compartment would be more likely to result in clarity, predictability, finality, low administrative burdens, fairness, or accuracy. Those concerns become very important and have more obvious implications in cases involving the procedures bearing on the conviction and treatment of criminals, which are the cases where Stevens now is well to the left of his colleagues. The question in those cases, viewed most generally, is the extent of the sacrifices—in time, money, and the risk that a guilty defendant will escape his just deserts—that are justified for the sake of giving defendants more opportunities to protest their innocence and contest the fairness of the proceedings against them.

These considerations describe both the nature of Stevens's liberalism and also the limitations of it. He is not a crusader for social justice or for civil liberties. He is a lawyerly type who regards his job as maximizing the accuracy and fairness of decisions in individual cases, so it is natural enough that his reaction to capital punishment was to micromanage rather than abolish it. Conservatives dislike his priorities and think he underestimates the costs of this approach, but it also makes him a frustrating if admired figure for ardent civil libertarians. Stevens has been a nibbler who prefers inconspicuous rulings to grand gestures, and it is frustrating to have a nibbler as the champion of one's hopes at the Court.

The other peculiarity of Stevens's usual penchant for casebound adjudication is that it coexists with an occasional tendency in the opposite direction. In certain politically charged areas noted at the start of this chapter, he is prone to offering rather immodest declarations of law—that property is not speech, for example, or that antiabortion legislation runs afoul of the Establishment Clause. Indeed, at times it seems that there are two strands in his judicial character: the instincts of the common law judge, but also the instinct for the grand statement that occasionally got the better of him. It probably is too early to say for sure whether those forays into grandeur will turn out to have been ahead of their time or will be confirmation of the soundness of Stevens's more usual aversion to them. At this writing it seems most likely that when students of the Court remember Stevens fondly, they will think of him in the common law mode that was his more usual signature. Whether or not it is the best way to be a Supreme Court justice, it is what he did best.

CONCLUSION: STEVENS AND LEGAL REALISM

As mentioned at the outset, Justice Stevens has occupied the seat held for the previous thirty-six years by William O. Douglas. The two men lend themselves to interesting and amusing comparisons. Both finished their careers regarded as the ranking liberals on their respective Courts in both politics and seniority, rather more surprisingly in Stevens's case. Both have been described as justices in the common law tradition,[104] rather more surprisingly in Douglas's case. Both were individualists who showed little interest in compromising to create coalitions, and both may have seen their influence suffer as a result. And yet in other respects they are perfect opposites. Stevens has been a conservative in method, Douglas a conservationist but not a conservative in anything. Stevens revels in doctrinal subtleties; Douglas was atheoretical and during most of his judicial career had little use for doctrine. Stevens has been considered the judge's justice, Douglas the "anti-judge";[105] Stevens is a lawyer, Douglas a crusader. Taken together they illustrate the great range of meanings that "liberalism" can have when applied to a member of the Court—and perhaps finally the uselessness of the term.

Douglas also was the Court's archrealist. He writes of a formative moment soon after he joined the Court when the chief justice, Charles Evans Hughes, "made a statement to me which at the time was shattering but that over the years turned out to be true: 'Justice Douglas, you must remember one thing. At the constitutional level where we work, ninety percent of any decision is emotional. The rational part of us supplies the reasons for supporting our predilections.'" Douglas went on to gain fame precisely for his habit of writing his point of view into the law without much mediation through doctrine or other legal materials. Justice Stevens was the other way, as suggested by one of his dissents:

> Some students of the Court take for granted that our decisions represent the will of the judges rather than the will of the law. This dogma may be the current fashion, but I remain convinced that such remarks reflect a profound misunderstanding of the nature of our work. Unfortunately, however, cynics—parading under the banner of legal realism—are given a measure of credibility whenever the Court bases a decision on its own notions of sound policy, rather than on what the law commands.[106]

And yet despite himself Stevens has been a marvelous study in realism. Here was the lawyerly judge, meticulously scrutinizing the facts and doctrine of each case and eschewing ideology and frequently offering idiosyncratic reasoning and arguments—and yet arriving at *results* in most politically sensitive areas that were about as predictable as those reached by Chief Justice Rehnquist, who at times has been accused of partisanship in rather blunt language.[107] Stevens's combination of meticulous methods and predictable outcomes can be understood as a lesson in how a minimalist style can give great sway to the underlying preferences of its user, though I do not mean to suggest that his colleagues were more constrained by their maximalism. More broadly it shows the difficulty any justice faces in preventing his decisions from being driven by his own values. A judge who eschews theory in favor of practical reason still cannot avoid expressing his own preferences through his decisions and cannot avoid the predictability that results—or at least a *justice* cannot. Judges in lower courts answer easier questions—that is, questions on which the legal materials bear clearly enough that most judges would answer them the same way. Those judges also are constrained by the chain of command. They have to worry about reversal and are bound by what the Court already has said in ways that the justices are not. But obedience to the will of the law generally does not produce answers to the kinds of questions the Supreme Court has to answer; decisions require background beliefs about the scope and style of a well-made decision and about the weight to give to the values in conflict in any case that finds its way onto the Court's docket. Those weights—the weights that very often separate Rehnquist from Stevens—generally cannot be found in the law itself. They have to be imported by the judge, implicitly or explicitly, consciously or not, which is why it so often was easy to guess where Stevens would come out on a question without knowing anything about the many factual or doctrinal details that he would rely on to get there.

There is no cause for embarrassment in this. It could not be otherwise. Or perhaps it could; for while a judge cannot avoid expressing values through his legal decisions, he can do it in ways more or less reverential to the forms of law. That is a principal difference between Douglas and Stevens. Douglas was a self-conscious legal realist and so was prone to express his views without mediating them much through legal forms. Stevens, too, has expressed his values through his decisions, but he has done it humbly. He played the law game; he took it very seriously; regardless of what he was saying, he generally said it in the language of picky, realist-hating analysis of doctrine and facts. This has been a salutary insistence. It has ensured that if his values were going to exert an influence on his decisions, they would have to be transformed along the way into a shape that would constrain the scope of their consequences and leave room for the values and choices of others. We learn from Stevens that what Hughes said to Douglas probably was true, but that judges do better by doubting and hedging against it than they do by trying to internalize it.

Yet while Douglas illustrates some of the hazards of trying to "do" realism, Stevens may illustrate some of the hazards of trying to "do" pragmatism of a certain type. It is doubtful that Stevens is a pragmatist in a self-conscious sense, but he has seemed to try to deliberately make decisions that would create the most reasonable results on the facts as he understood them. This strategy may sound sensible, but his jurisprudence suggests that a quest of this sort for "what works" may be too direct for its own good. Its benefits are obvious in the case at hand, while its costs may be long-run, less visible, and very significant. In Stevens's hands, at least, the approach has created unpredictability; it also has been expensive, as it promoted an extensive role for judges in human affairs, and it sometimes has required judgments and distinctions that Supreme Court justices are not in a particularly good position to make. Difficulties of this general nature often crop up when pragmatism takes the brute form of attempts to maximize the good too deliberately and directly. Put more generally, formalisms and generalities can serve valuable purposes and in some cases generate better results—better law, even judged pragmatically—than direct efforts to "be pragmatic" in a crude sense by weighing costs and benefits in every case.

Stevens's legacy is likely to be mixed in just the way these trade-offs suggest. He is an easy figure to admire, because a love of fairness in each individual case is an easy virtue to appreciate. But admiration and emulation are different things, and around Stevens there probably will always linger a sense that he also is a study in the limits and perils of pointillism as a style on the Supreme Court. As much as it is associated with fairness, his jurisprudence also will be associated with doctrinal unpredictability, a certain ad hoc quality, and a level of influence that—in part for those reasons—turned out to be minor.

NOTES

1. See, e.g., *Whitman v. American Trucking Associations,* 531 U.S. 457, 486 (2000) (Thomas, J., concurring); *United States v. Hubbell,* 530 U.S. 27, 49 (2000) (Thomas, J., concurring); *Saenz v. Roe,* 119 S.Ct. 1518, 1538 (1999) (Thomas, J., concurring); *Eastern Enterprises v. Apfel,* 524 U.S. 498, 538 (1998) (Thomas, J., concurring); *White v. Illinois,* 502 U.S. 346, 366 (1992) (Thomas, J., concurring).

2. See *United States v. Lopez,* 514 U.S. 549, 602 (1995) (Stevens, J., dissenting); *United States v. Morrison,* 529 U.S. 598 (2000).

3. *Kimel v. Florida Board of Regents,* 528 U.S. 62, 97–98 (2000) (Stevens, J., dissenting).

4. 492 U.S. 490, 566 (1989) (concurring opinion).

5. See, e.g., *Santa Fe Independent School District v. Doe,* 120 S.Ct. 2266 (2000); *Wallace v. Jaffree,* 472 U.S. 38 (1985); *Employment Division v. Smith,* 494 U.S. 872 (1990); *City of Boerne v. Flores,* 521 U.S. 507, 536–537 (1997).

6. See, e.g., *Committee for Public Education and Religious Liberty v. Regan,* 444 U.S. 646, 671 (1980) (dissenting opinion); *Wolman v. Walter,* 433 U.S. 229, 264 (1977) (concurring in part and dissenting in part); *County of Allegheny v. ACLU,* 492 U.S. 573, 651n7 (concurring in part and dissenting in part).

7. *City of Boerne v. Flores,* 521 U.S. 507, 536–537 (1997) (concurring opinion); *United States v. Lee,* 455 U.S. 252, 263 (1982) (concurring opinion).

8. 521 U.S., at 536–537, arguing that the Religious Freedom Restoration Act violated the Establishment Clause. For some discussion of the relationship between Justice Stevens's views of the religion clauses, see Michael W. McConnell, "Accommodation of Religion: An Update and a Response to the Critics," *George Washington Law Review* 60 (1992): 685–742, 730n205.

9. See, e.g., *Board of Education of Westside Community Schools v. Mergens,* 496 U.S. 226, 286–288 (dissenting opinion), characterizing religion as a "divisive" force and worrying that "student-initiated religious groups may exert a considerable degree of pressure even without official school sponsorship"; *Santa Fe Independent School District v. Doe,* 120 S.Ct. 2266 (2000), "the delivery of a pregame prayer has the improper effect of coercing those present to participate in an act of religious worship"; see also Stevens's views in *Cruzan v. Director, Missouri Dept. of Health,* 497 U.S. 261 (1990), discussed below.

10. *Regents of the University of California v. Bakke,* 438 U.S. 265 (1978); *Fullilove v. Klutznick,* 448 U.S. 448 (1980); *United Steelworkers v. Weber,* 443 U.S. 193 (1979); *City of Richmond v. J. A. Croson Co.,* 488 U.S. 469 (1989).

11. *Wygant v. Jackson Board of Education,* 476 U.S. 267 (1986); *Miller v. Johnson,* 515 U.S. 900 (1995); *Adarand Constructors v. Pena,* 515 U.S. 200 (1995); *Missouri v. Jenkins,* 515 U.S. 70 (1995).

12. 448 U.S., at 535n5 (dissenting opinion).

13. 476 U.S. 267 (1986).

14. 488 U.S. 469 (1989).

15. 515 U.S., at 242.

16. See *Shaw v. Reno,* 509 U.S. 630 (1993); *Holder v. Hall,* 512 U.S. 874 (1994); *Miller v. Johnson,* 515 U.S. 900 (1995); *Shaw v. Hunt,* 517 U.S. 899 (1996); *Bush v. Vera,* 517 U.S. 952 (1996); *Abrams v. Johnson,* 521 U.S. 74 (1997).

17. 429 U.S. 190, 211 (Stevens, J., concurring).

18. Ibid., at 197.

19. Ibid., at 211.

20. Ibid.

21. *Michael M. v. Superior Court,* 450 U.S. 464, 497n4 (1981) (Stevens, J., dissenting).

22. Ibid.

23. Ibid.

24. 430 U.S. 199 (1977), striking down a provision of the Social Security Act that imposed greater burdens on widowers than on widows seeking to collect benefits.

25. 450 U.S. 464 (1981), upholding a statutory rape law that applied to men but not to women; Stevens dissented.

26. 523 U.S. 420 (1998).

27. 427 U.S. 50 (1976), sustaining a zoning ordinance that forbade the operation of an adult theater within one thousand feet of similar establishment or within five hundred feet of a residential area.

28. 438 U.S. 726 (1978), finding constitutional the FCC's determination that the petitioner's broadcast of obscenities violated federal law.

29. Ibid., at 750–751 (citations and footnote omitted).

30. 521 U.S. 844 (1997).

31. See *R.A.V. v. City of St. Paul,* 505 U.S. 377, 416 (1992) (Stevens, J., concurring in the judgment).

32. See *Texas v. Johnson,* 491 U.S. 397, 436 (1989); *United States v. Eichman,* 496 U.S. 310, 319 (1990) (Stevens, J., dissenting).

33. See, e.g., *FEC v. Colorado Republican Federal Campaign Committee,* 121 S.Ct.

2351 (2001); *Nixon v. Shrink Missouri Government PAC,* 120 S.Ct. 897, 910 (2000) (Stevens, J., concurring); *Colorado Republican Federal Campaign Committee v. FEC,* 518 U.S. 604, 648 (1996) (Stevens, J., dissenting).

34. For a more complete discussion of the intersection between Stevens's judicial style and his speech jurisprudence—and for an excellent general discussion of Stevens—see Frederick Schauer, "Justice Stevens and the Size of Constitutional Decisions," *Rutgers Law Journal* 27 (1996): 543–562.

35. My definition of a criminal matter is expansive; it includes a case like *Hanlon v. Berger,* 119 S.Ct. 1706 (1999), where the plaintiff brought a *Bivens* suit complaining that his Fourth Amendment rights had been violated. Narrower definitions are possible, of course, but would not change the thrust of the numbers offered here.

36. This is a trick question; the answer is *United States v. Lopez,* where a 5 to 4 majority struck down the Gun-Free School Zones Act as beyond Congress's power to pass. *Lopez* is, of course, remembered as a very important decision about federalism; only incidentally was it a criminal case.

37. Robert J. Sickels, *John Paul Stevens and the Constitution* (University Park: Pennsylvania State University Press, 1992), ix, x, 5; Kermit Hall, ed., *The Oxford Companion to the Supreme Court of the United States* (New York: Oxford University Press, 1992), 836 (Stevens was "not easily associated with any particular voting bloc" and was "cast in a centrist, mediating role on an increasingly polarized Rehnquist Court"); Stuart Taylor, "The Last Moderate," *American Lawyer* (June 1990): 48.

38. See, e.g., *Fullilove v. Klutznick,* 448 U.S. 448 (1980); *City of Richmond v. J. A. Croson Co.,* 488 U.S. 469 (1989) (concurring opinion); *Parham v. Hughes,* 441 U.S. 347 (1979); *Rostker v. Goldberg,* 453 U.S. 57 (1981); cf. *Regents of the University of California v. Bakke,* 438 U.S. 265 (1978) (concurring opinion), arguing that the state's affirmative action program violated Title VI of the Civil Rights Act of 1964, and that the Court therefore did not need to reach the constitutional question.

39. *Nixon v. Shrink Missouri Government PAC,* 120 S.Ct. 897, 910 (2000) (Stevens, J., concurring).

40. 517 U.S. 559 (1996).

41. I generally will attribute the views and stylistic choices in opinions, including majority opinions, to their authors.

42. 517 U.S., at 583.

43. Ibid., at 584.

44. *Cruzan v. Director, Missouri Dept. of Health,* 497 U.S. 261, 331 (1990).

45. Ibid., at 331.

46. Ibid.

47. Ibid., at 350.

48. 521 U.S. 702 (1997).

49. Ibid., at 749–750, 752.

50. *Stenberg v. Carhart,* 120 S.Ct. 2597 (2000). Stevens argued in *Planned Parenthood of Southeastern Pennsylvania v. Casey* that the joint opinion of Justices O'Connor, Kennedy, and Souter did not go far enough; he would have held the counseling and spousal notification requirements at issue in that case invalid, as the "troika" did not. See 505 U.S. 833, 912 (1992).

51. 428 U.S. 52, 102 (1976).

52. 497 U.S. 417 (1990). The case also involved the constitutionality of a forty-eight-hour waiting period for abortions; I dispense with that aspect of the decision in order to keep the discussion manageable.

53. The state law in *Hodgson* provided that if its terms were invalidated, they would be replaced by identical provisions but with a "judicial bypass" option enabling the minor to avoid notification by appealing to a judge. A separate majority upheld this fallback position, but Stevens dissented: since the two-parent notification requirement was itself unreasonable, it could not be saved by the option of going to court instead.

54. 408 U.S. 238 (1972).

55. *Gregg v. Georgia*, 428 U.S. 153 (1976); *Proffitt v. Florida*, 428 U.S. 242 (1976); *Jurek v. Texas*, 428 U.S. 262 (1976); *Woodson v. North Carolina*, 428 U.S. 280 (1976); *Roberts v. Louisiana*, 428 U.S. 325 (1976).

56. *Godfrey v. Georgia*, 486 U.S. 356 (1980).

57. *Maynard v. Cartwright*, 486 U.S. 356 (1988).

58. *Walton v. Arizona*, 497 U.S. 639, 655 (1990) (internal quotation marks omitted).

59. *Arave v. Creech*, 507 U.S. 463 (1993).

60. In 1995 Congress passed the Anti-Terrorism and Effective Death Penalty Act, which codified many principles that the Court had announced over the preceding twenty years in interpreting the habeas corpus statute.

61. 455 U.S. 509 (1982).

62. Ibid., at 546 (dissenting opinion).

63. 477 U.S. 478 (1986).

64. Ibid., at 505 (concurring opinion).

65. Ibid., at 506.

66. See David A. Strauss, "Common Law Constitutional Interpretation," *University of Chicago Law Review* 63 (1996): 877–936.

67. Antonin Scalia, "The Rule of Law as a Law of Rules," *University of Chicago Law Review* 56 (1989): 1175–1188.

68. See Gary Lawson, *Cases and Materials on Administrative Law* (New York: Aspen Law and Business, 1999), xx.

69. Oliver W. Holmes Jr., "Codes and the Arrangements of Law," *Harvard Law Review* 44 (1931): 725–737.

70. See Mark F. Grady, "Positive Theories and Grown Order Conceptions of the Law," *Southwestern University Law Review* 23 (1994): 461–467.

71. This is one of Justice Scalia's complaints about standards; see "The Rule of Law," 1178–1179.

72. *New York v. Ferber*, 458 U.S. 747, 781 (1982) (concurring opinion).

73. See, e.g., *Burger v. Kemp*, 483 U.S. 776 (1987); *Bishop v. Wood*, 426 U.S. 341 (1976); *O'Sullivan v. Boerckel*, 526 U.S. 838 (1999) (dissenting opinion); cf. *Moore v. City of East Cleveland*, 431 U.S. 494, 514n1 (concurring opinion).

74. Cf. Kathleen Sullivan, "The Justice of Rules and the Justices of Standards," *Harvard Law Review* 106 (1992): 22–123, at 62. ("A decision favoring rules thus reflects the judgment that the danger of unfairness from official arbitrariness or bias is greater than the danger of unfairness from the arbitrariness that flows from the grossness of rules.")

75. 531 U.S., at x; 121 S.Ct. 525 (2000).

76. 121 S.Ct., at 542 (dissenting opinion).

77. See Scalia, "The Rule of Law."

78. John Paul Stevens, "Some Thoughts about a General Rule," *Arizona Law Review* 21 (1979): 599–605.

79. For another good example, see the opinions in *Landgraf v. USI Film Products,* 511 U.S. 244 (1994).

80. 505 U.S. 377 (1992).

81. Ibid., at 381.

82. Ibid., at 425.

83. Sickels, *John Paul Stevens and the Constitution,* 1; Norman Dorsen, "John Paul Stevens," *Annual Survey of American Law* (1992/1993): xxv–xxvii.

84. Sullivan, "The Justice of Rules," 90.

85. See Antonin Scalia, "Originalism: The Lesser Evil," *University of Cincinnati Law Review* 57 (1989): 849–866.

86. Richard A. Posner, *Overcoming Law* (Cambridge: Harvard University Press, 1995), 400–401.

87. See Ronald Dworkin, "Darwin's New Bulldog," *Harvard Law Review* 111 (1998): 1718–1729; Stanley Fish, "Almost Pragmatism: Richard Posner's Jurisprudence," *University of Chicago Law Review* 57 (1990): 1447–1475.

88. For another good example, see *Hopkins v. Reeves,* 524 U.S. 88 (1998) (dissenting opinion).

89. See Lea Brilmayer, *Conflict of Laws: Foundations and Future Directions,* 2d ed. (Boston: Little, Brown, 1995), chaps. 1–2; Larry Kramer, "Same-Sex Marriage, Conflict of Laws, and the Unconstitutional Public-Policy Exception," *Yale Law Journal* 106 (1997): 1965–2008, at 1992n105.

90. See Patrick J. Borchers, "Conflicts Pragmatism," *Albany Law Review* 56 (1993): 883–912, at 899–901.

91. See Michael H. Gottesman, "Draining the Dismal Swamp: The Case for Federal Choice of Law Statutes," *Georgetown Law Review* 80 (1991): 1–52, at 1–16 and n. 42. In addition, see Joseph W. Singer, "A Pragmatic Guide to Conflicts," *Boston University Law Review* 70 (1990): 731–820, at 731–741.

92. Oliver Wendell Holmes Jr., "Twenty Years in Retrospect," in *The Occasional Speeches of Justice Oliver Wendell Holmes,* ed. Mark DeWolfe Howe (Cambridge: Belknap Press of Harvard University Press, 1962), 154, 155.

93. *Baltimore and O. R. Co. v. Goodman,* 275 U.S. 66 (1927).

94. Oliver Wendell Holmes Jr., *The Common Law* (Boston: Little, Brown, 1881), 110.

95. Ibid.

96. Scalia, "The Rule of Law," 1182.

97. Stevens, "Mr. Justice Rutledge," in Dunham and Kurland, *Mr. Justice,* 319.

98. See Lee Epstein et al., *The Supreme Court Compendium: Dates, Decisions, and Developments,* 2d ed. (Washington, D.C.: Congressional Quarterly Press, 1996), 559–562.

99. See, e.g., *United States v. Leon,* 468 U.S. 897, 928 (1984) (concurring opinion); *New York Times Co. v. Sullivan,* 376 U.S. 254 (1964).

100. See Sullivan, "The Justice of Rules," 96–100.

101. See *Muscarello v. United States,* 118 S.Ct. 1911 (1998).

102. Other examples include *United States v. X-citement Video, Inc.,* 115 S.Ct. 464

(1995); *United States v. O'Hagan,* 117 S.Ct. 2199 (1997); *Bryan v. United States,* 118 S.Ct. 1939 (1998); *Holloway v. United States,* 119 S.Ct. 966 (1999); and *Fischer v. United States,* 120 S.Ct. 1780 (2000).

103. Justice Scalia dissented from the majority view endorsed by Justice Stevens in all of the cases cited in note 102.

104. See Melvin I. Urofsky, "William O. Douglas as a Common Law Judge," *Duke Law Journal* 41 (1991): 133–159.

105. See G. Edward White, "The Anti-Judge: William O. Douglas and the Ambiguities of Individuality," *Virginia Law Review* 74 (1988): 17–88.

106. *Trans World Airlines, Inc. v. Franklin Mint Corp.,* 466 U.S. 243, 282–283 (1984).

107. See Mark V. Tushnet, "A Republican Chief Justice," *Michigan Law Review* 88 (1990): 1326–1334, at 1328.

7

David H. Souter: Liberal Constitutionalism and the Brennan Seat

Thomas M. Keck

On July 23, 1990, President Bush nominated David Souter to replace the retiring Justice William Brennan on the Supreme Court. At the time, no one could have predicted the extent to which this relatively unknown New Hampshire judge would fill Brennan's shoes. No one could have predicted that this Republican appointee, who modeled himself on the great Warren Court dissenter, Justice Harlan, would become a leading advocate of liberal constitutionalism on the Court. But Souter has done just that. Broadly speaking, the two most significant constitutional developments on the Rehnquist Court have been the surprising survival of Warren Court–style liberal judicial activism, on the one hand, and the emergence of a new and distinctive conservative judicial activism, on the other, and in each of these broad contexts, Souter has consistently joined the Court's liberal wing.[1]

Along with Justices Stevens, Breyer, and Ginsburg, Souter has wholeheartedly supported the Court's liberal activism while sharply criticizing its conservative activism. Moreover, he has often led this group's efforts to persuade either O'Connor or Kennedy to provide a crucial fifth vote. Some scholars have described Souter, O'Connor, and Kennedy as a decisive centrist bloc on the conservative Court—particularly after their landmark opinions in *Planned Parenthood v. Casey* (1992) and *Lee v. Weisman* (1992) during Souter's second term—but this characterization is misleading. Souter has disagreed with O'Connor and Kennedy more often than not, and they have moved farther apart over time. His constitutional vision is fundamentally different from theirs, but where they have overlapped, they have generally spoken for the Court. In particular, the four liberal

I would like to thank Earl Maltz for his helpful comments on an earlier draft of this chapter, Akin Owoso for his invaluable research assistance, and John Fliter for sharing his work in progress on Justice Souter.

justices have often been successful in persuading O'Connor or Kennedy or both to join them in endorsing liberal judicial activism in defense of individual liberty and minority rights. Souter has firmly supported the Court's reaffirmation and even extension of landmark liberal precedents from the Warren and early Burger years in cases protecting abortion rights, gender equality, religious freedom, and the like. The *Casey* decision is only the most notable example here.

Souter has tempered Brennan's expansive and evolving rights-based constitutional vision, to be sure, but he has endorsed it to a surprising degree. Like Brennan, Souter has led the Court in defending an evolutionary, common law approach to constitutional interpretation that seeks to enforce those fundamental liberties that are essential to individual human dignity or to democratic governance. Where such principles are not at stake, in his view, the Court should exercise significant deference to the elected branches of government. Like Brennan, then, he has been sharply critical of conservative efforts to impose strict constitutional limits on government regulatory authority in the context of the modern welfare state. Here, however, the liberal justices have been much less successful in garnering a fifth judicial vote, as O'Connor and Kennedy have generally joined their conservative colleagues to form a decisive majority in favor of what might be called "New Right judicial activism" in areas such as federalism and affirmative action. As a result of these two trends, the Rehnquist Court has been exercising its power quite actively in pursuit of both liberal and conservative ends.[2]

Souter has been similar to Brennan in another way as well. Brennan was known for his persistent and often successful attempts to modify opinion drafts, written either by himself or another justice, in search of a five-justice majority for a reading of the Constitution as close as possible to his own.[3] In those few landmark cases of which we have some knowledge of the Rehnquist Court's internal deliberations, Souter has sought to play a similar role. This effort was particularly clear in the two most significant decisions discussed in this chapter — *Casey* and *Bush v. Gore* (2000) — the clearest examples, respectively, of Souter's remarkable success and his dramatic failure.

THE "STEALTH NOMINEE" JOINS THE COURT

President Bush nominated Souter to the Court just three days after Brennan announced his retirement in late July 1990. The fifty-year-old federal appellate judge had a distinguished record of academic achievement and public service, but he was virtually unknown outside the state of New Hampshire. He had served under state attorney general Warren Rudman for a number of years until Republican governor Meldrim Thomson appointed him to replace Rudman as attorney general in 1976. Two years later, Thomson named him as associate justice of the Superior Court of New Hampshire, and after five years as a trial judge, Souter was appointed to the state supreme court by new Republican governor John

Sununu, who had been persuaded to do so by Rudman, now the state's junior U.S. senator.[4] Souter served on the state supreme court until being named by President Bush to the First Circuit Court of Appeals, just two months before Brennan's retirement.

Journalists and scholars have widely interpreted Souter's nomination as an effort by Bush to find a "stealth nominee," someone who was not a well-known conservative ideologue and indeed had left such a sparse public record as to make him difficult to oppose on ideological grounds, but who nonetheless would prove to be a reliable conservative voice on the Supreme Court.[5] Brennan's retirement, after all, was the first since Justice Powell's, and Reagan's nomination of Robert Bork to replace Powell had led to the most divisive Senate confirmation battle in history—and to a stinging political defeat for President Reagan. Bush continued to face a Democratic Senate in 1990, and hence he repeatedly emphasized Souter's "fairness" and judicial temperament and insisted that there should be no "litmus test" for Supreme Court nominees.[6]

Nonetheless, the Court's role in a number of divisive political conflicts, particularly the issue of abortion rights, remained at the forefront of media coverage of the nomination, and President Bush still insisted that he had "selected a person who will interpret the Constitution, and . . . not legislate from the Federal bench."[7] Thus, in his own testimony before the Senate Judiciary Committee, Souter sought to assure the Democratic senators that he was no Robert Bork. He generally succeeded, beginning with the very first question asked of him. When Democratic senator Joseph R. Biden Jr. began by asking about the constitutional right to privacy, a right whose existence Bork had denied, Souter replied, "I believe that the due process clause of the 14th Amendment does recognize and does protect an unenumerated right of privacy." This view was part of his more general belief that due process liberty is not limited to the specific provisions of the Bill of Rights, and that the justices can and should rely on "principles that may be elucidated by the history and tradition of the U.S." Souter distanced himself from at least the most rigid form of Bork's constitutional originalism, emphasizing that the Court should not be bound by the specific intentions in the minds of the framers. Expressly disagreeing with the approach advocated by Scalia in a number of recent cases, Souter testified that the justices should identify the "principle that was intended to be established as opposed simply to the specific application that that particular provision was meant to have by—and that was in the minds of—those who proposed and framed and adopted that provision in the first place." In Souter's view, "principles don't change but our perceptions of the world around us and the need for those principles do." In support of this approach, he presented Justice Harlan as a model, emphasizing his effort to define unenumerated constitutional rights by examining our nation's history and traditions in search of "what might be called a bedrock concept of liberty."[8]

The senators also pressed Souter to articulate his positions on a number of specific constitutional questions. On some issues, he was relatively forthcoming, articulating a moderate posture on both race-conscious affirmative action and the separation of church and state, for example. On the particularly divisive question of abortion rights, however, he declined to indicate how he would decide: "I have not got any agenda on what should be done with *Roe v. Wade* if that case were brought before me. I will listen to both sides of that case. I have not made up my mind." He did observe that "whether I do or do not find [abortion] moral or immoral will play absolutely no role in any decision which I make, if I am asked to make it, on the question of what weight should or legitimately may be given to the interest which is represented by the abortion decision." He also noted, in a statement that would prove significant once he was actually faced with the issue, that to reconsider *Roe* would involve not only its original correctness but also "extremely significant issues of precedent." In reconsidering a precedent, Souter observed, judges need to ask "whether private citizens in their lives have relied upon it in their own planning to such a degree that, in fact, there would be a great hardship to overruling it now."[9]

Souter impressed the senators with his intellect and his moderate views, and he was confirmed without much opposition.[10] His testimony painted a picture, as he described himself, of "a moderate conservative . . . closer to the center than some but still on the right side."[11] The chief conflict among observers, however, was whether Souter's statements on the record could be trusted, or whether he was simply hiding his more conservative views until he secured his seat on the Court. Despite his extensive testimony, many conservatives and liberals alike were confident that Souter would turn out to be a reliably conservative justice.[12] Although he testified that "Justice Brennan is going to be remembered as one of the most fearlessly principled guardians of the American Constitution that it has ever had and ever will have," no one who was listening interpreted his statement to mean that he would follow in Brennan's constitutional footsteps.[13]

During his first term on the Court, this initial impression appeared correct. Souter drafted a relatively small number of opinions, in large part because he did not join the Court until the term's second week and hence struggled to catch up on the work of hiring staff, reading briefs, and the like. Those opinions that he did write, however, and his votes in the other cases as well generally served to solidify a narrow conservative majority on the Court. In the area of criminal procedure, for example, he joined the conservative majority in decisions that allowed the police broad leeway to search for drugs in passengers' belongings on public buses;[14] upheld the warrantless search of a car where the police had probable cause to believe it contained contraband or evidence;[15] allowed the admission of involuntary confessions under harmless error analysis;[16] limited the use of habeas corpus petitions to achieve federal review of state convictions and death sentences;[17] and allowed prosecutors to introduce "victim impact" testimony at capital sentencing hearings. In this last decision, the Court overturned two recent precedents, over a stinging Marshall dissent. Souter wrote separately to note that while he fully agreed with the majority's assessment of the earlier decisions' constitutional error, he would not have voted to overturn these precedents in the absence of some additional, "special justification." In his view, "overruling a precedent of this Court is a matter of no small import, for 'the doctrine of *stare decisis* is of fundamental importance to the rule of law.'" In this case, however, he found a special justification for doing so, in that the earlier decisions had created "an unworkable standard . . . that threatens . . . to produce such arbitrary consequences and uncertainty of application" as to diminish their precedential value.[18]

Souter also voted with the conservative majority in two significant equal protection cases. In *Gregory v. Ashcroft* (1991), the Court ruled that Missouri's mandatory retirement law for judges did not violate either the Age Discrimination in Employment Act or the Equal Protection Clause, and in *Hernandez v. New York* (1991), the Court held that the prosecutorial use of peremptory challenges to exclude Spanish-speaking jurors did not amount to unconstitutional racial discrimination.[19] In perhaps the term's most widely noted case, Souter voted with the conservatives on an important First Amendment issue as well, upholding the Reagan administration's "gag rule," under which doctors in federally funded family planning projects were prohibited from discussing abortion with their patients.[20]

In several other cases, however, Souter gave some indication that he would temper the Court's conservative approach with a dose of moderation. In the First Amendment context, for example, he joined the conservative justices in upholding Indiana's prohibition of nude dancing in *Barnes v. Glen Theatre* (1991), but he refused to join Rehnquist's opinion because it went too far in allowing the regulation of expression to promote the state's interest in "order and morality."[21] In two other cases, Souter joined with Justices O'Connor and Kennedy in a way that suggested their potential emergence as a decisive centrist bloc on the Court. In *Powers v. Ohio* (1991), these three joined the Court's more liberal justices to hold "that a criminal defendant may object to race-based exclusions of jurors effected through peremptory challenges whether or not the defendant and the excluded jurors share the same race."[22] And in *Harmelin v. Michigan* (1991), while these same three justices joined Rehnquist and Scalia to uphold a mandatory minimum sentence of life without parole for drug possession, they refused to join the portion of Scalia's opinion that held that the Eighth Amendment contains no proportionality guarantee, thus rendering the Court's conservative holding a much narrower one.[23]

THE EMERGENCE OF A CENTRIST BLOC?

During Souter's second term, he joined O'Connor and Kennedy in two dramatic decisions that led a number of observers to declare the surprising emergence of a centrist bloc on the Court.[24] In late June 1992, confounding expectations that the increasingly conservative Court would relax the constitutionally required separation of church and state, the Court invalidated the widespread practice of invocation and benediction prayers at public school graduation ceremonies. Over a sharp dissent from Scalia, Kennedy held for a five-justice majority in *Lee v. Weisman* that "at a minimum, the Constitution guarantees that government may not coerce anyone to support or participate in religion or its exercise, or otherwise act in a way which 'establishes a [state] religion or religious faith, or tends to do so,'" and Souter wrote separately to elaborate on his jurisprudential differences with Scalia.[25]

Even more dramatically, just five days later, Souter, O'Connor, and Kennedy issued their remarkable joint opinion in *Casey,* declaring that "the essential holding of *Roe v. Wade* should be retained and once again reaffirmed." These three Republican appointees began their opinion by explicitly rebuffing the Bush administration's request to overturn *Roe.*[26] Reaffirming the constitutional jurisprudence that they had been appointed to abolish, they held that "our law affords constitutional protection to personal decisions relating to marriage, procreation, contraception, family relationships, child rearing, and education. . . . These matters, involving the most intimate and personal choices a person may make in a lifetime, choices central to personal dignity and autonomy, are central to the liberty protected by the Fourteenth Amendment. At the heart of liberty is the right to define one's own concept of existence, of meaning, of the universe, and of the mystery of human life. Beliefs about these matters could not define the attributes of personhood were they formed under compulsion of the State."[27]

Joined also by Blackmun and Stevens to form a majority on these important points, the plurality made two independent arguments for upholding *Roe.* In section 2 of the opinion, they insisted that *Roe* was fundamentally correct in holding that the abortion decision is within the realm of constitutionally protected liberty. Citing a long line of cases, but relying in particular on Harlan's dissenting opinion in *Poe v. Ullman* (1961), they held that the Due Process Clause provides constitutional protection for "'all fundamental rights comprised within the term liberty.'" They acknowledged that "it is tempting, as a means of curbing the discretion of federal judges, to suppose that liberty encompasses no more than those rights already guaranteed to the individual against federal interference by the express provisions of the first eight Amendments to the Constitution. . . . It is also tempting, for the same reason, to suppose that the Due Process Clause protects only those practices, defined at the most specific level, that were protected against government interference by other rules of law when the Fourteenth Amendment was ratified." Just as Souter had testified before the Senate Judiciary Committee, however, they rejected each of these temptations—both Black's textualism and Scalia's modified version of that approach—as inadequate to the task of defining constitutional liberty. In the plurality's decisive view, "neither the Bill of Rights nor the specific practices of States at the time of the adoption of the Fourteenth Amendment marks the outer limits of the substantive sphere of liberty which the Fourteenth Amendment protects."[28] They acknowledged that this approach requires the exercise of "reasoned judgment" but insisted, supported by Harlan, that it "does not mean we are free to invalidate state policy choices with which we disagree."[29]

In section 3 of the opinion, the plurality held that whether or not *Roe* had been correct as an original matter, the principle of stare decisis demanded adherence to it. According to David Garrow's account, Souter drafted this section of the opinion, again picking up on a theme he had emphasized in his confirmation hearings.[30] He wrote that "because neither the factual underpinnings of *Roe*'s central holding nor our understanding of it has changed (and because no other indication of weakened precedent has been shown), the Court could not pretend to be reexamining the prior law with any justification beyond a present doctrinal disposition to come out differently from the Court of 1973." Under these circumstances, "a decision to overrule *Roe*'s essential holding . . . would address error, if error there was, at the cost of both profound and unnecessary damage to the Court's legitimacy, and to the Nation's commitment to the rule of law." In reaching this conclusion, the plurality offered the Court's most extensive and explicit discussion ever of the conditions under which a controversial precedent might legitimately be discarded, a discussion that is worth quoting at length:

> Where, in the performance of its judicial duties, the Court decides a case in such a way as to resolve the sort of intensely divisive controversy reflected in *Roe* and those rare, comparable cases, its decision has a dimension that the resolution of the normal case does not carry. It is the dimension present whenever the Court's interpretation of the Constitution calls the contending sides of a national controversy to end their national division by accepting a common mandate rooted in the Constitution.
>
> The Court is not asked to do this very often, having thus addressed the Nation only twice in our lifetime, in the decisions of *Brown* and *Roe*. But when the Court does act in this way, its decision requires an equally rare precedential force to counter the inevitable efforts to overturn it and to thwart its implementation. Some of those efforts may be mere unprincipled emotional reactions; others may proceed from principles worthy of profound respect. But whatever the premises of opposition may be, only the most convincing justification under accepted standards of precedent could suffice to demonstrate that a later decision overruling the first was anything but a surrender to political pressure, and an unjustified repudiation of the principle on which the Court staked its authority in the first instance. So to overrule under fire in the absence of the most compelling reason to reexamine a watershed decision would subvert the Court's legitimacy beyond any serious question.[31]

With these words, Souter helped craft a successful compromise that preserved the Court's practice of protecting unenumerated constitutional rights, emphasized that this practice was rooted in long-standing legal traditions, acknowledged that it would require the justices to exercise legal judgment, and insisted that this judgment could and would be principled and not partisan.

The plurality's holding was an effective compromise in another way as well: it reaffirmed *Roe*'s central promise that the government cannot legitimately outlaw abortion while also allowing a much greater degree of state regulation of abortion than had been permissible under *Roe*.[32] Their decision to uphold such regulations made clear that Souter, O'Connor, and Kennedy were advancing a vision of judicially enforceable constitutional liberty narrower than Justice Brennan's. As in *Weisman,* Blackmun and Stevens wrote separately to say that they fully joined Souter, O'Connor, and Kennedy's reasoning in striking down the challenged law, but that they would have gone still further. Nonetheless, the plurality opinion in *Casey* has rightly been viewed as an exemplary application of modern fundamental rights jurisprudence.[33] Consider, for example, its concluding statement:

> Our Constitution is a covenant running from the first generation of Americans to us, and then to future generations. It is a coherent succession. Each generation must learn anew that the Constitution's written terms embody ideas and aspirations that must survive more ages than one. We accept our responsibility not to retreat from interpreting the full meaning of the covenant in light of all of our precedents. We invoke it once again to define the freedom guaranteed by the Constitution's own promise, the promise of liberty.[34]

In this case, and a number of others to come, Souter declared his readiness to actively exercise judicial power in defense of constitutional liberty.

SOUTER'S DEFENSE OF LIBERAL ACTIVISM

Due Process Liberty

While Kennedy and O'Connor have tried to limit the reach of their *Casey* opinion, Souter has sought to build on its broad mandate. In *Washington v. Glucksberg* (1997), for example, when the Court unanimously upheld a state statute outlawing physician-assisted suicide, Souter insisted that the Court's holding should be taken as neither a rejection of substantive due process jurisprudence in general nor a final decision on the question of assisted suicide in particular:

> We are dealing with a claim to one of those rights sometimes described as rights of substantive due process and sometimes as unenumerated rights, in view of the breadth and indeterminacy of the "due process" serving as the claim's textual basis. The doctors accordingly arouse the skepticism of those

who find the Due Process Clause an unduly vague or oxymoronic warrant for judicial review of substantive state law, just as they also invoke two centuries of American constitutional practice in recognizing unenumerated, substantive limits on governmental action. . . . The persistence of substantive due process in our cases points to the legitimacy of the modern justification for such judicial review found in Justice Harlan's dissent in *Poe*, . . . while the acknowledged failures of some of these cases point with caution to the difficulty raised by the present claim.

Surveying the Court's long history of substantive due process jurisprudence—beginning with nineteenth-century state court decisions, moving through the Marshall and Taney Courts and the *Lochner* era, to Harlan's opinion in *Poe*—Souter adopted an "understanding of unenumerated rights . . . [which] avoids the absolutist failing of many older cases without embracing the opposite pole of equating reasonableness with past practice described at a very specific level. That understanding begins with a concept of 'ordered liberty,' comprising a continuum of rights to be free from 'arbitrary impositions and purposeless restraints.'"[35]

For Souter, this process of reasoned judgment amounted to a version of the common law method, but confined by two additional constraints. First, "a court is bound to confine the values that it recognizes to those truly deserving constitutional stature, either to those expressed in constitutional text, or those exemplified by 'the traditions from which [the Nation] developed,' or revealed by contrast with 'the traditions from which it broke.'" And second, "it is no justification for judicial intervention merely to identify a reasonable resolution of contending values that differs from the terms of the legislation under review. It is only when the legislation's justifying principle, critically valued, is so far from being commensurate with the individual interest as to be arbitrarily or pointlessly applied that the statute must give way." On the question of assisted suicide, Souter concluded that "while I do not decide for all time that respondents' claim should not be recognized, I acknowledge the legislative institutional competence as the better one to deal with that claim at this time."[36]

Writing for the Court, Rehnquist adopted a very different approach. Beginning with an extremely narrow reading of *Casey*, he framed the issue in *Glucksberg* as whether due process liberty includes "a right to commit suicide which itself includes a right to assistance in doing so," and he held that it does not. Rehnquist insisted that the Court should exercise substantive due process review only with great caution, and he complained that "Justice Souter . . . would largely abandon this restrained methodology, and instead ask 'whether [Washington's] statute sets up one of those "arbitrary impositions" or "purposeless restraints" at odds with the Due Process Clause.'" In his view, Souter's approach would exacerbate "the subjective elements that are necessarily present in due-process judicial review."[37] Rehnquist's opinion was joined not only by Scalia and Thomas, which was not surprising, but also by O'Connor and Kennedy despite its significant tension with their own opinion in *Casey*. Souter's approach was very different, and his debate with Rehnquist in this case replicated an earlier debate between Brennan and Scalia in *Michael H. v. Gerald D.* (1989), and before that, between Harlan and Black in *Griswold v. Connecticut* (1965), over the relative merits of "reasoned judgment" and rule-bound literalism in giving content to due process liberty.

The *Glucksberg* opinions, moreover, made clear that while the conservative vision of judicial restraint in the absence of a clear textual warrant has been widely influential in contemporary constitutional discourse, most of the justices have rejected this vision in favor of Harlan's more flexible approach to defining constitutional liberty. Harlan, of course, was no liberal, but in the structure of contemporary constitutional debate, it is his vision of "reasoned judgment" that has become the leading defense of liberal judicial activism. This liberal activism has been chastened, to be sure, but only at the margins. Due largely to the long-standing conservative critique of the Court's abortion jurisprudence, for example, not a single justice on the current Court was willing in *Glucksberg* to recognize a judicially enforceable constitutional right to assisted suicide. But while Scalia, Rehnquist, and Thomas wanted to rule definitively that no such constitutional right exists, the other justices insisted on leaving this door open for the future. Souter, Stevens, Ginsburg, and Breyer concurred only in the judgment, refusing to join Rehnquist's majority opinion for precisely this reason. And while O'Connor did join Rehnquist's opinion, she also wrote separately to insist that the decision had not fully settled the question of whether there was, in some circumstances, a constitutionally protected "right to die."

The following year, in *Sacramento v. Lewis* (1998), the Court again unanimously rejected a due process claim, but Souter again made clear that the "reasoned judgment" approach was alive and well. Holding that the Sacramento police did not violate Phillip Lewis's Fourteenth Amendment right to life when he was killed in a car accident during a police chase, Souter observed that "only a purpose to cause harm unrelated to the legitimate object of arrest will satisfy the element of arbitrary conduct shocking to the conscience, necessary for a due process violation." Kennedy and O'Connor joined Souter's opinion for the Court, but wrote separately to note that "the 'shocks the conscience' test . . . has the unfortunate connotation of a standard laden with subjective assessments. In that respect, it must be viewed with considerable skepticism." Souter had borrowed this test from Justice Frankfurter's opinion in *Rochin v. California* (1952), an opinion that had significantly influenced Harlan's approach to due process liberty, and Scalia and Thomas objected sharply to its revival. Concurring only in the judgment, Scalia noted that "just last Term, in *Washington v. Glucksberg,* the Court specifically rejected the method of substantive-due-process analysis employed by Justice Souter in his concurrence in that case, which is the very same method employed by Justice Souter in his opinion for the Court today." In fact, Scalia insisted, Souter's opinion in this case was even worse than his *Glucksberg* opinion, having replaced the standard of "arbitrary impositions" and "purposeless restraints," which was bad enough (in Scalia's view), with "the ne plus ultra, the Napoleon Brandy, the Mahatma Gandhi, the Cellophane of subjectivity, th' ol' 'shocks-the-conscience' test." Following his long-standing approach, Scalia insisted that Lewis had provided "no textual or historical support for this alleged due process right, and . . . I would 'decline to fashion a new due process right out of thin air.'"[38]

Again, however, Souter has been willing to engage Scalia on this point and has been surprisingly successful in pulling the Court in his direction. O'Connor and Kennedy have often stopped short of Souter's expansive view, but they have clearly rejected Scalia's narrow vision of judicially enforceable constitutional liberty under the Due Process Clause. Two years after *Sacramento v. Lewis,* the Court struck down Washington's "grandparent visitation" statute as a violation of the unenumerated "fundamental right of parents to make decisions concerning the care, custody, and control of their child," ignoring Scalia's objection that "judicial vindication of 'parental rights' under a Constitution that does not even mention them" would inevitably lead the Court to "usher in a new regime of judicially prescribed, and federally prescribed, family law." Kennedy urged the Court to vacate the state supreme court's broad ruling that the Due Process Clause requires a finding of harm before parental rights can be infringed and to remand the case for a careful consideration of whether this particular visitation order violated the parental rights that are indeed protected by the clause. O'Connor went one step further, vacating the state court decision but ruling that the statute had, in fact, been unconstitutionally applied in this case. Only Souter would have struck down the statute on its face.[39]

Similarly, when the Court struck down Nebraska's "partial birth abortion" law that same year, O'Connor wrote separately to note that a number of states have adopted similar laws that were narrower than Nebraska's and that might well be constitutionally valid. Kennedy sought to limit *Casey* even further, joining the Court's three anti-*Roe* conservatives in dissent and insisting that the statute served important state interests in the sanctity of life while placing no substantial obstacle in the path of a woman desiring an abortion. Souter, in contrast, joined Breyer's opinion for the Court in full.[40]

Religious Freedom

Along with the substantive due process cases, one of Souter's chief efforts to preserve Warren Court–style judicial activism in defense of constitutional liberty has been in the context of religious freedom. In the areas of both religious establishment and free exercise, the conservative justices of the Rehnquist Court have sought to displace the Warren Court's broad vision of religious liberty with a narrower emphasis on government neutrality. In each of these areas, Souter has been the Court's most articulate and consistent defender of the older view.[41] The conservative justices, for example, have sought to reduce the Establishment Clause to a principle of nonpreferentialism. Scalia and Thomas, in particular, have argued that the First Amendment requires neutrality among religious sects, but not neutrality between religion and irreligion. In their view, the government is perfectly free to, or perhaps even required to, provide generally available government benefits to religious organizations on neutral terms. They insist that the historical evidence of the framers' own practices reveals that they did not object to non-preferential government aid to religion. In the free exercise context, these same justices argue that the government is perfectly free to regulate religious exercise as part of a neutral, generally applicable criminal law, so long as it does not intentionally single out any particular religious group for unfavorable treatment.[42]

Souter has rejected each of these arguments, insisting that the Establishment Clause prohibits direct government funding of religious activity, even where such funding is provided on a neutral basis, and that the Free Exercise Clause prohibits governmental infringements on religious exercise, even where they are part of neutral, generally applicable regulations. Where he has been able to persuade O'Connor and Kennedy on these points, the Court has gone in his direction; where he has failed to do so, the Court has been rewriting the law in line with the conservative view.

As I have noted, these three justices cast the deciding votes to strike down the use of prayers at public school graduation ceremonies in *Weisman*. Writing for the Court, Kennedy held that public school graduation prayers violate the Establishment Clause in large part because they "carry a particular risk of indirect coercion" of students to participate. In dissent, Scalia agreed that coercion was a necessary element of an Establishment Clause violation but disagreed that any coercion had taken place in this instance. He also insisted that the Court should define the scope of the Establishment Clause by reference to historical practices and understandings. Insisting that "from our Nation's origin, prayer has been a prominent part of governmental ceremonies and proclamations," Scalia went so far as to complain that the Court was banishing from public school graduation ceremonies "the expression of gratitude to God that a majority of the community wishes to make."[43]

Weisman was Souter's first Establishment Clause case, and he wrote separately to reject Scalia's arguments as a dangerous threat to the liberty of religious minorities. Joined by Stevens and O'Connor, the length and thoughtfulness of Souter's opinion indicated that this was a constitutional value with which he was very much concerned. He opened by identifying the two key questions at issue in the case. First, does the Establishment Clause prohibit government actions that aid religion but do not grant preferential treatment to any particular religion? And second, does the clause prohibit all government actions that endorse religion or only those that coerce someone to participate in those actions?

On the first question, Souter disagreed sharply with Scalia, unequivocally rejecting the view that the Establishment Clause permits "non-preferential" aid to religion. Recalling the Court's landmark decision in *Everson v. Board of Education of Ewing* (1947), Souter noted that "forty-five years ago, this Court announced a basic principle of constitutional law from which it has not strayed: the Establishment Clause forbids not only state practices that 'aid one religion . . . or prefer one religion over another,' but also those that 'aid all religions.' Today we reaffirm that principle, holding that the Establishment Clause forbids state-sponsored prayers in public school settings no matter how nondenominational the prayers may be."[44] He acknowledged the opposing argument that, as originally understood, the Establishment Clause permitted "nondiscriminatory aid to religion," but he insisted that "while a case has been made for this position, it is not so convincing as to warrant reconsideration of our settled law; indeed, I find in the history of the Clause's textual development a more powerful argument supporting the Court's jurisprudence following *Everson*." Here, Souter offered his own review of the original meaning, concluding that the framers sought to prohibit nonpreferential aid for religion as well as preferences for particular faiths.[45]

On the second question, Souter departed from Kennedy by insisting that coercion is not a necessary element of an Establishment Clause violation. The school district had argued that government can endorse religion so long as it does not coerce religious conformity and had pointed to the framers' own political practices (along with other historical evidence) in support of this claim. Souter insisted, however, that while the early practices are relevant, they are not determinative evidence of constitutional meaning; the fact that the framers sometimes departed from their principles, he said, "cannot erase the principles." Again emphasizing the importance of precedent, he observed that the Court could not adopt "a 'coercion' analysis of the Clause . . . without abandoning our settled law, a course that, in my view, the text of the Clause would not readily permit. Nor does the extratextual evidence of original meaning stand so unequivocally at odds with the textual premise inherent in existing precedent that we should fundamentally reconsider our course." Reviewing the case law, he pointed out that the Court had prohibited many state laws and practices that were noncoercive but that conveyed a message of religious endorsement.[46]

Souter and Scalia continued their Establishment Clause debate in *Board of Education of Kiryas Joel Village School District v. Grumet* (1994). Writing for the Court, Souter ruled that the State of New York could not constitutionally create a special school district just for members of a Satmar Hasidic sect in the village of Kiryas Joel. This town, whose boundaries had been drawn in 1977 to include just the 320 acres inhabited entirely by Satmars, had a system of private religious schools but no public schools. The private schools, however, did not offer any special education services to handicapped children, and children who required such services thus had to attend public schools outside the town. As Souter noted, "their families found [this situation] highly unsatisfactory," given their strong emphasis on their own distinctive cultural and religious traditions. In response, the state legislature passed a statute that constituted Kiryas Joel as its own separate school district, allowing the Satmar community to elect a school board, establish curricular requirements and disciplinary rules, and the like.

Souter struck down this statute, holding that "a State may not delegate its civic authority to a group chosen according to a religious criterion." He acknowledged that the First Amendment requirement of government neutrality toward religion does not prohibit the government from accommodating religious belief and practice but insisted that this particular accommodation of the Satmar community's wishes went too far, "cross[ing] the line from permissible accommodation to impermissible establishment." In Souter's view, this "proposed accommodation singles out a particular religious sect for special treatment, and whatever the limits of permissible legislative accommodations may be, it is clear that neutrality as among religions must be honored."[47]

Scalia led the three conservative justices in dissent, mockingly accusing the Court of holding that the New York legislature had established Satmar Hasidim as the official state church. Souter characterized this accusation as just "one symptom of [Scalia's] inability to accept the fact that this Court has long held that the First Amendment reaches more than classic, 18th-century establishments. . . . An Establishment Clause diminished to the dimensions acceptable to Justice Scalia could be enforced by a few simple rules, and our docket would never see cases requiring the application of a principle like neutrality toward religion as well as among religious sects. But that would be as blind to history as to precedent, and the difference between Justice Scalia and the Court accordingly turns on the Court's recognition that the Establishment Clause does comprehend such a principle and obligates courts to exercise the judgment necessary to apply it."[48] Souter won this debate with Scalia because O'Connor and Kennedy joined most of his opinion, but they each wrote separately to note that they did not fully agree with Souter's analysis. They each noted, moreover, that New York's problem here had been caused in part by the Court's own case law, which had unduly restricted state and local governments from accommodating religion by providing special education services within private sectarian schools. They each suggested, in particular, that the Court's decision in *Aguilar v. Felton* (1985) should be reconsidered, a suggestion that Scalia, Thomas, and Rehnquist echoed in dissent.

With five justices having announced their willingness to overturn *Aguilar*, the original parties to that case filed an unusual procedural motion, under Federal Rule of Civil Procedure 60 (b), persuading the Court to rehear the case and reach the opposite result in *Agostini v. Felton* (1997). In the earlier case, the Court had held that the state could not send public school teachers into parochial schools to provide remedial education. It was this holding that had led the state instead to create a wholly separate public school district for Kiryas Joel. In *Agostini,* O'Connor wrote for a five-justice majority in holding that the state was free to provide remedial education in the parochial schools after all. Moving away from the strict wall of separation that the Warren and Burger Courts had generally required, the five conservatives announced that they would allow a much greater degree of legislative accommodation of religion. In dissent, Souter insisted that "the State is forbidden to subsidize religion directly and is just as surely forbidden to act in any way that could reasonably be viewed as religious endorsement." He appealed to stare decisis and complained that the Court was authorizing "direct state aid to religious institutions on an unparalleled scale, in violation of the Establishment Clause's central prohibition against religious subsidies by the government."[49]

Three years later, the Court upheld a related policy under which public school districts received federal funds to provide computer equipment and other instructional materials to both public and private schools, again overturning a precedent to reach this judgment. Writing for a four-justice plurality in *Mitchell v. Helms* (2000), Thomas emphasized the principle of neutrality, holding that the Establishment Clause generally allows governmental "aid that is offered to a broad range of groups or persons without regard to their religion."[50] Souter sharply rejected this doctrinal innovation. He had insisted in *Agostini* that the fact that the aid is "allocated under neutral, secular criteria is . . . a necessary but not a sufficient condition for an aid program to satisfy constitutional scrutiny. . . . If a scheme of government aid results in support for religion in some substantial degree, or in endorsement of its value, the formal neutrality of the scheme does not render the Establishment Clause helpless." He reiterated this point in *Mitchell*, objecting that the plurality "espouses a new conception of neutrality as a practically sufficient test of constitutionality that would, if adopted by the Court, eliminate enquiry into a law's effects." He provided a lengthy review of the numerous criteria of government aid, in addition to its evenhandedness, which the Court had long considered relevant. In Souter's view, the plurality's new approach "would replace the principle of no aid with a formula for generous religious support," and he repeatedly emphasized that this change would mark a sharp, and unwarranted, doctrinal break. He also took the opportunity to provide a lengthy and sweeping review of the purposes of the Establishment Clause itself, including the protection of individual freedom of conscience, which is violated by any compulsory support for religion; the prevention of the corruption of religion by reliance on government aid; and the prevention of divisive factional conflict among religious sects seeking government favors.[51]

The subtext in *Mitchell* was the constitutionality of school voucher policies, an issue that the Court was avoiding at the time, but eventually took up two years later. In his plurality opinion in *Mitchell,* Thomas noted that "as a way of assuring neutrality, we have repeatedly considered whether any governmental aid that goes to a religious institution does so 'only as a result of the genuinely independent and private choices of individuals.' We have viewed as significant whether the 'private choices of individual parents,' as opposed to the 'unmediated' will of government, determine what schools ultimately benefit from the government aid, and how much." Thomas spoke only for four justices, however, as O'Connor concurred only in the judgment. Souter continued to emphasize "the flat ban on subsidization" of religion as a central element of the Establishment Clause—and so it was clear that he would strike down a school voucher policy despite its even-handedness—but it was also clear that O'Connor would have the deciding vote.[52] In *Zelman v. Simmons-Harris* (2002), O'Connor joined her four conservative colleagues in upholding a school vouchers policy from Ohio in which the vast majority of participating schools were religious institutions. As in *Mitchell*, they emphasized the policy's neutrality among religious sects and the prominent role of private choice in directing the money to particular schools, and Souter objected that these arguments were no more persuasive here than they had been before.[53]

The vouchers case was just the latest of many examples in which Souter had objected to the Rehnquist Court's abandonment of the flat prohibition on government aid to religion. In *Rosenberger v. the University of Virginia* (1995) and *Good News Club v. Milford Central School* (2001), for example, the five conservative justices had held, first, that a public university cannot constitutionally exclude a student-run religious newspaper from generally available funding for student activities, and second, that a public school district could not exclude religious organizations from access to generally available school facilities. Writing for the Court, Justices Kennedy and Thomas had held that such exclusionary policies amounted to impermissible viewpoint discrimination under the free speech clause. Souter insisted, in contrast, that the free speech issue was irrelevant because the Establishment Clause flatly prohibits such direct government funding of, or support for, religious proselytizing. "[F]or the first time," he noted in *Rosenberger,* the Court was approving "direct funding of core religious activities by an arm of the State." Taking a close look at the student newspaper, entitled *Wide Awake,* he made clear that its avowed purpose was religious proselytizing: "The subject is not the discourse of the scholar's study or the seminar room, but of the evangelist's mission station and the pulpit. It is nothing other than the preaching of the word . . . [and u]sing public funds for the direct subsidization of preaching the word is categorically forbidden under the Establishment Clause." As in his other opinions, he provided a brief discussion of the clause's origins, emphasizing Madison's Memorial and Remonstrance against Religious Assessments and Jefferson's Virginia Bill for Establishing Religious Freedom, but he relied primarily on the Court's own precedents.[54]

Kennedy responded by treating the funding as akin to the evenhanded availability of university facilities, noting that the student fee program, shorn by the Court of its limits on funding religious groups, is "neutral towards religion" and so does not violate the Establishment Clause.[55] In yet another separate concurring opinion, O'Connor tried her best to balance Kennedy's principle of government neutrality and Souter's prohibition on state funding of religious activities, but she voted with Kennedy and the conservative majority. As this case makes clear, Souter has been a persistent defender of the expansive liberal vision of the

Establishment Clause. Where he has persuaded O'Connor or Kennedy or both to join him, he has led the Court's majority. Elsewhere, his dissenting arguments have clearly played a role in pulling O'Connor back from a full endorsement of Scalia's and Thomas's narrow Establishment Clause vision.[56]

Souter has played a similar role in the Court's free exercise decisions. In his first free exercise case, *Church of Lukumi Babalu Aye v. Hialeah* (1993), the Court unanimously held that the Hialeah City Council had unconstitutionally prohibited animal sacrifice with the purpose of interfering with the local practice of the Santeria religion. Scalia wrote a concurring opinion in which he reiterated his holding from *Employment Division of Oregon v. Smith* (1990) that if the ordinance had truly been a neutral, generally applicable criminal law, its incidental burden on religious exercise would not have sufficed to invalidate it. Souter also wrote separately, pointedly noting his disagreement with the *Smith* decision and refusing to join the section of Kennedy's plurality opinion that relied on it.

In Souter's view, the Free Exercise Clause requires not merely formal neutrality toward religion; in many circumstances, it also requires the affirmative governmental accommodation of religious practice. He called on the Court to overturn the *Smith* decision and to adhere to the Court's earlier, more expansive precedents. Given his concern for the principle of stare decisis, he took pains to explain why *Smith* could legitimately be reconsidered. He noted, first, that "the *Smith* rule was not subject to 'full-dress argument' prior to its announcement." Moreover, the broad new rule that Scalia announced in *Smith* appeared to be unnecessary to decide that case, and "the Court's better practice, one supported by the same principles of restraint that underlie the rule of *stare decisis,* is not to 'formulate a rule of constitutional law broader than is required by the precise facts to which it is to be applied.'"[57] Perhaps most important for Souter, the *Smith* rule was in his view flatly inconsistent with settled law. Since it did not purport to overturn the Court's free exercise precedents, it left a severe tension at the heart of free exercise law, and hence the Court was now faced not with the decision whether to overturn a precedent but rather the decision of which precedent to follow.

Finally, Souter noted that unlike the Court's Establishment Clause cases, its free exercise jurisprudence had been curiously devoid of any discussion of the history and original meaning of the First Amendment. He acknowledged that "there are differences of opinion as to the weight appropriately accorded original meaning. But whether or not one considers the original designs of the Clause binding, the interpretive significance of those designs surely ranks in the hierarchy of issues to be explored in resolving the tension inherent in free-exercise law as it stands today." And in his view, that history appeared to cut against the rule announced in *Smith.*[58] Four years later, when the Court struck down the Religious Freedom Restoration Act, an effort by Congress to write Souter's more expansive vision of the Free Exercise Clause into federal law, O'Connor marshaled extensive evidence of the original meaning of the clause and urged the Court to overturn *Smith.* In a brief concurring opinion, Souter noted that O'Connor's historical analysis had strengthened his opposition to *Smith,* but he insisted that that question was not properly presented in this case and so should not be decided.[59]

In sum, Souter has offered a broad interpretation of both of the First Amendment's religion clauses, following in the Warren Court tradition. This approach creates a problematic tension between the two, in that the Free Exercise Clause may sometimes be read to require a governmental accommodation of religion that the Establishment Clause is read to prohibit. In Souter's view, however, this approach is preferable to Scalia's and Thomas's narrow interpretation of both clauses, which avoids the tension only at the cost of abandoning the constitutional concern for religious freedom.[60] As with the area of due process liberty, the Rehnquist Court has surprisingly reaffirmed, and even built upon, a number of landmark liberal activist precedents on religious freedom, and Souter's votes and opinions have played a key role in these developments. Where the conservative justices have succeeded in chipping away at these precedents, Souter has been a leading dissenting voice.

SOUTER'S REJECTION OF THE NEW CONSERVATIVE ACTIVISM

Aside from the surprising survival of liberal judicial activism, the most significant development on the Rehnquist Court has been the emergence of a distinctive new style of conservative activism. In a variety of doctrinal areas, including affirmative action, federalism, property rights, campaign finance regulation, and commercial speech, the conservative justices of the current Court have proved quite willing to strike down state and federal statutes that conflict with their constitutional vision of limited government.[61] In the landmark case of *Bush v. Gore,* these same justices went so far as to enter the "political thicket" of vote counting in a presidential election. In each of these areas, Souter has objected both to the conservatives' substantive constitutional vision and to their willingness to overturn the majority will in the name of that vision.[62] As with his defense of liberal judicial activism in the areas of substantive due process, religious liberty, and the like, Souter has worked very hard to line up five judicial votes for his view, and where he has persuaded either O'Connor or Kennedy to join him, he has often spoken for the Court.[63] Most of the time, however, he has been unable to do so, and he has joined Stevens, Ginsburg, and Breyer in their dissenting calls for judicial restraint.

The Federalism Revival

Under Rehnquist's leadership, the conservative justices have turned to several preexisting strains in constitutional discourse in an effort to constitutionalize their critique of the modern welfare-regulatory state. In particular, they have returned to the long-abandoned practice of invalidating congressional statutes on federalism grounds, striking down nine separate provisions of federal law on such grounds from 1995 to 2001. In these decisions, the Court has revived pre–New Deal conceptions of the Interstate Commerce Clause, the Tenth Amendment, and state sovereign immunity as limitations on congressional regulatory authority and has signaled an increasing willingness to engage in the extensive judicial activism necessary to enforce those conceptions.

Except for one anomalous early vote (in *New York v. United States* [1992]), Souter has consistently rejected this conservative revival of federalism. In his view, the lesson of history is clear: the Court's prior efforts to enforce strict formalist limitations on national power have all proved disastrous. Dissenting in *U.S. v. Lopez* (1995), for example—the first case since the New Deal in which the Court had found a regulation of private activity to exceed congressional power under the Commerce Clause—Souter observed that "it seems fair to ask whether the step taken by the Court today does anything but portend a return to the untenable jurisprudence from which the Court extricated itself almost 60 years ago. The answer is not reassuring." He described the *Lochner* era as "one of this Court's most chastening experiences," which led the Court to develop its "rule of restraint" in the federalism context:

> The period from the turn of the century to 1937 is . . . noted for a series of cases applying highly formalistic notions of "commerce" to invalidate federal social and economic legislation. These restrictive views of commerce subject to congressional power complemented the Court's activism in limiting the enforceable scope of state economic regulation. It is most familiar history that during this same period the Court routinely invalidated state social and economic legislation under an expansive conception of . . . substantive due process.

Under each of these doctrinal lines, "the Court's character for the first third of the century showed itself in exacting judicial scrutiny of [legislative judgments]. . . . It was not merely coincidental, then, that sea changes in the Court's conceptions of its authority under the Due Process and Commerce Clauses occurred virtually together, in 1937." In the following years, the modern adoption of rational basis review in both of these contexts "expressed the recognition that the Court had no sustainable basis for subjecting economic regulation as such to judicial policy judgments, and for the past half-century the Court has no more turned back in the direction of formalistic Commerce Clause review . . . than it has inclined toward reasserting the substantive authority of *Lochner* due process."[64]

Similarly, Souter concluded his dissenting opinion in *Alden v. Maine* (1999) by again raising the specter of *Lochner*. In this case, the Court had continued its revival of the principle of state sovereign immunity as a limitation of federal legislative power, prompting Souter to observe that "the resemblance of today's state sovereign immunity to the *Lochner* era's industrial due process is striking.

The Court began this century by imputing immutable constitutional status to a conception of economic self-reliance that was never true to industrial life and grew insistently fictional with the years, and the Court has chosen to close the century by conferring like status on a conception of state sovereign immunity that is true neither to history nor to the structure of the Constitution. I expect the Court's late essay into immunity doctrine will prove the equal of its earlier experiment in laissez-faire, the one being as unrealistic as the other, as indefensible, and probably as fleeting."[65]

In addition to denouncing the Court's regrettable revival of discredited *Lochner*-era constitutional doctrines, Souter has also objected to the Court's reading of the founding generation's vision of federalism. In *Printz v. U.S.* (1997), for example, he engaged in a spirited debate with Scalia over Madison and Hamilton's understanding of whether Congress could require state government authorities to administer federal laws; in *Alden,* he criticized the Court for ranging beyond the text of the Eleventh Amendment to a broader "background principle" or "natural law" claim for state sovereign immunity. In Souter's view, the Court's references to sovereign immunity as "a 'fundamental aspect' of state sovereignty . . . [appear to refer] to a conception necessarily implied by statehood itself. The conception is thus not one of common law so much as of natural law, a universally applicable proposition discoverable by reason. This, I take it, is the sense in which the Court so emphatically relies on Alexander Hamilton's reference in *The Federalist* No. 81 to the States' sovereign immunity from suit as an 'inherent' right." In this light, "the Court's principal rationale . . . turns on history: was the natural law conception of sovereign immunity as inherent in any notion of an independent State widely held in the United States in the period preceding the ratification of 1788?" Souter answered this question in the negative and objected that "the Court's history simply disparages the capacity of the Constitution to order relationships in a Republic that has changed since the founding."[66]

In addition to contesting the substantive merits of the Court's reading of the constitutional structure of federalism, Souter has also argued that the Court should exercise a much more deferential role in this context. Dissenting in *Lopez,* he argued that a long line of modern precedents counsels that the Court should "defer to . . . [a] congressional judgment that its regulation addresses a subject substantially affecting interstate commerce 'if there is any rational basis for such a finding.'" He argued that this practice of judicial deference "reflects our respect for the institutional competence of the Congress on a subject expressly assigned to it by the Constitution and our appreciation of the legitimacy that comes from Congress's political accountability."[67]

Dissenting in *U.S. v. Morrison* (2000), he reiterated that "Congress has the power to legislate with regard to activity that, in the aggregate, has a substantial effect on interstate commerce. The fact of such a substantial effect is not an issue for the courts in the first instance, but for the Congress, whose institutional capacity for gathering evidence and taking testimony far exceeds ours. By passing legislation, Congress indicates its conclusion, whether explicitly or not, that facts support its exercise of the commerce power. The business of the courts is to review the congressional assessment, not for soundness but simply for the rationality of concluding that a jurisdictional basis exists in fact." Unlike the Gun-Free School Zones Act at issue in *Lopez,* moreover, Congress had here assembled a "mountain of data . . . showing the effects of violence against women on interstate commerce." Souter provided an extensive summary of these data and denounced the Court's majority for failing to give Congress's findings any deference. He relied on *Gibbons v. Ogden* (1824), *Wickard v. Filburn* (1942), *Garcia v. San Antonio Metropolitan Transportation Authority* (1985), as well as a brief review of the founding history to condemn the majority for rejecting "the Founders' considered judgment that politics, not judicial review, should mediate between state and national interests as the strength and legislative jurisdiction of the National Government inevitably increased through the expected growth of the national economy."[68]

Souter's argument that the Court's federalism revival will necessitate an unwarranted degree of judicial activism has influenced the Court's more pragmatic conservatives, leading them to hedge on just how far they are willing to carry this revival. Both O'Connor and Kennedy have expressed some fear that the Court's approach could threaten a vast and disruptive expansion of the judicial role in enforcing limits on congressional power.[69] They are each clearly troubled by the extraordinary degree of judicial activism that would be required to enforce the original understanding of federalism in the context of the modern welfare-regulatory state. They have been willing to go along with the revival of the federalism-based limits on congressional power while preventing the Court from adopting Rehnquist's, Scalia's, and Thomas's sweeping vision of that revival. Souter's arguments against this entire line of cases, however, have remained in dissent.

Affirmative Action and the "Color-blind" Constitution

A similar pattern has characterized the Rehnquist Court's divisions on the constitutionality of race-based affirmative action policies. In a series of decisions beginning in 1989, the Court has invalidated a number of such policies for violating the Fourteenth Amendment's Equal Protection Clause. Influenced by the New Right's rejection of multicultural egalitarianism in favor of an individualistic conception of "merit," the Court has built on a long-standing, though contested, color-blind vision of the Constitution and has proven willing to engage in the extensive judicial activism necessary to enforce that vision.

In cases such as *Adarand Constructors, Inc. v. Pena* (1995), the Court has applied this vision of the Equal Protection Clause to prohibit policies favoring minority-owned businesses in government contracting decisions. And in *Shaw v. Reno (Shaw I)* (1993) and its progeny, the Court has applied it to prevent states from considering race when drawing legislative districts, even if such consideration is necessary to preserve an effective political voice for racial minorities. In *Miller v. Johnson* (1995), for example, the Court held that regardless of whether a districting scheme dilutes the votes of or otherwise disadvantages any particular group, it will recognize an equal protection claim whenever "the State has used race as a basis for separating voters into districts."[70]

Thus, in these cases, the Rehnquist Court has struck down a range of state and federal affirmative action programs and has even gone so far as to enter the "political thicket" of legislative apportionment, marking a sharp departure from the settled conservative view that the Court has no proper business in this area. The extent to which constitutional conservatives have abandoned their traditional commitment to judicial restraint in this area has been remarkable; following the logic of the high court's holdings, federal judges have been actively scrutinizing the admissions standards of public universities and have even thrown out the results of democratic elections.[71] Scalia and Thomas have gone the farthest in this regard, while O'Connor has limited the scope of these conservative holdings, consistently casting the deciding vote to support them, but regularly characterizing their reach more narrowly than her fellow conservative justices would wish.[72]

Souter and his fellow dissenting justices have objected to these decisions on two key grounds. First, they have insisted that the principal purpose of the Equal Protection Clause is to protect relatively powerless minority groups from majoritarian discrimination, a value that is not threatened by race-conscious policies that discriminate against the white majority. In other words, they have rejected the color-blind vision of equality and urged the adoption of the alternative approach rooted in Justice Stone's *Carolene Products* footnote.[73] In the racial gerrymandering cases, for example, Souter has repeatedly emphasized that no racial group—let alone a relatively powerless one—is in any way disadvantaged by the creation of majority-minority electoral districts. In his view, racial classifications in the law are not illegitimate per se, but only when they operate to injure a disadvantaged class. Dissenting in *Shaw I,* he observed that unlike race-conscious decisions in government contracting and college admissions, "the mere placement of an individual in one district instead of another denies no one a right or benefit provided to others."[74] And in *Bush v. Vera* (1996), he objected to the Court's rejection of "the very understanding of equal protection as a practical guarantee against harm to some class singled out for disparate treatment."[75]

Second, the dissenting justices have argued that the Court's active scrutiny of affirmative action policies violates the tenet of judicial restraint. In *Bush v. Vera,* for example, Souter observed that this series of decisions has resulted in a "shift in responsibility for setting district boundaries from the state legislatures, which are invested with front line authority by Article I, to the courts, and truly to this Court, which is left to superintend the drawing of every legislative district in the land."[76] In the government contracting context, he had urged the Court in *Adarand* to adhere to stare decisis and follow its own decision in *Fullilove v.*

Klutznick (1980) "that discrimination in the construction industry had been subject to government acquiescence, with effects that remain and that may be
addressed by some preferential treatment falling within the congressional power
under Section 5 of the Fourteenth Amendment." In his view, this section 5
authority created an interest "sufficiently important" to satisfy strict scrutiny.[77]

Most fundamentally, Souter noted that "a majority of the Court today reiter-
ates that there are circumstances in which Government may, consistently with the
Constitution, adopt programs aimed at remedying the effects of past invidious
discrimination." This was true because O'Connor refused to join her fellow conservatives in enacting an absolute principle of color-blind law, insisting instead
that color-blindness must be balanced against competing considerations and that
the application of strict scrutiny would not necessarily be fatal for a race-conscious affirmative action policy.[78] As in the federalism context, O'Connor has
hedged her support for conservative activism in response to Souter's (and the
other dissenters') call for judicial restraint. In a role reversal from the Warren
Court years, Souter and his fellow dissenting liberal justices have sharply
denounced the conservative majority for interfering with the operation of the
political branches. Their demonstration of the sharp conflict between the conservatives' enforcement of their color-blind vision and their commitment to judicial
restraint, moreover, has led the more moderate conservatives—in this case,
O'Connor—to blink.

Bush v. Gore and Political Thickets

The affirmative action and federalism cases are emblematic of a broader pattern
of decision-making on the Rehnquist Court. Across a number of areas of constitutional doctrine, the five conservative justices have developed a distinctive style
of conservative judicial activism. Souter has dissented in these cases and has
worked very hard to persuade O'Connor and Kennedy to his view. He has generally failed, but O'Connor or Kennedy or both frequently heed his arguments to
some degree and hence seek to hedge the conservative holding by limiting it to
its particular facts, by relying on a narrow legal principle, or by balancing a broad
legal principle against competing considerations. The clearest, and most significant, example of this pattern is the Court's decision settling the outcome of the
2000 presidential election.

Souter's important role in this case is not to be found in his opinion. He provided no eloquent critiques of the Court's illegitimate action, as Stevens, Breyer,
and Ginsburg all sought to do, though he did note that he was in "substantial
agreement" with each of their dissenting opinions. In his own dissent, Souter simply summarized and responded to Bush's three legal arguments, which he characterized as straightforward and easily resolved. In Souter's view, Bush's only
meritorious argument was the equal protection claim "that unjustifiably disparate
standards are applied in different electoral jurisdictions to otherwise identical

facts." He could "conceive of no legitimate state interest served by these differing treatments of the expressions of voters' fundamental rights. The differences appear wholly arbitrary." And so he would have remanded the case to the state courts to establish uniform standards under which the recount could continue. To recount manually the approximately sixty thousand uncounted "undervotes" in a short period of time "would be a tall order," he acknowledged, but "there is no justification for denying the State the opportunity to try to count all disputed ballots."[79]

More important than these straightforward legal arguments was Souter's behind-the-scenes role, in which he tried valiantly to persuade O'Connor or Kennedy to provide a fifth vote for allowing the recount to continue. Just as Brennan would have done, Souter sought to craft a compromise that could garner five judicial votes, and he reportedly said after the decision that given one more day, he would have persuaded Kennedy.[80] Souter's efforts in this regard became clear, at least in hindsight, during the Court's oral arguments, when his questions revealed that he was searching for a compromise resolution in which the Court would remand the case to the Florida courts to resume the manual recount under a more uniform standard for determining the voters' intent.[81] Unlike his dramatic success under similar circumstances in *Casey,* however, here he dramatically failed.

CONCLUSION: SOUTER AND THE BRENNAN SEAT

When Souter praised Justice Brennan's constitutional vision before the Senate Judiciary Committee, no one thought that he would follow in Brennan's footsteps. The Court has moved significantly to the right over the past generation, and hence Brennan's constitutional aspirations have inevitably been chastened. Within this context, however, Souter has been a remarkably clear defender of what Mark Tushnet has called "the New Deal/Great Society constitutional order."[82] Souter's understanding of the Court's role is captured pretty well by Justice Stone's *Carolene Products* footnote, emphasizing the active judicial protection of minority rights and the democratic process, supplemented by an evolving common law conception of constitutional liberty borrowed chiefly from the second Justice Harlan. This constitutional vision leads Souter to a good deal of "judicial activism," in the sense of a willingness to strike down democratically enacted statutes that conflict with fundamental constitutional principles. Like Harlan, however, he has tempered this approach with a healthy dose of history, precedent, and self-restraint. Taking his place in Brennan's seat, Souter has elaborated on Brennan's argument, regularly articulated in debates with Justice Scalia, that while the Court must always look to the nation's traditions as a guide to constitutional interpretation, those traditions are flexible and evolving and leave significant room for the judicial elaboration of constitutional principle. Among the liberal justices, moreover, he has been the most willing to engage in historical debates with the conservatives over the original understanding of particular provisions of the constitutional text.

In case after case, Souter has worked to marshal five judicial votes in support of this liberal constitutional vision. On the conservative Rehnquist Court, moreover, he has been remarkably successful at this task when it comes to preserving liberal, Warren Court–style judicial activism in defense of individual liberty and minority rights. He has been much less successful, however, when it comes to curtailing the newer conservative activism advocated by Justices Scalia and Thomas. The best examples here are *Casey* and *Bush v. Gore* respectively.

In addition to the areas of constitutional law that I have discussed, there are others that fit this pattern. Souter's unanimous opinion in *Hurley v. Irish-American Gay, Lesbian, and Bisexual Group of Boston* (1995), for example, contained the Court's first respectful discussion of gays and lesbians, marking a sharp rhetorical shift from the majority and concurring opinions just nine years earlier in *Bowers v. Hardwick* (1986). One year after *Hurley,* Souter joined Kennedy's opinion for the Court in the landmark case of *Romer v. Evans* (1996), the first significant victory for gay rights arguments under the Equal Protection Clause. Souter has also consistently supported the Court's protection of gender equality under the Equal Protection Clause, joining, for example, Ginsburg's landmark opinion for the Court in *U.S. v. Virginia* (1996).[83]

There are other areas of the law that appear to fit less well. In particular, Souter's jurisprudence in the area of criminal procedure has been in some ways more conservative than his views elsewhere, though this tendency has often been overstated. Consider, for example, his widely noted opinion for a bare majority in *Atwater v. Lago Vista* (2001), upholding the use of a warrantless custodial arrest for a misdemeanor violation of Texas's seatbelt law. Such decisions make clear that Souter's vision of liberal constitutionalism is less sweeping than Brennan's, but in the context of the chastened aspirations of the current Court, Souter has written or joined liberal activist opinions on prison conditions,[84] habeas corpus,[85] and capital punishment.[86] His vote in *Atwater,* moreover, is explained by his reading of the legal history and traditions regarding peace officers' authority to make warrantless misdemeanor arrests.

Following his usual practice, he surveyed the early common law, colonial era treatises and legal dictionaries, and the English statutes, all of which were relevant to assessing the framers' understanding of whether such arrests were "unreasonable" (and hence prohibited by the Fourth Amendment). He also noted that since the founding, the nation had witnessed "two centuries of uninterrupted (and largely unchallenged) state and federal practice permitting warrantless arrests for misdemeanors not amounting to or involving breach of the peace," and that all fifty states currently have legislation authorizing such arrests. In his view, moreover, "both the legislative tradition of granting warrantless misdemeanor arrest authority and the judicial tradition of sustaining such statutes against constitutional attack are buttressed by legal commentary that, for more than a century now, has almost uniformly recognized the constitutionality of extending warrantless arrest power to misdemeanors without limitation to breaches of the peace." In sum, Atwater was asking the Court to develop "a new and distinct body of constitutional law," and Souter could find no justification, outside the facts of this unusual case, for taking such a step.[87]

Pointing to decisions such as *Atwater,* some scholars have argued that "[t]here are no liberals on this Court," only centrist conservatives and extreme conservatives, but this characterization is plainly inadequate.[88] It may be useful to characterize O'Connor and Kennedy as centrist conservatives, though this label tells us little about the actual content of their particular brand of conservatism. Souter, however, has clearly refused to join these justices to form a coherent centrist bloc on the Court, disagreeing with their constitutional vision more often than not, though always exhibiting a willingness to compromise. The Court that has decided *Casey, Romer, Weisman, U.S. v. Virginia, Saenz v. Roe* (1999), and *Dickerson v. U.S.* (2000) clearly includes some liberal justices, even if they do not support every feature of the Warren Court tradition. And David Souter, surprising though it may be, has been a leading defender of this Court's liberal constitutionalism.

NOTES

1. Consider, for example, the Court's decisions striking down antiabortion laws in the former category and its decisions striking down affirmative action policies in the latter. By "judicial activism," I mean simply to suggest the opposite of judicial restraint—in other words, a relative willingness to declare constitutional limitations on government or a relative willingness to become involved in heated political conflicts. These competing visions of the proper role of the Supreme Court in our democratic system represent what Ronald Kahn, *The Supreme Court and Constitutional Theory, 1953–1993* (Lawrence: University Press of Kansas, 1994): 20–22, calls "polity principles," i.e., "deeply held ideas about where decisionmaking power should be located when deciding questions of constitutional significance. Polity principles involve beliefs about whether courts or electorally accountable political institutions are the more appropriate forum for constitutional decisionmaking" and together with constitutional "rights principles," these structural norms are what make up any particular substantive vision of the Constitution.

2. For a sustained explanation of how a judicial conservatism born in reaction against the liberal judicial activism of the Warren Court has come to create not judicial restraint but instead its own version of judicial activism, see Thomas M. Keck, *The Supreme Court and Modern Constitutional Conservatism, 1937–2003* (Chicago: University of Chicago Press, forthcoming).

3. See, for example, Lee Epstein and Jack Knight, *The Choices Justices Make* (Washington, D.C.: CQ Press, 1998), 67–70.

4. David J. Garrow, "Justice Souter Emerges," *New York Times Magazine,* 25 September 1994, 41.

5. Perhaps the most humorous indication of Souter's anonymity was Justice Marshall's statement in a televised interview that the first thing he did upon hearing of the nomination was call his wife to ask, "Have I ever heard of this man?" When his wife replied, "No. I haven't either," he then called the newly retired Justice Brennan. Brennan's wife answered the phone and said, "He's never heard of him either" (quoted in "Bush 'Dead' on Civil Rights, Says Justice Marshall," *St. Louis Post-Dispatch,* 27 July 1990, 16A).

6. John Anthony Maltese, *The Selling of Supreme Court Nominees* (Baltimore: Johns Hopkins University Press, 1998), 130–131. Note also President Bush's comments at the press conference announcing Souter's nomination; reprinted as "Comments by President on His Choice of Justice," *New York Times,* 24 July 1990, A18. Souter was not completely unknown to Bush administration officials themselves, of course. He had just been nominated and confirmed to the First Circuit that year, and he had made the short list for Kennedy's seat on the Court two years earlier, all of which had been due to the efforts of Senator Rudman.

7. See "Comments by President on His Choice of Justice."

8. *Nomination of David H. Souter to Be Associate Justice of the Supreme Court of the United States: Hearings before the Senate Committee on the Judiciary,* 101st Cong., 2d sess. (Washington, D.C.: Government Printing Office, 1991), 54, 140, 274, 276–277, 303.

9. Souter characterized the principle of stare decisis as "a bedrock necessity if we are going to have in our judicial systems anything that can be called 'rule of law' as opposed to random, case-by-case decision-making" (ibid., 68, 189, 211).

10. The votes were 13 to 1 in the Judiciary Committee and 90 to 9 in the full Senate. On the senators' positive impressions of Souter, see Ellen Goodman, "The Judge Who Speaks in Two Voices," *Boston Globe,* 20 September 1990, 23.

11. Quoted in Tony Mauro, "Time Will Tell Where Souter Sits; Putting Him in a Niche May be Tough," *USA Today,* 9 October 1990, 3A.

12. See, for example, Terry Eastland, "How to Win a Seat on the Court," *Los Angeles Times,* 4 October 1990, B7; Edward M. Kennedy, "Souter Nomination Should Be Rejected," *USA Today,* 1 October 1990, 12A; Ruth Marcus, "Senators Left Wondering after Hearing: Which Is the Real David Souter?" *Washington Post,* 23 September 1990, A4; Tony Mauro, "Brennan's Absence, Legacy to Loom Large," *USA Today,* 1 October 1990, 13A.

13. *Nomination of David H. Souter to Be Associate Justice,* 186. In a similar vein, upon taking the oath of office on October 9, he noted that he hoped some years hence "to pass on the Constitution 'in as vigorous condition as I have received it this afternoon, as it were, from Justice Brennan'" ("Souter Takes Preliminary Oath, Joins Court Today," *St. Petersburg Times,* 9 October 1990, 9A).

14. *Florida v. Bostick,* 501 U.S. 429 (1991).

15. *California v. Acevedo,* 500 U.S. 565 (1991).

16. *Arizona v. Fulminate,* 499 U.S. 279 (1991).

17. *McCleskey v. Zant,* 499 U.S. 467 (1991).

18. *Payne v. Tennessee,* 501 U.S. 808, 839–843 (1991).

19. 501 U.S. 452 (1991); 500 U.S. 352 (1991).

20. *Rust v. Sullivan,* 500 U.S. 173 (1991).

21. 501 U.S. 560, 581–587 (1991). Souter also joined the liberal justices in *UAW v. Johnson Controls,* 499 U.S. 187 (1991), and *Parker v. Dugger,* 498 U.S. 308 (1991).

22. 499 U.S. 400, 402 (1991).

23. 501 U.S. 957, 997 (1991).

24. See, e.g., James F. Simon, *The Center Holds: The Power Struggle inside the Rehnquist Court* (New York: Simon and Schuster, 1995).

25. 505 U.S. 577, 587 (1992). I take up Souter's Establishment Clause jurisprudence more fully below.

26. The joint plurality opinion began with these words: "Liberty finds no refuge in a jurisprudence of doubt. Yet, 19 years after our holding that the Constitution protects a woman's right to terminate her pregnancy in its early stages, that definition of liberty is still questioned. Joining the respondents as *amicus curiae,* the United States, as it has done in five other cases in the last decade, again asks us to overrule *Roe*" (505 U.S. 833, 846, 844 [1992]).

27. Ibid., at 851.

28. In support of their alternative approach, they quoted Harlan's argument that "the full scope of the liberty guaranteed by the Due Process Clause cannot be found in or limited by the precise terms of the specific guarantees elsewhere provided in the Constitution. This 'liberty' is not a series of isolated points pricked out in terms of the taking of property; the freedom of speech, press, and religion; . . . and so on. It is a rational continuum which, broadly speaking, includes a freedom from all substantial arbitrary impositions and purposeless restraints" (ibid., at 846–850, quoting *Poe,* 367 U.S. 497, 543 [1961]).

29. 505 U.S., at 849–850.

30. Garrow, "Justice Souter Emerges," 38. On the decision-making and opinion-drafting process in *Casey,* see also Simon, *The Center Holds,* 144–157.

31. 505 U.S., at 864, 866–867, 869.

32. Applying O'Connor's "undue burden" standard, the plurality struck down the state's spousal notification requirement, but upheld extensive record-keeping and reporting requirements, provisions requiring informed consent and a twenty-four-hour waiting period, and a parental consent requirement for minors; ibid., at 877, 880–901.

33. Note, for example, Ronald Dworkin's observation that *Casey* "may prove to be one of the most important Court decisions of this generation . . . because three key justices . . . reaffirmed a more general view of the nature of the Constitution which they had been appointed to help destroy" (*Freedom's Law: The Moral Reading of the American Constitution* [Cambridge: Harvard University Press, 1996], 117). Or David Garrow's observation that "the *Casey* Court formally and explicitly buried *Lochner*'s ghost. Substantive due process is—as it should be—a fundamental and fully accepted aspect of present-day American constitutional doctrine" ("From *Brown* to *Casey:* The U.S. Supreme Court and the Burdens of History," in *Race, Law, and Culture: Reflections on Brown v. Board of Education,* ed. Austin Sarat [New York: Oxford University Press, 1997], 83).

34. 505 U.S., at 901.

35. 521 U.S. 702, 755–756, 765 (1997).

36. Ibid., at 767, 768, 789.

37. Ibid., at 721–722.

38. 523 U.S. 833, 836, 857, 860, 861, 862 (1998).

39. *Troxel v. Granville,* 530 U.S. 57, 92, 93 (2000).

40. *Stenberg v. Carhart,* 530 U.S. 914 (2000).

41. See generally John A. Fliter, "Keeping the Faith: Justice David Souter and the First Amendment Religion Clauses," *Journal of Church and State* 40 (1998): 387.

42. See Thomas's concurring opinion in *Rosenberger v. University of Virginia,* 515 U.S. 819 (1995), Scalia's dissenting opinion in *Weisman;* and Scalia's opinion for the Court in *Employment Division, Department of Human Resources of Oregon v. Smith,* 494 U.S. 872 (1990).

43. 505 U.S. 577, 592, 631, 633, 646 (1992).

44. Ibid., at 609–610, quoting *Everson v. Board of Education of Ewing,* 330 U.S. 1, 15 (1947).

45. 505 U.S., at 612.

46. Ibid., at 619, 625. When the Court reaffirmed and extended *Weisman* in *Santa Fe Independent School District v. Doe,* 530 U.S. 290 (2000), Souter joined Stevens's opinion for the Court.

47. 512 U.S. 687, 692, 698, 706–707, 710 (1994).

48. Ibid., at 709.

49. 521 U.S. 203, 240–241, 242 (1997).

50. 530 U.S. 793, 809 (2000).

51. 521 U.S., at 253; 530 U.S., at 869, 900.

52. 530 U.S., at 810.

53. 122 S.Ct. 2460 (2002).

54. 515 U.S. 819, 829, 863 (1995). See also *Good News Club v. Milford Central School,* 533 U.S. 98 (2001).

55. 515 U.S., at 868.

56. Ibid., at 847, 849, 852.

57. 508 U.S. 520, 571–572 (1993), quoting Brandeis's concurring opinion in *Ashwander v. TVA,* 297 U.S. 288, 347 (1936).

58. 508 U.S., at 577.

59. *City of Boerne v. Flores,* 521 U.S. 507, 565–566 (1997).

60. See generally Suzanna Sherry, "*Lee v. Weisman:* Paradox Redux," *The Supreme Court Review* (1992): 123–153.

61. In this light, it is misleading (or at least incomplete) to describe the conservative jurisprudence of the Rehnquist Court as a jurisprudence of restraint, as Keith Whittington, Ralph Rossum, and Mark Silverstein all do in this book. For my elaboration of this argument, see Keck, *The Supreme Court and Modern Constitutional Conservatism.*

62. In the area of property rights, for example, see Souter's dissenting opinion in *Phillips v. Washington Legal Foundation,* 524 U.S. 156 (1998).

63. Note, for example, Souter's effort to curtail the Rehnquist Court's active scrutiny of democratically enacted campaign finance regulations. Since *Buckley v. Valeo* (1976), the Court has held that the First Amendment prohibits all limitations on campaign expenditures, but that the government has significantly greater leeway to regulate campaign contributions. Whether made by candidates themselves or by individuals or organizations acting independently of any candidate (so-called "independent expenditures"), the Court has held that such expenditures amount to constitutionally protected acts of political speech. In *Colorado Republican Federal Campaign Committee v. FEC,* 518 U.S. 604

(1996), Souter and O'Connor joined Breyer's plurality opinion striking down the FEC's application of independent expenditure limits to the political parties themselves, reiterating *Buckley*'s holding that restrictions on expenditures are more constitutionally suspect than those on contributions. Breyer's opinion was an effort to mark out a middle ground between the views of Scalia, Thomas, Rehnquist, and Kennedy on the one hand and Stevens and Ginsburg, on the other. The conservatives insist that virtually all government restrictions on either contributions or expenditures are constitutionally suspect, while the liberals insist that the Court should defer to government efforts to rid the electoral process of corruption. Souter joined Breyer in holding that the parties do have a First Amendment right to make independent expenditures, uncoordinated with any candidate's campaign, without interference by the government. Scalia and his conservative colleagues would have gone further, holding that the government may not limit party spending even if it is coordinated with the candidate. The Court refused to address this broader claim at the time, but five years later, Souter wrote for the Court in rejecting it. Here, he held that a party's coordinated expenditures, unlike its truly independent ones, can be restricted consistently with the First Amendment, accepting Stevens's and Ginsburg's argument that the government was free to try to close this significant soft money loophole in the existing law and crafting that argument in such a way as to keep Breyer and (even more important) O'Connor on board. See *FEC v. Colorado Republican Federal Campaign Committee,* 121 S.Ct. 2351 (2001).

Souter had also written for the Court in *Nixon v. Shrink Missouri Government PAC,* 528 U.S. 377 (2000), upholding contribution limits that were stricter than those that had been upheld in *Buckley.* In doing so, he offered significant deference to the Missouri legislature on the necessity of relatively low contribution limits to deal with the problem of corruption or the appearance of corruption in the democratic process. In dissent, Rehnquist, Scalia, Thomas, and Kennedy insisted that these contribution limits should be struck down on First Amendment grounds.

64. 115 S.Ct. 1624, 1651–1653 (1995).

65. 527 U.S. 706, 814 (1999). Souter advanced a similar argument in his dissenting opinions in *Seminole Tribe of Florida v. Florida,* 517 U.S. 44, 165–166 (1996), and *U.S. v. Morrison,* 120 S.Ct. 1740, 1766–1768 (2000).

66. 527 U.S., at 760–761, 763. See also his dissenting opinion in *Morrison,* 120 S.Ct., at 1769–1770.

67. 514 U.S. 549, 603–604 (1995).

68. 529 U.S. 598, 628–629, 647 (2000).

69. Note, for example, O'Connor's concurring opinion in *Printz* and Kennedy's concurring opinion in *Lopez.*

70. 515 U.S. 900, 911 (1995).

71. See, for example, *Hopwood v. Texas,* 78 F.3d 932 (5th Cir. 1996); *Vera v. Bush,* 933 F. Supp. 1341 (S.D. Tex. 1996).

72. See, for example, O'Connor's opinion for the Court in *Adarand* and her concurring opinion in *Bush v. Vera,* 517 U.S. 952 (1996).

73. *U.S. v. Carolene Products,* 304 U.S. 144, 152–153n4 (1938).

74. 509 U.S. 630, 681–682 (1993).

75. 517 U.S. 952, 1053 (1996).

76. 517 U.S., at 1045–1046.

77. 515 U.S. 200, 266 (1995).

78. Ibid., at 269–270. See also *Hunt v. Cromartie,* 532 U.S. 234 (2001), in which O'Connor voted with the four liberals to uphold North Carolina's 12th Congressional District (which was before the high court for the fourth time), despite what the other four conservatives characterized as a persistent pattern of race-conscious districting.

79. 531 U.S. 98, 129, 134, 135 (2000).

80. See David A. Kaplan, "The Accidental President," *Newsweek,* 17 September 2001.

81. For a wonderfully helpful account of these oral arguments, see Howard Gillman, *The Votes That Counted: How the Court Decided the 2000 Presidential Election* (Chicago: University of Chicago Press, 2001), 129–137.

82. I have borrowed the notion of the recent "chastening of constitutional aspiration" from Tushnet as well. See Mark V. Tushnet, "The Supreme Court, 1998 Term—Foreword: The New Constitutional Order and the Chastening of Constitutional Aspiration," *Harvard Law Review* 113 (1999): 29.

83. 518 U.S. 515 (1996). Souter also joined Ginsburg's dissenting opinion in *Miller v. Albright,* 523 U.S. 420 (1998), and O'Connor's dissenting opinion in *Tuan Anh Nguyen v. INS,* 533 U.S. 53 (2001).

84. See, for example, *Hudson v. McMillian,* 503 U.S. 1 (1992), *Helling v. McKinney,* 509 U.S. 25 (1993), *Farmer v. Brennan,* 511 U.S. 825 (1994), *Sandin v. Conner,* 515 U.S. 472 (1995), and *Lewis v. Casey,* 518 U.S. 343 (1996).

85. See, for example, *Withrow v. Williams,* 507 U.S. 680 (1993), *Kyles v. Whitley,* 514 U.S. 419 (1995), and *Lindh v. Murphy,* 521 U.S. 320 (1997).

86. See, for example, *Herrera v. Collins,* 506 U.S. 390 (1993), *Johnson v. Texas,* 509 U.S. 350 (1993), and *Graham v. Collins,* 506 U.S. 461 (1993). See generally John A. Fliter, "Justice David Souter and Criminal Law" (unpublished manuscript on file with author).

87. 532 U.S. 318, 121 S.Ct. 1536, 1550, 1552, 1557 (2001).

88. Stephen E. Gottlieb, *Morality Imposed: The Rehnquist Court and Liberty in America* (New York: New York University Press, 2000), 197.

8

Advocate on the Court:
Ruth Bader Ginsburg and the
Limits of Formal Equality

Judith Baer

Justice Ruth Bader Ginsburg has been called "the Thurgood Marshall of sex discrimination law" and "a judge's judge."[1] The first label is as apt as it is irresistible. As general counsel for the ACLU Women's Rights Project in the 1970s, Ginsburg did the job Marshall had done for the NAACP a generation earlier. Their career paths, from advocate of constitutional change to author of constitutional law, are not only symmetrical; they are virtually unique in Supreme Court history. Equally striking similarities are apparent in their judicial careers. Both judges were members of a stable minority voting bloc, dissenting from rulings that became increasingly conservative during their tenure.

But the comparison between Ginsburg and Marshall obscures as much as it illuminates. It is difficult to imagine anyone calling Thurgood Marshall "a judge's judge" with a straight face. But it is equally unlikely that anyone will ever describe Ruth Ginsburg as an "American revolutionary." She appears more comfortable on the Court than Marshall ever did.[2] Marshall was unable to influence race discrimination law on the Court as powerfully as he did arguing before it; his impact on constitutional doctrine was frustrated by the Court majority. Ginsburg, by contrast, has continued as a justice to influence the development of constitutional doctrine on gender discrimination. She has succeeded in moving the law closer to where she wants it to be. If Marshall's signature opinion was his dissent in *San Antonio Independent School District v. Rodriguez,* Ginsburg's star turn is surely her opinion for the Court in the VMI case, *U.S. v. Virginia.*[3] Her impact, like Marshall's, is limited both by her minority status on the Court and by entrenched constitutional principles. But, unlike Marshall, she is also constrained by her own limited vision.

The author gratefully acknowledges the support of the Center for Humanities Research, Texas A&M University.

"TRYING MOST OF THE TIME TO STAY ALIVE"[4]

The familiar stations on the route to the Supreme Court include the law firm, the lower court, the legislative or executive office, and, of course, the prosecutor's or attorney general's office. Few if any of these possibilities were open to Ruth Ginsburg when she graduated from Columbia Law School in 1959. The obstacles she confronted as "a woman, a Jew, and a mother to boot" were as formidable as those facing Sandra Day O'Connor in California and Arizona, or the challenges awaiting Thurgood Marshall when he graduated from Howard University in 1933, the year Ginsburg was born.[5] Although she tied for first place in her graduating class, no law firm would hire her. Like O'Connor, she was forced to look for vulnerable spots in the male supremacist fortress. For O'Connor, the entry point was the prosecutor's office; for Ginsburg, it was the law school.

Ginsburg entered academia on the ground floor in 1963, as an assistant professor at Rutgers University Law School. She rose to full professor at Rutgers and returned to Columbia in 1972 as the law school's first tenured woman professor. Specializing in civil procedure, she published law review articles in that field and also in comparative law, conflict of laws, and constitutional law. Each of her two books combined one or more of these fields: the first on Swedish civil procedure, the second on gender discrimination.[6] Ginsburg was no more daunted by her status as "token woman" than she had been by any earlier obstacles. She earned a reputation as an excellent scholar and teacher. Within her profession, she was respected; outside it, her academic career, like that of most professors, attracted little attention. It was in the courtroom, not the classroom, that her work commanded notice.

Ginsburg's "professional interest in the crusade against gender discrimination" began at Rutgers. Not surprisingly for the 1960s, it was her students who stimulated this interest.[7] She developed a course on women and the law and argued sex discrimination cases pro bono for the ACLU. At the time, gender discrimination was not yet the hot topic it would become. The rebellions of the 1960s did not include a women's rights movement until the very end of the decade. But by the time Ginsburg joined the Columbia faculty, the field of women and the law was burgeoning. Ginsburg ranks with such pioneers as Barbara Babcock, Herma Hill Kay, Pauli Murray, and Leo Kanowitz as one of the founders of the field.[8]

Ruth Ginsburg became general counsel for the ACLU Women's Rights Project the same year she joined the Columbia faculty. She had already participated in *Reed v. Reed,* the first Supreme Court case invalidating a sex-based discrimination under the Equal Protection Clause of the Fourteenth Amendment.[9] By 1980, she had argued six cases before the Court, won five, briefed three, and filed amicus curiae briefs in numerous others.[10] The impact of these efforts is difficult to exaggerate. Neither women's rights nor equal protection would ever be the same again. Ruth Ginsburg did not accomplish all this alone. She had no part at all in many landmark cases. More important, the new judicial receptivity toward gender discrimination claims was due at least as much to the resurgence of feminist activism in the 1970s as to the work of any individual. Nevertheless, today's equal protection law might be very different without the participation of Ruth Bader Ginsburg.

"THE EMPTY CUPBOARD"[11]

In a contest for Worst Supreme Court Prophecy, predictions about the impact of the Equal Protection Clause would be prominent on the top-ten lists. The doubts expressed by Justice Samuel Miller about "whether any action of a State not directed against the negroes as a class, or on account of their race, will ever be held to come within the purview of this provision" were as groundless as Justice Oliver Wendell Holmes's reference to the clause as "the traditional last resort of constitutional arguments" was inapt.[12] By 1971, the provision had long since been interpreted to protect all people, first from arbitrary classifications and later from certain kinds of disfavored classifications. The "two tier" approach was fully entrenched in constitutional law. On the lower tier were ordinary, innocuous classifications: discriminations based on age, for instance, or the size of a city's population or the value of property. These were upheld as long as they bore a rational relationship to a legitimate governmental purpose. Most laws survived this minimal scrutiny. The upper tier contained classifications that were "inherently suspect"; discriminations based on these characteristics were subjected to "the most rigid scrutiny." Race was the paradigm example of a suspect classification.[13] The fact that this rule originated in *Korematsu v. U.S.*—a non–equal protection case, where the author of the rule failed to apply it and in which the law was upheld— did not prevent the Court from using it to strike down racial classifications.[14]

Sex-based discrimination was entrenched on the lower tier. The notion that sex, like race, could be an inherently suspect classification received no serious judicial consideration until the California Supreme Court adopted the rule in 1971.[15] The judicial scrutiny accorded laws that treated men and women differently was minimal indeed. Given the prevailing social attitudes in the century after the ratification of the Fourteenth Amendment, it might seem reasonable to suppose that a rational basis would be found for some discriminatory laws but not for others. But in effect, courts had given legislatures a blank check in this area.

Judges had taken their cue from *Muller v. Oregon,* decided in 1908. *Muller* upheld an hours limitation for women workers because a "woman's physical structure and the performance of maternal functions" differentiated her "from the other sex." Therefore, "she is appropriately placed in a class by herself."[16] Applied to laws affecting sweated workers in the female job ghetto, this ruling might be defensible; applied to laws reserving good jobs for male workers or limiting women's jury service, it was highly problematic.[17] But courts found it impossible to distinguish between laws "designed for her protection" and laws that were harmful or merely silly. Judges acted as if *Muller* had ruled that women were different from men and that, therefore, any law treating women differently from men was reasonable. The Constitution became and remained an "empty cupboard" for women.

In trying to fill the cupboard, Ginsburg and the Women's Rights Project looked for a "clear winner" to litigate. The criteria included sympathetic clients, archaic laws, and cost-free outcomes.[18] Ginsburg was especially eager to argue cases brought by men; she thought judges might look more favorably on claims made by people of their own gender.[19] Except for the last criterion, *Reed v. Reed* could hardly have been better suited to her strategy. An Idaho law gave males automatic preference over equally qualified females in appointing the adminis-trator of a dead person's estate. Eligibility for this position was determined by the closeness of the applicant's relationship by marriage or blood to the deceased: spouse first, children second, and so on. The number of appointments to which the gender preference applied was surely not large. The issue could arise only if you died intestate and unmarried, if one male and one female relative of the same degree of consanguinity survived you, and if they could not agree on who would administer your estate. But Sally and Cecil Reed had been separated for several years before their son, Richard, committed suicide. Sally blamed Cecil (who had custody) for the young man's death. The legislature repealed the law while the litigation was pending.

Ruth Ginsburg prepared what became the "grandmother brief" for sex dis-crimination cases.[20] While she emphasized the absurdity of this particular law, she laid the doctrinal foundation for future cases in which laws would be less absurd, plaintiffs less sympathetic, and remedies more costly. This discrimina-tion, the brief argued, was premised on the acceptance of traditional gender roles: men at work, women at home. Laws posited on these stereotypes denied equal protection to both men and women. Court decisions had done to women what *Plessy v. Ferguson* had done to African Americans: generated "a separate and unequal place" for them.[21] Sex, like race, should be assigned to the top tier of inherently suspect classifications. Although Ginsburg doubted that the Court would accept the suspect classification argument on the first try—and her own behavior as a judge suggests she might not have voted that way herself—she strove to get the justices to take the argument seriously.[22]

Ginsburg needed to include some critical analysis of the idea that men and women belonged in separate spheres, a notion still alive and well in American law at the time. She reviewed precedents that identified the distinguishing fea-ture of a suspect classification as its basis on "an unalterable identifying trait."[23] She relied on the California Supreme Court's argument:

Sex, like race and lineage, is an immutable trait, a status into which the class members are locked by the accident of birth. What differentiates sex from nonsuspect statuses, such as intelligence or physical disability, and aligns it with the recognized suspect classifications, is that the characteristic frequently bears no relation to ability to perform or contribute to society. The result is that the whole class is relegated to inferior legal status without regard to the capabilities or characteristics of its members.[24]

The Supreme Court did not go this far in *Reed*. It voted unanimously to strike down the law while keeping sex discrimination on the lower tier. An automatic preference for males represented "the very kind of arbitrary legislative choice" forbidden by the Equal Protection Clause.[25] That was all the Court had to do in this case. Nevertheless, the decision sent a signal to lower courts, legislatures, and litigants that the blank check for sex discrimination had been withdrawn. Ginsburg's success in *Reed* brought her and the Women's Rights Project many more cases to argue.

The closest she came—tantalizingly close—to achieving her doctrinal goal was *Frontiero v. Richardson* in 1973. The Court came within one vote of declaring sex a suspect classification in striking down a law making it harder for women military personnel to qualify for dependents' benefits than for their male counterparts. Justice William J. Brennan's plurality opinion quoted verbatim from the same California case that Ginsburg often cited. However, the four other justices in the majority either wanted to stick with the rational basis test or were reluctant to take such a step while the proposed Equal Rights Amendment was before the states.[26]

Craig v. Boren, decided in 1976, represented the farthest point to which the Court was prepared to move for the next twenty years. *Craig,* to which Ginsburg contributed an amicus brief, ruled that "classifications by gender must serve important governmental objectives and be substantially related to these objectives."[27] This "intermediate scrutiny" standard was a compromise between the rational relationship to a legitimate purpose required by the rational basis test and the compelling justification needed to sustain a suspect classification. *Craig* also changed the two-tier structure of equal protection analysis, adding a third tier, or possibly a mezzanine, between the original two.

Once again, judges had placed women in a class by themselves. But it was a very different class from *Muller.* Between 1971 and 1981, the Court filled the new cupboard it had built in a reasonably intelligent way. Discrimination based on "old notions" or stereotyped characterizations—denying survivors' benefits to widowers but not to widows, establishing different ages of majority for women and men, or giving sole power to a husband, as "head and master" of the household, to mortgage property—was invalidated.[28] Laws based on physical differences between the sexes, especially the capacity to become pregnant, or on women's legal ineligibility to serve in combat were sustained, however tenuous the relationship between the gender difference and the law at issue.[29] Ginsburg's participation ended in 1980, when President Jimmy Carter appointed her to the

Court of Appeals for the District of Columbia Circuit. Thirteen years later, when she went to the Supreme Court, nothing had changed.

THE SECOND ACT: FROM LAWYER TO JUDGE

Ruth Ginsburg's experience as a professor and litigator unequivocally qualified her for a seat on an appellate court. Her gender was probably a plus for the first president to prioritize diversity and affirmative action in making judicial appointments. She was not the first or the only woman to serve on the D.C. court. Patricia Wald, another Carter appointee, had preceded her there a year earlier. By 1992, Ginsburg was one of three women among eleven active judges. If she was a token, at least she was not the only token. This lack of uniqueness no doubt made her adjustment to her new role easier,[30] but she still had some adapting to do.

Of all the lawyers who become appellate court judges, perhaps none is better prepared than the law school professor. Both the judge and the scholar must be learned in the law. Both professions require public speaking, Socratic dialogue, heavy reading, and, especially, writing. The ability to think on one's feet is useful to both judge and professor, but less important to either than to a trial judge or a litigator; the reading of briefs, the writing of articles, and the preparing of classes allow, and indeed demand, ample time for advance preparation. But a judge on a federal circuit court confronts at least two demands that law professors need not face unless they want to. First, she must collaborate with her colleagues on opinions. Second, she must be a polymath, knowledgeable in any area of law likely to come before her.

Ginsburg's success on the first dimension is undisputed. Her working relationships with the other judges were generally good. The efficient management for which the D.C. circuit is celebrated may have facilitated collegial amity. And the fact that the judges usually sit in panels of three, in which the membership varies and includes district judges, may have reduced interpersonal conflict. At any rate, Ginsburg settled in and made friends, even across ideological lines. Her friendship with Antonin Scalia began on the court of appeals and has continued on the Supreme Court.

One reason Judge Ginsburg fit in well may have been the fact that her "crusading liberal lawyer's views" at the bar gave way to a "moderate political ideology" on the bench. One study describes her as a "swing vote" who "sided more with Republican-appointed colleagues than with Democratic counterparts" (and most frequently with Judge Kenneth Starr).[31] Assessments of the quality of her work are mixed. According to one commentator, she earned a "reputation as an intelligent, highly competent jurist." But another study characterized her performance as "lackluster at best" and commented further that her record "lacked any significant achievements in gender-related issues."[32]

Ruth Ginsburg's judicial "hero" is John Marshall Harlan II. Her admiration for Harlan derives from neither his gentle, dignified manner nor his conservatism. Instead, Ginsburg strives to emulate his elegantly crafted opinions, his respect for judicial restraint and precedent, and his commitment to federalism, fairness, and procedural regularity.[33] Although Harlan did not seek to initiate doctrinal change as Ginsburg has done, he did not automatically resist it.[34] But he opposed what he saw as efforts to circumvent the limits of judicial procedure, to go too fast, or to ignore the consequences of activist rulings.[35] Ginsburg has demonstrated a similar style of what might be called restrained activism or activist restraint. She has actively promoted change, at least in equal protection doctrine, but she has sought to ground constitutional change in precedent and doctrine. In a 1984 speech, she asserted that *Roe v. Wade* "ventured too far in the change it ordered."[36] Although it is fruitless to speculate about what Harlan would have done in *Roe,* Ginsburg's statement is reminiscent of his criticism of the "cosmic view" of the judicial function "that all deficiencies in our society that have failed of correction by other means should find a cure in the courts."[37]

MODERATE OR LIBERAL? GINSBURG ON THE SUPREME COURT

Byron White's retirement in 1993 made Bill Clinton the first Democratic president in twenty-six years to get to fill a vacancy on the Supreme Court. Clinton's nominee would become the first Democrat to join the Court since Thurgood Marshall. Ruth Ginsburg had the correct politics, but she was no Robert Bork of the left. Her judicial opinions and legal scholarship established an ample "paper trail," but the paper put her in the ideological center rather than either the left or right wing. If her appellate court performance had been less than spectacular, neither had it brought her negative attention. A federal appeals court judge who is not disqualified by age or infirmity has to make an effort in order to be considered ineligible for the Supreme Court, and Ginsburg's record was free of any such blemish. She was rated "well qualified" by the ABA and confirmed by the Senate, 93 to 2.

Ginsburg has brought to the Court many of the characteristics of the law professor she once was. She questions lawyers as relentlessly as any seminar teacher might question students. She has also maintained the scholar's footnote habit; her opinions are replete with citations of precedents. Her work (like that of Stephen Breyer, her fellow Clinton appointee) is indicative of the rightward trends in American politics in the last generation. Commentators label her as one of the Court's "liberals," along with Breyer, John Paul Stevens, and David Souter. Some of Ginsburg's votes, like those in both important gay right cases decided during her tenure, support that label. In *Romer v. Evans,* she joined the majority in striking down Colorado's Proposition 2, a ballot initiative excluding homosexuals from state antidiscrimination policies.[38] She joined the "liberal" bloc in dissent in *Boy Scouts v. Dale,* in which the organization's exclusion of gays prevailed against a state ruling.[39] However, it is difficult to imagine any of the Warren Court liberals concurring, as Ginsburg did, in upholding the power of a school district to require drug tests for student athletes.[40] When she wrote for the Court in *Chandler v. Miller*, invalidating mandatory urine tests for candidates for state office under the Fourth Amendment, she spoke for every justice except William Rehnquist.[41]

In criminal cases, Ginsburg has not notably distinguished herself either from the other justices or from the "tough on crime" president who appointed her. Her record here seriously compromises her as a "liberal," for it is these unpopular causes involving unsympathetic litigants that provide the toughest test of one's liberalism. Ginsburg's votes reveal little evidence of an enduring affinity with the views of the ACLU. For example, she dissented from only one of a series of rulings in the mid-1990s that broadened the "automobile exception" to the probable cause requirement.[42] On death penalty cases where the Court is divided, Ginsburg often joins a minority composed of herself, Breyer, John Paul Stevens, and David Souter.[43] But when the majority is lopsided, it usually includes her.[44] Neither Ginsburg nor any other sitting justice has taken on Justice Harry Blackmun's role as skeptic and contrarian with respect to either the death penalty or the "war on drugs" that has generated so many of the search and seizure cases.[45] As far as the present Court is concerned, these issues appear closed.

But other civil liberties issues—like establishment of religion—provoke more disagreement. Although Ginsburg has been all but silent, her votes do not suggest that she has rejected the prevailing, though precarious, *Lemon* test. She is unpersuaded either by the accommodationist approach of Chief Justice Rehnquist or by Justice O'Connor's attempt at compromise: "The Establishment Clause prohibits making adherence to a religion relevant to a person's standing in a political community."[46] Two decisions clarify the difference between Ginsburg's position and O'Connor's. Both voted against student-led prayer at football games (*Santa Fe Independent School District v. Doe* [2000]). But Ginsburg dissented and O'Connor concurred in *Agostini v. Felton*, a 1997 ruling sustaining state aid to parochial schools.[47]

Other Establishment Clause votes hint that Ginsburg might regard even the *Lemon* test of secular purpose, neutral primary effect, and avoidance of excessive entanglement as too friendly toward government involvement with religion.[48] In *City of Boerne v. Flores*, decided the same week as *Agostini*, she voted to overrule the Religious Freedom Restoration Act (RFRA), thus deserting a stable minority bloc and adding one vote to an equally stable majority bloc in cases involving federalism and congressional power (see below).[49] Inferring an opinion from a silent response is always a risky enterprise, but Ginsburg may well have voted as she did because her conviction that the First Amendment forbids the government to favor religion overrode her commitment to federal supremacy.

The one opinion Ruth Ginsburg has written on the merits in an Establishment Clause case suggests that she may come closer than any justice in the last fifty years to embracing the all but obsolescent separationist approach. The premise that "the First Amendment has erected a wall between church and state" that "must be kept high and impregnable" has fallen into disuse since it was honored in the breach by Hugo Black and in the observance by Robert Jackson in *Everson v. Board of Education.*[50] But Ginsburg's dissent in *Capital Square v. Pinetti* (1995) read the Establishment Clause to *forbid* precisely what seven other justices insisted that the Free Speech Clause *required.*[51] The majority affirmed an Ohio decision that refusing to allow the Ku Klux Klan to display a cross on state property constituted an impermissible content-based speech regulation. Even if conformity to the Establishment Clause had constituted a compelling justification for such a rule, permitting the display of a cross did not constitute an establishment of religion. In a curt opinion, Ginsburg insisted that it did. She cited *Everson* as authority that "the aim of the Establishment Clause is genuinely to uncouple government from church." The Klan "failed to state unequivocally that Ohio did not endorse the display's message," so "the relief ordered by the District Court thus violated the Establishment Clause."[52]

Although Ginsburg often dissents, she is not a "great dissenter" in the style of Holmes, Brandeis, or Black. It is noteworthy that her *Capital Square* opinion does not really propound the separatist doctrine; she does little more than allude to it. She is usually willing to let other justices speak for her. One commentator suggests that she "crafts her opinions strategically, with a mind to creating precedent for the future."[53] Her silence on civil liberties issues may reflect a suspicion that she would be wasting her time. Her dissent in *Adarand v. Peña* (1995) suggests that her goals are proximate and pragmatic. In *Adarand,* a fragmented majority of five remanded a lower court decision sustaining a federal minority preference program. Ginsburg's dissent emphasized the "majority's acknowledgment of Congress's authority to act affirmatively, not only to end discrimination, but also to counteract discrimination's lingering effects. . . . Congress surely can conclude that a carefully designed affirmative action program may help to realize, finally, the 'equal protection of the laws.'"[54] This opinion announces her belief that the Fourteenth Amendment has not been interpreted broadly enough. It also sends a message to Congress not to give up. But it is not "an appeal to the brooding spirit of the law, to the intelligence of a future day."[55]

Rights and liberties are not the predominating issues in the Rehnquist Court. The landmark cases increasingly tend to involve separation of powers and federalism. In a series of decisions since the mid-1990s, the Court has taken the initiative in demarcating the powers of the branches of the national government and adjudicating the relationship between federal and state governments. All but two of these cases were decided by a 5 to 4 vote, and the same four justices—Ginsburg, Stevens, Souter, and Breyer—dissented every time.[56]

The Court has essentially rejected the cooperative federalism of the past two generations in favor of a doctrine reminiscent of pre–New Deal dual federalism. It has cited as binding authority nineteenth-century cases long considered moribund[57] and revisited issues that were presumed settled to jeopardize precedents on which lawmakers had relied.[58] It has struck down all or part of recent federal laws enacted with overwhelming bipartisan support and signed by enthusiastic presidents. These statutes include the RFRA, the Brady Bill, the Americans with Disabilities Act (ADA), and the Violence against Women Act (VAWA). And, most extraordinary of all, the Court determined the results of the 2000 presidential election.[59]

Some of these rulings asserted that Congress had exceeded its lawmaking power and invaded the powers of the states. *U.S. v. Lopez* (1995) and *Printz v. U.S.* (1997) found the commerce power inadequate to support, respectively, the Gun-Free School Zones Act of 1990 and the Brady Handgun Violence Prevention Act of 1993.[60] The RFRA met an analogous fate under section 5 of the Fourteenth Amendment.[61] The Court also ruled that Congress had exceeded its Fourteenth Amendment enforcement power when it authorized damage against states under the Age Discrimination in Employment Act and the ADA.[62] *U.S. v. Morrison* (2000) held that neither the Commerce Clause nor section 5 authorized the VAWA.[63]

Chief Justice Rehnquist's declaration in *Lopez,* which he quoted five years later in *Morrison,* is illustrative of the majority's approach to federalism: "The Constitution requires a distinction between what is truly national and what is truly local."[64] But does this distinction reflect reality? The history of gun control and violence against women provides strong evidence that these problems cannot be solved locally. Like defense and economic regulation, they are prime examples of things states may not be able do alone; in *Lopez* and *Printz,* the states were hardly screaming for Congress to leave them alone. The recent commerce cases also emphasize a distinction between economic activity (regulation permissible) and noneconomic activity (regulation prohibited); how solid is that distinction after the Civil Rights Act of 1964?[65]

Several recent decisions appear to misread the Constitution outright. Although the Eleventh Amendment prohibits lawsuits between one state and citizens of another state, *Seminole Tribe v. Florida, Kimel v. Board of Regents,* and *Board of Trustees v. Garrett* extended the doctrine of sovereign immunity to citizens' suits against their own state.[66] And it is difficult to read *Bush v. Gore* without doubting whether these decisions are really about federalism at all. When the very majority that has constrained Congress's Fourteenth Amendment powers over the states invokes that same provision to stop a state from resolving an election, it seems plausible that the majority is more protective of the Court's power than that of the states.[67] The dissenting "liberal" justices occupy an atypical position for liberals on the Court. They become the advocates of judicial restraint.

Ginsburg's dissent in *Bush v. Gore* (the only one of these cases in which she has written separately) displays the respect for both judicial restraint and federalism that she shares with her hero, the second Justice Harlan.[68] Her opinion lacks the angry eloquence of Justice Stevens's dissent or the historical sophistication of Justice Breyer's. Although she omits the customary "respectfully," she takes a conciliatory tone: "I might join the Chief Justice were it my commission to interpret Florida law." While "this Court must sometimes examine state law in order to protect federal rights," the petitioners "have not presented a substantial equal protection claim," and the time squeeze was of the Court's own making. The majority has violated "the ordinary principle that dictates [this case's] proper resolution: Federal courts defer to state high courts' interpretations of their own law."[69]

GENDER DISCRIMINATION: FINISHING WHAT SHE STARTED

When Ginsburg arrived on the Court, the constitutional doctrine of gender equality remained essentially that of *Craig v. Boren*. The intermediate scrutiny standard of substantial relationship to an important purpose still prevailed. However, the Court had not had occasion to use the test since 1984.[70] Ginsburg has participated in two equal protection cases involving gender discrimination during her tenure. *J. E. B. v. Alabama ex rel. T. B.* was decided in her first term. She voted with five other justices to invalidate gender-based peremptory challenges in jury selection but did not write a separate opinion.[71] The second case was *U.S. v. Virginia*. Here, Ginsburg wrote her first opinion for the Court in her three years of service.

The story of the Virginia Military Institute's losing battle to exclude women is too notorious to require extensive retelling. Since it took place while another southern military college with a similar educational philosophy was waging the same war with the same result, the difference between VMI and the Citadel should be clarified. The Citadel is a private institution in South Carolina. VMI, as its full name suggests, is a state institution and therefore bound by the Equal Protection Clause.

This case recalls John Marshall's words in *Marbury v. Madison:* "deeply interesting" but "not of an intricacy proportioned to its interest."[72] The single-sex state college had been ruled unconstitutional in 1982, in Justice O'Connor's first opinion for the Court.[73] The principle of *Brown v. Board of Education*—"in the field of public education the doctrine of 'separate but equal' has no place"—to sex discrimination rendered dubious at best the status of the "Virginia Women's Institute for Leadership" by means of which the state had tried to preserve VMI as a male bastion.[74] In fact, VWIL bore an uncomfortable resemblance to the law school at the Texas State University for Negroes, founded to keep Homer Sweatt out of the University of Texas.[75]

The interest generated by the case arose from the passion with which students, faculty, administrators, and alumni of VMI defended the status quo. Loyalist after loyalist praised VMI's "adversative" training, which seeks "to instill mental and physical discipline in its cadets and impart to them a strong moral code." They lauded the school's emphasis on "physical rigor, mental stress, absolute equality of treatment, absence of privacy, minute regulation of behavior, and indoctrination in desirable values" (not including, apparently, correct word usage). "Rats" who stick it out for four years emerge "educated and honorable men, . . . confident in the functions and attitudes of leadership, possessing a high sense of public service, advocates of the American democracy and free enterprise system, and ready as citizen-soldiers to defend their country."[76] Whether or not women could tolerate this treatment—a matter about which VMI loyalists evinced some doubt-—they insisted, to a man, that coeducation would destroy the unique character of the institution. "Allowance for personal privacy would have to be made"; physical education requirements "would have to be altered, at least for the women"; and "the adversative environment could not survive unmodified."[77]

Two federal courts, both located in Virginia, sided with VMI. The district court insisted that VMI contributed to the diversity of Virginia's system of higher education and that coeducation would destroy this diversity.[78] The Court of Appeals for the Fourth Circuit vacated this judgment, suggesting several ways that VMI might have its cake and eat it too.[79] The state proposed to establish a parallel institution. Both the district court and the circuit court approved; "providing the option of a single-gender college education may be considered a legitimate and important aspect of a public system of higher education."[80] These judges proved no less impervious than VMI defenders were to the lessons of military history. Twenty-five years after the integration of the military academies, a change opposed by most of the people responsible for implementing it has been absorbed into the system.[81] At roughly the same time, the integration of women into the Corps of Cadets at Texas A&M University was proceeding with even less enthusiasm. Despite a history of nasty incidents, the women are here to stay. A generation earlier, Dwight D. Eisenhower changed his mind about the Women's Army Corps. Initially "opposed to the use of women," he saw them "perform so magnificently in various positions, including service in anti-aircraft batteries, that I had been converted."[82] The WACS are long gone now, and women serve in all branches of the military on an equal basis with men. All these institutions have undergone significant change, but their character and mission have endured.

This kind of case was ideally suited to Ruth Bader Ginsburg's expertise and talents. Writing this opinion put her in a position similar to that of an experienced actor playing Lady Macbeth or Hamlet. She had the opportunity to do something she had spent years preparing to do. Ginsburg seemed to enjoy summarizing the long since discredited notions about the unsuitability of education for women that had once been commonplace and, in some locales, apparently still were. Nevertheless, doctrine and precedent led to the inescapable conclusion:

Without equating gender classifications, for all purposes, to classifications based on race or national origin, the Court, in post-*Reed* decisions, has carefully inspected official action that closes a door or denies an opportunity to women (or to men). To summarize the Court's current directions for cases of official classification based on gender: . . . the reviewing court must determine whether the proffered justification is "exceedingly persuasive." The burden of justification is demanding and it rests entirely on the State. The State must show "at least that the [challenged] classification 'serves important governmental objectives' and that the discriminatory means employed are 'substantially related to the achievement of those objectives.'" The justification must be genuine, not hypothesized or invented *post hoc* in response to litigation. And it must not rely on overbroad generalizations about the different talents, capacities, or preferences of males and females. . . .

"Inherent differences" between men and women, we have come to appreciate, remain cause for celebration, but not for the denigration of members of either sex or for artificial constraints on an individual's opportunity.[83]

The majority, "measuring the record of this case against the review standard just described," concluded "that Virginia has shown no 'exceedingly persuasive justification'" for excluding women from VMI.[84] Ginsburg dismissed the lower courts' "diversity" argument as inadequate to justify "a plan to afford a unique educational opportunity only to males. However 'liberally' this plan serves the State's sons, it makes no provision for her daughters. That is not *equal* protection."[85] As for VWIL, Ginsburg devoted several pages to showing that it "affords women no opportunity to experience the rigorous military training for which VMI is famed"[86] and a few more pages to the precedential value of *Sweatt v. Painter.*[87]

U.S. v. Virginia represents a triumph for individuality over conformity, autonomy over convention, and reason over emotion. Ginsburg's opinion is a masterful combination of intelligence, erudition, and eloquence. It will probably not win much grudging admiration from opponents of the decision; the readers who admire it most are likely to approve of the result. But the same observation might be made about, say, Robert Jackson's opinion in *West Virginia Board of Education v. Barnette* or William O. Douglas's opinion in *Terminiello v. Chicago.*[88] The majority opinion in *U.S. v. Virginia* ranks with these essays. All three opinions are clear, concise, well organized, and intelligently argued. All contain powerful, but not excessive, rhetorical flourishes; *Barnette* and *Terminiello* are still quoted half a century after they were decided. And all make a compelling case against violating individual rights just because some people feel strongly that we should.[89]

Barnette struck down a compulsory flag salute in the public schools, reversing a three-year-old ruling. The plaintiffs, Jehovah's Witnesses, were asserting their religious freedom, but the Court decided the case on free speech grounds: no child may be forced to salute. "If there is any fixed star in our constitutional constellation," wrote Jackson, "it is that no official, high or petty, can prescribe what shall be orthodox in politics, nationalism, religion, or other matters of opinion or force citizens to confess by word or act their faith therein."[90] *Terminiello* invalidated a "breach of the peace" ordinance applied to silence an inflammatory speaker. Douglas held that "a function of free speech is to invite dispute. It may indeed best serve its high purpose when it induces a condition of unrest, creates dissatisfaction with conditions as they are, or even stirs people to anger."[91] The VMI decision contains similar powerful language.

Like its ancestors, *U.S. v. Virginia* is a perfectly *liberal* opinion. The situation is right out of John Stuart Mill: individuals wanted to do something that society would not let them do. (*Barnette* presented the mirror image of this problem.) Of course, the Fourteenth Amendment does not enact Mill's *Essay on Liberty*, but doctrine and precedent led inexorably to the same result. Most cases are nowhere near this simple, therefore the precedential value of this decision may be limited. Nevertheless, Ginsburg's opinion is notable for two accomplishments. First, it is far more readable and quotable than most of her opinions. Second—and perhaps more important to her—it nudges the law closer to her preferred doctrine.

Craig v. Boren is followed, but not verbatim. "Substantially related to the achievement of [important] objectives" is modified by "at least." The justification for sex-based discrimination must be "exceedingly persuasive." This modifier sounds less like "substantial" than it does like "compelling justification," the standard that inherently suspect classifications must meet. In the words of one commentator, "The increased standard of scrutiny may be cloaked in a new 'skeptical scrutiny' or 'exceedingly persuasive' language, but the undisputed fact is that the Court had adopted a new heightened standard of scrutiny."[92]

If Ginsburg is trying to elevate sex to the status of a suspect classification, she is not without past and present collegial support. The phrases she uses are not original with her. "Exceedingly persuasive justification" comes from *Mississippi University for Women v. Hogan*, Justice O'Connor's first majority opinion. The "at least" qualifier of *Craig* is a quotation from a 1980 Court opinion by Justice Byron White, whom Ginsburg replaced. White had joined the plurality opinion in *Frontiero*.[93] One law review article asserts that *J. E. B. v. Alabama* has already accomplished this change. If the Court's ruling "that the exercise of peremptory challenges based on gender stereotypes constitutes invidious discrimination because it reinforces prejudicial views about the relative abilities of women and men" can be reconciled with a 1975 decision invalidating gender discrimination in jury selection "because women and men bring separate and unique perspectives to the courtroom . . . the standard of review must be strict scrutiny."[94]

Two decisions since *Virginia* suggest that this statement was overly optimistic. Both rulings upheld sections of the immigration law that made it easier for the children of single citizen mothers to become citizens than children of single citizen fathers. Neither *Miller v. Albright* (1998) nor *Nguyen v. INS* (2001) mention suspect classification or exceedingly persuasive justification; the precedents on which the Court relies are cases involving single fathers. Although Ginsburg wrote a dissent in *Miller*, it was Justice Breyer who invoked the VMI case.[95]

WOMEN'S RIGHTS IN THE COURTS: PAST, PRESENT, AND FUTURE

Thirty years after *Reed v. Reed*, Ruth Bader Ginsburg can look back on a record of extraordinary accomplishment in the area of women and the law. Sexual equality comes closer and closer to being a legal reality. The Social Security and military cases like *Wiesenfeld* and *Frontiero* gave women equal opportunities to protect their own futures and those of their families, even after their deaths. *Kirchberg v. Feenstra,* in overturning a state law that made the husband "head and master" of his household, effectively abolished the traditional law of marriage.[96] The VMI decision made clear to the states that the Constitution means "equal" when it says "equal." These are tangible gains; they cannot fairly be disparaged or trivialized. As lawyer and judge, Ginsburg has helped produce an extraordinary change.

Suppose the Supreme Court, explicitly or *sub silentio,* makes gender a suspect classification. What impact would this doctrinal change have? Two cases decided twenty years ago under the *Craig* standard continue to provoke criticism. *Michael M. v. Superior Court of Sonoma County* upheld a "statutory rape" law that applied only to males having sex with underage females. The Court majority found a substantial relationship between this policy and the important state objective of discouraging teenage pregnancy.[97] *Rostker v. Goldberg* upheld male-only draft registration because only men were then allowed to serve in combat.[98]

Under strict scrutiny, women's reproductive role might provide compelling justification for some discriminatory policies. Suppose, for instance, there is not enough rubella vaccine for all the children who need it; a state that immunized only the girls could defend that choice. Equal protection cases involving the rights of single fathers with respect to newborn infants might hinge on the mother's experience of pregnancy, childbirth, and the postpartum period.[99] But the *Michael M.* argument failed to convince the dissenters and much of the Court's attentive public even under the old rules; it is difficult to see how it could survive the more rigorous standard of review. The fate of *Goldberg* under strict scrutiny is less clear. The Court's reliance on women's ineligibility for combat is obsolete, now that the ban is gone; only inertia seems to keep single-sex registration in place.

Making gender a suspect classification would produce some different results and change the terms of discourse about sexual equality and constitutional law. But what impact would this change have? An examination of the Supreme Court's post-*Craig* output reveals two striking facts. First, there are only a few cases. Second, most of them involve men. The Court has decided only nineteen gender cases on equal protection grounds since 1976. The most recent case, *U.S.*

v. Virginia, was won on behalf of women. The last such case before 1996 was *Feenstra*—in 1981. Fourteen of the cases decided since *Craig* were brought by men. Lower court cases exhibit a similar pattern. The women's won-lost record is better than the men's; moreover, victories by men do not necessarily harm women and may benefit them. But so far men have been the primary beneficiaries of the new sexual equality doctrine.[100]

Ruth Ginsburg has given no indication that this outcome troubles her. She continues to regard sex equality not as requiring the elimination of male supremacy, but as a problem of *discrimination,* of basing decisions on a person's sex. A law "enshrining and promoting the woman's 'natural' role as selfless homemaker, and correspondingly emphasizing the man's role as provider, . . . impeded both men and women from pursuit of the very opportunities and styles of life that could enable them to break away from traditional patterns and develop their full, human capacities."[101] Discrimination against men is "just as bad" as discrimination against women. In the VMI decision, Ginsburg repeatedly cited *MUW v. Hogan.* Joe Hogan sued to get into an all-female state nursing school and won. Ginsburg has given no indication that she perceives any important difference between these two cases.

As far as VMI and MUW are concerned, she may be right. An all-female nursing school and an all-male military college do reinforce the old stereotypes she has criticized. Many all-female institutions have claimed as their mission the education of "young ladies" in "needlework, cooking, housekeeping and such other industrial arts as may be suitable to their sex and conducive to their support and usefulness."[102] However, some women's schools and colleges attempt to provide a rigorous academic education in an atmosphere free of social distractions. Many educators who welcomed the admission of women to Harvard and Yale do not therefore conclude that Bryn Mawr and Wellesley must admit men. The admission of girls to the elite academic Stuyvesant High School in New York City does not vitiate the case for Hunter College High School, but both institutions became coeducational.[103]

Ginsburg's dissent in a 1995 legislative districting decision applies the neutral antidiscrimination principle to racial classifications. Defending the creation of a predominantly black district against a successful equal protection challenge, she carefully writes of "race" and the "reality of ethnic bonds."[104] It would be difficult for her to change the evenhanded approach to discrimination even if she wanted to. *Regents v. Bakke* categorically refused to distinguish between invidious and benign racial discrimination back in 1978.[105] Subsequent decisions have entrenched this single standard rather than weakened it; one need only think of *City of Richmond v. Croson, Shaw v. Reno, Adarand v. Pena,* and *Miller v. Johnson.*[106] These decisions reflect a preference for the *Frontiero* version of suspect classification, which emphasizes the ground for discrimination rather than the group disadvantaged by it, over Justice Lewis Powell's formulation in *Rodriguez.* Powell's "traditional indicia of suspectness" included being "saddled with such disabilities, or subjected to such a history of purposeful unequal treatment, or relegated to such a position of political powerlessness as to command extraordinary protection from the majoritarian political process."[107] Whether or not women qualify as such a class, men definitely do not.

Judicial reluctance to make sex a suspect classification has not prevented the Court from extending other components of race discrimination doctrine to sex discrimination. The justices have applied both the neutral antidiscrimination principle and the requirement that any racially biased impact must have been intentional in order to be unconstitutional.[108] The intent requirement makes it difficult to challenge jury verdicts, sentencing, divorce settlements, child custody awards, and the like. It also renders fanciful any suggestion that there might be an equal protection issue in, say, the definition of self-defense to include a homeowner confronted by a stranger but to exclude a domestic abuse victim who returns violence for violence. These legal issues raise some of the most troubling questions about race and sex equality today, and doctrine makes constitutional challenges to prevailing practices impossible.[109]

But these doctrines and principles were not firmly in place when Ginsburg began her work. The first key decisions on neutrality and intent date from the 1970s, the same years when she was arguing her cases. Ginsburg had choices, and she chose to frame the legal questions as involving discrimination rather than subjection. Suppose her arguments had included more *Rodriguez* and less *Frontiero;* would the result have been fewer decisions benefiting men and more protection of women's interests in situations that formal equality cannot resolve? Possibly, but hindsight is a tool best used with caution.

Ginsburg's approach to women's rights has received persistent criticism from scholars for reasons that transcend constitutional doctrine. Feminist theorists have described her work as dependent on "standards set by the male norm"; one author criticized her "phallocentric" viewpoint and "assimilationist" stance.[110] "Difference" feminists assert that this approach presumes women's similarity to men; therefore, it fails women where genuine differences exist in women's and men's concrete reality and experience.[111] Radical feminists insist that adherence to formal equality is self-defeating for women because the system is already structured around male needs and priorities.[112]

Ginsburg often cites Wendy Williams, an adamant defender of formal equality.[113] Williams has argued that decisions like *Goldberg* and *Michael M.* "absolve women of personal responsibility in the name of protection."[114] But many feminist jurists doubt that different results in these cases would have benefited women. After all, Michael M. was accused of forcible rape and tried on a lesser charge; reversing the lower court might have let a rapist go free. Some scholars insist that accommodating women's traditional roles is more important than ensuring equal opportunity. True, even the most committed difference theorist might agree that women who want to attend VMI should be able to. But those who believe that equal opportunity is *incompatible* with such changes as recognizing women's interests as primary caregivers in custody cases or the connection between domestic violence and self-defense will reject the formal equality model outright.[115] Several feminist scholars find the formal equality model not so much wrong as inadequate.[116] Refusing Wendy Williams's invitation to presume that "we can't have it both ways," these scholars see no need to "decide which way we want to have it."[117] Equal opportunity is incompatible with pregnancy and postpartum leaves, single-sex statutory rape and alimony laws, a male-only draft, child custody rulings that accommodate nursing mothers, and other woman-friendly policies only if we rigidly confine our thinking within the existing doctrinal categories.

Formal equality can accomplish some goals very well. It can get rid of laws that are based on gender-role stereotypes, are obsolescent, or are just plain stupid. But the last thirty years of constitutional adjudication are evidence of how little formal equality can do. It is an inadequate tool for securing gender equality in reality as well as on paper. Constitutional law may not be the best means toward that end. Were Ginsburg's hero, Justice Harlan, alive today, he might consider male supremacy one of those social ills that the judicial system cannot and should not resolve. Court decisions are not the only possible remedy for sexist policies. Gender-neutral statutes that rank traditional female activities and concerns equally with those of men are feasible; some, like the Family Medical Leave Act of 1993, do exist. Ruth Ginsburg and the contemporary feminist movement may have accomplished all the legal change possible for one generation. To put her accomplishments in perspective, we should remember that she began her career in the days of sex-segregated want ads, mandatory unpaid maternity leaves, and men-only graduate and professional schools. Nevertheless, Ginsburg's success may come back to haunt us. The antidiscrimination approach may ultimately do more harm than good to the cause of women's equality.

CONCLUSION

Ruth Bader Ginsburg seems destined to spend her Supreme Court career as a member of a minority bloc. Turnover on the Court may make the bloc even smaller. With Republicans in control of the presidency and the Senate, the Court is likely to become more rather than less conservative with respect to civil rights and liberties. But the Bush administration has not yet demonstrated the extent of its commitment to the new judicial federalism or the priority it will give to this issue in making judicial appointments. Nor do we know yet how successful the administration will be in predicting the behavior of its appointees. A new justice could become part of a 5 to 4 majority reversing the recent trend of hostility toward federal power.

Ginsburg's frequent presence on the losing side limits her opportunities to write binding precedent. She has chosen to dissent in silence much of the time and does not go out of her way to be original or eloquent. When she does write, her opinions stay firmly in the present; they speak to actual audiences, not hypothetical future ones. She shows no tendency to strike out on her own, to express ideas nobody else has thought of. Her majority opinions are too few, and her dissents too ordinary, to make it likely that posterity will remember her for them.

She is not an innovator; even her opinions in gender cases adhere firmly to the venerable suspect classification doctrine. But she is far from being a marginal justice. She appears to be an active and influential participant on the Court, someone to whom others pay attention. Her impact both before the Court and on it has been profound. She will be remembered mostly for her contributions to the law of sexual equality. As a member of the first cohort of women lawyers to reach the top of the profession, her influence has gone far beyond cases won and opinions written. Like Sandra Day O'Connor, she has been a trailblazer and role model for younger generations of women lawyers. Ginsburg's work as litigator and judge has produced rulings whose effect on women's situations is limited, and it has not pleased everyone. Her impact is probably weakened by the same lack of creativity and vision she displays in general. But the once empty cupboard for women is overflowing. The blank check for sex discrimination has been replaced by skeptical and rigorous scrutiny. Ruth Bader Ginsburg's work has brought American women closer to full equality under the law than anyone could have imagined when she entered the legal profession.

NOTES

1. Respectively, "Ruth Ginsburg: Carving a Career Path through a Male-Dominated Legal World," *Congressional Quarterly Weekly Report,* 17 July 1993, 1876–1877; Peter W. Haber and Richard Taranto, "Ruth Bader Ginsburg: A Judge's Judge," *Wall Street Journal,* 15 June 1993, A18.

2. Juan Williams, *Thurgood Marshall: American Revolutionary* (New York: Times Books, 1998); Bob Woodward and Scott Armstrong, *The Brethren* (Simon and Schuster, 1979), 424.

3. Respectively, 411 U.S. 1 (1973); 518 U.S. 515 (1996).

4. "We worked, we married, . . . had children, served their schools, tried to do it all, have it all, be it all; never forgetting, particularly, that we were supposed to be living greatly in the law, and that we were, in fact, just trying most of the time to stay alive" (Judith Richards Hope, quoted in Ruth Bader Ginsburg, "Remarks on Women's Progress in the Legal Profession in the United States," *University of Tulsa Law Journal* 33 [Fall 1997]: 13–21).

5. "Ruth Ginsburg," note 1 above.

6. Respectively, Ruth Bader Ginsburg and Anders Bruzelius, *Civil Procedure in Sweden* (The Hague: M. Nijhoff, 1965); Kenneth M. Davidson, Ruth Bader Ginsburg, and Herma Hill Kay, *Text, Cases and Materials on Sex-Based Discrimination* (St. Paul, Minn.: West Publishing, 1974).

7. "The House That Ruth Built: Justice Ruth Bader Ginsburg, Gender and Justice," *New York Law School Journal of Human Rights* 14 (1997): 311, 314; Toni J. Ellington et al., "Justice Ruth Bader Ginsburg and Sex Discrimination," *University of Hawaii Law Review* 20 (1998): 699, 708; Ruth Bader Ginsburg, "The Progression of Women in the Law," *Valparaiso University Law Review* 28 (1994): 1161.

8. See Barbara A. Babcock et al., *Sex Discrimination and the Law: Cases and Remedies* (Boston: Little, Brown, 1975); Davidson, Ginsburg, and Kay, *Sex-Based Discrimination,* note 6 above; Pauli Murray and Mary Eastwood, "Jane Crow and the Law: Sex Discrimination and Title VII," *George Washington University Law Review* 34 (1965): 232; Leo Kanowitz, *Women and the Law: The Unfinished Revolution* (Albuquerque: University of New Mexico Press, 1969).

9. 404 U.S. 71 (1971).

10. The cases she argued were *Frontiero v. Richardson,* 411 U.S. 677 (1973), military benefits; *Kahn v. Shevin,* 416 U.S. 351 (1974), property tax exemption; *Weinberger v. Wiesenfeld,* 420 U.S. 636 (1975), Social Security; *Edwards v. Healy,* 421 U.S. 772 (1975), jury service; *Califano v. Goldfarb,* 430 U.S. 199 (1977), Social Security; and *Duren v. Missouri,* 439 U.S. 357 (1979), jury service. *Kahn* was the only case she lost. She was on the brief in *Reed,* note 9 above; *Struck v. Secretary of Defense,* cert. granted, 409 U.S. 947, judgment vacated, 409 U.S. 1071 (1972), pregnancy and the military; and *Turner v. Department of Employment Security,* 423 U.S. 44 (1975), pregnancy and unemployment compensation. Prominent cases in which she participated in amicus briefs include *Geduldig v. Aiello,* 417 U.S. 484 (1974), disability benefits and pregnancy; *General Electric v. Gilbert,* 429 U.S. 125 (1976), pregnancy and Title VII; *Craig v. Boren,* 429 U.S. 190 (1976), drinking age; *Califano v. Webster,* 430 U.S. 313 (1977), Social Security; *Dothard v. Rawlinson,* 433 U.S. 321 (1977), employment; *Nashville Gas v. Satty,* 434 U.S. 136 (1977), seniority benefits and pregnancy; *Los Angeles Department of Power and Water v. Manhart,* 435 U.S. 702 (1978), pension funds; *Orr v. Orr,* 440 U.S. 268 (1979), alimony; *Califano v. Westcott,* 443 U.S. 76 (1979), Social Security; and *Wengler v. Druggists Mutual Insurance,* 446 U.S. 142 (1980), workers' compensation.

11. "The Constitution is an empty cupboard for women." Ruth Bader Ginsburg, "Sex Equality and the Constitution," *Tulane Law Review* 52 (1978): 451, 452–453.

12. Respectively, *Slaughter-House Cases,* 83 U.S. 36, 83 (1873); *Buck v. Bell,* 274 U.S. 200, 208 (1927).

13. *Korematsu v. U.S.,* 323 U.S. 214, 216 (1944).

14. See *McLaughlin v. Florida,* 379 U.S. 184, 191–194, 196 (1964).

15. *Sail'er Inn, Inc. v. Kirby,* 485 P.2d 529, 540–541. See note 24 and accompanying text. Justice Brennan quoted verbatim from this opinion in *Frontiero v. Richardson,* 411 U.S. 677, 686–687.

16. 208 U.S. 412, 421–423.

17. Defensible, but not necessarily justifiable. See Judith A. Baer, *The Chains of Protection: The Judicial Response to Women's Labor Legislation* (Westport, Conn.: Greenwood Press, 1978). Later cases include *Goesaert v. Cleary,* 335 U.S. 464 (1948), and *Hoyt v. Florida,* 368 U.S. 57 (1961).

18. Deborah L. Markowitz, "In Pursuit of Equality: One Woman's Work to Change the Law," *Women's Rights Law Reporter* 14 (1992): 335, 339–340. See also Ellington et al., "Justice Ruth Bader Ginsburg," note 7 above, 722–727; Ruth Bader Ginsburg, "Con-

stitutional Adjudication As a Means of Advancing the Equal Stature of Men and Women under the Law," *Hofstra Law Review* 26 (1997): 263, and "Remarks on Women's Progress," note 4 above; Kenneth L. Karst, "'The Way Women Are': Some Notes in the Margin for Ruth Bader Ginsburg," *Hawaii Law Review* 20 (1998): 619.

19. Joyce Ann Baugh et al., "Justice Ruth Bader Ginsburg: A Preliminary Assessment," *Toledo Law Review* 26 (1994): 1, 26.

20. "The House That Ruth Built," note 7 above, 320.

21. Ellington et al., "Justice Ruth Bader Ginsburg," note 7 above, 723.

22. Markowitz, "In Pursuit of Equality," note 18 above, 340–342. See also Note, "Justice Ruth Bader Ginsburg and the Virginia Military Institute: A Culmination of Strategic Success," *Cardozo Women's Law Journal* 4 (1998): 541. As a judge, Ginsburg has shown a respect for precedent and a cautious approach to doctrinal change. See "Ruth Bader Ginsburg and John Marshall Harlan: A Justice and Her Hero," *Hawaii Law Review* 20 (1998): 97.

23. Ellington et al., "Justice Ruth Bader Ginsburg," note 7 above, 725.

24. *Sail'er Inn, Inc. v. Kirby,* note 15 above, 540–551.

25. 404 U.S. 71, 76.

26. 411 U.S. 677, 691–692.

27. 429 U.S. 190, 197.

28. Respectively, *Stanton v. Stanton,* 412 U.S. 7 (1975); *Weinberger v. Weisenfeld* and *Califano v. Goldfarb,* note 10 above; *Kirchberg v. Feenstra,* 450 U.S. 455 (1981).

29. Respectively, *Michael M. v. Superior Court of Sonoma County,* 450 U.S. 464 (1981), statutory rape; *Rostker v. Goldberg,* 453 U.S. 57 (1981), draft registration. *Kahn v. Shevin,* note 10 above, sustained a widows-only property tax exemption as a compensation for women's lower earnings. It is unlikely that *Kahn* would survive judicial scrutiny today. Now that women do serve in combat, *Rostker,* too, rests on dubious grounds.

30. Ginsburg has indicated that this was true on the Supreme Court, describing Justice O'Connor as "my savvy, sympatique colleague and counselor" ("Progression of Women," note 7 above, 14.

31. Respectively, "Ruth Bader Ginsburg," note 1 above; Baugh et al., "Justice Ruth Bader Ginsburg," note 19 above, 5.

32. Respectively "Ruth Bader Ginsburg," note 1 above; Note, "Justice Ruth Bader Ginsburg," note 22 above, 557, 577.

33. See "A Justice and Her Hero," note 22 above, 797–816.

34. For example, he voted to extend the right of counsel to state courts, *Gideon v. Wainwright,* 372 U.S. 335 (1963), and wrote a concurring opinion in *Griswold v. Connecticut,* 381 U.S. 479, 499–502 (1965).

35. See, for example, his dissents in *Mapp v. Ohio,* 367 U.S. 643, 672–685 (1961), and *Miranda v. Arizona,* 384 U.S. 436, 504–526 (1966).

36. 410 U.S. 113 (1973). Ruth Bader Ginsburg, "Some Thoughts on Autonomy and Equality in Relation to *Roe v. Wade,*" *North Carolina Law Review* 63 (1985): 375, 382.

37. Address, American Bar Center, 13 August 1963.

38. 517 U.S. 620 (1996).

39. 530 U.S. 640 (2000). Ginsburg did not write an opinion in either case.

40. *Vernonia School District 47J v. Acton,* 515 U.S. 646 (1995). By "Warren Court liberals," I mean Earl Warren, Hugo L. Black, William O. Douglas, William J. Brennan Jr., Thurgood Marshall, Arthur J. Goldberg, and Abe Fortas.

41. 520 U.S. 305 (1997).

42. She dissented in *Wyoming v. Houghton,* 526 U.S. 295, 309–313 (1999). See also *Whren v. United States,* 517 U.S. 806 (1996); *Ohio v. Robinette,* 519 U.S. 33 (1996); *Maryland v. Wilson,* 519 U.S. 408 (1997).

43. See, for example, *Calderon v. Coleman,* 525 U.S. 141 (1999); *Smith v. Robbins,* 528 U.S. 259 (2000); *Ramdass v. Angelone,* 530 U.S. 156 (2000).

44. See, for example, *Edwards v. Carpenter,* 529 U.S. 446 (2000).

45. *Callins v. Collins,* 114 S.Ct. 1127, 1128 (1994) (dissenting from denial of certiorari); *Employment Division, Department of Human Resources v. Smith,* 494 U.S. 872, 907–909 (1990).

46. Respectively, *Wallace v. Jaffree,* 472 U.S. 38, 91–114 (1985) (dissenting opinion); *Lynch v. Donnelly,* 465 U.S. 668, 687 (1984) (concurring opinion).

47. Respectively, 530 U.S. 290; 521 U.S. 203. Both Ginsburg and O'Connor joined the majority in *Board of Education, Kiryas Joel Village School District v. Grumet,* 512 U.S. 687 (1994).

48. *Lemon v. Kurtzman,* 403 U.S. 602 (1971).

49. 521 U.S. 907 (1997).

50. 330 U.S. 1, 18 (1947).

51. 515 U.S. 753. Ginsburg's dissent in *Agostini v. Felton,* 521 U.S. 203, 255–260 dealt with procedural rules, not doctrine.

52. 515 U.S. 753, 817–818.

53. "A Justice and Her Hero," note 22 above, 818.

54. 515 U.S. 200, 271.

55. Charles Evans Hughes, *The Supreme Court of the United States* (New York: Columbia University Press, 1928), 68.

56. The exceptions were *City of Boerne v. Flores,* note 49 above, 6 to 3, and *Dickerson v. United States,* 530 U.S. 428 (2000), 7 to 2.

57. For example, in *U.S. v. Morrison,* note 63 below, Rehnquist cites *Civil Rights Cases,* 100 U.S. 3 (1883), and *Harris v. U.S.,* 106 U.S. 629 (1883).

58. For example, *Garcia v. San Antonio Metropolitan Transit Authority,* 469 U.S. 578 (1985), congressional power to regulate labor conditions in state government; *Katzenbach v. Morgan,* 384 U.S. 641 (1966), section 5 of the Fourteenth Amendment.

59. *Bush v. Gore,* 121 S.Ct. 525 (2000).

60. 514 U.S. 549; 521 U.S. 848.

61. *City of Boerne v. Flores,* note 49 above.

62. Respectively, *Kimel v. Board of Regents,* 528 U.S. 62 (2000); *Board of Trustees v. Garrett,* 2001 U.S. LEXIS 1700 (2001).

63. 529 U.S. 598.

64. Note 60 above, 568; note 63 above, 677.

65. See *Heart of Atlanta Motel v. United States,* 379 U.S. 241 (1964).

66. Respectively, 517 U.S. 44 (1996); 528 U.S. 62 (2000); 2001 U.S. LEXIS 1700 (2001).

67. This tension between federal *judicial* supremacy and principles of federalism emerged long before the conservative majority took hold. See *Michigan v. Long,* 463 U.S. 1032 (1983). Here, the Burger Court weakened the settled rule that a state supreme court is the final interpreter of that state's constitution. The justices' reversal of the Michigan

court found insufficient emphasis on an adequate independent state ground for a search and seizure ruling. *Boy Scouts of America v. Dale,* note 39 above, revealed a similar choice of priorities.

68. "A Justice and Her Hero," note 22 above, 806–813.

69. 121 S.Ct. 525, 546, 547, 549.

70. *Heckler v. Matthews,* 465 U.S. 778, Social Security.

71. 511 U.S. 127 (1994).

72. 1 Cranch 137, 176 (1803).

73. *Mississippi University for Women v. Hogan,* 458 U.S. 718.

74. 347 U.S. 483, 495 (1954).

75. *Sweatt v. Painter,* 339 U.S. 629 (1950).

76. 518 U.S. 515, 520, 521, 522 (1996).

77. Ibid., at 524.

78. 766 F.Supp. 1407 (1991).

79. 976 F.2d 890 (1992).

80. 852 F.Supp. 471 (1994); 44 F3d 1229, 1238 (1995).

81. See Judith Hicks Stiehm, *Bring Me Men and Women: Mandated Change at the U.S. Air Force Academy* (Berkeley: University of California Press, 1981).

82. Dwight D. Eisenhower, *Crusade in Europe* (New York: Doubleday, 1948), 141.

83. 518 U.S. 515, 532–533. The interior quotes are from *MUW v. Hogan,* note 73 above, 724; *Wengler v. Druggist Mutual Insurance Company,* 446 U.S. 142, 150 (1980); *Craig v. Boren,* note 10 above, and the briefs and oral arguments.

84. 518 U.S. 515, 534.

85. Ibid., at 540 (emphasis added).

86. Ibid., at 548.

87. Ibid., at 553–554.

88. Respectively, 319 U.S. 624, 625–642 (1943); 337 U.S. 1, 2–5 (1949).

89. The flag-burning case, *Texas v. Johnson,* 491 U.S. 397 (1989), is similar.

90. 319 U.S., at 642, reversing *Minersville School District v. Gobitis,* 310 U.S. 546 (1940).

91. 337 U.S., at 4.

92. Note, "Justice Ruth Bader Ginsburg and the Virginia Military Institute," note 22 above, 582. See also Comment, "Ruth Bader Ginsburg: Extending the Constitution," *John Marshall Law Review* 32 (1998): 197; Kenneth L. Karst, "'The Way Women Are': Some Notes in the Margin for Ruth Bader Ginsburg," *Hawaii Law Review* 20 (1998): 619; and Deborah Jones Merritt, "Hearing the Voices of Individual Women and Men: Justice Ruth Bader Ginsburg," *Hawaii Law Review* 20 (1998): 635. Ginsburg,"Constitutional Adjudication," note 18 above, herself makes no claim to have changed constitutional doctrine.

93. 446 U.S. 442.

94. Note, "Strictly Speaking: Viewing *J. E. B. v. Alabama ex rel. T. B.* as Sub Silentio Application of Strict Scrutiny to Gender-based Classifications," *Houston Law Review* 32 (1995): 869, 885, 888, 890. The 1975 case is *Taylor v. Louisiana,* 419 U.S. 522. The notion that cases must be reconciled doctrinally may strike a political scientist as quaint, but a law student may be a better reader of the judicial mind than a nonlawyer.

95. Respectively, 523 U.S. 420, 460–471 (Ginsburg), 471–489 (Breyer); 99–2071.

96. See notes 10 and 28 above.

97. See above, note 29.

98. See above, note 29.

99. See, for example, *Lehr v. Robertson,* 463 U.S. 248 (1983).

100. See Judith A. Baer, "Women's Rights and the Limits of Constitutional Doctrine," *Western Political Quarterly* 44 (1991): 821, and *Our Lives before the Law: Constructing a Feminist Jurisprudence* (Princeton: Princeton University Press, 1999), chap. 5.

101. Ginsburg, "Constitutional Adjudication," note 18 above, 270.

102. *Williams v. McNair,* 316 F.Supp. 134, 136n3 (D.S.C. 1970). See also Judith A. Baer, *Women in American Law: The Struggle toward Equality from the New Deal to the Present,* 3d ed. (New York: Holmes and Meier Publishers, 2003), chap. 6.

103. Private colleges are not covered by the Fourteenth Amendment, although they must obey antidiscrimination laws in order to receive federal funds. Title IX of the Education Amendments Act of 1972 allowed historically black, women's, and men's colleges to continue as such. Public schools, of course, are bound by the Constitution; the old elite single-sex schools have become coeducational, at least on paper. Hunter College High has admitted boys since 1974. Boys are free to apply to the Philadelphia High School for Girls and Western High School in Baltimore, but none has ever chosen to attend. The U.S. Department of Education's Office of Civil Rights has found this situation constitutional. See Note, "The Young Women's Leadership School: A Viable Alternative to Traditional Coeducational Public Schools," *Cardozo Women's Law School* 4 (1998): 455, 479–480.

104. *Miller v. Johnson,* 515 U.S. 900, 944–945.

105. 438 U.S. 265.

106. Respectively, 488 U.S. 469 (1989); 509 U.S. 630 (1993); 515 U.S. 220 (1995); and 515 U.S. 900 (1995).

107. 411 U.S. 1, 28 (1973).

108. For race discrimination, see *Washington v. Davis,* 426 U.S. 229 (1976); *Arlington Heights v. Metropolitan Housing Development Corporation,* 429 U.S. 252 (1977); and *McCleskey v. Kemp,* 481 U.S. 279 (1977). For sex discrimination, see *Personnel Administrator v. Feeney,* 442 U.S. 256 (1979).

109. See Baer, *Our Lives,* note 100 above, chap. 5.

110. Respectively, Markowitz, "In Pursuit of Equality," note 18 above, 338; David Cole, "Strategies of Difference: Litigating for Women's Rights in a Man's World," *Law and Inequality* 2 (1984): 33, 35.

111. See Ann M. Scales, "The Emergence of Feminist Jurisprudence: An Essay," *Yale Law Journal* 95 (1986): 1373.

112. See, for example, Catharine A. MacKinnon, *Feminism Unmodified* (Cambridge: Harvard University Press, 1987), 37: "Day one of taking gender into account was the day the job was structured with the expectation that its occupant would have no child care responsibilities."

113. For example, Ginsburg, "Some Thoughts on Autonomy," note 36 above, 386; "Constitutional Adjudication," note 18 above, 271; and "Speaking in a Judicial Voice," *New York University Law Review* 67 (1992): 1185n108.

114. Wendy Williams, "The Equality Crisis," in *Feminist Legal Theory,* ed. Katharine T. Bartlett and Rosanne M. Kennedy (Boulder, Colo.: Westview Press, 1991), 15, 21.

115. See, for example, Mary Becker, "Prince Charming: Abstract Equality," in *Feminist Jurisprudence: The Difference Debate*, ed. Leslie Friedman Goldstein (Lanham, Md.: Rowman and Littlefield, 1992), 99; Mary Ann Mason, *The Equality Trap* (New York: Simon and Schuster, 1988).

116. Those who reject the need for choice include Baer, *Our Lives,* note 100 above; MacKinnon, *Feminism Unmodified,* note 112 above; and Joan C. Williams, "Deconstructing Gender," in *Feminist Jurisprudence,* note 115 above, 31.

117. Williams, "Equality Crisis," note 114 above, 26.

9

The Synthetic Progressivism of Stephen G. Breyer

Ken I. Kersch

A few days before the opening of the Senate hearings on the nomination of Boston-based federal appellate Judge Stephen Breyer to the U.S. Supreme Court, the Washington press corps peppered Deputy White House Counsel Joel Klein with questions about whether Breyer, who was reputed for his decisional pragmatism, believed in any transcendent constitutional principles that he would put beyond balancing. Klein brushed off the question. Breyer had not thought much about the Constitution at all, Klein declared. His intellectual interests had always lain elsewhere.[1]

In another time and place, given the importance and large complement of constitutional cases on the Supreme Court docket, this admission might have raised eyebrows. But in 1994, the press and President Bill Clinton alike understood that appointing a brilliant scholar who was reflexively liberal but who had not mused much either privately or publicly about equal protection or civil liberties set the president on the highest political ground possible.

Breyer's nomination came in the immediate wake of a succession of bitter political struggles between ideologically polarized political parties over nominees to the Court and high positions in the executive branch.[2] The presidential appointments cycle of the late 1980s and early 1990s left more blood soaking the soil than the denouement of a Greek tragedy. It began with the concerted and successful effort of liberal interest groups, especially abortion rights groups, to defeat Ronald Reagan's 1987 appointment of federal judge and former Yale law professor Robert Bork to the Supreme Court (Bork positively brimmed with constitutional principles that he put beyond balancing). George H. W. Bush's nominee for defense secretary, John Tower, went down in 1989 in a cloud of allegations of womanizing and hard drinking, and his nomination of Clarence Thomas to the Supreme Court was nearly defeated by a storm over yet another "woman's issue," this time allegations of sexual harassment (no fool, Thomas smoothly insisted that he had not given abortion rights a moment's thought). Although confirmation fights had certainly occurred in the past (Louis Brandeis's and Thurgood Marshall's had both been particularly brutal), the broadcast of these seriatim confirmation battles on national television at the dawn of the era of the twenty-four/seven news cycle converted the Reagan and Bush administration fights from beltway battles into transfixing national donnybrooks.

When Bill Clinton took office it was payback time. In 1993, his first two nominees for attorney general (both women, as Clinton insisted on appointing a woman to the office), Zoe Baird and Kimba Wood, were forced to step aside over "nanny problems." Gay rights activist Roberta Achtenberg was nearly defeated in her bid to become assistant secretary of housing and urban development. And University of Pennsylvania law professor Lani Guinier was forced to take herself out of the running for the position of assistant attorney general for civil rights in the face of staunch Republican objections to her well-documented support for racial preference policies.

The searing political heat of the Supreme Court appointments battles of the Reagan and George H. W. Bush administrations had ultimately been doused in cold water by the appointment to the Court of a slew of so-called "pragmatists" or "minimalists."[3] The seat slated for Judge Bork went to low-profile Ninth Circuit judge Anthony Kennedy. Warren Era pillar William Brennan's seat was handed over to Granite State stealth candidate David Souter. Clinton's high court appointments ended up as his own cold-water counterparts to his troubled series of first-term executive branch nominations. As part of an effort to rachet down the chaos of his early administration, in 1993 Clinton settled on the relatively uncontroversial federal judge Ruth Bader Ginsburg to be his first high court pick. Although Ginsburg had a background as a women's rights crusader for the ACLU who had once argued such landmark cases as *Frontiero v. Richardson* (1973) and *Craig v. Boren* (1976) before the justices, in more recent years she had consolidated a reputation as a legal craftsman through her well-bottomed administrative law rulings on the D.C. Circuit.[4] She sailed through her Senate confirmation hearings with little trouble.

Judge Breyer had been among those considered by Clinton for appointment to Justice Ginsburg's seat. He had, however, been quickly dropped from contention in large part because of a Baird-and-Wood-like nanny problem of his own, a problem that at the time was a bright red cape in the hands of the administration's appointments picadors. By the time liberal Republican and Nixon appointee Harry Blackmun stepped down in 1994, however, dudgeon over the nanny issue had all but exhausted itself. The need to keep controversy to a minimum, however, remained a high priority for a poll-conscious president who was particularly concerned with the future in Congress of his ambitious national health care plan spearheaded by his wife, Hillary Rodham Clinton. Former Maine senator, Senate Majority Leader, and federal district court judge George Mitchell, said to be Clinton's first choice, set his sights on becoming baseball commissioner instead and took his name out of the running. Interior Secretary Bruce Babbitt, another much bruited possibility, had already become entangled in a series of nasty political battles with western land interests (and their defenders in Congress), and the scholarly Arkansas federal judge, and Friend of Bill, Richard Arnold had made some purportedly less than ironclad abortion rulings, been associated in the past with an all-male social club, and was bedeviled by heart troubles to boot. Judge Breyer's name marched to the head of Bill Clinton's Supreme Court short list once again.

Breyer had made a name for himself as one of the nation's leading scholars of regulation and of administrative and antitrust law, abstruse subjects that he had taught as a professor at Harvard Law School beginning in 1967. When he was named to the Court in 1994, pundits and analysts were at first at a loss as to how to categorize the judge's legal ideology. Many settled on calling attention to Breyer's "non-ideological pragmatic philosophy," his "moderation," and his "technical skill." His opinions both for the First Circuit Court of Appeals in Boston (where he was a Carter appointee) and, subsequently, on the Rehnquist Court have since been praised for being "free of rhetoric, crisply-stated, organized, and well-written, with little jargon or any ideological bent or message." Others have called Breyer the quintessence of the "techno-judge": the dull, uncontroversial craftsman of the sort whose chief virtue is his ability to slide through the process of nomination to accession untouched by the sharp knives of a contentious political age. One commentator has simply defined Breyer as the Court's reliable "purveyor of common sense."[5]

The substantive foundations of one age's simple common sense, however, are often hard fought and long in the making. And Justice Breyer's "common sense" is no exception. It seems bland, technocratic, and devoid of substantive foundations only to those whose understandings of the ideal liberal or progressive appointment to the Court were formed in the Warren era, which had an unusual fixation on big rulings, big principles, and big hearts.

One of those people, it is worth saying, was Bill Clinton. While running for president in 1992, Clinton, harking back no doubt to the heroic Warren Court of his youth, made it clear that he wanted to appoint justices to the high court who had some life experience that extended beyond the courtroom and the ivory tower. Thinking of people like Alabama senator Hugo Black and California governor and vice presidential candidate Earl Warren, Clinton called Mario Cuomo, the sharp but silver-tongued governor of New York, "the kind of person I would want on the Court."[6]

The Breyer appointment ended up as the spawn of the Warren Court, but not in the simple way that Clinton had hoped. In the 1950s and 1960s, the Court had asserted its power to a degree that had not been seen since the New Deal standoff. That Court mobilized political forces that rallied around opposition to judicial activism (these forces helped elect Richard Nixon to the Presidency in 1968), including a powerful Right to Life Movement (which helped elect Ronald

Reagan). Conservative chief executives pledged to support the appointment of federal judges who would follow the law and not legislate from the bench, and who would interpret the Constitution according to the intent of its drafters rather than according to fluctuations in the perceived needs of the times. At the same time, however, both the Warren Court's rulings and federal legislation opened up the courts to all sorts of interest groups that formerly had to look elsewhere for political victories. These groups now also had a serious stake in who was appointed to the federal bench. In the era of divided government, judicial appointments became front-burner political issues in a way in which they had not been for most of American history.[7]

The Clinton administration alighted on techno-judges as a solution to the problems caused by the open politicization of the judicial selection process. To fixate on the big-hearted, broad-principled Warren-era justice as the progressive ideal, an ideal to which Justice Breyer is seen as "falling short," is to miss the very real ways in which he is a well-anchored—and, indeed, pioneering—substantive progressive. Breyer's jurisprudence, constitutional and otherwise, embodies a synthesis of twentieth-century legal progressive commitments, past, Warren era, and future.

Justice Breyer has not by any means rejected the liberal jurisprudence of the Warren Court. Rather, he assumes it. Breyer's pragmatism and minimalism stand firmly on the shoulders of the Warren Court's giants, and if he is permitted the luxury of presenting his rulings as pragmatic, restrained, and commonsensical, it is only because he can congenially refer to settled liberal precedent that, situated as he is in political time, he need not trouble to defend or discuss.[8] The existence of this deep reservoir of Warren era–precedent allows Breyer to simultaneously lend his support to the jurisprudence of the Court's liberal activism while spending most of his intellectual energy drawing upon an older, pre-Warren era constitutional progressivism suspicious of Court power, enamored of systematic empirical analysis, and confident of the virtues of administrative expertise. It appears to be Breyer's ambition to transform this older progressive outlook into a blueprint for an emergent twenty-first-century progressive imperative that looks to European and world standards as a yardstick against which to measure the development of the United States as an advanced nation.

Far from being a just-the-facts techno-judge, Justice Breyer's jurisprudence represents an effort to synthesize the divergent strands of twentieth-century constitutional progressivism and to update them for a new global order. It is because the path to doing so effectively does not involve grand, principled pronouncements in big cases that it has looked to many as if Breyer is not doing much of anything at all. It is when politics seems to be nothing more than movement toward a more expert rational order that constitutional progressivism most successfully avoids backlash politics and becomes deeply institutionalized as part of the architecture of a quasi-permanent governing order.

BACKGROUND AND INTELLECTUAL ROOTS

A former denizen of Cambridge, Massachusetts, and a man who married into the monied aristocracy of England, Justice Breyer is a good-natured man known for his polish and mild eccentricity. He alternates between riding the bus and his bike to work at the Court. And he takes a keen pleasure in debating—declaiming, even — the literary classics ("Oh Daddy—not the *Epic of Gilgamesh* again!").[9] Perhaps the Democrats who had appointed him were protesting too much by calling attention to the fact that Breyer once worked as a ditchdigger for the Pacific Gas and Electric Company during the summer as a young man growing up in San Francisco in the 1950s. But when it was discovered that the Supreme Court nominee had a criminal record, it was unclear whether the populist-inclined Democrats were pleased or nonplussed by the fact that Breyer's arrest for underage drinking was a consequence not of youthful dockside debauchery but rather of a stab at sophistication in the San Francisco opera house. At the age of nineteen, the future justice had boldly ponied up a couple of dollars for a glass of red wine in blithe defiance of California law.[10]

Justice Breyer came by his pragmatism in the first instance less as a by-product of *la vie active* than as a matter of serious metaphysics. When not digging ditches for the Pacific Gas and Electric Company, he studied pragmatism systematically at Stanford (from which he graduated with highest honors in philosophy in 1959) and, after a stint as a Marshall Scholar at Oxford, at Harvard Law School, where he wrote his third-year paper on Charles Sanders Pierce, William James, and Willard Quine. The American pragmatists, many of whom, like Breyer, had been members of the Harvard faculty, exerted a strong gravitational pull in Cambridge, especially at Harvard Law School. There, the pragmatist philosophers had a profound effect on the protorealism of Oliver Wendell Holmes Jr., a skeptic about judicial power who famously declared that "the life of law has not been logic, but experience," and on the sociological jurisprudence of the school's dean, Roscoe Pound, a botanist-turned-lawyer who argued with much influence for the proposition that, figments of formalism aside, at base law is policy and, as such, legal decisions are best made by judges who are able to avail themselves of the insights of social science.[11]

Holmes died in 1932 and Pound (who lived until 1964) was inactive by the time Breyer arrived at Harvard in September 1961, but even in the early 1960s, debates over their arguments and understandings of the nature of law retained a prominent place on the intellectual chess board at Harvard and, indeed, at law schools throughout the country. The formalism against which Holmes and Pound had honed their understandings had been vanquished politically at the time of the New Deal, aided in no small part in its efforts by swarms of freshly minted Harvard Law School graduates, including Professor Felix Frankfurter's "Happy Hot Dogs."[12] This regime change in legal thought and practice set the stage for the next intellectual move. With the triumph of the New Deal, realism and sociological jurisprudence had moved from outsider status to the corridors of power, and thus taking on formalism was no longer necessary. The new call to duty for Harvard progressives was to fashion a serviceable theory of the proper role for judges, law, and courts in a postformalist world. The pioneering scholars of this new world were New Deal veteran Henry Hart and his student, Albert Sacks, who constructed a new and highly influential "legal process" approach to law, which spoke to the new, post–New Deal progressive imperatives. Stephen Breyer was a devoted student of Hart and Sacks.

"We are," Oscar Wilde once pronounced, "other people." But might it be too simple to associate Justice Breyer's jurisprudence with the views of Hart and Sacks? After all, four other members of the Rehnquist Court, Justices Scalia, Kennedy, Souter, and Ginsburg, also took Hart and Sacks's famed legal process course while students at Harvard. Each has fashioned his or her own distinctive jurisprudence, and none are carbon copies of Breyer. Nonetheless, all within this group, with the exception of Antonin Scalia, have been rather consistently classed as "pragmatists" or "judicial minimalists." And of all these justices, it is Breyer who seems to have taken legal process thinking most fervently to heart. Only he went on to make legal process–type concerns the engine of his intellectual development.

The legal process approach sought, as Morton Horwitz has put it, "to absorb the temper and insights of Legal Realism after the triumph of the New Deal."[13] Legal realism as a school of thought endeavored to unmask the much revered doctrines and formalities of Anglo-American law as jurisprudential covers for what, stripped bare, amounted to raw policymaking by judges. Legal decisions, the realists declared, did not involve the application of preexisting (and apolitical) legal doctrine to a distinctive set of facts, a process in which a judge is a purely legal actor applying given law rather than making law. Rather, judicial decision-making required judges to actively exercise discretion in choosing applicable doctrine, emphasizing (and ignoring) selected facts, and choosing results that seemed to be socially useful and situationally just. As such, judges inevitably directed their work toward the advancement of some social purpose or purposes. Judges, in short, made law, and it was high time that scholars admitted this fact and analyzed law accordingly.[14]

Before the 1930s, legal realists, despite their prominence both in intellectual circles and the academy, had by and large been forced to situate themselves on the outside of political power looking in. With the election of Franklin Roosevelt to the presidency, however, they and their New Deal successors finally anchored themselves firmly in positions of administrative and judicial power. The question for the New Deal generation, which included Henry Hart (a veteran of Roosevelt's Office of Price Administration), was now no longer whether law amounted to the exercise of discretionary power, a matter long since assumed by jurisprudential progressives, but rather how one might go about exercising that discretionary power legitimately and in the best interests of society.

The legal process approach of Hart and Sacks was influential because it offered a serviceable answer. Law, scions of the realists well knew, was inevitably purposive. Given this purposiveness, the goal of those who govern should be to take care that the law worked effectively for people. Judges, Hart and Sacks were told by reflection and experience, were not likely to take a leading role in that process. As progressives and New Dealers, the Harvard professors were skeptical of the institutional capacity of judges (who had long relied on outdated constitutional and common law touchstones—what FDR had maligned as "horse and buggy" constitutionalism) to effectively address the full panoply of modern economic and social problems. The problem ran deeper than the fact that late-nineteenth- and early-twentieth-century judges were pillars of conservatism. As generalists and as government actors making policy as a by-product of the resolution of discrete, bipolar disputes in which they were apprised only of the facts brought to them by interested advocates, judges were simply not well positioned institutionally to make wise policy.[15] What was now needed in a post-realist world was a theory of institutional competence, a theory of which institutions—courts, administrative agencies, or private orderings—were best suited to make policy in which substantive areas and regarding which questions of governance.

The legal process approach amounted to a theory of proper processes and sensible institutional settlement. Because they provided for the orderly, if provisional, resolution of disputes over policy, sensible legal processes and settlements possessed "a moral claim to acceptance."[16] According to this new outlook, while judges certainly could not lay claim to the privileged position they had been accorded under the reign of legal formalism, they still had an important, if lesser, role to play. Hart and Sacks claimed that judges should read both statutes and precedent purposively and that, with purpose in mind, they should engage in a process of "reasoned elaboration."[17] In doing so, they should be especially attentive to questions of institutional competence. Judges, of necessity, had their place within the new, postformalist legal order. But many more decisions, the process scholars decided, should be made not by the generalists on the bench but rather by trained experts in the field. These experts would not be members of the bar but experts within Washington's new administrative agencies. Administrative experts were best positioned to gather facts, assess the consequences of decisions, and set informed and reasonable public policy.

As a progressive imperative for the new post–New Deal world, legal process had a famously unusual history. In its friendliness to expertise and federal administrative power and its suspicion of judicial power and of the formalities of federalism and the separation of powers, it has been (and remains) profoundly influential. At the very moment Hart and Sacks were announcing a new, process-oriented progressivism for a post–New Deal world, however, the progressive imperative was undergoing a radical shift in response to the civil rights movement and the subsequent "Rights Revolution" of the Warren years. The emergent progressive imperative lionized judges and judicial power and was simultaneously heeding the call of deep principles over pragmatism. The tension between these two apparently warring forms of constitutional progressivism between the mid-1950s and the mid-1960s so whipsawed Hart and Sacks that they could never bring themselves to publish their famous legal process text in this new jurisprudential environment. In their hearts, and rather poignantly, they knew it failed to speak effectively to the new progressive constitutionalism that, at the time of *Brown v. Board of Education* (1954), was just then struggling to be born.

STEPHEN BREYER'S SYNTHETIC PROGRESSIVISM

Although Stephen Breyer decided early to live greatly in the law, the intellectual road he took proved to have more in common with the pre–New Deal era's non-lawyer progressives than with the legal crusaders of the Warren years. Breyer was always less Thurgood Marshall than Charles Francis Adams, the pioneering head of the Massachusetts Board of Railway Commissioners in the late nineteenth century. Adams, who had forsaken the study of law early, trained his sights not on empathy and "simple justice," but on the construction of a serviceable institutional infrastructure that focused on problems of aggregate economic growth and the methods by which, through expert guidance, corporate interests and the wider public interest could be harmonized.

Where the imperatives of Adams's time involved the imposition of some sort of governing order on economic chaos, those of Breyer's involved, for the first sustained period in American history, the dismantling of sclerotic, competition-stifling regulatory regimes such as that governing the airline industry, the railroads, banking, and telecommunications. An authority on the economics of regulation associated with the Harvard wing of the law and economics school, Breyer made a name for himself in Washington, and in regulatory history, as the driving intellectual force behind Massachusetts senator Edward Kennedy's 1975 hearings on airline deregulation. The Breyer-initiated hearings set the stage for President Carter's 1977 appointment of Cornell economist Alfred Kahn as head of the Civil Aeronautics Board and for Kahn's successful leadership in first transforming the CAB and then, in short order, persuading Congress to eliminate it. The Breyer-Kahn initiated reform, in the tradition of Charles Francis Adams, helped to both vivify an industry and bring affordable air travel within the budget of a wide swathe of middle-class America. As Adams did with the Massachusetts railroads, Breyer played a leading role in devising and institutionalizing a regulatory structure that benefited capitalists and consumers alike.[18]

If being a "techno-judge" means lacking in a substantive legal vision, Justice Breyer is no techno-judge. If, however, it means an affinity with rationalist, scientific, antiformalist systems–regarding progressivism of the early twentieth century, Breyer fits the bill. What he adds to this progressivism is an inclination to look beyond the formalities of national boundaries in the same way and for the same reasons that his early-twentieth-century progenitors insisted upon leaping over the making of "formalist" distinctions between the national and state governments. In doing so, Justice Breyer's jurisprudence represents a synthesis of the various faces of twentieth-century constitutional progressivism, including a sense that the progressive institutional ethic is poised to take the next step toward globalism.

The first imperative of this synthetic progressivism is that the judge should serve as a helpmeet in the formulation of wise policy. Wise policymaking is first and foremost a matter of empirics and thus proceeds to make decisions only after all the relevant facts have been gathered. In his lengthy dissent from the majority's decision in *U.S. v. Lopez* (1995) to strike down the federal Gun-Free School Zones Act because it did not regulate interstate commerce, Breyer placed heavy emphasis on congressional findings that the law did affect commerce. "Courts must give Congress a degree of leeway" on these matters, which require "an empirical judgment of the kind that a legislature is more likely than a court to make with accuracy."[19] Although the fact that Congress made its empirical findings only after Antonio Lopez was prosecuted under the act was constitutionally significant for the Court's majority, Breyer found this constitutionally irrelevant: to rely on this distinction, he wrote, "would appear to elevate form over substance."[20]

In his apparent commitment to looking at facts on a case-by-case basis hardly and directly, as free as possible from ideological, formalist, and traditional constitutional categories, Breyer has praised "the genius of the Framers' pragmatic vision,"[21] but he is especially fond of citing Oliver Wendell Holmes Jr., the justice whose scholarship and jurisprudence emphasized the pragmatic policy adjustments underlying all legal rules, in arriving at a nonlegal approach to those adjustments. In a dissent in the line-item veto case of *Clinton v. New York* (1998), which was joined by Justices O'Connor and Scalia, Breyer cited Holmes for the proposition that the constitutional separation of powers does not "divide the branches into watertight compartments." "I recognize," he concluded, "that the Act before us is novel. In a sense it skirts a constitutional edge. But that edge has to do with means, not ends." And in a Brandeisian coda, Breyer concluded that the means at issue, the line-item veto, "represent[s] an experiment that may, or may not, help representative government work better. The Constitution, in my view, authorizes Congress and the President to try novel methods in this way."[22]

Like the pragmatism with which Holmes came to be associated, Breyer's synthetic progressivism is skeptical of the promise of judicial power. Since wise policymaking is at base an empirical matter, it is best conducted by experts who have gathered the relevant facts, whether they be in Congress or (as is more likely) in expert administrative agencies. The question is not one of the democratic legitimacy of the courts (as is often the case in considerations of judicial review). It is instead primarily one of institutional competence.

As a committed antiformalist skeptical of courts, judges, and the usefulness of legal categories, Breyer seems to have a particularly difficult time abiding the frankly categorical jurisprudence of Clarence Thomas, whom he frequently needles in his opinions with an evident exasperation at Thomas's untiring resurrection of thoughtways that adherents of the Harvard progressive constitutional tradition (such as Breyer) thought they had vanquished a very long time ago. In an abortion rights decision, Breyer first states Thomas's reading of the relevant precedent upon a disputed point of law and then states dismissively, "He is wrong."[23] In a free speech decision assessing the constitutionality of restrictions on "patently offensive" programming on cable television, Breyer sharply criticizes Justice Thomas's blithe (in Breyer's view) importation of standard free speech doctrine concerning public forums into the regulation of leased access cable channels as decidedly unhelpful.[24]

In addition to being policy-minded, empirical, and anticategorical, Breyer's synthetic progressivism is particularly attentive to the recognition of the existence of system effects, or the notion that decisions in one area typically have complicated, and often unanticipated, spillover effects upon outcomes in many areas and, as such, one can rarely act with confidence to alter one part of a system without simultaneously altering the dynamics of others.[25] Far from advancing rational policymaking within complex systems, traditional constitutional categories easily serve to thwart them. So in *U.S. v. Morrison* (2000), a case in which the Court followed up on its 1995 *Lopez* decision by striking down the federal Violence against Women Act as exceeding the scope of Congress's power under the Commerce Clause, Breyer, in dissent, chided the majority for moving to institute "complex Commerce Clause rules creating fine distinctions that achieve only random results." "How much would be gained," he asked, "were Congress to reenact the present law in the form of 'An Act Forbidding Violence Against Women Perpetrated at Public Accommodations or by Those Who Have Moved in, or Through the Use of Items that Have Moved in, Interstate Commerce'?"[26]

The most innovative feature of Breyer's synthetic progressivism is that, in a trend pioneered by international environmental and human rights groups, ethicists such as Peter Singer, and even the animating political vision of popular vote winner Al Gore, it inclines toward looking beyond national boundaries to the "global system" in setting the context for wise policymaking and the standard for a just order. Just as it was considered an aberrant constitutional formalism to refer to the Great Depression not as a national problem but rather as "the widespread similarity of local conditions," so the new synthetic progressivism is inching toward declaring aberrant a reliance only on national empirical evidence, national effects, and national sources of law.[27]

This inclination is a novel but logical extension of the New Deal constitutionalism as articulated by Justice Hughes in *West Coast Hotel v. Parrish* (1937), the "switch-in-time" Washington State minimum wage case. In rejecting the liberty of contract argument that had governed in the *Adkins* case (1923) (which *West Coast Hotel* overruled), Hughes emphasized that "liberty of contract" was a fiction under conditions, as here, of unequal bargaining power and thus was detrimental to the health and well-being of the worker. But he went beyond this statement to add an innovative systems argument that the failure of the employer to pay the legally stipulated minimum wage "casts a direct burden for their support on the community." "What these workers lose in wages the taxpayers are called upon to pay," he continued. "The bare cost of living must be met. We may take judicial notice of the unparalleled demands for relief which arose during the recent period of depression and still continue to an alarming extent despite the degree of economic recovery which has been achieved. . . . The community is not bound to provide what is in effect a subsidy for unconscionable employers."[28]

So, for example, in the *Lopez* decision Breyer makes a point of emphasizing the importance of primary and secondary education in light of "increasing global competition" and citing data for the proposition that "lagging worker productivity has contributed to negative trade balances and to real hourly competition that has fallen below wages in 10 other industrialized nations." He continues by spotlighting the problem of American students "emerg[ing] from classrooms without the reading or mathematical skills necessary to compete with their European or Asian counterparts," which has global systems effects. It lowers the nation's "standing" in the "international marketplace" and affects decisions by firms about whether to build production facilities here or overseas. All this he considers relevant to the constitutionality of the Gun-Free School Zones Act.

In the *Morrison* case, a reaffirmation of the *Lopez* ruling (by the same one-vote margin), from which Breyer also dissented, he goes beyond citing data regarding global economic systems to appealing to the example of the federalism of the European Union. In *Morrison*, Breyer cites article 5 of the treaty establishing the European Community and several law review articles that contemplate and, in some cases, propose European federalism as a model that America would do well to take into account. In his *Printz* dissent, although noting defensively, in response to a barb from Justice Scalia, that "of course, we are interpreting our own Constitution, not those of other nations, and there may be relevant political and structural differences between their systems and our own," Breyer, citing law review articles and the experiences of Switzerland, Germany, and the EU, declares nonetheless that "at least some other countries . . . have found that local control is better maintained through application of a principle that is the direct opposite of the principle that the majority derives from the silence of our Constitution." These foreign experiences are cited to "cast an empirical light on the consequences of different solutions to a common legal problem."[29] In a similar move in the right-to-die case, he contrasts the palliative care system of the terminally ill of England to that of the Netherlands to shed light on the American case.

Justice Breyer's interest in foreign law sources and global systems is even more evident in his scholarship. In fact, since he has ascended to the high court, a preoccupation with these issues seems to be well on its way to replacing his formerly predominant intellectual interest in regulatory and administrative law issues. Breyer's most recent work takes up the very issue of the relationship between national and supranational courts in Europe, a dynamic that he apparently believes is likely to become only more important in the United States.[30]

There are intimations of these inclinations even in his earlier work on regulation. In one of his books on regulatory reform, *Breaking the Vicious Circle* (delivered as the 1992 Holmes Lectures at Harvard), Breyer argues for the need to consider side by side the problems of toxic waste spills in New Hampshire with defoliation in Madagascar in thinking about wise policymaking.[31] The book's culminating prescription for the appropriate means of effectuating a rational, systems-inclined policy order is to create in America a French-style civil service and an American analogue of the French Conseil D'Etat, which he praises for its marriage of substantive and legal expertise and for taking "a general, perhaps a global, view of government programs."[32] In line with his pragmatic approach to reform, Breyer declares that he considers the creation of such a body in America to be politically feasible because it could be created piecemeal, through a series of small, low-profile changes that will individually prove their worth and gradually accumulate over time to culminate ultimately in a new and novel government body. This declared preference for transforming institutions through low-profile, piecemeal steps, it is worth noting, amounts to a statement in microcosm of the method underlying Justice Breyer's broader intellectual and jurisprudential project.[33]

Finally, while Warren Era constitutional progressives like William Brennan on the Court and Ronald Dworkin in the academy have emphasized the need for the meaning of the Constitution to change with the moral evolution of society, Justice Breyer's synthetic progressivism, in contrast, emphasizes the need for governing institutions to change not in response to shifts in the moral order but rather to the economic, technological, and social-institutional landscape. Law, as an instrument of policy in a dynamic world, is always in flux. In allowing the sexual harassment lawsuit against President Clinton to go forward while he was in office in the face of separation of powers and executive privilege objections, for example, the majority opinion by Justice Stevens in *Clinton v. Jones* (1997) made much of the fact that, historically speaking, private civil damages actions against sitting presidents were extremely rare. In his concurrence in the case, however, Breyer placed considerable—and, it turned out, prescient—emphasis on the ways in which the legal system had changed since the 1960s, citing evidence of what Walter K. Olson has dubbed "the litigation explosion" and noting the increased time, expense, and scope of discovery in this unwonted new world. Because the balance of power between the judiciary and individuals and other institutions had shifted, reliance on past evidence alone is not a guide for sound policy. The Court, Breyer felt, should consider formulating "a constitutionally based requirement that district courts schedule proceedings so as to avoid significant interference with the President's ongoing discharge of his official responsibilities."[34]

The "minimalism" First Amendment scholar and constitutional theorist Cass Sunstein has praised in Justice Breyer's free speech decisions—a pragmatic approach that eschews abstractions and hews closely to the case's unique facts in rendering a decision—is most readily on display in cases involving the regulation of new technologies, where he commonly cites social and technological change in reaching his decisions. In a case involving sexually oriented programming on cable television, Breyer cited social science evidence on the increased numbers of latchkey children "home alone."[35] In a case involving the constitutionality of cable broadcast must-carry rules, he relied in part on the changing position of cable television within the overall market for the delivery of television programs to American homes. In a political speech case, Breyer asked that the controlling precedent of *Buckley v. Valeo* be reconsidered "in light of the post-Buckley experience."[36]

SYNTHETIC PROGRESSIVISM AND THE COURT'S GOVERNMENTAL POWERS DECISIONS

Justice Breyer's synthetic progressivism has an unmistakable rhetorical commitment to the limitation of judicial power vis-à-vis the nation's legislative and executive branches. In this commitment, he echoes Progressive, New Deal, and legal process thinking, all variants of pre–Warren Era progressivism. This skepticism is animated by considerations of institutional capacity. Unlike legislatures and administrative experts, judges typically lack the empirical resources to set, and to experiment with the end of setting, wise public policy. For this reason, Breyer has arrived at traditionally liberal positions giving the broadest possible meaning to Congress's power under the Commerce Clause while, like the New Deal justices before him, reading the Tenth Amendment as "a truism"[37] and a flexible interpretation of constitutional separation of powers requirements. For Breyer, all of these are areas in which the judiciary should by and large stay its hand.

This skepticism regarding judicial power was in evidence in *Clinton v. Jones,* where, although concurring in the Court's judgment that while in office the president did not possess an automatic temporary immunity from civil damages suits arising out of nonofficial actions that took place prior to his assuming the duties of president, Breyer insisted that federal district courts should be constitutionally required to limit themselves "so as to avoid significant interference with the President's ongoing discharge of his official responsibilities."[38] In the same spirit, in *Boerne v. Flores* (1997), a religious liberties decision in which a prickly Supreme Court jealously defended its institutional prerogatives against a perceived assault by the U.S. Congress, he demurred. His brief dissent attempts to diffuse a stand-off by raising a point of doctrinal consistency: the Court needed first to determine whether *Employment Division v. Smith* (1990), the opinion that the Religious Freedom Restoration Act at issue in *Boerne* was directed at overruling, was correctly decided before it could rule on this case. The question was one of crafting a consistent legal landscape with regard to these issues.[39] Justice Breyer's dissent in *Bush v. Gore* (2000) cited both New Deal–era cautions against runaway judicial power and similar warnings from Alexander Bickel.[40]

Notwithstanding a substantive skepticism about judicial power in some doctrinal areas and a rhetorical skepticism about it in all, Justice Breyer has departed markedly from the old progressivism in joining the majority opinion in the *BMW v. Gore* (1996), in which for the first time since the New Deal, the Court deployed the doctrine of economic substantive due process, the bête noire of the old progressives, to invalidate a state action.[41] The use of "due process," whether concerning economic or other matters, is typically understood in constitutional law to represent the epitome of activist judicial policymaking, with judges substituting their own view for those of the people's elected legislators in making law.

In his *BMW* concurrence, Breyer concluded that an Alabama state court's $2 million punitive damage award in a case in which a man was sold a $40,000 new car that he had not been told had been repainted to the tune of $600 was arbitrary and hence violated Fourteenth Amendment due process guarantees. In doing so, however, Breyer and the other members of the majority acted to limit the power not of the Alabama legislature but of the Alabama courts.[42] In his opinion in this case, Breyer suggests the same awareness he evinced in *Clinton v. Jones* that we live in a changed and more litigious era, in which not only are there more lawsuits but also their damage awards can be unusually high and seemingly randomly so. The award here, he noted, "is extraordinary by historical standards, and . . . finds no analogue until relatively recent times."[43] Breyer's conclusion that the award was unconstitutionally excessive stemmed from his long-standing concerns for the systemic operation of a rational legal order. Due process, or "requiring the application of law, rather than a system of caprice," he explained, citing the Magna Carta, "does more than simply provide citizens notice of what actions may subject them to punishment; it also helps to assure the uniform general treatment of similarly situated persons that is the essence of law itself. . . . The standards the Alabama courts applied here are vague and open-ended to the point where they risk arbitrary results." [44]

The due process problem for Breyer, in other words, is not that the Alabama court's award was excessive by an objective measure, though certainly its amount raised red flags, but that it was not made pursuant to a rational system. In his concurrence, he suggests that several rational systems for calculating punitive damages awards have been offered by legal scholars (he cites fellow law and economics scholars for possible formulas), but makes it clear that he is not advocating a particular economic theory of punitive damages but rather some economic theory to provide structure to the system. This requirement is especially important where courts review punitive damage awards arrived at by juries who do not "work within a discipline and hierarchical organization that normally promotes roughly uniform interpretation and application of the law," as judges do.[45]

Due process requires that some system—any rational, guiding system—structure the legal order.

Given his longstanding legal process interest in the proper allocation of institutional powers within political systems, it is not surprising that Breyer has written in a high proportion of the Court's most important federalism and separation of powers cases. Although the form of his analysis is unique, his ultimate votes in federalism and separation of powers cases are vintage New Deal progressivism. Breyer's dissent in *U.S. v. Lopez* (1995), in which the Court for the first time since the New Deal invalidated a statute on the grounds that it exceeded Congress's enumerated power to "regulate Commerce . . . among the several States," was lengthy and showcased many of his substantive constitutional commitments, in particular a stated skepticism about judicial power, a reliance on empiricism, and a vision of contemporary life as constituting a grand, interconnected system that extends beyond the formal fictions of both state and national boundaries.

For Breyer, the test in *Lopez* was whether the activity in question (in this case, the possession of guns in a school zone) had a "significant effect" on interstate commerce, with the significance of that effect to be determined cumulatively. The effects of all the individual gun possessions in school zones, in short, would have to be added up to provide a bird's-eye view of the total effect on national commerce. Determining the connection between this gun regulation and commerce "requires an empirical judgment of a kind that a legislature is more likely than a court to make with accuracy," and thus was a matter for Congress and not the courts.[46] One of the problems with the Gun-Free School Zones Act, at least for the majority, was that Congress had not actually written into the law its findings concerning the effects of guns in school zones on interstate commerce. Breyer considered this omission a matter of mere form: Congress made the requisite findings after *Lopez* had been prosecuted, and it is the social facts, rather than the form of enactment, that are ultimately determinative.

In his dissent, Breyer went on to canvas a wide array of ways in which Congress had noted that guns near schools affect commerce ("violence victims suffer academically"; "teachers unable to teach, students unable to learn"; "Education . . . has long been inextricably intertwined with the Nation's economy"). He made special, and characteristic, mention of "increasing global competition" and took pains to compare the educational performance of American students with their counterparts in Europe and Asia, adding that "today, more than ever, many firms base their location decisions upon the presence, or absence, of a work force with a basic education." Breyer's affinity for pointing out interconnectedness went so far as to note the likely effect on book and school supply sales in places where violence disrupts learning. "Commerce among the several states," he said, quoting Holmes in *Swift and Co. v. United States* (1905), "is not a technical legal conception, but a practical one, drawn from the course of business."

On the Court, Breyer has proved to be a committed cooperative federalist. Under cooperative federalism, an outgrowth of the early-twentieth-century and New Deal progressive ethic to which he pledged allegiance in *Lopez*, there are no effective constitutional limits on national power. Such limits exist only as matters of institutional prudence, through, that is, politically agreed-upon, pragmatic cooperation with the states. Cooperative federalism is federalism denuded of all its formal requirements. In cooperative federalist judicial rulings, judges are partners in the ongoing process of the formulation of serviceable institutional arrangements. Or, as Justice Breyer put it in another context in praising a fellow judge, in "mak[ing] past precedent reveal the legal principle that is its driving force [i.e., federalism], and then, with intelligence, shap[ing] that principle in light of its basic purposes, enabling it to work better within the society of which it is a part."[47]

In federalism cases, Breyer has voted to declare state-imposed term limits for members of a state's congressional delegation to be unconstitutional. Citing the dynamics of European federalism in which, in his assessment, the commandeering of local officials to administer national programs serves to enhance rather than limit the decentralization of power (it offers an alternative to the creation of large, centralized bureaucracies), Breyer would have held a congressional order that local sheriffs conduct background checks for gun buyers to be consistent with principles of American constitutional federalism. Along the same limes, he has consistently rejected state claims of sovereign immunity in the face of private lawsuits authorized by federal statutes (despite, it is worth noting, the immense power this approach puts in the hands of judges), in one case on the grounds that, although the formal Fourteenth Amendment remedy of direct federal remedial action against the state remains, such action is not likely to be taken and thus, for this reason, for constitutional purposes effectively does not exist.[48]

In separation of powers cases, Justice Breyer's jurisprudence is somewhat less predictable, perhaps because in this area he finds that, measured by the yardstick of current needs, the formal institutional arrangements set up by the founders work relatively well. And, unlike federalism claims involving state sovereignty, they do nothing to thwart a national interconnected governing system but rather constitute that system. Separation of powers formalist Antonin Scalia (and Justice O'Connor) joined a Breyer dissent that would have upheld the constitutionality of the Line Item Veto Act. The reasoning of the dissent was vintage Breyer, however, in its praise of "the genius of the Framers' pragmatic vision" and its declaration that "we are to interpret nonliteral separation of powers principles in light of the need for 'workable government.'"[49] The fact of the matter is that the act served a useful principle, and it was a practical impossibility for Congress to "divide such a bill into thousands or tens of thousands, of separate appropriations bills." The legislation "represent[s] an experiment that may, or may not, help representative government work better." As such, the Constitution does not stand in its way.[50]

SYNTHETIC PROGRESSIVISM AND CIVIL RIGHTS AND LIBERTIES

As noted earlier, scholars have speculated persuasively that the likely reason that Henry Hart and Joseph Sacks, Breyer's legal process mentors at Harvard Law School, could never rouse themselves to publish their influential and widely read casebook manuscript was that the professors understood that the book's preoccupation with the proper allocation of institutional power within an efficient system of governance failed to speak at all to what everyone was coming to recognize in the middle to late 1950s would become the most importunate and disputed matters of American law—issues of civil rights and civil liberties. When substance, particularly in the form of "simple justice," has beckoned, the refinements of institutional arrangements seem beside the point.[51]

This is hardly to say that legal process approaches proved impossible to apply to civil rights and civil liberties questions. Many, such as Herbert Wechsler, John Hart Ely, and Alexander Bickel, among others, did so with great prominence. The fact remained, however, as many critics of these scholars pointed out, that process alone was not enough. Justice Breyer's opinions on civil rights and civil liberties questions are written in legal process style. Rather than penning oracular appeals to fundamental constitutional principles, for instance, he is usually careful to recognize that on important issues society consists of individuals who hew to "virtually irreconcilable points of view" and that "constitutional law must govern a society whose different members sincerely hold directly opposing views."[52] While others leap to answer constitutional questions, Breyer often demurs on the grounds that the issue has not been squarely joined in the case and thus has not been debated adequately enough to bode well for wise policy change.[53] He is fond of citing the empirical evidence relied on by legislatures in arriving at their decisions as a prelude to an argument concerning legislative expertise and the limits of judicial competence.[54]

At the same time, however, with a few exceptions, Breyer's civil rights and civil liberties votes are predictably liberal and, moreover, commonly violate many of the core legal process tenets to which he has ostensibly committed himself in his governmental powers opinions. For example, he considered empirical evidence on the value of the unique form of single-sex education provided by the Virginia Military Institute irrelevant to the constitutionality of the institute's all-male admissions policies. Skepticism about judicial competence has not prevented him from backing increased judicial supervision of sexual speech in the workplace or judicial management of school systems in the interest of numerical racialism.[55] The existence of the landmark civil rights decisions of the 1960s and 1970s has allowed Breyer to more or less play the role of the reluctant suitor to constitutional liberalism, as someone whose decisions in the area are based not on his substantive views but on the nature of the evidence and of a rational institutional order.[56]

As a scholar, rights and liberties issues were never a preoccupation of Breyer's. His adoption of these positions seems to be part of his furnished soul as a Cambridge Democrat. Interestingly enough, and reflecting the political biases of the party that appointed him to the high court, his concerns regarding the limits of judicial power, the costs of regulation, and systems effects, including those involving the overlegalization of the policymaking process (a skepticism about what Jonathan Rauch has recently called "bureaucratic legalism")[57] seem to be hermetically sealed off from his decisions regarding rights and liberties. Few liberal justices have come to the Court as well equipped intellectually to rethink the shibboleths of 1960s and 1970s constitutional liberalism in light of our post-1970s experiences as Breyer has consistently done with regard to matters of economic regulation. With some marginal albeit interesting exceptions, however, his votes and views in this area are standard issue.[58]

In one way, however, Breyer might yet prove to be an innovator in this area, though it seems likely that his innovation will amount to a matter of method rather than substance. Given his penchant for transnationalism, it is quite possible that, over time, he will increasingly borrow what he deems to be serviceable "human rights" precedent from foreign or international courts and other such bodies with the aim of bringing American constitutional jurisprudence concerning rights and liberties up to what transnational progressive activists and their political allies in the academy consider the superior standards of Europe and of international bodies and conventions. In this endeavor, it seems that Breyer is less likely to rethink Warren era liberalism than, having found its domestic wellsprings to have run dry, to import that liberalism back into the United States from Europe where in recent years, like underappreciated American jazz musicians, it has been living in glorified exile on the Continent.[59]

As a clerk for Arthur Goldberg in 1965, the future Justice Breyer was actually present at the creation of the Warren Court's right to privacy, a right that eight years later would become the anchor for abortion rights in *Roe v. Wade*. He did the research for and wrote the first draft of Justice Goldberg's opinion in *Griswold v. Connecticut,* an opinion that found the right to privacy in the provision for the protection of unenumerated rights in the Constitution's Ninth Amendment. Despite these marked beginnings, although a committed adherent to Warren era precedent, Justice Breyer has to date been more cautious in finding such rights in his own career on the bench.[60]

Where Justice Breyer has been bold in his rights jurisprudence, it concerned economic rights (his background as a scholar with a thorough command of and respect for market economics and a business-sensitive statutory jurisprudence made him relatively popular among Republicans for a Clinton appointee and incurred the disapproval of the Naderite Left in his Senate confirmation hearings). He joined in the Court's stunning ruling in *BMW v. Gore* (1995), in which the Court issued its first post–New Deal economic substantive due process decision. In *BMW,* the justices held that an Alabama jury's punitive damage award for minor damage to a luxury car was unconstitutionally arbitrary and excessive.

In noneconomic substantive due process decisions involving abortion,

Breyer has signed on to the liberal position that abortions are constitutionally protected by the same right to privacy that he helped to fashion as a young law clerk. Unlike either his mentor Justice Goldberg or his predecessor Harry Blackmun, however, Breyer has been able to argue his abortion rights decisions as "straightforward application[s]" of the relevant precedent established "over the course of a generation," thus avoiding the flack that comes in controversial areas from grounding one's opinions in deep political or constitutional principle.[61] At the time of his appointment to the Court, it was not clear to some that he would take this path. At that time, some abortion rights groups were concerned because, while sitting on the First Circuit, Breyer dissented from the appellate court's vote in *Bellotti v. Baird* to strike down the Massachusetts parental notification statute. In doing so, however, he pleaded plain Supreme Court precedent. He did the same in his opinion for the Court that struck down a Nebraska ban on "partial birth abortions." But when parental notification laws of the sort at issue in *Bellotti v. Baird* came before the Court, Breyer, no longer a lowly appellate court judge, sided with the most liberal justices in dissent, voting that the laws be struck down as unconstitutional.[62] So far as abortion was concerned, the confirmation worries proved to be misplaced.

Breyer has expressed a willingness to consider substantive due process claims in other noneconomic contexts as well. In *Washington v. Glucksberg* (1997), the decision concerning the so-called "right to die," he concurred in the opinion upholding the constitutionality of a state statute making it a felony to knowingly aid another in a suicide attempt in the face of a claim that the law violated the Fourteenth Amendment liberty interest of physicians and others who were acting to help the terminally ill. Breyer opined that the right at issue in the case was not (as the majority opinion would have it) a "right to commit suicide with another's assistance" but rather the "right to die with dignity." As "the avoidance of severe physical pain (connected with death)," he argued speculatively, "would have to constitute an essential part of any successful claim and . . . the laws before us do not force a dying person to undergo that kind of pain" because palliative care was available, no constitutional right was violated on the facts of the case before the Court.[63]

Predictably enough, despite a supposed commitment to empiricism, in sex discrimination cases Justice Breyer tends to take a categorical approach that denies sex differences between men and women and inclines toward treating empirically observable differences as "stereotypes" rather than as social and biological facts. In *Miller v. Albright* (1998), a case in which the Court voted 6 to 3 to uphold a statutory provision granting automatic citizenship at birth to an out-of-wedlock, foreign-born child of an alien father and an American mother but requiring the similar child of an alien mother and an American father to meet certain affirmative statutory requirements concerning proof of identity and relationship, Breyer, in a dissent joined by Justices Ginsburg and Souter, wrote that the statutory distinctions at issue "depend for their validity upon the generalization that mothers are significantly more likely than fathers to care for their children, or to develop caring relationships with their children," and hence were unconstitutional.[64] This, he argued, was the result dictated by the Court's equal protection precedent in sex discrimination cases, including the precedent in *United States v. Virginia* (1996), the Virginia Militiary Institute case, a decision in which Breyer joined Ruth Bader Ginsburg's majority opinion.[65]

Despite a supposed skepticism about judicial power, Breyer has been a committed advocate of the increased judicial supervision of sex-related speech and conduct in the workplace and, notwithstanding his solicitude for systems effects in other contexts, has largely ignored the way in which an increasingly litigious environment has both chilled constitutionally protected speech and cut swathes through basic considerations of personal privacy (an environment increasingly satirized by a less earnest post–baby boom generation in classic situation comedies such as *Seinfeld* and the popular Comedy Central cartoon series, *South Park,* which constructed a classic episode around the Ur-sexual harassment case of *Everyone v. Everyone*).[66] Breyer's enthusiasm for judicial policing of the workplace in Title VII and Title IX cases has been duplicated in his statutory jurisprudence under the Americans with Disabilities Act, where he has joined Justice Stevens as the Court's lone dissenters from decisions that held that it was not a violation of the act for an airline to require that its pilots have twenty-twenty uncorrected vision or for a package delivery system to refuse to give a strenuous job requiring extensive manual labor to an employee with chronically high blood pressure.[67]

Despite Justice Breyer's stated refusal in sex discrimination cases to give constitutional sanction to stereotypes—regardless of empirical observations about identifiable groups of people—in the Court's voting rights decisions he has been eager to cite empirical evidence to reinforce the stereotype that black people by and large vote their kind when deciding between candidates for elective office. In *Abrams v. Johnson* (1997), a redistricting case arising under the Voting Rights Act, Breyer's dissent, which was joined by Justices Stevens, Souter, and Ginsburg, cited extensive evidence of voting "polarization" in support of the proposition that the drawing of legislative districts with race in mind is a form of "benign" as opposed to "invidious" discrimination.[68]

To date, *Abrams* is the rare race case in which Justice Breyer has actually written for himself. For the most part, in racial equality decisions he joins the Court's liberal wing, citing legislative authority and a skepticism concerning judicial power as a means of voting to uphold the constitutionality of interest group racialism. Breyer has been a consistent supporter, for example, of affirmative action and racially derived electoral districts. In cases raising these issues, he often signs on to opinions of Ruth Bader Ginsburg arguing that the government should be accorded broad authority to employ racialist remedies in an attempt to make up for the disadvantages occurring to blacks as a group because of the nation's racist past.

Pragmatic empiricism is back in the footlights again in Breyer's freedom of speech decisions. In many of the Rehnquist Court's free speech cases, the pragmatic, fact-specific, pragmatic minimalism praised by Cass Sunstein, an approach of which Justice Breyer is one of Sunstein's exemplars, has led to decisions so fragmented as to amount nearly to a return to the issuance of seriatim opinions.[69] Perhaps because of his background as a scholar of regulatory law and policy, Breyer has tended to write his own opinions in speech cases involving the legal regulation of elections and of broadcast and cable technologies.

In these decisions, Breyer commonly takes sustained judicial notice of the changing nature of the technological and legal environment that he argues strenuously makes categorical approaches to constitutional questions in the area particularly inappropriate. In *Denver Area Educational Telecommunications Consortium v. FCC* (1995), he wrote for the Court in holding that federal "segregate and block" requirements concerning "patently offensive" sexual programming on leased access cable television channels violated constitutional requirements concerning free speech. He reached this conclusion citing the existence of less restrictive technological means to achieve the same ends. But in so doing, Justice Breyer rejected the contention, supported by five others on the Court, that giving cable television companies the choice of whether to provide or prohibit patently offensive programming on leased access channels violated the First Amendment because such channels comprised a constitutionally protected "public forum." He noted prominently "the changes taking place in the law, the technology, and the industrial structure, related to telecommunications" and dismissed analogies drawn by Justices Thomas and Kennedy to other areas of free speech law to reach a result, asserting that "we believe it unwise and unnecessary definitively to pick one analogy or one specific set of words" to decide the case. The Court must balance all of the relevant interests in light of the shifting context while leaving the law flexible enough to accommodate future technological developments.[70]

Similarly, Justice Breyer concurred in the Court's holding that the "must carry" provisions of the Cable Television Consumer Protection and Competition Act of 1992 were consistent with the First Amendment. He did so on the grounds that, at the moment, a considerable portion of the American public does not have access to cable television but only to broadcast stations. In this situation, the must carry rules are essential to keeping broadcast TV on the air and thus ensuring "access to a multiplicity of information sources" for a large segment of the population, an important government interest. Breyer admitted frankly that the must carry rules imposed a "serious First Amendment price" on cable operators. Nonetheless, the statute's purpose of "prevent[ing] too precipitous a decline in the quality and quantity of programming choice for an ever shrinking non-cable subscribing segment of the public" is an interest that outweighs the cost.[71] Although he did not write separately in the case, Breyer joined in the Court's opinion in *ACLU v. Reno* (1996), holding that the Communications Decency Act

262   KEN I. KERSCH

of 1996 aimed at protecting minors from harmful material on the Internet amounted to an unconstitutional, content-based restriction on speech. In reaching its decision, the Court, in a Breyer-esque turn, specifically noted the unique nature of the Internet and hence distinguished regulation there from regulation appropriate to broadcast and other communications media.[72]

Breyer's jurisprudence in cases involving the regulation of elections has been as narrowly drawn as his cable regulation opinions. In *Colorado Republican Federal Campaign Commission v. FEC* (1996), he closely applied the distinction made in *Buckley v. Valeo* (1976) between limits on campaign contributions and limits on campaign expenditures to conclude that the First Amendment permitted political parties to spend freely on campaign ads when, as here, the party bought ads attacking the likely Democratic candidate for the U.S. Senate prior to the time his Republican opponent had been selected.[73] He joined the Court majority in a decision holding that it was an unconstitutional infringement of core free speech protections to impose a regulatory scheme banning the anonymous distribution of campaign literature, and he also joined in a decision holding that it was an infringement of constitutional rights to free association for a mayor to remove a tow truck service from the city's pool of independent contractors for refusing to contribute to the mayor's reelection campaign and instead backing the opposition candidate.[74]

Breyer's approach to speech issues in other contexts also parses facts closely. "Words take meaning from context," he announced at the outset of a decision concurring in part and dissenting in part in a clinic access case in which he refused to state any opinion on the constitutionality of so-called "floating bubbles" (movable buffer zones of stipulated distances that center around people coming and going from clinics). As he read the facts in the case, such a bubble had not yet been either affirmatively imposed by the district court nor had anyone been charged with its violation. Justice Breyer was on board for the Court's judgment that commercial speech was entitled to significant constitutional protection, but rather than signing on to a broad pronouncement of the principle, he joined Justices O'Connor, Rehnquist, and Souter in arguing that the ban on the advertisement of liquor prices outside the confines of stores amounted to a ban broader than the regulation necessary to serve the state's interests in keeping alcohol prices high in order to lower consumption. The state might, these justices noted, set minimum prices or impose liquor taxes to achieve the same results without any attendant restrictions on the freedom of speech.[75]

In cases involving the Establishment Clause and questions of the free exercise of religion, Justice Breyer's votes tend to array themselves with those of the Court's most liberal justices. In *Rosenberger v. University of Virginia* (1995), for example, a case involving the constitutionality of the University of Virginia's policy of funding a wide variety of student publications without regard for their content, but refusing to accord similar funding to student-run religious publications, he joined Justice Souter's strident dissent from the Court's landmark ruling striking down the policy.[76] Perhaps because of a vague awareness that few advanced democratic nations of the world have found it either necessary or helpful to hew to the strict separationist tenets created by the U.S. Supreme Court in the middle years of the twentieth century, however, Justice Breyer does stray from the Court's left in favor of its moderate center in some of the Court's religion cases. In *Good News Club v. Milford* (2001), for instance, he parted ways from the Court's liberals to join the conservative majority to hold that barring a Christian group from after-hours access to school buildings violated its members' rights to the freedom of speech.[77] In *Mitchell v. Helms* (2000), a case involving the distribution of federal funds to both public and private schools (secular and parochial) for secular uses, Breyer joined Justice O'Connor's moderate concurrence, once again leaving the Court's liberals in dissent. In *Capital Square v. Pinette* (1995), a decision holding unconstitutional the state of Ohio's refusal to permit the Ku Klux Klan's erection of a cross on the statehouse lawn alongside the display of a wide variety of other religious symbols, he signed on to Justice Scalia's majority opinion and joined Justices Souter and O'Connor's middle-ground concurrences (Justices Stevens and Ginsburg, the former appealing to Jefferson's famous "wall of separation" metaphor, dissented).[78] And in *Boerne v. Flores* (1997), Justice Breyer would have joined in upholding the constitutionality of the Religious Freedom Restoration Act, passed by Congress in response to the Court's earlier (and, many contended, erroneous) decision in *Employment Decision v. Smith*. Rather than reasoning from grand principles, however, his dissent argued that the matter could not be resolved authoritatively unless the Court squarely reconsidered whether it should follow or overrule the *Smith* precedent, which it had not done in the *Boerne* case.

Justice Breyer comes to the Court's criminal law cases with not only judicial but also administrative experience in the area. He was one of seven members of the U.S. Sentencing Commission formed by Congress in 1984 to impose order on the system that determined the severity of punishments for federal crimes. When the panel's efforts to reach a consensus on the appropriate punishment and penalties for particular crimes stalled, Breyer pitched in with a pragmatic, political solution: he proposed that the commission use data to get average sentences that judges have applied and set the new penalties according to calculated averages. In this way, an attempt was made to bridge substantive differences by procedural methods. The result, however, turned out to be quite substantive—the penalties were very harsh. And the new sentencing guidelines have since been subject to repeated criticism for their severity, inflexibility, and (in many cases) irrationality.

In his criminal process decisions, however, Justice Breyer is, with one pronounced exception, a reliable member of the Court's liberal voting bloc. He typically votes with Justice Stevens and the Court's other liberals in habeas and other cases involving the death penalty (which he has never concluded is per se unconstitutional), in cases involving the treatment of the incarcerated, in Fifth

Amendment due process cases, and in a variety of other matters of criminal procedure.[79] When it comes to Fourth Amendment search and seizure cases, however, Breyer commonly sides with the Court's conservatives. Although he makes no reference to European trends in this area in his opinions, one might spy a global sensibility here, as this is one important sector of criminal law in which Europeans give considerably more power to the police than liberal American jurisprudes would provide.[80] In *Minnesota v. Carter* (1998), for example, a case in which a policeman, tipped off by a neighbor that people were bagging cocaine in a nearby apartment, looked through the imperfectly closed blinds of the apartment, saw the criminal activity, secured a warrant, and made an arrest, Justice Breyer joined the Court in concluding that a guest visiting the apartment did not have a legitimate expectation of Fourth Amendment privacy as a visitor to the building.[81] Breyer has also joined the Court's more conservative justices to uphold the constitutionality of a random drug test testing program for high school athletes, to hold that bus passengers have no legitimate expectation of privacy in the soft luggage they store in the bus's overhead bins, and to rule that seizure and admission of evidence from a car following a routine traffic stop on the basis of an outstanding warrant issued because of a clerical error did not violate Fourth Amendment guarantees.[82]

CONCLUSION

Self-styled progressives have long had a troubled relationship with the strictures of American constitutionalism. In the early years of the twentieth century, progressive historians like Charles Beard, advancing his "economic" theory of the Constitution, animadverted against the charter as a plot by a cabal of wealthy and powerful men to advance and preserve their own interests at the expense of the broader interests of the American people.[83] At midcentury, in his deep and broadly influential study of American race relations, *An American Dilemma,* Swedish socialist Gunnar Myrdal declared in frustration that "the worship of the Constitution is a most flagrant violation of the American Creed which, as far as the technical arrangements, is strongly opposed to stiff formulas." Myrdal pragmatically declared that the path of progress required a studied following of the spirit rather than the letter of the law.[84] Whereas Beard, who was writing in the Lochner era against the countermajoritarian exercise of judicial review, saw the Constitution as barrier to democratic rule, Myrdal read it as an obtacle to the appropriate elite leadership in the name of progress. "The 150 year old Constitution," he wrote, "is in many respects impractical and ill-suited for modern conditions and . . . furthermore, the drafters of the document made it technically difficult to change *even if there were no popular feelings against change.*"[85] The conclusion of Myrdal's formulation jettisoned a concern for democracy in favor of an emphasis on the achievement, in the name of antiformalism, of concrete substantive results.

It is no coincidence that at this very moment the Supreme Court began to appeal not to our own country and traditions but beyond our borders for the principled authority to take the next progressive step. It was not likely that the Court, following Myrdal, would dismiss the written Constitution as "impractical and ill-suited to modern conditions," or that it would unmask American veneration of the document as "a most flagrant violation of the American creed." What it did instead was to look to international agreements—the United Nations Charter (1945), the Universal Declaration of Human Rights (1948), the Convention on the Prevention and Punishment of the Crime of Genocide (1948), and the Proposed Covenant on Human Rights (1948)—as potential authorities for the proper resolution of domestic issues. In *Oyama v. California* (1948), the Court came within a single vote of overturning the state of California's Alien Land Law as a violation of articles 55 and 56 of the UN Charter. In that case, Justice Murphy declared that the law "does violence to the high ideals of the Constitution of the United States and the Charter of the United Nations."[86] In the face of virulent domestic objection to the effort of the Court to change American law through the importing of foreign standards and authorities, expressed in the heated dispute in the 1950s over the Bricker Amendment, the Court stopped citing foreign sources and altered its readings of clauses of the American Constitution to achieve the same result.[87]

Justice Breyer's "common sense" cosmopolitanism, as it turns out, involves a more circumspect revival of 1950s globalism—transnationalism for the latest era of "The End of Ideology."[88] Politics is over, and the age of sensible, humane governance according to universal standards, the great progressive hope since at least the Wilson administration, is at hand.

In his recent book on the approach taken to constitutional questions by the Rehnquist Court, Cass Sunstein has classed Justice Breyer as one of the Court's emblematic "judicial minimalists," justices who promote democratic deliberation by crafting what Sunstein terms "narrow" and "shallow" case-specific constitutional decisions that leave broad issues of principle open for public discussion and debate. He classes Breyer alongside Justices Ginsburg, O'Connor, Souter, and Kennedy as the justices who "have adopted no unitary 'theory' of constitutional interpretation." "Instead of adopting theories," Sunstein writes, "they decide cases."[89]

Although Sunstein focuses on what he takes to be the effects of Justice Breyer's constitutional jurisprudence on democratic deliberation, the wellsprings of Breyer's "minimalism" are quite far from the sort of civil republicanism that Sunstein has consistently promoted in his own scholarly work. Justice Breyer's primary concern is not deliberative democracy but rather the proper allocation of institutional expertise and competence within a rational and coordinated system of public policy. He may not have a unitary theory of constitutional interpretation, but this does not at all mean he lacks a unitary theory of governance. Breyer's substantive theory of governance is deep and has been applied again and again in his constitutional decisions.

The fact that Justice Breyer's "minimalism" arises out of a concern for a rationally ordered system of institutional expertise and not civil republicanism may actually turn out to matter a great deal as he gains seniority and is assigned the task of writing more, and more important, constitutional opinions for the high court. In certain ways that become more significant with each passing year, the distinctive wellsprings of Breyer's pragmatism may actually help lead the Court away from playing a constructive role in promoting democratic deliberation and toward a high-handed, transnational elitism, particularly as it concerns civil rights and liberties. Evidence of this inclination in Justice Breyer's jurisprudence and recent scholarship is readily apparent.

Frustrated with their inability to achieve their policy goals within the deliberative processes of American government, a variety of interest groups on the liberal left, including environmental and "human rights" groups, have turned their attention to lobbying foreign and international organizations and then acting behind the scenes to apply their policy victories outside the United States back within this country via little noticed treaty provisions and obscure clauses within international agreements.[90] These groups have taken the democratic processes within the borders of sovereign nations to be barriers rather than benefits to their substantive programs. Justice Breyer, in pioneering the introduction of foreign and international precedent and sources into his Supreme Court opinions, represents, albeit still in cautious and embryonic form, the jurisprudential adjunct to this elite progressive globalism. Through the novel use of these foreign and international law sources, he is beginning to lay the basis for a postsovereign constitutionalism in which the wisdom of policies, including our substantive commitments regarding rights and liberties, is assessed by global rather than American standards. As Jeremy Rabkin has noted, the antisovereignty thrust of these trends is decidedly antidemocratic.[91] And that thrust will likely influence Breyer's opinions, and perhaps eventually the jurisprudence of other federal judges and Supreme Court justices, regardless of the fact that Breyer continues to craft his decisions, as he almost certainly will, in pragmatic, case-by-case terms.

Justice Breyer, of course, is hardly likely to take aggressively radical steps in the globalist direction. He will work by intimation and degrees, with the hope that gradually, over time, the decisions of the American Supreme Court will be more like those of other countries, which regularly cite foreign (including American) precedent as the basis of their decisions. In this project of "forg[ing] . . . from . . . several different legal systems a single workable system that . . . would serve as the voice of human decency," as Justice Breyer has recently praised Justice Jackson for doing at Nuremberg, he is hardly lacking an overarching constitutional vision.[92] Breyer may be possessed of common sense and act, as a political pragmatist would, by small steps, but like his "pragmatist" compatriots in the academy, his substantive commitments are clear to anyone who has the inclination to look.

"Techno-judge" or not, Justice Breyer is a quintessential progressive in that he is often impatient with the rigidities and formalities of tradition and law and thrills in the opportunity to begin and to build systems anew. For this reason, in recent years he has become taken by the genesis of the creation of the European Union. It is there—and not in Washington—that the processes of institutional design are under way before his very eyes. That is where the new thinking is being done, and Justice Breyer will do what he can, pragmatically, common-sensically, to make sure that the United States reaps the benefits of this new intel-lectual and constitutional project taking place beyond our shores. He takes his ideas from the old progressives, his instincts from the Warren Era, and his aspi-rations from the new progressive globalists. He may not be Justice Brennan, but when considered from a broader perspective, Breyer is a progressive justice through and through.

NOTES

1. Nat Hentoff, "The Breyer Coronation," *Progressive,* October 1999, 19.

2. See Benjamin Ginsberg and Martin Shefter, *Politics by Other Means: The Declin-ing Importance of Elections in America* (New York: Basic Books, 1990); Stephen L. Carter, *The Confirmation Mess: Cleaning Up the Federal Appointments Process* (New York: Basic Books, 1994).

3. Cass Sunstein, *One Case at a Time: Judicial Minimalism on the U.S. Supreme Court* (Cambridge: Harvard University Press, 1999), x–xii. Sunstein has advanced the term "judicial minimalism" for judging that promotes "democratic deliberation" by eschewing abstractions and, while accepting agreed-upon core principles in making deci-sions, sticks closely to the relevant facts of unique, individual cases. "Pragmatism" involves a similar mistrust of abstraction and reliance on broad principles, but may refer to anything from (colloquially) political realism in decision-making to (philosophically) the antifoundationalist political philosophies of Pierce, James, and Dewey. For our pur-poses, it is enough to note that mimimalists and pragmatists reject the role of judges as openly assuming a leadership role in the discovery and enforcement of new rights. When it was first advanced in philosophical circles and subsequently imported in various forms into American legal discourse, pragmatism had radical jurisprudential implications. Sun-stein's minimalism, however, is, at base, a conservative disposition aimed at preserving the core principles of the liberal Warren Court. It does so by attempting to stigmatize as "anti-democratic" judicial efforts by the current Court to repudiate the Court-created prin-ciples of the 1950s and 1960s.

4. Ginsburg had argued these cases as head of the ACLU's Women's Rights Project: *Frontiero v. Richardson,* 411 U.S. 677 (1973), holding unconstitutional on equal protec-tion grounds differing rebuttable presumptions in the U.S. military concerning the finan-cial dependency of married men and married women; *Craig v. Boren,* 429 U.S. 190 (1976), holding unconstitutional on equal protection grounds Oklahoma drinking laws that, taking statistical evidence of relative dangers into account, set different minimum drinking ages for men and women. Ginsburg had been friendly with Justice Scalia on the

U.S. Court of Appeals for the District of Columbia and won some points from conservatives for being a critic of the constitutional jurisprudence of *Roe v. Wade,* 410 U.S. 113
(1973), though hardly a critic of abortion rights per se. Sunstein, *One Case at a Time,* cat-
egorizes all of these relatively uncontroversial appointments—Kennedy, Souter, Ginsburg, and Breyer (to which he adds O'Connor)—as "judicial minimalists."

5. Jeffrey S. Lubbers, "Justice Stephen Breyer: Purveyor of Common Sense in
Many Forums," *Administrative Law Journal of American University* 8 (Winter 1995):
775; Richard J. Pierce Jr., "Symposium: Justice Breyer: Intentionalist, Pragmatist, and
Empiricist," *Administrative Law Journal of American University* 8 (Winter 1995): 747;
Mark Silverstein and William Haltom, "You Can't Always Get What You Want: Reflec-
tions on the Ginsburg and Breyer Nominations," *Journal of Law and Politics* 12 (Summer
1996): 459; Walter E. Joyce, "Essay: The Early Constitutional Jurisprudence of Justice
Stephn G. Breyer: A Study of the Justice's First Year on the United States Supreme
Court," *Seton Hall Constitutional Law Journal* 7 (Fall 1996): 149. See also Ted Gest,
"Breyer Lists from Port to Starboard," *U.S. News and World Report,* 18 July 1994.

6. Quoted in Silverstein and Haltom, "You Can't Always Get What You Want,"
460.

7. See generally Cornell Clayton, "Law, Politics, and the Rehnquist Court: Struc-
tural Influences on Supreme Court Decisionmaking," in *The Supreme Court in American
Politics: New Institutionalist Interpretations,* ed. Howard Gillman and Cornell Clayton
(Lawrence: University Press of Kansas, 1999), 151–177.

8. Sunstein declares that "any minimalist will operate against an agreed-upon background. Anyone who seeks to leave things undecided is likely to accept a wide range of
things, and these constitute a 'core' of agreement about constitutional essentials" (*One
Case at a Time,* x). Sunstein's newly conservative focus on the "core of agreements about
constitutional essentials" represents a repudiation of his own earlier works on constitutional theory. See Ronald Kahn, "A Critique of Judicial Minimalism: The Outside World
in Supreme Court Decision-making," paper presented at the Annual Meeting of the American Political Science Association, San Francisco, September 2001. The concept of "political time" emphasizes the importance of appreciating the changing constraints and
opportunities of political actors as they are situated within offices and institutions that
alter across time. See Stephen Skowronek, *The Politics That Presidents Make: Leadership
from John Adams to George Bush* (Cambridge: Belknap Press of Harvard University
Press, 1993).

9. Jeffrey Rosen, "Breyer Restraint: Is Clinton's Court Pick Too Good to Be True?"
New Republic, 11 July 1994.

10. Ibid., 19.

11. Oliver Wendell Holmes Jr. "The Common Law," *Harvard Law Review* 10 (1897):
61; Roscoe Pound, "The Need of a Sociological Jurisprudence," *Green Bag* 19 (1907): 610,
and "The Scope and Purpose of Sociological Jurisprudence," *Harvard Law Review* 24
(1911): 591, 25 (1912): 140, 25 (1912): 489; Arthur Sutherland, *The Law at Harvard: A
History of Ideas and Men, 1817–1967* (Cambridge: Belknap Press of Harvard University
Press, 1967); Robert Stevens, *Law School: Legal Education in America from the 1850s to
the 1980s* (Chapel Hill: University of North Carolina Press, 1983); Grant Gilmore, *The
Ages of American Law* (New Haven: Yale University Press, 1977). See generally Louis
Menand, *The Metaphysical Club* (New York: Farrar, Straus, and Giroux, 2001).

STEPHEN G. BREYER   269

12. See Peter Irons, *The New Deal Lawyers* (Princeton: Princeton University Press, 1982); *Lochner v. New York,* 198 U.S. 45 (1905); *West Coast Hotel v. Parrish*, 300 U.S. 379 (1937); *Home Building and Loan Association v. Blaisdell,* 290 U.S. 398 (1934); *Hammer v. Dagenhart,* 247 U.S. 251 (1918); *United States v. Darby,* 312 U.S. 100 (1941).

13. Morton Horwitz, *The Transformation of American Law 1870–1960: The Crisis of Legal Orthodoxy* (New York: Oxford University Press, 1992).

14. Jerome Frank, *Law and the Modern Mind* (Gloucester, Mass.: Peter Smith, 1970); Benjamin Cardozo, *The Nature of the Judicial Process* (New Haven: Yale University Press, 1921). See also Laura Kalman, *Legal Realism at Yale, 1927–1960* (Chapel Hill: University of North Carolina Press, 1986).

15. For a more recent articulation of the institutional limits of courts as policymakers, see Donald Horowitz, *The Courts and Social Policy* (Washington, D.C.: Brookings Institution, 1977).

16. William N. Eskridge Jr. and Philip P. Frickey, "An Historical and Critical Introduction" to *The Legal Process: Basic Problems in the Making and Application of Law,* by Henry M. Hart Jr. and Albert M. Sacks, ed. Eskridge and Frickey (Westbury, N.Y.: Foundation Press, 1994), lxxiv.

17. Eskridge and Frickey, "Historical and Critical Introduction," xcii. Eskridge and Frickey suggest that it was an awareness of this disconnectedness between the text's preoccupations and the hotly emerging questions of constitutional law that led the authors never to publish it (p. cvi). They do point out, however, that a whole generation of constitutional theorists, such as Herbert Wechsler, Alexander Bickel, and John Hart Ely, were plainly influenced by the approach's commitment to purposiveness, rationalism, and questions of institutional competence (pp. cxv–cxvi).

18. See Thomas K. McCraw, *Prophets of Regulation: Charles Francis Adams, Louis D. Brandeis, James M. Landis,* and *Alfred E. Kahn* (Cambridge: Belknap Press of Harvard University Press, 1984), 35, 248–251, 266. Breyer sets out his views on (and experiences in) regulation in detail in *Regulation and Reform* (Cambridge: Harvard University Press, 1982). Alfred Kahn had, perhaps not coincidentally, famously made a public commitment to clarity as one of his first moves as the new head of the CAB, an institution that he had concluded routinely used clouds of obfuscatory language to hide what was an entrenched pattern of arbitrary and irrational decision-making. Kahn insisted upon clear writing at the CAB, hectoring his staff, often personally, with assertions that "if you can't explain what you are doing to people in simple English, you are probably doing something wrong." In a campaign for administrative clarity that received wide press coverage in that late 1970s, Kahn explained that he had "very profound not only aesthetic but philosophical objections to people in government hiding behind a cloud of pompous verbiage which creates a gulf between them and the people." Breyer replicated this commitment to clarity in declarations about how as a justice he would craft his Supreme Court opinions. It is likely that this commitment came out of the same concern about the cloaking of administrative unreason that had motivated his fellow reformer Alfred Kahn. This experience was not Breyer's first stint in government service. Following his clerkship for Justice Goldberg in 1965, he worked for two years in the Justice Department as special assistant to the assistant attorney general for antitrust. In 1973, he was an assistant special prosecutor in the Watergate investigation. Just before his appointment to the First Circuit, Breyer served as chief counsel to the Senate Judiciary Committee.

19. *United States v. Lopez,* 514 U.S. 549, 616–617 (1995).

20. Ibid., at 618.

21. *Clinton v. New York,* 534 U.S. 399, 435 (1998).

22. Ibid., at 440, 449, citing *Springer v. Philippine Islands,* 277 U.S. 189 (1928) (J. Holmes, dissenting). In *New State Ice v. Liebmann,* 285 U.S. 262 (1932), 311 (J. Brandeis, dissenting), Justice Brandeis famously stated that governments must have the constitutional power "to remold, through experimentation our economic practices and institutions to meet changing social and economic needs."

23. *Stenberg v. Carhart,* 530 U.S. 914, 931 (2000).

24. *Denver Area Telecommunications v. FCC,* 518 U.S. 727, 740 (1996): "For Justice Thomas, the case is simple because the cable operator who owns the system over which access channels are broadcast, like a bookstore owner with respect to what it displays on its shelves, has a predominant First Amendment interest. [This categorical approach] . . . import[s] law developed in very different contexts into a new and changing environment, and [it lacks] the flexibility necessary to allow government to respond to very serious practical problems without sacrificing the free exchange of ideas the First Amendment is designed to protect." See also *Colorado Republican Federal Campaign Committee v. FEC,* 518 U.S. 604, 626 (1996): "Justice Thomas . . . would reach the broader constitutional question notwithstanding . . . prudential considerations. In fact, he would reach a great number of issues neither addressed below, nor presented by the facts of this case, nor raised by the parties, for he believes it appropriate here to overrule *sua sponte* this Court's entire campaign finance jurisprudence, developed in numerous cases over the last 20 years."

25. See Robert Jervis, *System Effects: Complexity in Political and Social Life* (Princeton: Princeton University Press, 1997).

26. *United States v. Morrison,* 529 U.S. 598, 659 (2000).

27. Hughes was reflecting an ethic of interconnectedness that came to be pervasive in the social and social scientific thought of this era. This ethic was reflected in both the Court's new progressive and New Deal jurisprudence. See Morton White, *Social Thought in America: The Revolt against Formalism* (Boston: Beacon Press, 1957); Thomas L. Haskell, *The Emergence of Professional Social Science: The American Social Science Association and the Nineteenth-Century Crisis of Authority* (Urbana: University of Illinois Press, 1977); Theodore J. Lowi, "The Welfare State: Ethical Foundations and Constitutional Remedies," *Political Science Quarterly* 101 (1986): 197–220. For examples of the new emphasis on transnational interconnectedness, see Peter Singer, "The Singer Solution to World Poverty," *New York Times Magazine,* 5 September 1999, 60, arguing that moral considerations of a just income distribution must be considered without regard to national boundaries; Nicholas Lemann, "Gore without a Script," *New Yorker,* 31 July 2000, describing Gore's intellectual fixation on global systems—of governance and otherwise; and Al Gore, *Earth in the Balance: Ecology and the Human Spirit* (Boston: Houghton Mifflin, 1992).

28. *West Coast Hotel v. Parrish,* 300 U.S. 379 (1937); see also *Wickard v. Filburn,* 317 U.S. 111 (1942).

29. In making this claim, Breyer cites Madison as also looking to European federalisms in designing American federalism. The distinction that he fails to note, however, is that Madison was designing and writing the Constitution, which was subsequently debated

and ratified, whereas Breyer is a federal judge appointed not to invent a constitution but to interpret one. One article cited by Breyer specifically advocates the importation of an emergent European model of federalism into American constitutionalism: Stephen Gardbaum, "Rethinking Constitutional Federalism," *Texas Law Review* 74 (March 1996): 795. Another makes a general argument that it is legitimate for federal judges to move aggressively and creatively beyond the confines of the constitutional text to restore the original balance of American federalism through novel doctrinal means: Lawrence Lessig, "Translating Federalism: *U.S. v. Lopez*," *Supreme Court Review* (1995): 125. In the Jackson article, the advocacy is more limited and implicit, while in the Bermann article, the directionality is reversed, with the lessons of American federalism applied to questions of European constitutional design: Vicki Jackson, "Federalism and the Uses and Limits of Law: *Printz* and Principles," *Harvard Law Review* 111 (June 1998): 2180; George A. Bermann, "Taking Subsidiarity Seriously: Federalism in the European Community and the United States," *Columbia Law Review* 94 (March 1994): 332.

30. Stephen Breyer, "Constitutionalism, Privatization, and Globalization: Changing Relationships among European Constitutional Courts," *Cardozo Law Review* 21 (February 2000): 1045. See also Breyer, "Speech: Crimes against Humanity: Nuremberg, 1946," *New York University Law Review* 71 (November 1996): 1161. These interests are likely to endear Justice Breyer to contemporary legal academics, who currently share similar preoccupations.

31. Stephen Breyer, *Breaking the Vicious Circle: Toward Effective Risk Regulation* (Cambridge: Harvard University Press, 1993), 20.

32. Ibid., 70–71.

33. Ibid., 79.

34. *Clinton v. Jones*, 520 U.S. 681, 722, 724 (1997). See Walter K. Olson, *The Litigation Explosion: What Happened When America Unleashed the Lawsuit* (New York: Thomas Talley Books–Dutton, 1991).

35. *United States v. Playboy Entertainment Group*, 529 U.S. 803 (2000).

36. See *Reno v. ACLU*, 521 U.S. 844 (1997); *Nixon v. Shrink Missouri Government PAC*, 528 U.S. 377 (2000).

37. *United States v. Darby*, 312 U.S. 100 (1941) (J. Stone).

38. *Clinton v. Jones*, 520 U.S. 681, 724 (1997).

39. *Boerne v. Flores*, 117 U.S. 2159 (1997); *Employment Division v. Smith*, 494 U.S. 872 (1990). See also *Raines v. Byrd*, 521 U.S. 811 (1997), in which Justice Breyer dissented from the holding that members of Congress lacked standing to challenge the constitutionality of the line-item veto prior to the exercise of that veto by the president (the issue was eventually adjudicated in *Clinton v. New York*). Breyer argued that legislator standing of the sort asserted in *Raines* was constitutional under a key (1939) precedent, but expressed a willingness to reconsider that precedent should the point have been argued in the *Raines* case.

40. At the same time, Breyer allowed for exceptions in cases involving either "a fundamental constitutional principle" or "a basic human liberty"; *Bush v. Gore*, 531 U.S. 98, 157–158 (2000). The implication, of course, is that restraint was in order because no fundamental constitutional principle was involved. One report has it that Justice Breyer was apoplectic about *Bush v. Gore* and angrily pronounced it to be "the most outrageous, indefensible thing" the Court has ever done. See David A. Kaplan, *The Accidental President: How 413 Lawyers, 9 Supreme Court Justices, and 5,963,110 (Give or Take a Few)*

Floridians Landed George W. Bush in the White House (New York: William Morrow, 2001), 292. Richard Posner, *Breaking the Deadlock: The 2000 Election, the Constitution, and the Courts* (Princeton: Princeton University Press, 2001), the most prominent contemporary proponent of judicial "pragmatism," reached a different conclusion. While giving due notice to the weaknesses in the Court's hastily reasoned opinion, he crafted a careful defense of the Court's ultimate decision in the case. My own view is that, jurisprudentially speaking, *Bush v. Gore* was a sport. The case will have little practical significance in constitutional development except to serve as a reminder of the institutional confidence of the contemporary Supreme Court. In taking this confidence to new heights, of course, the *Bush v. Gore* dissenters (and their partisans) have been at least as culpable (and, indeed, probably more so) than those who composed the *Bush v. Gore* majority.

41. See, for example, *Allgeyer v. Louisiana,* 165 U.S. 578 (1897); *Lochner v. New York,* 198 U.S. 45 (1905); *Adkins v. Children's Hospital,* 261 U.S. 525 (1923).

42. It is for this reason that Tinsley Yarbrough, *The Rehnquist Court and the Constitution* (New York: Oxford University Press, 2000), 114, is off the mark in calling it "ironic" that Breyer, a *Lopez* dissenter and vocally concerned with judicial overreaching, would join the majority in *BMW v. Gore.* The *BMW* case, unlike *Lopez,* involved the assertion of judicial power in the interest of limiting judicial power.

43. *BMW v. Gore,* 517 U.S. 559 (1995), 594.

44. Ibid., at 587, 588.

45. Ibid., at 596.

46. 514 U.S., at 616–617.

47. Stephen Breyer, "Articulos: Introduction," *Revista Juridica Universidad de Puerto Rico* 65 (1996): 427. This purposive approach, incidentally, mirrors Justice Breyer's approach to statutory interpretation, which is not discussed in this chapter.

48. *U.S. Term Limits v. Thornton,* 514 U.S. 779 (1995); *Printz v. United States,* 521 U.S. 98 (1997); *Seminole Tribe v. Florida,* 517 U.S. 44 (1976); *Alden v. Maine,* 527 U.S. 706 (1999); *West v. Gibson,* 527 U.S. 212 (1999).

49. 534 U.S., at 435, 436, citing *Youngstown Sheet and Tube v. Sawyer,* 343 U.S. 579, 635 (1952) (J. Jackson, concurring).

50. 534 U.S., at 434, 443, 450. See also *Clinton v. Jones,* 520 U.S. 681 (1997); *Department of Commerce v. U.S. House of Representatives,* 525 U.S. 316 (1999), census sampling case.

51. The phrase is Richard Kluger's and part of the title of his book on the *Brown v. Board of Education* case: *Simple Justice: The History of Brown v. Board of Education and Black America's Struggle for Equality* (New York: Knopf, 1976).

52. 530 U.S., at 921.

53. See *Adarand v. Pena,* 515 U.S. 200 (1995), joining Souter's dissent based in part on the fact that the issue of overruling *Fullilove v. Klutznick,* 448 U.S. 448 (1980), was not joined before the Court; *Washington v. Glucksberg,* 521 U.S. 702 (1997), suggesting that there may well be a fundamental due process right to "die with dignity," but that that issue was not squarely joined by the facts of the case; *Stenberg v. Carhart,* 530 U.S. 914, 938 (2000), striking down Nebraska's ban on partial-birth abortions on the grounds that the decision was a "straighforward application" of precedent.

54. See *U.S. v. Lopez,* 514 U.S. 549 (1995); *Abrams v. Johnson,* 521 U.S. 74 (1997).

55. *Gebser v. Lago Vista,* 524 U.S. 274 (1998); *Burlington Industries v. Ellerth,* 524

U.S. 742 (1998); *Faragher v. Boca Raton,* 524 U.S. 775 (1998); *Davis v. Monroe County,* 526 U.S. 629 (1999); *Missouri v. Jenkins,* 515 U.S. 70 (1995).

56. See generally Ronald Kahn, "The Social and Political Construction of Abortion Rights in Supreme Court Decision-making," paper presented at the Annual Meeting of the Western Political Science Association, Las Vegas, March 2001.

57. Jonathan Rauch, "Courting Danger: The Rise of Antisocial Law," Bradley Lecture, American Enterprise Institute, 11 December 2000, and "Law and Disorder: Why Too Much Due Process Is a Dangerous Thing," *New Republic,* 30 April 2001.

58. It is indeed quite possible that the fundamental distinction between the Harvard and the Chicago approaches to law and economics is that the adherents of the former school are unwilling to follow the logic of their insights to the point at which they would begin to undermine the authority of their shibboleths.

59. It seems that the intellectual groundwork for such a project is already being laid in the academy, which has shown a burgeoning affinity for studying the ways in which pressures from abroad played a prominent role in supporting and advancing the civil rights movement during the Court's Warren years. See, for example, Mary L. Dudziak, *Cold War Civil Rights: Race and the Image of American Democracy* (Princeton: Princeton University Press, 2000); Azza Salama Layton, *International Politics and Civil Rights Policies in the United States, 1941–1960* (Cambridge: Cambridge University Press, 2000). See also Michael Sandel, *Democracy's Discontent: America in Search of a Public Philosophy* (Cambridge: Belknap Press of Harvard University Press, 1990), 338–351. The new "constructivism" in international relations theory, not coincidentally, is supportive of a similar domestic agenda. See, for example, Margaret Keck and Kathryn Sikkink, *Activists Beyond Borders: Advocacy Networks in International Politics* (Ithaca: Cornell University Press, 1998); Thomas Risse, Stephen C. Ropp, and Katherine Sikkink, eds., *The Power of Human Rights: International Norms and Domestic Change* (New York: Cambridge University Press, 1999). See generally Jeffrey T. Checkel, "The Constructivist Turn in International Relations Theory," *World Politics* 50, no. 2 (January 1998): 324–348; Christian Reus-Smit, "The Constitutional Structure of International Society and the Nature of Fundamental Institutions," *International Organization* 51, no. 4 (Autumn 1997): 555–590; John G. Ruggie, *Constructing the World Polity* (London: Routledge, 1998). These ideas are now in the process of being imported into the legal academy.

60. Rosen, "Breyer Restraint," 19.

61. *Stenberg v. Carhart,* 530 U.S. 914, 921, 938 (2000), citing *Roe v. Wade,* 410 U.S. 113 (1973), and *Planned Parenthood v. Casey,* 505 U.S. 833 (1992).

62. *Lambert v. Wicklund,* 520 U.S. 292 (1997); *Mazurek v. Armstrong,* 520 U.S. 968 (1997).

63. *Washington v. Glucksberg,* 521 U.S. 702 ,790, 791 (1997) (J. Breyer, concurring).

64. *Miller v. Albright,* 523 U.S. 420, 482 (1998). See also *Tuan Anh Nguyen v. INS,* 533 U.S. 53 (2001) (J. Breyer joining Justices O'Connor, Souter, and Ginsburg in dissent).

65. *United States v. Virginia,* 518 U.S. 515 (1996).

66. *Gebser v. Lago Vista,* 524 U.S. 775 (1998); *Burlington Industries v. Ellerth,* 524 U.S. 742 (1998); *Faragher v. Boca Raton,* 524 U.S. 775 (1998); *Davis v. Monroe County,* 526 U.S. 629 (1999). See Jeffrey Rosen, *The Unwanted Gaze: The Destruction of Privacy*

in America (New York: Random House, 2000); Eugene Volokh, "How Harassment Law Restricts Free Speech," *Rutgers Law Review* 47 (Winter 1995): 563.

67. *Sutton v. United Airlines,* 527 U.S 471 (1999); *Murphy v. United Parcel Service,* 527 U.S. 516 (1999). See also *PGA Tour v. Martin,* 532 U.S. 661 (2001) (JJ. Scalia and Thomas, dissenting), where Justice Breyer joined the Court's majority in holding it a violation of the Americans with Disability Act for the PGA Tour not to grant a player with a circulatory disorder a waiver of a tournament regulation forbidding the use of golf carts by competitors. For a highly activist reading by Breyer of an immigration statute as applied to aliens, see *Zadvydas v. Davis,* 533 U.S. 678 (2001).

68. *Abrams v. Johnson,* 521 U.S. 74, 112 (1997).

69. See, for example, *44 Liquormart v. Rhode Island,* 517 U.S. 484 (1996); *Denver Area Educational Telecommunications Consortium v. FCC,* 518 U.S. 727 (1996); *Colorado Republican Federal Campaign Committee v. FEC,* 518 U.S. 604 (1996); *Turner Broadcasting System v. FCC,* 520 U.S. 180 (1997).

70. 518 U.S. 727. But see *United States v. Playboy Entertainment Group,* 529 U.S. 803 (2000), where Justice Breyer, in what he deemed "the application, not the elucidation of First Amendment principles," wrote for Justices Scalia and O'Connor in dissent from the Court's opinion striking down a law on the regulation of sexual programming on cable television on the grounds that, on the facts of the case, there was a legitimate problem to be addressed by regulation, and Congress had wide leeway to address it.

71. *Turner Broadcasting System v. FCC,* 520 U.S. 180 (1997).

72. *Reno v. ACLU,* 521 U.S. 844 (1997).

73. *Colorado Republican Federal Campaign Commission v. FEC,* 518 U.S. 604 (1996). See also *Buckley v. American Constitutional Law Foundation,* 525 U.S. 482 (1999).

74. *McIntyre v. Ohio Elections Commission,* 514 U.S. 334 (1995); *O'Hare Truck Service v. City of Northlake,* 518 U.S. 712 (1996). See also *Federal Election Commission v. Colorado Republican Federal Campaign Committee,* 533 U.S. 431 (2001).

75. *Schenck v. Pro-Choice Network of Western New York,* 519 U.S. 357 (1997); *44 Liquormart v. Rhode Island,* 517 U.S. 484 (1996).

76. *Rosenberger v. University of Virginia,* 515 U.S. 819 (1995). See also *Agostini v. Felton,* 521 U.S. 203 (1997) (J. Breyer joining JJ. Stevens, Souter, and Ginsburg in dissent); *Santa Fe Independent School District v. Doe,* 530 U.S. 290 (2000) (J. Breyer joining liberal majority).

77. *Good News Club v. Milford Central School District,* 533 U.S. 98 (2001).

78. In *Capital Square Review and Advisory Board v. Pinette,* 510 U.S. 1307 (1993), Justice Breyer signed on as a backer of the Court's "Endorsement Test," which asks whether a reasonable, informed viewer in the circumstances presented would interpret the government's action as an endorsement or a disapproval of religion or of particular religious beliefs. See also *Allegheny v. Greater Pittsburgh ACLU,* 492 U.S. 573, 625–628 (1989) (J. O'Connor, concurring in part and concurring in the judgment).

79. See, for example, *Jones v. United States,* 527 U.S. 373 (1999); *Calderon v. Thompson,* 523 U.S. 538 (1998); *Kansas v. Hendricks,* 521 U.S. 346 (1997); *Lewis v. Casey,* 516 U.S. 804 (1996), prison libraries; *O'Dell v. Netherland,* 521 US. 151 (1997), habeas corpus.

80. See, for example, Doris Marie Provine, "Courts in the Political Process in

France" (206–230), and Herbert M. Kritzer, "Courts, Justice, and Politics in England" (97–99), in *Courts and Law in Comparative Perspective,* ed. Herbert Jacob, Erhard Blankenburg, Herbert M. Kritzer, Doris Marie Provine, and Joseph Sanders (New Haven: Yale University Press, 1996).

81. *Minnesota v. Carter,* 525 U.S. 83 (1998) (JJ. Ginsburg, Stevens, and Souter, dissenting).

82. *Venonia School District v. Acton,* 515 U.S. 646 (1995) (JJ. O'Connor, Stevens, and Souter, dissenting); *Bond v. United States,* 529 U.S. 334 (2000) (JJ. Breyer and Scalia, dissenting); *Arizona v. Evans,* 514 U.S. 1 (1995) (JJ. Ginsburg and Stevens, dissenting). See also *Wyoming v. Houghton,* 526 U.S. 295 (1999) (JJ. Stevens, Ginsburg, and Souter, dissenting); *Florida v. White,* 526 U.S. 559 (1999) (JJ. Stevens and Ginsburg, dissenting); *Illinois v. McArthur,* 531 U.S. 326 (2001) (J. Breyer, for the Court; J. Stevens, dissenting). But see also *Atwater v. City of Lago Vista,* 532 U.S. 318 (2000); *Indianapolis v. Edmond,* 531 U.S. 32 (2000).

83. Charles A. Beard, *An Economic Interpretation of the Constitution of the United States* (New York: Macmillan, 1935).

84. Gunnar Myrdal, *An American Dilemma* (New York: McGraw Hill, 1964), 12–13.

85. Ibid., 12 (emphasis added).

86. *Oyama v. California,* 332 U.S. 633, 673 (1948). See also *Youngstown Sheet and Tube Co. v. Sawyer,* 343 U.S. 579, 668–669; *Sei Fujii v. California,* 217 P.2d 481 (1950), declaring the UN Charter to be a self-executing part of U.S. law.

87. See Duane Tananbaum, *The Bricker Amendment: A Test of Eisenhower's Political Leadership* (Ithaca: Cornell University Press, 1988). See also Lawrence Preuss, "Some Aspects of the Human Rights Provisions of the Charter and Their Execution in the United States," *American Journal of International Law* 46 (1952): 289, 296, advocating use of the Fourteenth Amendment rather than the UN Charter to advance civil rights in the United States; Charles Fairman, "Editorial Comment: Finis to Fujii," *American Journal of International Law,* 46 (1952): 682–690. Neither Dudziak, *Cold War Civil Rightrs,* nor Layton, *International Politics and Civil Rights Policies in the United States,* mentions the heated constitutional debate over the Bricker Amendment.

88. See Grant Gilmore, *The Ages of American Law* (New Haven: Yale University Press, 1977), 106, in which he describes the legal outlook of the 1950s as in large part an outlook subservient to the "cheerfully meaningless slogans" of "The End of Ideology" and "World Peace Through World Law." The case was made with regard to the 1950s by Daniel Bell, *The End of Ideology: On the Exhaustion of Political Ideas in the Fifties* (New York: Free Press, 1962), and today by Francis Fukuyama, *The End of History and the Last Man* (New York: Free Press, 1992).

89. Sunstein, *One Case at a Time,* 9.

90. See Robert Putnam, "Diplomacy and Domestic Politics: The Logic of Two-Level Games," *International Organization* 42 (Summer 1988): 427–460, political entrepreneurs bringing international influence to bear on domestic politics while domestic politics shapes international positions in a two-level game.

91. For discussions of the antidemocratic nature of these developments, see Jeremy Rabkin, *Why Sovereignty Matters* (Washington, D.C.: AEI Press, 1998), and *Law without Nations?* (Princeton: Princeton University Press, forthcoming).

92. Stephen Breyer, "Speech: Crimes against Humanity, Nuremberg, 1946," *New York University Law Review* 71 (1996): 1161. Whether this "single workable system" would follow or depart from the protections accorded under the American constitutional system is not clear.

Conclusion:
Politics and the Rehnquist Court

Mark Silverstein

William Rehnquist has sat on the Supreme Court since 1971, and the Court that bears his name has been in place for over fifteen years. In the academic world, such longevity invariably produces works of retrospection and critical assessment. The Rehnquist Court, however, is very much alive and well, rendering any effort to assess its work subject to continual revision. The chapters in the current volume minimize that risk, for they proceed, as Professor Maltz notes in his introduction, on the premise that for now the jurisprudence of the Rehnquist Court can best be understood as the result of the interaction of individual justices, each with a particular understanding of the problems of interpreting the Constitution and the role of the Supreme Court in American politics. By concentrating our attention on the parts, we ultimately will come to better understand the whole, and these extraordinary essays on the justices of the Rehnquist Court illustrate the wisdom of this approach.

In concluding this book, I too wish to approach the Rehnquist Court by concentrating on the composition of the Court. In my view, the Rehnquist Court marks a distinct period in Supreme Court history precisely because the justices currently serving are cut from a different mold than their predecessors dating back to the New Deal era. The justices of the current Court are the product of a nomination and confirmation process that has undergone a major transformation in the last several decades, and this transformation—itself a result of shifts in the larger political setting—has produced a new genre of Supreme Court justice. Phrased another way, the background and pre-Court careers of the members of the current Court are dramatically different from the background and careers of many of the justices who served on earlier Courts. Regardless of whether one applauds or mourns the arrival of this new Court with a "new type" justice (and I suspect I am perhaps among the mourners while Professor Maltz is with the applauders), appreciating the impact of the new politics of nomination and confirmation on the Court may well help us begin to assess the Rehnquist Court.

A COLLAPSE OF DEFERENCE

Chief Justice Warren Burger's announcement that he would retire at the conclusion of the 1985 term of the Court presented President Ronald Reagan with the welcome opportunity to name a new chief. It was, one might imagine, a stimulating prospect, but one nevertheless fraught with potential political liabilities. For years, Reagan had successfully linked previously apolitical evangelicals and religious conservatives with the Republican Party by combining pious rhetoric with the resolute promise to recast the ideological makeup of the Supreme Court. The new chief justice would, without question, need to be a conservative but ideally one of greater intellectual depth than the retiring Burger, capable of leading a true conservative judicial revolution. The religious right now formed an important component of the Republican Party, and the administration, early in its second term, was determined to reward the faithful. On the other side of the ledger, however, was the undeniable reality of the upcoming 1986 midterm elections and the unsettling possibility that Republicans would fail to retain their slim majority in the Senate. A delay in either nomination or confirmation might result in a Democratic controlled Senate vetting the new chief justice. On the other hand, to nominate a moderate to enhance the likelihood of quick confirmation was certain to trigger the wrath of the Republican right.

The decision to elevate Associate Justice William Rehnquist to the chief justiceship and name D.C. Circuit Judge Antonin Scalia to Rehnquist's vacant associate seat was the result of an intricate and exquisite political calculation. As the Burger Court's most forceful conservative, Rehnquist was certain to draw substantial liberal opposition. But the fact that he was already on the Court made speedy hearings far more likely and, absent a credible threat of filibuster, the votes for confirmation were secure. The nomination of William Rehnquist to succeed Warren Burger would fuel liberal opposition, but in the end the administration was confident he would survive the attack. With liberal interests focused on the futile attempt to deny their longtime nemesis Rehnquist the chief justiceship, the administration made a second calculation that the Scalia nomination would draw relatively little attention. It was correct on both its bets. A heated attack on Rehnquist's politics and credibility produced thirty-three negative votes in the Senate, an extraordinary showing of Senate antipathy considering that Rehnquist had been a Supreme Court justice for more than fourteen years prior to this vote. Scalia, however, managed the associate position without a single senator registering opposition. Reagan had seemingly made good on his promise to recast the Supreme Court and just in the nick of time; within the year the Senate would return to Democratic control.

The Rehnquist and Scalia appointments began a new chapter in the history of the Supreme Court if only because we have traditionally (albeit often mistakenly) pronounced the coming of a new chief as the beginning of a "new" Court. In this case, however, the hype may well have been warranted. In much the same way that the presidency of Ronald Reagan heralded a more decisive end to the New Deal/Great Society governing coalition than did the presidencies of either Richard Nixon or Gerald Ford, so too did the ascendancy of William Rehnquist to the chief justiceship appear to signal the end of the Warren Court era in a far more stark and telling manner than did the years of Warren Burger's stewardship. The transition, however, was not celebrated by a spasm of judicial activism on the part of the justices of the Rehnquist Court that laid waste to the most notable decisions of the Warren Court. Quite the contrary, Chief Justice Rehnquist has presided over what at most could be characterized as a judicial rebellion (hardly a revolution) in which the Court lowered its visibility and output and altered some of the basic assumptions of New Deal/Great Society constitutional jurisprudence (favoring the states over the national government is the prime example) while nevertheless engaging in a decison-making that, when all the votes were tallied, supported a good deal of doctrinal continuity. Trying to puzzle out why this Court should strike a tone so different from its immediate predecessors while at the same time preserving so much of what those Courts did leads, I think, to an examination of recent developments in the process through which we select and confirm justices of the Supreme Court of the United States.

The common thread that links the diverse men and women who make up the Rehnquist Court is that each attained this position after enduring a conspicuously new and different politics of nomination and confirmation, a politics that reflects what Samuel H. Beer, in another context, once termed the "collapse of deference."[1] Professor Beer was writing about British politics of the midsixties through the seventies, a time in which the ideals of a more "radical democracy"—participatory, egalitarian, and individualistic—overtook old traditional values and transformed the British polity. He was quick to note that there was much to lament as well as celebrate about this transformation, and a similar experience took place in the United States, although, given the inherently democratic ethos of American politics, to a lesser degree. An example of the "Americanization" of the collapse of deference may be found in the process of nominating and confirming Supreme Court justices.

From the turn of the century until the late 1960s, the nomination and confirmation process was marked by "passivity," "trust," and "deference to authority and competence" (phrases used by Beer to describe British politics prior to the 1960s). There might be isolated instances of revolt—the battle over the Brandeis nomination early in the century and the defeat of John Parker in 1940, for example—but the process, on the whole, was distinguished by widespread acceptance of presidential prerogative and deference on the part of the typical senator to both Senate elders and presidential choice. It was low-visibility politics in which insider deals paved the way for men of excellence and mediocrity to find their way to the nation's highest court without a great deal of public scrutiny or involvement.

The failure of the Senate to confirm Abe Fortas as chief justice in 1968 marked the coming of a new politics of nomination and confirmation. The process today is nasty, brutish, and anything but short. Threats of potential Senate filibusters by the opposing party or simply independent senators hang over the proceedings and constrain presidential options. Televised hearings enhance the opportunity for dramatic confrontations and encourage independent action by senators constantly in need of campaign funds and national media exposure. Powerful group interests are motivated and mobilized to begin grassroots campaigns even before a nomination is formally announced. No longer the preserve of a few political insiders, nominations to the federal bench are now governed by a robust and unruly brand of participatory democracy. Indeed, one might say that the modern confirmation process encompasses the best and worst of modern American politics; it has become, in short, a uniquely American instance of the "collapse of deference."

A NEW POLITICS OF NOMINATION AND CONFIRMATION

The Rehnquist Court is distinctive and a "new" Court precisely because it is the first of the modern era to be completely a product of the new politics of nomination and confirmation. Franklin Roosevelt transformed the Supreme Court in the 1930s through the appointment power, but the controversy of the New Deal was fixed on the executive's opportunity to name new justices. Once FDR had the chance to place his choices on the Court, the process of nomination and confirmation was essentially a formality. Hugo Black, Felix Frankfurter, William O. Douglas, and Frank Murphy were highly visible and politically controversial before being selected by FDR, and yet they assumed their places on the Court with relative ease. Much the same could be said of the appointments of Warren Court era. Acknowledged liberals like Arthur Goldberg and Abe Fortas and well-known political figures like Warren secured their seats without undue difficulty. Race played an ugly role in the Thurgood Marshall hearings, but ultimately America's preeminent activist lawyer was confirmed to the Court by a wide margin.

It was the Senate's refusal in 1968 to confirm Fortas as chief justice that signaled the beginning of a new era of contentious, disorderly, and unpredictable proceedings that defines the current Court. I have made the argument that the modern confirmation process is directly linked to the decision-making of the Warren Court in another context and will spare the reader an extended discussion in the current volume.[2] Stated simply, the most enduring legacy of the Warren years may well be the effort made by the Court during the 1960s to open the federal courts to a host of new claims and litigants and to fashion creative forms of judicial relief to serve these new interests. The motivation for the men of the Warren Court was undoubtedly to make judicial relief more readily available to the politically weak and disadvantaged. Disregarding traditional rules of standing or relaxing the requirements for class actions, for example, did ultimately enhance the ability of civil rights groups to employ federal judicial power to secure the goal of a more egalitarian society.

Making it easier to invoke the power of the federal courts, however, had wide-ranging consequences beyond even the beneficent expectations of the Warren Court justices. By the 1970s, divided government and the gridlock produced by a fragmented political system combined with the zero-sum nature of modern legislative activity (i.e., for every proposed new legislative program, the modern legislator faces the unappealing choice of either raising taxes or cutting existing programs) compelled even politically powerful interests to seek alternative arenas for the implementation of policy preferences. It quickly became apparent that a federal judiciary with relaxed justiciability standards and expanded remedies fit that bill quite nicely.

For much of the twentieth century, the decision about who sat on the nation's highest court was a matter of low-key, insider politics. Only rarely would a presidential nomination to the Court arouse intense public scrutiny. One quite unforeseen consequence of the Warren Court's effort to open wide the doors of the federal courts to an array of interests and claims, however, was to make the staffing of that federal judiciary a matter of deep concern to an ever-increasing range of politically powerful groups. The Bork nomination in 1987 stands out as a particularly sharp example of this development when over three hundred identified interest groups signed on to battle the nomination. The fact that interests as dissimilar as the United Mine Workers and the National Gay and Lesbian Task Force could find a common ground in opposing (or supporting, for that matter) a judicial nomination—even at the level of the Supreme Court—is powerful evidence that the staffing of the federal judiciary has emerged as a critical issue to a wide variety of powerful political groups.

Conventional wisdom of the last fifty years has been that an activist judiciary most often serves the needs of forces traditionally aligned with the Democratic Party. There is much to this notion; civil rights organizations have traditionally been more welcome in the party of Roosevelt, and the more affluent interests that often employed the judiciary in the 1970s (to realize liberal policy goals) tend to identify with the Democratic Party. But an activist judiciary has also played an important, if unique, role in the development of the modern Republican Party. Many of the hot-button social issues (abortion rights, school prayer, obscenity) that Republicans employed in the last three decades to link Protestant evangelicals and urban Catholics to the Republican Party have been insulated from legislative change by constitutional decisions of the modern Supreme Court. Efforts to secure a conservative social agenda through political action inevitably hinged on wholesale changes in the federal courts, and both Ronald Reagan and George Bush, the elder, adroitly rewarded social and religious conservatives for their electoral support by ceding judicial appointments to the right wing of the party. The net result is that powerful forces in the Republican Party now join equally powerful forces within the Democratic Party in a shared obsession with judicial appointments.

At almost the same time that the Warren Court was reworking the nature of judicial power, the U.S. Senate was undergoing a major transformation.[3] The old Senate was marked by a clublike atmosphere in which newcomers kept a low profile and leaders from both parties cooperated to further collective goals. The institution was governed by widely shared, albeit unwritten, norms of behavior that served to restrict the autonomous power of each member and ensure the orderly flow of Senate business. The norms of cooperation, apprenticeship, civility, and specialization worked to confirm the primacy of the institution over the ambitions of individual members. Thus the typical senator of the 1950s labored in what today would be considered virtual obscurity, concentrating on committee work, rarely being heard on the floor of the Senate, and even more rarely being acknowledged in the media. A handful of senior senators spoke for the institution and dispensed its resources to those members who played by the unwritten rules. Phrased very simply, the Senate of the 1940s and 1950s was a highly predictable institution marked by a high degree of conformity among members.

It goes almost without saying that the modern Senate is a far more unruly institution. Veteran senators pursue a host of goals independently of party leadership, and newcomers arrive with an ambitious agenda and the wherewithal to pursue that agenda. The constant search for campaign funds demands higher visibility on a wide array of issues, and, as a result, committee assignments no longer define a senator's range of interests. Activity on the Senate floor has increased, and the modern senator does not hesitate to employ the rules of the Senate to pursue personal ambition at the expense of institutional goals. As Barbara Sinclair has recently noted, "The Senate ha[s] become a body in which every member, regardless of seniority, fe[els] entitled to participate on any issue of interest for either constituency or policy reasons."[4] The Senate, like the House of Representatives, is today a more partisan body with votes often defined strictly by party affiliation. Filibusters have increased dramatically both on the part of individual senators seeking to disrupt the operation of the Senate and on the part of the minority party seeking to undercut the agenda of the majority. The modern Senate, Burdett Loomis tells us, is now distinguished by "declining trust, rising partisanship and entrenched individualism."[5]

The paradox of a highly partisan yet individualistic Senate accords the president a terribly complex arena in which to attempt to secure confirmation of a nominee to any appointed position, much less to the Supreme Court. No longer will private negotiations with a few key senators virtually assure a president's choice easy passage through the Senate. In the modern era, a president must heed the concerns of any interested senator, and substantial partisan opposition is a disquieting possibility on any nomination. The activism of the modern judiciary has ratcheted the difficulty level still higher, making certain that every nomination will receive intense scrutiny from powerful interests across the political

spectrum. These organizations, skilled in mobilizing grassroots politics and producing modern media campaigns, have the resources and the political acumen to
make even the presidential selection of a nominee as daunting a task as navigat-
ing that nominee's passage through an increasingly fractious Senate.

THE CONFIRMATION PROCESS AND THE REHNQUIST COURT

In my view, to place the Rehnquist Court in historical perspective requires an
appreciation of the fact that the current Court is the end result of a nomination and
confirmation process that now severely circumscribes presidential choice and
encourages (requires?) the elevation of experienced, competent, invisible jurists
at the expense of nominees with an extensive political and public background
who have played a prominent role in the life of the nation prior to appointment.
The inescapable political reality of the last two decades dictates that a nominee
of great prominence and public visibility facilitates the mobilization of opposition. Bill Clinton faced this reality in 1993 when Justice White announced his
retirement from the Court. Conservative groups immediately floated the names of
Mario Cuomo, Laurence Tribe, and other well-known liberals as likely Clinton
replacement choices. Whether the Clinton administration actually intended to
make such an appointment was beside the point; names like Cuomo and Tribe
were certain to trigger conservative ire, and floating these names was a useful
device to mobilize opposition to a Clinton nominee even before the president
announced his choice. Republican presidents faced and will continue to face a
similar mobilization of liberal opposition whenever a vacancy appeared (or
appears) on the Court. In an age of divided government and the decline of deference, it will be a rare president indeed who is willing to expend the political capital necessary to shepherd a controversial nominee through the process.

The operative question becomes not who the president might prefer to nominate but which acceptable candidate will trigger the least resistance on the part
of opposition forces. In the modern era, presidents have responded to the new
confirmation reality by avoiding well-known, prominent political nominees in
favor of little known jurists of no readily discernible political inclinations. After
reviewing the history of recruitment patterns to the Supreme Court, Professor
Larry Baum concluded that the most distinctive recent trend is "the steady and
sharp decline in the proportion of justices who had experience as candidates for
elective office."[6] For example, from 1968 to the present, Justice O'Connor is the
only member of the current Court who ran for elective office, and her career as
a state legislator was quite brief. Baum's research shows, however, that for the
period 1933–1968, one of every three nominees had run for political office prior
to coming to the Court, and well over half (61.9 percent) were holding a political post at the time of appointment. Equally revealing is the fact that only one in
four (28 percent) were judges at the time of elevation to the high court. Contrast

this statistic with the modern period beginning in 1968, when 83.6 percent of the individuals selected by the president were serving as judges just prior to nomination. In Baum's words, the modern period is unique in that "the legal path to the Court has been dominant to an unprecedented degree."[7]

There is another way to approach this trend, perhaps another "spin" on the collapse of deference and its impact on the Rehnquist Court. FDR named eight new justices to the Court during his years in office; he was personally acquainted with seven of them. Only Wiley Rutledge was unknown personally to FDR at the time of his nomination, and Rutledge, perhaps not coincidentally, was the only federal judge that FDR elevated to the Supreme Court. Many of the men nominated by Roosevelt were his close personal friends, some were trusted advisers, and all were ardent New Dealers. Harry Truman made four appointments to the Court; each was an individual well known to the president. Byron White had known and worked for John Kennedy for over twenty years before Kennedy made White his first appointment to the Court, and Arthur Goldberg, the other Kennedy appointment, served as his secretary of labor. Abe Fortas was a close friend and adviser to Lyndon Johnson for years prior to his appointment in 1965, and it was LBJ, with little if any consultation with political aides, who made the inspired decision to elevate his solicitor general, Thurgood Marshall, to the Court. During this era, only the Eisenhower appointments to the Court were neither advisers nor friends of the president. Nonetheless, for a variety of political reasons (and certainly not friendship) Eisenhower did nominate a most prominent Republican politician, Earl Warren, in what would be his most famous (or, perhaps for Eisenhower, infamous) appointment to the Court.

During this period, the White House and the Supreme Court were at the apex of separate branches in the constitutional scheme, but were significantly linked by personal contact and, more often than not, by shared political aspirations and goals. By way of contrast, on the current Court only Chief Justice Rehnquist could arguably be said to have even met the president prior to the actual nomination process. Indeed, we can safely assume that for the last thirty years, one manifestation of the collapse of deference is simply that too close an association with the president (for example, Fortas in 1968) or with national politics would almost certainly guarantee substantial Senate opposition to a nomination. Once again, the Clinton experience provides a ready example.

Prior to his victory in 1992, Clinton, at various times, made it quite clear that his ideal pick for a Supreme Court justice would be an individual with a broad political background and an appreciation of the impact of law on people's lives. But after assuming the presidency, Clinton found that a "homerun" (his word) appointment was easier to conjure on the campaign trail than to realize as president. After Justice White announced his resignation, the Clinton administration focused attention on Secretary of Interior Bruce Babbitt as a potential successor to White. Babbitt, a former governor of Arizona and dark horse candidate for president years earlier, lacked judicial experience but did have the broad political experience that Clinton apparently considered necessary for the Court. Influential Republicans, including Orrin Hatch, the ranking Republican on the Senate Judiciary Committee, however, quickly made clear their opposition to Babbitt as an individual likely to "legislate from the bench." Unwilling to face down such potent opposition, Clinton abandoned the search for the nominee with the "big heart" (his phrase once again) and spent months moving from one potential nominee to another, ultimately giving both friends and foes alike veto power during the selection process. Eighty-seven days after Justice White's retirement announcement, Clinton nominated Judge Ruth Bader Ginsburg, whom the president met for the first time just prior to his announcement of her nomination.

One year later, following Justice Blackmun's retirement, the administration once again went through the process of floating names and weighing potential support and opposition before settling on Judge Stephen Breyer. Clinton had met Breyer during the search for White's successor, and although he reportedly was unimpressed with Judge Breyer at their first meeting, a year later he found him a safe and, most important, an easily confirmable pick. In the case of both the Ginsburg and Breyer nominations, Clinton, despite the luxury of a Democratic majority in the Senate, abandoned his acknowledged preference for the well-known, political appointment who surely would have triggered a fight in the confirmation process for the highly competent, technically skilled, and publicly unknown lower court federal judge who was assured an uneventful elevation to the high court. The fact that both the Breyer and Ginsburg confirmations proceeded without a hitch should not obscure from the student of the modern Supreme Court the level of conflict at the nomination stage and the constraints imposed on presidential prerogative.

Detailing how each justice on the Court attained his or her position would certainly exceed the scope of this chapter. Even the brief descriptions, however, contained in the other chapters of this volume highlight how the professional experience of the justices of the Rehnquist Court differ from the justices who preceded them. The biographies of the members of the current Court are, in many cases, markedly similar: graduation, after service on the law review, from a national law school, a clerkship with a federal judge or association with a prestigious law firm, typically followed by either a teaching career or government service before being appointed to the U.S. Court of Appeals. In almost every case, elevation to the Supreme Court was the result of presidential compromise or careful calculation or both of the variables involved in securing confirmation. Frequently (certainly more frequently than other periods in the twentieth century) the deciding factor that motivated presidential selection was that the nominee would attract minimal opposition or had qualities (gender, race, and so on) that might deflect potential opposition. A confirmation process that so brackets presidential choice has produced a Court controlled by highly competent, intelligent, former lower court judges who share, in varying degrees, a skepticism regarding the capacity as well as the suitability of the judiciary to impose dramatic change on the body politic.

PRAGMATISTS VERSUS IDEOLOGUES

The new politics of nomination and confirmation, in short, have produced a new Supreme Court staffed with a new type of justice. None of the justices of the Rehnquist Court is linked to the president and presidential politics and aspirations in the same manner as were the justices of the Warren and Roosevelt Courts. Nor is the Rehnquist Court marked by sharp ideological battles led by partisan justices. The most ideological of the justices—the chief justice together with Justices Scalia and Thomas—are opposed not by a Left (there is no Left on this Court) but rather by pragmatic moderates who appear to define themselves less through ideology and more through simply being competent lawyers and judges. For a variety of reasons peculiar to each, Rehnquist, Scalia, and Thomas overcame or outlasted a selection and confirmation process that rewards legal expertise and judicial experience coupled with political blandness. Their colleagues, however, are distinctly a product of this process. Ranging from the political center to the moderate right, these justices form the heart (if not the soul) of the Rehnquist Court, frequently eschewing the "big" opinion grounded on broad, fundamental principles in favor of what Cass Sunstein has characterized as "judicial minimalism."[8] Neither liberal nor conservative, the core of the Rehnquist Court fears deciding too much and labors mightily to avoid that fate. "Justices in the new regime," Mark Tushnet astutely noted, "seek to show they are technically competent lawyers who do small things very well."[9]

This is, nevertheless, a conservative Supreme Court, particularly if one uses the Warren or Roosevelt Courts for comparison. (It is, it should be emphasized, hardly a conservative interpreter of the Constitution when measured against the entire history of the Supreme Court.) The mood of the nation has taken a decided turn to the right and, as Robert Dahl observed many years ago, Supreme Court decision-making eventually will reflect the governing ideology of the day.[10] The existence of a reliable conservative bloc of three votes will inevitably skew results in that direction on a Court that has no consistent ideological counterbalance. In spite of this conservative trend, the Scalia, Rehnquist, and Thomas bloc certainly gives the impression of being outside the mainstream on the current Court. Mirroring in a curious way the ideological loneliness of Justices Brennan and Marshall in the twilight of their careers, the conservative trio appears at times to suffer a comparable isolation.

Justice Scalia lashes out in opinions at colleagues with whom he disagrees, and his influence on the Court unquestionably has been diminished by the abrasive tenor of his writing and his overbearing manner in the courtroom. In this regard, Scalia may be following in the footsteps of his fellow academic Felix Frankfurter, whose ill-disguised contempt for many of his colleagues undercut his influence on the Court. Justice Thomas remains an enigmatic figure, seemingly more comfortable hobnobbing with right-wing political groups and staking out occasionally extreme libertarian positions than seeking to establish influence and rapport with the other justices. When compared to Scalia and Thomas, the chief justice offers a mellower tone but an equally conservative agenda. If that agenda is to become a matter of constitutional law, then the chief justice—and to the outside observer the task does seem to fall to Rehnquist—must persuade at least two other justices to join the conservative trio. These votes must come from the pragmatic, technically competent justices who make up the remainder of this Court, and hence, even when the chief justice is successful, the votes often come hedged with enough qualifications to undermine the ideological import of the decision. Too often (certainly for Scalia and Thomas and most likely for the chief justice as well), what might be seen as a conservative victory on the merits is undercut by a multiplicity of concurring opinions that strive to emphasize precisely how little new law is really being established.

No cases illustrate the estrangement of the ideologues and the ascendancy of the technically skilled than the Court's most recent abortion decisions. *Planned Parenthood of Southeastern Pennsylvania v. Casey*[11] and *Stenberg v. Carhart*[12] represent archetypal Rehnquist Court opinions and present a snapshot of the workings of the current Court. Substantively, the joint opinion in *Casey* authored by Justices O'Connor, Souter, and Kennedy was a judicial effort to achieve, in effect, a middle ground in the already decades-old abortion debate: retain the "core right" to an abortion while permitting the states expanded latitude to regulate around that core principle. When all is said and done, that is the obvious point of the "undue burden test," and its ultimate justification can only rest on the notion of compromise. Freed from the automatic results compelled by either strict scrutiny or rational basis analysis, undue burden permits pragmatic jurists to proceed through the abortion thicket employing narrow rulings that decide little, turn on factual determinations, and avoid articulating fundamental principles. For a Court made up of a majority of justices seeking to make big cases quite small, the undue burden test makes perfect sense.

For any observer of the Rehnquist Court, what is particularly striking about *Casey* is that of the six justices who failed to sign on to the undue burden approach, it was the conservative trio that appeared most distraught by the outcome. *Casey*, in spite of everything, upheld all but one of the Pennsylvania legislature's efforts to regulate the abortion procedure, and yet one could spend months searching the volumes of *U.S. Reports* and fail to come upon any piece of judicial writing that approaches the harsh words and tone found in Justice Scalia's concurring and dissenting opinion. In my view it trumps his effort in *Webster v. Reproductive Health Services*[13] in which he savages Justice O'Connor, characterizing her analysis as "irrational" and all but labeling her a coward for the failure to vote to overrule *Roe*.

Years later in *Carhart*, a 5 to 4 Court struck down Nebraska's so-called "partial-birth" abortion ban. Justices Breyer and Ginsberg signed on to the "undue burden" standard and helped form a majority holding that the ban failed to provide an exception for the preservation of the health of the mother as well as constituting an undue burden on the choice of abortion itself. The majority left for another day the potentially significant question of whether the state could offer interests other than maternal health or protection of potential life to justify regulating previability abortions. On this issue Justice Kennedy broke with the majority and joined Scalia, Thomas, and the chief justice in dissent.

Once again, the intensity of several of the dissenting opinions is startling. Justice Scalia likened the majority's result to that in *Korematsu* and *Dred Scott,* while Justice Thomas spent pages graphically describing the procedure at issue. The reaction again seemed out of sync with the limited scope of the majority's decision and the frankly infrequent use of the partial-birth procedure. Perhaps the stridency of the Thomas and Scalia dissents can be attributed to the personal sensitivities of the justices or the shock value of media treatment of the contested procedure. But I suspect it is also in the nature of a cri de coeur springing from the true believers who have witnessed the infidels (and pragmatic infidels, no less), in effect, seize the day.

Although the minimalist and pragmatic nature of much of the work of the Rehnquist Court has been the subject of a good deal of scholarly comment, the Court, nonetheless, has altered several long-standing and fundamental assumptions of constitutional interpretation. One area where this trend is particularly evident is the justices' willingness to challenge the deference to national power articulated by every Court since the New Deal. In this effort to reorient federal-state relations, the conservative trio can typically count on the votes of Justices Kennedy and O'Connor. Despite a solid majority on the Court and despite the fact that this majority appears to be "swimming with the political tide rather than against it,"[14] the cautious, pragmatic justices on the Rehnquist Court quite often take pains to emphasize exactly how narrow the holdings really are, while the ideologues push to extend new doctrine.

United States v. Lopez,[15] in which the Court appeared to alter a half century's interpretation of federal power under the Commerce Clause, provides a ready example. Justice Thomas used his concurring opinion to conclude that the Court simply did not go far enough; in his view, the entire body of law that extended federal power to local activities that "substantially effect" interstate commerce was an illegitimate interpretation of the Constitution. At the same time, Justice Kennedy, joined by Justice O'Connor, concurred with the majority, writing to emphasize the majority's "necessary though limited holding." It is a scenario that is repeated throughout the decision-making of the Rehnquist Court.

Another example can be found in the Court's affirmative action decisions. In *Adarand Construction v. Pena,*[16] the Court by a 5 to 4 margin held that strict scrutiny would apply to federal as well as state race-based affirmative action plans. Although the holding in *Adarand* could signal the demise of all affirmative action plans (a result quite expressly in line with the thinking of Rehnquist, Thomas, and Scalia), Justice O'Connor, joined by Justice Kennedy, took pains to emphasize that strict scrutiny did not require a court to strike down the statute under consideration and that the government was not precluded from race-based programs to remedy racial discrimination as long as it could satisfy an apparently now more lenient strict scrutiny test. If it is indeed to be the case that strict scrutiny as employed by the centrists on the Court in affirmative action cases will no longer inevitably be fatal, then *Adarand* may come to herald yet another small victory for the pragmatists and further estrangement of the right wing of the Court.

A NEW COURT FOR A NEW AGE

Mark Tushnet has characterized the transformation of politics and political institutions that took place during the Rehnquist years as the coming of "a new constitutional order," a period in which the institutions through which the nation made its important decisions as well as the principles that guided those decisions underwent important and distinct changes.[17] The old order—the era of the New Deal and the Great Society—was conclusively put to rest during the Reagan presidency. Much of President Reagan's most powerful rhetoric rested on the basic premise that more government was not the solution but indeed the problem, and the ascendancy of this new order was confirmed in Bill Clinton's State of the Union Address in 1996 when he announced that the "era of big government is over." A general skepticism regarding the capacity of government to enact beneficial change is the new public philosophy, and it is reflected in a judiciary with diminished constitutional expectations as well. In Mark Tushnet's words, "the end of big government means the end of a big Court, too."[18]

Twenty years ago, Martin Shapiro described the awkward relationship that linked the Warren Court with the scholars who filled the law reviews and scholarly journals with commentary about what the Court was doing.[19] Many of those commentators were academic lawyers who came of age during the New Deal, and the defining constitutional event of their generation was the battle over the institutional role of the judiciary that reached its zenith during the Roosevelt years. Judicial modesty, for these scholars, became the mark of the modern judiciary; judicial activism, they believed, was incompatible with progressive national politics led by an assertive and dominant executive branch. The conviction that an activist judiciary could neatly coexist with an activist president was, for the New Dealers, heresy. Thus, during the Warren Court years, some of the most powerful critiques of the Court came not from the academic Right, but instead from old liberals faced with the apparent transgressions of a new generation of liberals. The subtlety of this almost "family" dispute was perfectly captured by Shapiro: "Because the Warren Court was engaged in a consistent and comprehensive constitutionalization of the New Deal's fundamental vision of social justice, while violating its fundamental political theory of a strong presidency, the New Deal commentators loved what the Court was doing but hated the fact that it was doing it."[20]

The Warren Court, in turn, produced its own generation of academic lawyers who found their way to law school inspired in no small part by a Supreme Court that appeared to consistently link constitutional law to social justice (I count myself among those academic lawyers). The justices of the Warren Court became almost mythic figures, unhampered by legalisms and procedural niceties in the quest to issue the "big" decision and do "justice." And the big decision was inevitably an effort to redirect the law—and constitutional law in particular—to serve the needs of America's most disadvantaged. To a new generation brought to the law by a faith in the Warren Court and what it was doing, the capacity of judges to employ the law for progressive change seemed almost limitless.

Those who might generously be termed "the Warren Court children" are now part of that generation of scholars that chronicles the Rehnquist Court. To many, a Court that shrinks its own caseload, that struggles to minimize the impact of the cases it does consider, that favors state power over national power, that treats racial discrimination as a private rather than public issue and that considers the death penalty a reasonable method of crime control is also a Court that no longer makes human dignity the central tenet of constitutional interpretation. A Court made up of technically skilled but virtually invisible lawyers seems so much smaller in comparison to Courts populated by larger-than-life figures like Hugo Black, William Douglas, William Brennan, Felix Frankfurter, Earl Warren, and Thurgood Marshall. For many of those who came of age during the Warren Court era, this is, simply put, a much diminished Court.

Of course, the New Deal and the Great Society are no more, and the Warren Court is long part of history. To a degree perhaps not appreciated at the time, the former were a necessary precondition for the existence of the latter. Linked through the appointment power with the president and the seemingly boundless political aspirations of the times, the Warren Court was an activist Court in an era that celebrated activist government. A new governing regime and a new public philosophy, however, must beget a new Court, and the lessened prominence and ambition of the current Court are the natural outcomes of the politics of a new day. Perhaps we should abandon the retrospective effort to place particular Courts in "historical perspective" and focus greater attention on how the politics of the moment shapes the role and workings of the Court. It is not a little unfair and perhaps not particularly useful to measure the current Court by what came before it. In the final analysis, the Rehnquist Court must be assessed as part of a new order and a new public philosophy that despairs of the capacity of public institutions (particularly at the national level) to govern wisely and well. The Rehnquist Court's critics may remember a brighter day, but perhaps it is those critics, and not the Court, that are out of joint. When all is said and done, this is a Court that mirrors the times.

NOTES

1. Samuel H. Beer, *Britain against Itself: The Political Contradictions of Collectivism* (New York: Norton, 1982).

2. See, for example, Mark Silverstein, *Judicious Choices: The New Politics of the Supreme Court Confirmations* (New York: Norton, 1994).

3. See Barbara Sinclair, *The Transformation of the U.S. Senate* (Baltimore: Johns Hopkins University Press, 1989).

4. Barbara Sinclair, "Individualism, Partisanship, and Cooperation in the Senate," in *Esteemed Colleagues: Civility and Deliberation in the U.S. Senate,* ed. Burdett Loomis (Washington, D.C.: Brookings Institution Press, 2000).

5. Burdett Loomis, "Civility and Deliberation: A Linked Pair?" in ibid.

6. See Lawrence Baum, "Recruitment and the Motivations of Supreme Court Justices," in *Supreme Court Decision-Making: New Institutionalist Approaches,* ed. Cornell Clayton and Howard Gillman (Chicago: University of Chicago Press, 1999). The data that follow are taken from this chapter.

7. Ibid.

8. Cass Sunstein, *One Case at a Time: Judicial Minimalism on the Supreme Court* (Cambridge: Harvard University Press, 1999).

9. Mark Tushnet, "Foreword: The New Constitutional Order and the Chastening of Constitutional Aspiration," *Harvard Law Review* 113 (November 1999): 91.

10. Robert Dahl, "Decision Making in a Democracy: The Supreme Court as a National Policy Maker," *Journal of Public Law* 6 (1958): 279.

11. 505 U.S. 833 (1992).

12. 530 U.S. 914 (2000).

13. 492 U.S. 490 (1989).

14. Keith E. Whittington, "Taking What They Give Us: Explaining the Court's Federalism Offensive," *Duke Law Journal* 51 (2001): 519.

15. 514 U.S. 549 (1995).

16. 515 U.S. 200 (1995).

17. See Tushnet, "The New Constitutional Order," 91.

18. Ibid., 64.

19. Martin Shapiro, "Fathers and Sons: The Court, the Commentators, and the Search for Values," in *The Burger Court: The Counter-Revolution That Wasn't,* ed. Vincent Blasi (New Haven: Yale University Press, 1983).

20. Ibid., 219.

Contributors

JUDITH A. BAER is professor of political science at Texas A&M University. She received her Ph.D. from the University of Chicago. Among her many works are *Women in American Law: The Struggle toward Equality from the New Deal to the Present* and *Our Lives before the Law.*

WARD FARNSWORTH is associate professor of law at Boston University. He received his J.D. from the University of Chicago and is the author of "Women under Reconstruction: The Congressional Understanding," published in *Northwestern University Law Review.*

MARK A. GRABER is associate professor of government at the University of Maryland. He received his J.D. from Columbia University and his Ph.D. from Yale University. Among his many works are *Transforming Free Speech, Rethinking Abortion,* and the forthcoming *Dred Scott and the Problem of Constitutional Evil.*

THOMAS M. KECK is assistant professor of political science at Syracuse University. He received his Ph.D. from Rutgers University and is the author of the forthcoming *The Supreme Court and Modern Constitutional Conservatism, 1937–2003.*

KEN I. KERSCH is assistant professor of politics at Princeton University. He received his Ph.D. from Cornell University and is the author of the forthcoming *The Constitution of Progress: Discontinuous Development in American Constitutional Law.*

EARL M. MALTZ is distinguished professor of law at Rutgers University. He received his J.D. from Harvard University. Among his many works on constitutional law and constitutional history is *The Chief Justiceship of Warren Burger.*

NANCY MAVEETY is associate professor of political science at Tulane University. She is the editor of the forthcoming *The Pioneers of Judicial Behavior* and the author of *Representation Rights in the Burger Years* and *Sandra Day O'Connor: Strategist on the Court.*

RALPH A. ROSSUM is the Salvatori professor of political science and American constitutionalism at Claremont-McKenna University. He received his Ph.D. from the University of Chicago. He is the author of many journal articles and six books, including the two-volume *American Constitutional Law.*

MARK SILVERSTEIN is professor of political science at Boston University. He received his Ph.D. from Cornell University and his J.D. from Columbia University. Among his many publications are *Constitutional Faiths: Felix Frankfurter, Hugo Black, and the Process of Judicial Decisionmaking* and *Judicious Choices: The New Politics for Supreme Court Confirmations.*

KEITH E. WHITTINGTON is assistant professor of politics at Princeton University. He received his Ph.D. from Yale University. Among his many publications are *Constitutional Construction: Divided Process and Constitutional Meaning* and *Constitutional Interpretation: Textual Meaning, Original Intent, and Judicial Review.*

Index

Iowa Law Review, Wald in, 45
Irving Independent School Dist. v. Tatro,
    Thomas and, 80

Jackson, Robert H., 132, 139n88, 224, 228,
    266
    Brown and, 11
    Rehnquist and, 10, 15, 21, 26
Jaffa, Harry V., 42
James, William, 245, 267n3
James B. Beam Distilling Company, Scalia
    and, 54
J.E.B. v. Alabama ex rel. T.B., 4, 229
    Ginsburg and, 226
    Kennedy and, 148
Jefferson, Thomas, 42, 46, 200, 263
Jehovah's Witnesses, 228
Jim Crow laws, 85, 89
Johnson, Lyndon B., 9, 284
Johnson v. DeGrandy, O'Connor and,
    138n69
Judicial activism, 4–5, 26, 90, 114, 132, 194,
    209
    Ginsburg and, 222
    New Right, 186, 205
    restrained, 222
    Souter and, 185, 186, 195, 203, 205,
        210n1
    Thomas and, 96n129
Judicial power, 282
    Breyer and, 260
    Scalia and, 60n3, 67n118
Judicial restraint, 21, 210n2
    O'Connor and, 131
    Rehnquist and, 22, 27
    Souter and, 210n1

Kahn, Alfred, 248, 269n18
Kahn v. Shevin, Ginsburg and, 235n10,
    236n29
Kanowitz, Leo, 217
Kansas v. Hendricks, Thomas and, 75
Kay, Herma Hill, 217
Kennedy, Anthony M., 75, 89, 107, 125,
    186, 242, 288
    Breyer and, 261, 265
    early career of, 140
    Hart/Sacks and, 246
    nomination of, 141, 142
    O'Connor and, 109, 117, 118, 119, 123,
        124, 130
    opposition by, 6
    role of, 140
    Scalia and, 55, 58, 68n161

Souter and, 185, 189, 190, 192, 194, 195,
    198, 200, 201, 202, 205, 207, 208, 209,
    210
Stevens and, 181n50
Thomas and, 80, 95n94
vote of, 5, 6
Kennedy, Edward, 14, 248
Kennedy, John F., 284
Kent, James, 38
Kimel v. Florida Board of Regents, 131, 225
Kirchberg v. Feenstra, Ginsburg and, 230,
    231
Kirkland, Lane, 141, 142
Kiryas Joel, 197, 198
Klarman, Michael J., 89
Klein, Joel, Breyer and, 241
Kluger, Richard, 272n51
Korematsu v. U.S., 218, 288
Ku Klux Klan, 96n113, 224, 263
Kyllo v. United States, Scalia and, 46–47

*Lamb's Chapel v. Center Moriches Union
    Free School District,* O'Connor and,
    123–24
Lawsuits, immunity against, 20, 24–25
Lechmere Inc. v. NLRB, Thomas and, 75
Lee v. Weisman, 2
    O'Connor and, 123, 124
    Scalia and, 38, 68n161
    Souter and, 190, 192, 196
Legal process, Breyer and, 246, 247, 257
Legal Realism, 173
    Breyer and, 246
    Stevens and, 177–79
Legislative history, Scalia and, 43–46, 64n73
Legislative powers, 19
    individual protections and, 16
    Rehnquist and, 21
    Scalia and, 51, 60n3
Lemon test
    Ginsburg and, 223
    O'Connor and, 122, 123, 124
    points of, 137n45
Lemon v. Kurtzman, 122
Lewis, Phillip, 194
Lex loci delicti, 173
Liberal activism, 4–5
    defense of, 192–202
Liberalism, 107, 258
    Douglas and, 177
    O'Connor and, 103
    Souter and, 209
    Stevens and, 158–59, 162–63, 175, 176
Line Item Veto Act, 256